SCIENCE OF SUSTAINABLE DESIGN

THIRD EDITION

Edited by Mary Myers

TEMPLE UNIVERSITY

cognella® | ACADEMIC PUBLISHING

Bassim Hamadeh, CEO and Publisher

Kassie Graves, Director of Acquisitions

Jamie Giganti, Senior Managing Editor

Jess Estrella, Senior Graphic Designer

John Remington, Senior Field Acquisitions Editor

Natalie Lakosil, Senior Licensing Manager

Allie Kiekhofer and Kaela Martin, Associate Editors

Kat Ragudos, Interior Designer

Cover images: Copyright © Depositphotos/Pakhnyushchyy.
               Copyright © 2012 iStockphoto LP/Susan Chiang.
               Copyright © 2015 iStockphoto LP/RomoloTavani.

Printed in the United States of America

ISBN: 978-1-63487-428-1 (pbk) / 978-1-63487-429-8 (br)

CONTENTS

PART 3

DESIGNING SUSTAINABLE CITIES AND SUBURBS   233

PART 4
ETHICS

ACKNOWLEDGMENTS

BY MARY MYERS

I am very grateful to K. Daryl Carrington, Ph.D., for contributing to this and former editions of *The Science of Sustainable Design*, and for co-teaching the course over the years. His perspective as an architect and researcher has helped to shape both the course and this book. Additionally, I would like to thank colleagues Lynn Mandarano, Jeff Harris, Shirley Loveless, and Kristen Ford Haaf for co-teaching the course and providing valuable discourse on the topics of planning and landscape architecture. Jeff Featherstone and Deborah Howe participated in the brainstorming of the concept. Kate Benisek and Charlene Briggs have brought enthusiasm and thoughtfulness to their teaching of the course as it has expanded with new sections.

The proposal to establish the course would not have succeeded without the support and critical review of Professor Lolly Tai, Professor and Temple University General Education Director Terry Halbert, and the General Education Committee. These people and many others have helped to move the course (and book) toward its current form. Finally, this book is dedicated to my students, whose creative insights, questions and thirst for knowledge have been a source of constant inspiration.

INTRODUCTION

BY MARY MYERS

This is the third edition of an anthology whose idea took root in an interdisciplinary course proposal in 2005. At that time, Temple University was rethinking the core requirements of its undergraduate curriculum. A team of professors from environmental studies, landscape architecture, community and regional planning, and architecture met to discuss a course that would integrate science and design. Over the next two years, ideas were discussed and reviewed by a university committee, texts researched and read, schedules and syllabi drafted and revised, until a final proposal emerged called "The Science of Sustainable Design."

First taught in spring 2008, content is continually reassessed by the teaching team to reflect the most current information in science and design. This version of the book contains more original material by the author. Some of the chapters were shaped from student comments about the desire to know more about a topic. Others originated in peer-reviewed presentations or research investigations. All reflect the desire to enhance critical thinking by demonstrating the relevance of empirical information to sustainable design. Interest in environmental sustainability has increased considerably during the past three decades and now permeates many subjects such as political science, literature, law, economics, business, art and architecture. Peer reviewed scientific articles on the topic abound, supporting new understanding and prompting new questions. This revised edition refers to the current science related to sustainability, acknowledging that the science is changing at a very fast rate.

WHAT IS SUSTAINABLE DESIGN?

The term "sustainability" has been common parlance for several decades. It was defined by the Brundtland Commission (1987) "To meet the needs of the present generation without compromising the ability of future generations to meet their needs." Designer Buckminster Fuller articulated the difficulty of this task, when he characterized our planet as a "spaceship." All of the supplies we have are onboard, and the only external resource is energy from the Sun, so we must take great care in their use (*Operating Manual for Spaceship Earth*, 1969). In order to ensure the ability of future generations to meet their needs, we must live within the carrying capacity of spaceship Earth's natural systems and husband our resources. Every action we take to produce or consume goods or food has impacts and repercussions. The negative impacts are manifest in global climate change, environmental degradation, and loss of species.

Design is defined as the modification of an object, place, or process with intention or purpose. Our culture has given considerable thought to functional and aesthetic aspects of design, but "sustainable design" is relatively new. Sustainable design looks at a range of a human artifact, (such as a house, transportation network, car, or toothbrush) and tries to move toward a position that does not compromise the earth's carrying capacity. Thoughtful design can reduce negative impacts through consideration of matter and energy flows, reduction or elimination of waste, and renewal of degraded cities and natural environments. The intention of these readings is to show the relevance of design to an improved relationship between humans and the environment. Sustainable design is ultimately evidence-based and must be tied to the scientific laws governing our planet.

Based upon this framework, the definition of sustainable design can be made more specific and to articulate the important link between scientific laws and design. Aldo Leopold's concept of rightness is used as a basis for building toward this. Leopold wrote: "A thing is right when it tends to preserve the integrity, stability and beauty of the biotic community. It is wrong when it tends otherwise" (Leopold, p. 224).

Reinterpreted to relate to human artifacts:

> A design (building, object, landscape, or city) is sustainable when it supports the healthy function of the laws of matter and energy, and promotes biodiversity and ecological services. It is unsustainable when it adversely impacts the natural laws or reduces biodiversity and ecological services.

The anthology has four parts: scientific laws and principles; human impacts; sustainable design case studies; and environmental ethics. The readings begin with an introduction explaining sustainable design's relevance to current and future generations. This is followed by a presentation of the science that must inform design: biology, the Laws of Matter and Energy and explanation of Biodiversity. The science is followed by a discussion of human impacts on the environment and design approaches to mitigate impacts. Case studies illustrating sustainable design are third. An environmental ethics reading is included because ultimately sustainable design is an ethical practice directed toward supporting the needs of future generations of humans and other life forms.

PART ONE:
SCIENTIFIC LAWS AND PRINCIPLES

The Law of Conservation of Matter and the two Laws of Energy are the basic underpinnings of sustainability. Derived from thousands of experiments and observations, the laws are accepted by the scientific community. They cannot be changed or broken, and they apply universally. Thus, we are in a zero-sum game, things are either sustainable or they are not.

Conservation of Matter:
IN ANY PHYSICAL OR CHEMICAL TRANSFORMATION, MATTER CANNOT BE CREATED OR DESTROYED.

Earth has all of the matter it will ever have (aside from meteor hits). We manipulate matter to become different things, such as the computer used to write this work, which is mainly aluminum (originally bauxite), and plastic (originally oil). We cannot "make" new matter; we can only change it from one form to another.

Laws of Energy (Thermodynamics):
IN ANY PHYSICAL OR CHEMICAL TRANSFORMATION, ENERGY CANNOT BE CREATED OR DESTROYED.

The first energy law is similar to the conservation of matter. We cannot create energy, only change its form. Nearly all of earth's energy is provided by the sun. Supplemental energy used to transform matter and transport humans and goods comes from other sources. We drill and mine the earth's surface and under its seas withdrawing oil, coal, and natural gas. These fossil fuels were laid down millions of years ago with the death of animals and plants. The extracted fuels are burned to create electricity and high-temperature heat, capable of running industrial machinery; trucks, trains, cars, and buses; and heating and cooling buildings, powering washing machines and kitchen equipment, and so forth.

The Second Law of Energy:
WHEN ENERGY IS TRANSFORMED FROM ONE FORM TO ANOTHER, SOME ENERGY IS DEGRADED TO LOWER QUALITY, MORE DISPERSED ENERGY.

The Second Law of Energy is very important to sustainable design. It tells us that each time a conversion occurs, some energy is lost and the remaining energy is less capable of doing work. Thus when electricity arrives at your apartment or house, it is more dispersed and "weaker" after having traveled from a centralized power plant. Sustainable design focuses on energy efficiency and conservation (involving fewer transformations) to respond to the Second Law of Energy.

Biogeochemical Cycles

Materials that are essential to life, including carbon, water, nitrogen, phosphorous, and sulfur, are constantly cycled through the biosphere, ensuring global distribution and reuse. Manmade change to the carbon and hydrologic cycles is a critical area to be considered in sustainable design.

PART TWO:
SUSTAINABLE APPROACHES AND CASE STUDIES

Sustainable design is being rapidly adopted worldwide in response to climate change and human pressure on the environment. There are many methods and examples for the practice of sustainable design. Research by ethnobotanists indicates that people have lived within and sustainably managed their environments for millennia. This information can be useful to contemporary design and planning. We also see that beautiful design endures---another hallmark of sustainability.

The selected case studies demonstrate the principles that need to guide design in the 21st century: creativity; reliance upon scientific evidence; openness to other ways of thinking; respect for the environment and other life forms; and a spirit of social inclusiveness and justice. Decisions must be based upon the best scientific evidence available.

PART THREE:
DESIGNING SUSTAINABLE CITIES AND SUBURBS

There are four essential points to this section. The first is that sustainable design ideas are transferable, because they operate, as does the rest of the planet, according to the scientific laws of matter and energy. Second, sound solutions are useful at a variety of scales, from residential gardens to cities and regions. Third, natural solutions, such as those put forth in the chapter on "Conjoined Nature" are now found in a variety of buildings and cities around the world. Fourth, biodiversity is foundational to the functioning of the biogeochemical cycles and is increasingly recognized as providing important ecological services. The chapter on retrofitting a suburban garden focuses on how biodiversity can be maximized at the local scale.

PART FOUR:
ETHICS

Thoughtful actions stem from ethical positions, which make ethical understanding essential to sustainable design and sustainable living. The dominant ethos of the industrial age has been to exploit the environment without thought for the consequences. Humans have subjugated the entire planet to their will, but have done so at the peril of future generations. It is obvious that a sustainable planet is in our interest, but many, perhaps most people and industries are not making appropriate choices. American culture is focused primarily on profit and obtaining an affluent lifestyle, behaving as if the Earth has unlimited resources and ability to absorb environmental impact.

A new ethos is necessary. It must be less anthropocentric and allow us to redress the damage that has been done. Leopold puts forth a land ethic, calling upon us to re-think our responsibility as stewards of the planet and other species. We are traveling on spaceship Earth with many other species and depend upon the land for our survival. Leopold's land ethic underpins action in environmental conservation, preservation, and restoration.

Finally, humans have evolved within nature and recent scientific studies reveal the important relationship between green space and health. This emerging area of research portends a deeper reason for an environmental ethic.

MOVING FORWARD

Students who read this anthology will have varied backgrounds and majors. But sustainable design thinking is needed in every area of our culture and within every profession to meet the challenges of global warming, environmental degradation, and loss of species. These readings provide information and rationale integral to that thinking. The scientific principles might be considered the substance, or the *what* of sustainable design; methods and case studies are examples of *how* the principles are applied; and the readings related to ethics constitute the reasons for applying the principles, the *why*. I anticipate that the content, especially that which relates to case studies, will change in future editions to respond to expanded adoption of sustainable design. Recommendations from students prompted me to include more content on sustainable cities than previous editions. Discussion and interaction with students has been invaluable in developing this book. I am grateful for their insights, engagement and comments.

WHY IS SUSTAINABLE DESIGN IMPORTANT?

Population, Affluence, Technology, and Climate Change

BY MARY MYERS

Environmental degradation is occurring at a rapid rate. This is due to anthropocentric (human-centered) activities, rather than natural or geologic activities. Three major factors are coalescing to effect environmental degradation: increased human population, increased affluence, and climate change. Climate change is now unequivocally accepted by the scientific community as a threat to the earth's climate-regulation system and consequently to ecosystem stability. Climate change adds to environmental degradation through increased floods, rising sea levels, and desertification.

Sustainable design attempts to ameliorate environmental degradation and slow and mitigate climate-change impacts by considering how matter and energy are converted and used in buildings, objects, landscapes, and transportation. Sustainable design also seeks to reduce or completely counteract environmental destruction by restoring ecosystems. The case studies included in later chapters demonstrate how sustainable design works to reduce, eliminate, or reverse environmental degradation. This chapter examines population trends, effects of affluence, and climate-change projections and impacts.

HUMAN POPULATION—2050 AND BEYOND

Humans, *Homo sapiens*, are an intelligent and adaptable species. We have proven that we are capable of living anywhere on earth and may demonstrate the capability to live on other planets. Our technologies have enabled us to expand our territories and our populations. In approximately 10000

B.C. many humans shifted from a nomadic existence of hunting and gathering to an agricultural existence. This was called the Neolithic Revolution and is estimated to have taken a few thousand years for the majority of humanity to make this shift (Miller, 2006). It was revolutionary for our species because for at least 200,000 years, we had flourished as hunters and gatherers.

Significant societal changes occurred with the shift to agriculture. Humans were able to store large quantities of food and to accumulate and store material goods. More people could live in one place, bringing about exchange of knowledge. Archaeological evidence indicates that reading and writing evolved around 3000 B.C. in Sumeria, a city-state in the Middle East (Woods 2010, pp. 36–37). Stratification of classes became distinct and hierarchies arose. For example, Sumeria (present-day Iraq) had a king or ruler at the top of the hierarchy supported by the military and priest classes; followed by a professional class made up of lawyers, educators, physicians, scientists; a trade class of blacksmiths, potters, builders, and others who worked with their hands; farmers; herdsmen, servants, and slaves (Jellicoe and Jellicoe, pp. 22–23). The emergence of city-states brought about trade and advances in technology.

Each major technological change resulted in increased human population. In 10000 B.C., the world's population is estimated to have been about 7 million. It grew relatively slowly over the next 12,000 years to be about 600 million in 1700 A.D. The Industrial Revolution began around that time with the discovery that combusting fossil fuel could create high enough temperatures to transform matter relatively easily. Agrarian-based economies and societies were abandoned for industrial societies where people worked in factories to create all sorts of commodities. By 1850, the population was 1 billion. A little more than a century later, by 1960, the population was 3 billion. This time period ushered in the Science and Computer Revolution. In mid year 1996, world population was 5.8 billion. . In May 2016, (the time of this writing) the world population was close to 7.4 billion. One billion six hundred million people had been added in 20 years (http://esa.un.org/wpp/Excel-Data/population).

The United Nations (UN) Department of Economic and Social Affairs, Population Division tracks world population using up-to-date census information and health statistics. " The world population is projected to increase by more than one billion people within the next 14 years, reaching 8.5 billion in 2030, and to increase further to 9.7 billion in 2050 and 11.2 billion by 2100 (World Population Prospects: The 2015 Revision p.2)." .The UN 2300 Report makes certain assumptions about fertility and death rates. It has projected that there will be lower fertility rates overall (1.85 children per woman) in 2100 but that replacement rates will return and continue indefinitely beyond 2200.

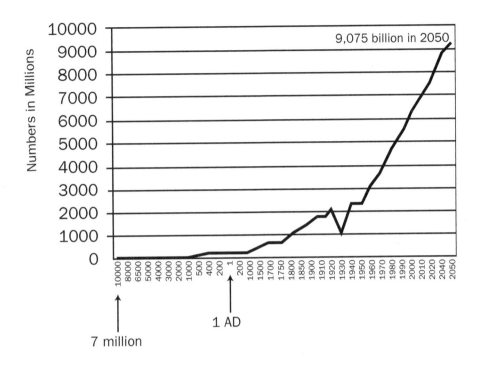

Figure 2.1. Population density graph

As of mid 2015, according to the United Nations 2015 Report:

"Sixty percent of the global population live(d) in Asia (4.4 billion), 16 per cent in Africa (1.2 billion), 10 per cent in Europe (738 million), 9 per cent in Latin America and the Caribbean (634 million),and the remaining 5 per cent in Northern America (358 million) and Oceania (39 million). China (1.4 billion) and India (1.3 billion) remain(ed) the two largest countries of the world, both with more than 1 billion people, representing 19 and 18 per cent of the world's population, respectively (*World Population Prospects: The 2015 Revision* p. 2)."

In 2015, the six most populous countries were China, India, USA, Indonesia, Brazil, and Pakistan. In 2050, the six most populous are predicted to be India, China, Nigeria, USA, Pakistan, Indonesia, and Pakistan. In the United States, the population has grown from 285 million people in 2000 to 324 million in 2016. It will reach 408.7 million (43.4% growth) in 2050.

Table 2.1 Population (in billions) of the World and Major Areas, 2015, 2030, 2050 and 2100

MAJOR AREA	2015	2030	2050	2100
World	7.35	8.50	9.725	11.21
Africa	1.19	1.68	2.48	4.39
Asia	4.34	4.92	5.27	4.89
Europe	0.74	0.73	0.71	0.65
Latin America and Caribbean	0.63	0.72	0.78	0.72
Northern America	0.36	0.40	0.43	0.50
Oceana	0.04	0.05	0.06	0.07

Source: United Nations Department of Economic and Social Affairs, Population Division (2015), *World Population Prospects: The 2015 Revision.* New York, United Nations

Table 2.2 Ten most populous countries in 2015, 2050 and 2100.

POPULATION IN BILLIONS			
RANK	2015	2050	2100
1	China, 1.38	India, 1.70	India, 1.66
2	India, 1.31	China, 1.35	China, 1.00
3	USA, 0.32	Nigeria, 0.40	Nigeria, 0.75
4	Indonesia, 0.26	USA, 0.39	USA, 0.45
5	Brazil, 0.21	Indonesia, 0.32	Congo, DR, 0.39
6	Pakistan, 0.19	Pakistan, 0.31	Pakistan, 0.36
7	Nigeria, 0.18	Brazil, 0.24	Indonesia, 0.31
8	Bangladesh, 0.16	Bangladesh, 0.20	Tanzania, UR, 0.30
9	Russian Federation, 0.14	Congo, DR 0.195	Ethiopia, 0.24
10	Mexico, 0.13	Ethiopia, 0.19	Niger, 0.24

Source: United Nations Department of Economic and Social Affairs, Population Division (2015), *World Population Prospects: The 2015 Revision.* New York, United Nations

Migration from lesser developed countries to more developed countries has been a trend for centuries. Better pay, quality of life, access to material goods, education, etc. in high-income countries attracts immigrants from lower or middle-income countries. Between 2000 and 2015, high income countries received an average of 4.1 million net migrants per year. "Economic and demographic asymmetries across countries are likely to remain powerful generators of international migration within the medium-term future. Large-scale refugee movements have also had a profound influence on the level of net migration experienced by some countries, including those affected recently by the Syrian crisis (*World Population Prospects*, p. 11)"

Around the world, a profound change in density and population will occur in the next three decades. This means that today's youth will be responsible for many pressing decisions. An objective of this book is to demonstrate that scientific evidence should underpin decisions about the environment. At the same time decision makers should utilize designers' visionary scenarios to project and build a better future. It will be interesting to see how the current generation meets the challenges of planning for population growth, climate change mitigation/adaptation, and shifts in cultural expectations.

Table 2.3 Population Density (persons/sq. kilometer of land)

	1950	2000	2050	2100
N. America	9.2	16.9	23.9	25.3
E. Africa	10.8	41.7	101.5	133.6
W. Europe	129.5	168.6	169.5	156.7
India	120.3	342.0	515.1	490.5
China	59.5	136.7	149.5	126.7
Australia, NZ	1.3	2.9	3.8	3.6

Source: *UN World Population to 2300 Report*, p.64
Note: 1 square kilometer = 0.39 square miles or 247 square acres

How do we ensure that all people have a good quality of life, access to food and health care, clean water and air? How do we ensure that other life forms, animals and plants, are not extinguished in the process? How should we plan our cities, suburbs, farms, and wildernesses to accommodate a nearly 4 billion more people by 2100? Decisions about where and what form growth should take are important. A very densely populated high-rise city might allow for more useable open space beyond its borders—but requires flows of food, water, goods, etc., and may have an intense impact due to sewage and other wastes.

THE DOUBLE WHAMMY:
AFFLUENCE IS ADDED TO POPULATION GROWTH

The US has a relatively low population density when compared with other parts of the world. However, to live sustainably we need to consider more than population size and density. We must also look at the amount of land used to support a certain lifestyle, or *affluence* (level of consumption). This is done by examining our ecological footprints. The ecological footprint is defined as:

> The aggregate area of land and water in various ecological categories that is needed to produce all the resources we consume and to absorb all the wastes we generate on a continuous basis. (Wackernagel and Reese, 1997, p. 7)

Americans have one of the largest ecological footprints in the world. The equivalent of from 3 to 5 earths is required for the USA to maintain its current mode of living. Sustainable design coupled with sustainable lifestyle can reduce our footprint. A few aspects of our lifestyle that have great impact upon the environment are: home size (we tend to live in large homes that consume lots of fossil fuels for heating and lighting); transportation (we tend to drive private vehicles, which also use lots of fossil fuel); and diet (we tend to have a meat-heavy diet, which requires more fossil fuel to produce than a plant-based diet).

People everywhere aspire to a high quality of living. Current American culture associates a high quality of living with affluence or material wealth and consumption. It is likely that people in developing countries will also adopt a more affluent lifestyle at the same time that population is growing. This is the "double whammy" that will directly increase environmental impact.

The dilemma was identified and given a formula in 1971 by Ehrlich and Holdren:

Environmental Impact (I) = Population (P) x Affluence (A) x Technology (T), or I = PAT.

Ehrlich and Ehrlich (1997) later amended the formula, substituting E_{pc} or per capita energy consumption for A and T, stating: "almost all of a society's most environmentally damaging activities involve the mobilization and use of energy at high levels" (Ehrlich and Ehrlich, p. 1188). Regardless of how it is defined, population growth plus affluence will take a very heavy toll on the environment.

Ehrlich and Ehrlich point out that humans rely upon the environment for many benefits, including "the maintenance of the quality of the atmosphere; regulation of climate, provision of food from the sea, replenishment of soils, control of pests, and other vital underpinnings of agriculture, (timber production), medicines...and regulation of freshwater flows (including controlling floods and droughts) and other forms of weather amelioration" (Ehrlich and Ehrlich, p. 1189). They suggest that it may be difficult to halt the juggernaut of population that is propelling us toward 9 billion in 2050. However, it is desirable to "move as rapidly as is humanely possible to an optimum sustainable population size" (Ehrlich and Ehrlich, p. 1189). The Ehrlichs maintain that for all of the people in the world to enjoy a maximum quality of life over the long term, human population should be about 2 billion, or less than 1/3 of the current population. But the UN does not project that this is likely to happen during the next few centuries.

THE TRIPLE WHAMMY:
CLIMATE CHANGE

Warming of the climate system is unequivocal, as is now evident from observations of increases in global average air and ocean temperatures, widespread melting of snow and ice and rising global average sea level. (Bernstein, et al. 2007. IPCC).

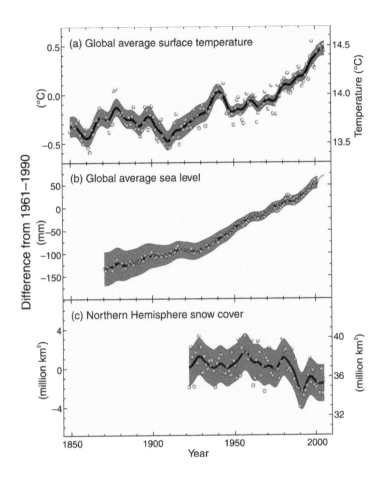

Figure 2.2 Effects of Rising Temperatures

These charts show climate change trends that have occurred over the past two centuries. While minor "dips" have occurred, the general trend has been toward hotter temperatures and higher sea levels. Snow cover in the northern hemisphere has dropped since 1990. This is largely due to the melting of Greenland and the polar ice cap. (http://www.ipcc.ch/graphics/syr/fig1-1.jpg).

Burning fossil fuels (beginning around 1700) has allowed humans to create and operate new technologies, such as trains, autos, airplanes, home appliances, farm machines, and computers. But the combustion of oil, coal, and gas emits waste gases, including CO_2, NO_2, and others, into the atmosphere, creating the greenhouse effect. These emissions have altered the global climate, initiating a trajectory of warming temperatures and rising sea levels.

"The primary drivers of climate change are tropical deforestation and the burning of fossil fuels (such as coal and oil)—activities that release carbon dioxide (CO_2) and other heat-trapping or 'greenhouse' gases into the atmosphere. The resulting CO_2 concentrations, now at their highest levels in at least the past

800,000 years, are largely responsible for annual average temperature increases over the last century of more than 0.5°F in Pennsylvania and 1°F in the mid-Atlantic region" (Union of Concerned Scientists 2008, p. 6).

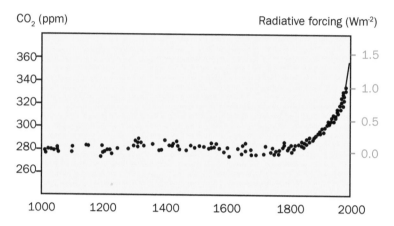

Figure 2.3 Indicators of the human influence on the atmosphere during the industrial era.

This chart shows that atmospheric carbon dioxide has increased from about 280 ppm (parts per million) in the pre-industrial era to over 360 ppm in 2000. It is continuing to rise. "Greenhouse Gas (GHG) missions were the highest in human history from 2000 to 2010 and reached 49 (±4.5) GtCO2eq/yr in 2010. The global economic crisis 2007/2008 only temporarily reduced emissions (IPCC,2014, Summary for Policy Makers, p. 18)."

The increased concentration of CO2 has resulted in radiative forcing (or watts per square meter). The earth is not able to radiate the sun's heat back into space due to the CO2 concentrations, resulting in 1.5 watts per square meter now being absorbed as opposed to a little over 0 in the pre-industrial era.

THE REALITY OF CLIMATE CHANGE

The Intergovernmental Panel on Climate Change (IPCC) has studied climate change for nearly three decades. It is composed of thousands of scientists from 195 countries working on a voluntary basis to "provide the world with a clear scientific view on the current state of knowledge in climate change and its potential environmental and socio-economic impacts" (http://www.ipcc.ch/organization). The IPCC scientists do not conduct research but assess current scientific and socio-economic research and policy.

IPCC is highly confident that climate change is inevitable and has developed models to predict likely trends. It is very important to do whatever we can to reduce and halt combustion of fossil fuels and destruction of ecosystems, especially forests, which convert carbon dioxide to oxygen. These actions will slow climate change. However, the IPCC predicts that even with reduction of combustion, it is likely to take centuries for the planet's thermostat to recover (IPCC).

PREDICTED IMPACTS TO TWO CONTINENTS

Two continents are used to exemplify the impacts of climate change: Africa and North America. Africa, which has a rapidly growing population but relatively low affluence, is expected to be impacted with up to 50% less yield from rain-fed agriculture by 2020. By 2080, arid and semi-arid land is expected to increase by 5–8% in Africa, exacerbating food and water shortages. By around 2100, adapting to sea-level rise could cost at least 5–10% of Africa's GNP (IPCC, 2007 p. 50).

The western part of North America is predicted to have decreased snow pack causing increased competition for already short water supply. In the early decades of the 21st century (the present), N. America will have increased yield of rain-fed agriculture...but not in all regions. Cities are expected to have an increased number, intensity, and duration of heat waves in the 21st century. Coastal communities and habitats will be increasingly stressed by climate change (IPCC, 2007 p. 52).

ECOSYSTEM AND SPECIES IMPACTS

According to the IPCC, some ecosystems are very likely to be especially affected by climate change. The sea-ice biome, tundra, and boreal forests will be affected by warming. Mediterranean-type ecosystems and some tropical forests will be affected by less precipitation. Mangroves, salt marshes, and coral reefs will have multiple stresses.

Coastal ecosystems will be impacted by sea-level rise and extreme weather events. The IPCC has also stated that "approximately 20–30% of species assessed so far are likely to be at increased risk of extinction if increases in global average warming exceed 1.5–2.5 degrees C (relative to 1980–99). If temperatures exceed 3.5% degrees C, model projections suggest significant extinctions of 40–70% of species assessed around the globe" (IPCC, 2007, p. 52–53).

ADAPTING TO AND MITIGATING CLIMATE CHANGE

Societies can respond to climate change by adapting to its impacts and by reducing GHG emissions (mitigation), thereby reducing the rate and magnitude of change. (IPCC, p. 56)

There is opportunity to mitigate (reduce) climate change through policy decisions. Humans are a fairly resilient and adaptable species, able to adjust to new conditions. In the 21st century we will need to adapt to the changes brought about from greenhouse gases and carbon dioxide persisting in the atmosphere. IPCC states that "there is much evidence of substantial economic potential for the mitigation of global GHG emissions over the coming decades that could offset the projected growth of global emissions or reduce emissions below current levels" (IPCC,2006, p. 58).

According to the IPCC, "the next two decades present a window of opportunity for mitigation in urban areas, as a large portion of the world's urban areas will be developed during this period...urban land cover is projected to expand by 56–310 % between 2000 and 2030 (IPCC, 2014, p.25)."

Cities can bundle policies and designs to help mitigate climate change. For example, designing flood regulation, water quality, food and transport systems to form a mutually reinforcing "grid" could have a significant effect.

Energy infrastructure is a key area of potential mitigation. Between 2005 and 2030, over $20 trillion will be invested in energy infrastructure. If non-polluting and low-carbon technologies are selected over polluting technologies, CO_2 can be reduced or at least not increased from current levels (IPCC, p. 58). Subsidies and tax credits are frequently used by governments to reward positive change and to overcome barriers to change. National and international policies emphasizing cooperation and mitigation can be the basis of large-scale societal change. Implementing regulations and standards and taxing polluters will also be effective. Public education and awareness can also contribute to positive behavioral changes.

A FORMULA FOR REDUCING ENVIRONMENTAL IMPACTS AND MITIGATING CLIMATE CHANGE

Along with population reduction, there is a need for affluence reduction or redistribution of wealth worldwide. For Americans this might mean that they use less-polluting forms of transportation (i.e., trains, buses, bicycles) or non-polluting forms (walking); live in smaller homes powered by renewable energy; and eat a different diet.

Carrington and Myers (2012) propose that a critical means of counteracting environmental degradation is through ecological restoration and regenerative design. Restoration of native plant communities on urban vacant lots, for example, will provide habitat for native insect and animal species and replenish ecological services. We propose amending the I = PAT formula to:

Environmental Impact (I) = Population (P) x Affluence (A) x Technology (T) – **Ecological restoration/regenerative Design (R)**

Regenerative design is design that produces more energy than it uses or up-cycles the matter that it contains. An example of regenerative design is a house that has more photovoltaic panels than it needs and puts the excess energy produced back into the grid. A raingarden that absorbs more than the stormwater runoff associated with its own property is regenerative. And the garden is expected to absorb more as the plants mature and have more leaf surface area and more extensive root zones. Ecological restoration is the restoration of degraded, simplified environments to healthier, more diverse ecosystems. Ecological restoration sets a trajectory in motion toward ever-increasing diversity.

The revised formula suggests that sustainability can apply to a spectrum of design disciplines (architecture, landscape architecture, and planning) at a variety of scales. It will be increasingly difficult to protect and conserve intact ecosystems, so we need to discover design ideas for buildings, landscapes, cities, and regions that can restore degraded ecosystems and provide healthier environments. Together, restored landscapes and improved buildings, transportation systems and infrastructure systems, can add up to have an aggregate positive value to reduce I (environmental impact) and to reduce GHG from many products, structures, and places used by humans.

QUESTIONS

1. How much food and material wealth could hunters/gatherers store?
2. How do you think this influenced their societies?
3. Does social stratification continue today? Where and in what way?
4. If world population increases to 9.7 billion in 2050, from 6.1 billion in 2000, what is the percent increase?
5. What are the environmental ramifications of that increase? How can we project how to manage earth's resources over the long term?
6. What will be the impact of increased life expectancy on world population?
7. Do you agree with Ehrlich and Ehrlichs' proposal that the earth's population should be reduced to 2 billion?
8. What ethical issues need to be dealt with in reducing population? Can it occur in a humane manner?
9. Why are bicycles considered *less* polluting forms of transportation rather than *non*-polluting forms?
10. What should cities do to adapt to the effects of climate change—especially as related to heat waves?
11. Can Africa afford to spend 5–10% of its GNP on adapting to sea-level rise? How can the monies be raised?
12. Do you think there is a link between political stability and climate change impacts?
13. In 2050, the most populous countries will be in which regions of the world? Do those regions currently have food or water shortages?

REFERENCES

Bernstein, et al. 2007. *Climate Change 2007: Synthesis Report*. Intergovernmental Panel on Climate Change. (http://www.ipcc.ch/organization).

Carrington, K. Daryl and Mary Myers. 2012. "The Fidelity Hypothesis." *Abstract. Finding Center: Council of Educators in Landscape Architecture* conference. March 28–31, 2012.

Ehrlich, Paul R. and Anne H. Ehrlich. 1997. "The Population Explosion: Why We Should Care and What We Should Do About It." *Environmental Law* 27: 1187–1197.

Ehrlich, Paul R. and John P. Holdren. 1971. "Impact of Population Growth." *Science*, 171:1212–17.

Illustrations on Climate Change from IPCC: (http://www.grida.no/climate/ipcc_tar/slides/index.htm).

IPCC, 2014: Summary for Policymakers. In: Climate Change 2014: Mitigation of Climate Change. Contribution of Working Group III to the Fifth Assessment Report of the Intergovernmental Panel on Climate Change [Edenhofer, O., R. Pichs-Madruga, Y. Sokona, E. Farahani, S. Kadner, K. Seyboth, A. Adler, I. Baum, S. Brunner, P. Eickemeier, B. Kriemann, J. Savolainen, S. Schlömer, C. von Stechow, T. Zwickel and J.C. Minx (eds.)]. Cambridge University Press, Cambridge, United Kingdom and New York, NY, USA.

Union of Concerned Scientists. October 2008. *Climate Change in Pennsylvania: Impacts and Solutions for the Keystone State.* UCS Publications: Cambridge, MA.

United Nations Department of Economic and Social Affairs/Population Division

World Population Prospects: The 2015 Revision, Key Findings. New York: the United Nations.

http://esa.un.org/unpd/wpp/publications/files/key_findings_wpp_2015.pdf

United Nations. 2004. *World Population to 2300.* Report by the Department of Social and Economic Affairs. ST/ESA/SER.A/236 (http://www.un.org/esa/population): accessed January 14, 2013.

Wackernagel, Mathis and William Rees. 1997. "Perceptual and Structural Barriers to Investing in Natural Capital: Economics from an Ecological Footprint Perspective." *Ecological Economics* 20: 3–24.

Woods, Christopher. 2010. "The Earliest Mesopotamian Writing," in Woods, Christopher, *Visible Language. Inventions of Writing in the Ancient Middle East and Beyond*, Oriental Institute Museum Publications, 32, Chicago: University of Chicago, pp. 33–50.

Scientific Laws and Principles

THE FRAMEWORK OF BIOLOGY

BY JOELLE PRESSON AND JAN JENNER

Mount Vernon Man Dies from Hantavirus

November 9, 2003

Panic and Concern: Four Corners disease. In May 1993 a fatal epidemic erupted in the Four Corners area, triggering an intensive effort to identify the cause of the disease and find a cure.

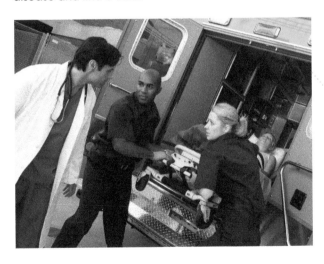

Threads ...

Four Corners Disease

Local woman dies of Hantavirus

May 10, 2003

Four Corners Disease

On May 14, 1993, a young Navajo man was brought to the medical center in Gallup, New Mexico (**see chapter-opening photo**). He was feverish and gasping for air and his condition rapidly worsened. As a medical team struggled to save him, his blood pressure dropped, his breathing became more strangled, and quite suddenly he died.

Because the young man died of unknown causes, an autopsy was ordered. The pathologist who performed it noted something odd. Just five days earlier he had seen another case just like this one: a young woman who had died from similar, flulike symptoms. Odder still, the pair turned out to be an engaged couple, and the young man had been brought to the emergency room while traveling to his fiancée's funeral.

Because the young couple's deaths were mysterious, swift, and similar, the hospital notified the New Mexico Department of Health. They warned doctors throughout the state that a fatal epidemic might be developing in the Four Corners region—an area where Arizona, Colorado, New Mexico, and Utah join. Doctors were asked to be alert for reports of other, similar deaths. Within days what the media were calling Four Corners disease had claimed more victims. All were young and otherwise healthy; all had had flulike symptoms; all the deaths were swift and agonized.

News of Four Corners disease spread panic and concern among the general population, and authorities at the Centers for Disease Control and Prevention (CDC) in Atlanta, Georgia, responded swiftly. Within just *one month* workers identified the cause of the disease and tracked it to its source. By mid-June the outbreak was understood in a larger context, and people in the region were given practical advice on how to prevent, detect, and get early treatment for the disease. This success story is an outstanding example of how science solved a problem and provided fast answers that saved lives.

If you were a member of a team assigned to solve a new disease, how would you proceed? What assumptions about nature and life would guide your work? What rules of logic would help you to draw conclusions? How would you decide which of the many possible explanations to believe and act on? In this chapter you will be introduced to the scientific approach to solving problems that has been so successful in revealing life's secrets.

Table 3.1 Biology in the News.

HEADLINE	DESCRIPTION OF STORY
From a Few Genes, Life's Myriad Shapes. *New York Times*, June 2007.	Researchers in the field of "evo-devo"—evolution and development—have found that only a handful of genes controls the diversity of body shapes found in animals. Studies in evo-devo are allowing scientists to understand how genetics, evolution, and development combine to produce animal diversity and human diversity.
Over-the-Counter DNA Testing: Wave of the Future or Waste of Money? Walgreens Rolls Out a Genetic 'Spit Kit' Test With Pathway Genomics. *ABC News* Medical Unit, May 11, 2010.	The kits allow genetic testing for risks of a variety of disorders, including cystic fibrosis, Alzheimer's, and breast cancer. It remains to be seen how effectively people can use this kind of genetic information.
The Ethics of Genetic Tests for Would-Be Parents. *NPR*, January 13, 2011.	New genetic tests allow parents to find out their own risks of passing on a genetic disorder, and to test their own embryos and choose to birth children who do not carry a particular genetic mutation. Parents will have to be well-informed about genetic testing and about the genetic disorders in order to make ethical decisions in this complex arena.
Athletes Beware, Scientists Hot on Gene Doping Trail. *Wired Magazine*, February 4, 2010.	Some companies are trying to sell genetic engineering kits to athletes, promising that athletic performance can be increased by taking a "pill" that will alter their genes. It is not at all clear whether such "kits" would actually work. Scientists are already trying to find ways to detect evidence of gene doping.
Children who form no racial stereotypes found. *Nature News*, April 2011.	Scientists have long suspected that racial stereotyping is an expression of the fear of strangers and of those who are "not like us". New research has found a genetic mutation that supports this view.
Genetic Ancestral Testing Cannot Deliver On Its Promise, Study Warns. *Science News*, October 2007.	Many companies promise the ability to find out a person's ancestral heritage through genetic testing. But, these tests come with assumptions, scientific underpinnings, and caveats, which prospective buyers must understand in order to interpret their results.

3.1

BIOLOGY TOUCHES EVERY ASPECT OF YOUR LIFE

Science is an intellectual pursuit that has a profound influence on your life. If you compare how you live with life in the 1800s, changes wrought by technology are obvious. Sanitation, convenience foods, cars, computers, cell phones, and e-mail are just a few examples of everyday applications of scientific discoveries that make your life so different from your great-great-grandparents'. Many other far-reaching applications of scientific discoveries that affect how you live come from **biology**, the study of life. Medical advances are an example. When you go to the doctor for antibiotics to treat an infection, you probably don't think about the biologists who made your treatment possible. From scientists of the 1700s who first peered into microscopes and saw tiny life-forms to present-day researchers who reveal how those life-forms can cause diseases, the treatment of infectious diseases is based on biological science.

biology the study of life

Discoveries in biology have made headlines in recent years. These include new antibiotics; contraceptives; drugs for high cholesterol and high blood pressure; treatments for clogged arteries, cancer, diabetes, and AIDS; genetic tests for a variety of diseases; and techniques that can ensure that your child does not inherit a serious genetic disease. All of these recent medical advances are rooted in biology. **Table 3.1** shows other less well-publicized areas where biology affects modern life. For example, microbes routinely are used to help clean up toxic waste sites and oil spills. Insights from studies of how living things depend on their environments can help us to predict what Earth's future will be like if humans continue to overpopulate, deplete, and pollute environments. Other applications of biology allow scientists to construct machines that can sense the environment, make decisions, mimic movements of people and other animals, and even surpass human mental abilities. In these and many other ways, biological science has daily impacts on your life.

Biology is a sprawling science. It encompasses a wide range of topics from electrons to ecosystems. This range is reflected in the work of people who "do" biology. For instance, many biologists focus their studies on cells. Such investigations include the chemicals that make up cells, how cells use energy, build complex structures, or reproduce. Studies of **organisms**, defined as entire living things, reveal how cells work together in plants, fungi, or animals. Other biologists concentrate on the ways different organisms interact with one another and with their environments, such as the interactions within families of elephants, the effects of pollutants on various species of algae, how birds migrate to their winter homes, or how new species evolve. All of these studies and many more are part of the science of biology.

organism the entire body of a living thing

Four Major Themes Run Through Your Study of Biology

Although biology is a large and complex field, it has several recurrent themes. In the chapters ahead you will encounter four of these biological themes. One theme is that complex things happen when simpler things interact. This idea is known as *emergent properties,* and you will discover it repeatedly during your study of biology. A second theme can be expressed as *unity and diversity.* This means that living things share fundamental structures and functions and are similar in many ways, yet each individual organism is unique and slightly different from all others. A related biological theme is *evolution by means of natural selection*, a process that explains the unity and diversity of life. This principle describes how some traits remain the same, while others change over generations. It also explains how these changes over the course of Earth's history have led to the evolution of totally new kinds of organisms. As a final theme, wherever feasible this book will explain the *scientific processes* that generate biological knowledge. Watch for these four themes throughout the chapters ahead. They will help you to make better sense of the new information you will learn.

In this introductory chapter you will explore some of the most important findings and conclusions in biology and consider how scientists use scientific approaches to reach their conclusions. This chapter is not a summary of the text. Rather, it provides the framework for your study of biology and gives you the basic vocabulary and concepts needed before you begin your journey into the study of life.

3.2
LIFE IS DEFINED BY A SET OF FEATURES THAT ALL LIVING THINGS SHARE

Biology is the study of life, but what exactly is life and how are living things different from nonliving things? For instance, what is there about you, the bacteria in yogurt, or a potted plant that is different from a watch, a yogurt container, or a flowerpot? Although living things are remarkably diverse, all have common features that collectively make each of them alive. Non-living things might have some of these features, and only a living thing will have all of them. Here are some of the most obvious ones.

- Life happens only within cells. All organisms are made up of one or more cells; each cell is limited by a physical boundary.
- Living things are highly complex and organized.
- Living things strictly control their internal environments and keep internal conditions within certain limits.
- Living things respond to and interact with the external environment.
- Living things use energy to power their internal processes, build internal structures, and grow.
- Living things carry instructions for conducting their internal processes and use these instructions to reproduce.

cell the smallest structural unit of life

cell membrane the boundary that separates a cell from other cells and from the environment while it allows a cell to communicate with the environment

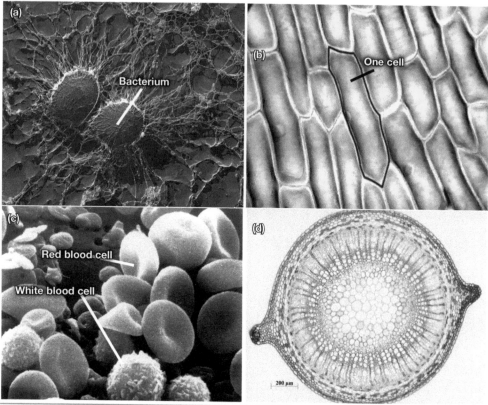

(a) Bacterium

(b) One cell

(c) Red blood cell
White blood cell

(d) 200 µm

Figure 3.1 All Living Things Are Made of Cells. **(a)** Bacterial cells, **(b)** Cells of an onion, **(c)** Human blood cells, **(d)** Tissues in the stem of a plant are made of many individual cells. (a: Erik Erbe & Christopher Pooley; b: kaibara87; c: Bruce Wetzel & Harry Schaefer; d: Rolf Dieter Mueller)

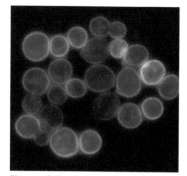

Figure 3.2 A Membrane Surrounds a Cell. **When yeast cells are stained in a particular way the proteins in their cell membranes absorb the dye and fluoresce red, orange, yellow, or green.** (Masur)

Let's briefly consider each of these characteristics that collectively differentiate something that is alive from something that is not alive.

Life Happens Inside Cells That Are Complex, Highly Organized, and Homeostatic

One universal aspect of life on Earth is that it happens inside cells. A **cell** is the basic structural unit of life. Cells come in many sizes and shapes, and organisms consist of one or more cells. **Figure 3.1** shows how varied cells can be; their variety reflects the amazing diversity of life.

How do you know if something is a cell? One characteristic feature of a cell is the boundary that separates the life within the cell from the nonlife outside of the cell. You are familiar with the boundaries of living things such as your own skin, the bark of a tree, or the shell of a crab, but you may be less familiar with the boundary around each cell, called the **cell membrane** (**Figure 3.2**). It protects the delicate processes of life from the environment surrounding the cell and allows a cell to communicate with the environment.

It is the processes that go on inside of a cell that make it alive. These processes are complex and highly organized. What does this mean? *Complex* means that cells have many different structures and a multitude of chemical processes; *organized* means that these structures and processes are not in disarray. It might help to think of a room before and after you straighten it. Of course your room is complex. Not only does it contain your "stuff"—clothes, books, and furniture—but also it houses the complex activities that happen in your room, what biologists would call your "processes." For instance, you might study, listen to music, watch TV, and pet your cat—all in this same room. Before you tidy up, things are scattered everywhere. Once you have straightened the room, the things in it still are complex, but they are more organized because you have shelved the books, put away your clothes, and gathered up your dirty laundry. This may even inspire you to focus time just on your cat, then read awhile, and then listen to music. You can see that both situations—before and after straightening—are complex, but the room is organized only after you have cleaned it up.

In a similar way, life is both complex and organized. Every living cell has an ordered, complex, internal structure. Of course, you cannot see subcellular structures with unaided vision, but you can observe the complexity and organization characteristic of life at other levels. An oak tree provides a good example. Its roots, trunk, branches, twigs, buds, leaves, flowers, and acorns give the tree a complex structure (**Figure 3.3**), but there is order in this complexity. Roots are underground, the trunk supports the branches, and the branches repeatedly fork and diverge to form the canopy that reaches upward. Leaves have characteristic structures and are arranged in a pattern on the tree. Flowers are reproductive structures that appear only at a specific season of the year. Pollinated flowers may mature into seed-bearing acorns, and in organized ways staining yeast cells with a special dye allows the

Figure 3.3   An Oak Tree Has a Complex and Organized Structure.

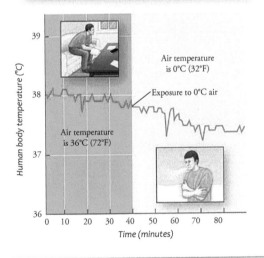

Even 40 minutes after exposure to 0°C air, human body temperature remains relatively constant and has fallen only about 0.5°C. Internal body mechanisms, including shivering, help maintain a steady body temperature.

Figure 3.4   Maintenance of a Steady Body Temperature Is a Homeostatic Mechanism. **Why has the person's body temperature fallen only 0.5°C when the outside air temperature is about 38°C colder than indoor air?**

Figure 3.5 Predator Eats Predator. This robber fly has wrestled a dragonfly to the ground and is sucking out its body fluids. (Thomas Shahan)

Figure 3.6 Predator and Prey. The cat's body will convert the mouse's tissues to energy and useful chemicals. (Lxowle)

homeostasis the stable internal conditions of an organism that support life's cellular and chemical processes

proteins in their cell membranes to become visible as they glow shades of red, orange, yellow, and green. Seeds within acorns grow into new mature oak trees. If you take a few moments to look at the natural world, you will find other examples of the complexity and organization of life.

Life accomplishes this order and organization because the activities that go on inside an organism are strictly controlled. Again, think of your room. If you want to *keep* your room and your activities organized, you must control where you put each item and what you do at each moment. For instance, a book could go either on the desk or on the shelf and still be organized, but it can't go into the pile of laundry. Cells and organisms also have ways to control structures and activities to ensure that the ordered life of a cell does not fall into chaos.

To manage life's chemical processes, living things also must regulate the quantities and characteristics of the chemicals they contain. The inside of a cell is mostly water, but many chemicals are dissolved in that water—and these are critically involved in the structures, processes, and activities that collectively are called *life*. While external environmental conditions may fluctuate wildly, the internal environment of a cell cannot. Factors such as the amount of water, amount of salt and other chemicals, and acidity are carefully regulated. Some organisms also regulate more complex traits such as body temperature or food intake.

The delicate balance of internal aspects that all living organisms maintain is called **homeostasis.** If this internal chemical balance is upset—that is, if homeostasis is disrupted—an organism easily can die. Homeostasis is reflected in the way many systems of the human body work. Control of body temperature is a good example (**Figure 3.4**). If a mammal, such as a human, is suddenly put in a very cold environment, body temperature will not fall dramatically. Body systems respond to the cold and maintain body temperature close to normal. Only after a long time in the cold will body temperature begin to fall.

Living Things Respond to and Interact with Their Environments, Use Energy, and Reproduce

To survive, every organism must interact with its environment. Plants must locate and grow toward a source of light or water. Other organisms must locate and take in food (**Figure 3.5**). An individual might move toward a potential mate, or its offspring, or need to know how wet, or hot, or salty the environment is. You might need to know if the person walking behind you is an innocent stranger, an old classmate, or someone to run from. All cells must sense and respond to their environments.

Another important point about living organisms is that they are active. Structures inside of cells move, cells move, and organisms that are made of many cells move. To carry out all of these activities living organisms must have a source of **energy**. For now energy will be defined as something objects have that gives them the ability to do work. In its need for a source of power, life is no different from a lawnmower, an electric toothbrush, or a cell phone. The Sun is the ultimate source of energy for nearly all organisms. While plants, some bacteria, and algae can harvest the Sun's energy directly, the rest of us obtain energy by eating plants or other living things (**Figure 3.6**). Living organisms spend much time getting energy and converting it to a form their cells readily can use.

When people work together to complete a complex set of tasks, it helps if they have instructions. In a similar way cells need instructions to carry out the processes of life. The instructions for the activities that go on in a cell are contained in large molecules called **DNA**, an acronym for deoxyribonucleic acid (**Figure 3.7**). Although the details of the DNA molecule differ, the instructions it carries are made of the same chemicals and work in the same way in all organisms. The structure of DNA and the consistent way it works to direct living processes are the basis for the unity of life. As you will read in later chapters, though, DNA molecules differ slightly between individuals, and these subtle variations are responsible for the incredible diversity of life.

In addition to providing instructions for a cell's activities, DNA gives organisms the special ability to reproduce. The DNA molecule can be copied exactly, and the copy can be given to new cells, which can outlive the parent cell. Without this special ability, life would not continue over time. When DNA is successfully copied and a new cell is made, the process ensures that the new cell has the same instructions and operates by the same rules as did its parent cell.

Figure 3.7 DNA molecules carry the instructions for all the processes of life for all organisms.

Quick Check   **3.2**

What is the function of the cell membrane?

Describe homeostasis, using adjustments in body temperature as an example.

3.3
LEVELS OF ORGANIZATION ARE CHARACTERISTIC OF LIFE

The complex interactions within and between living organisms can seem baffling, but you can begin to comprehend them by considering something that biologists call *levels of organization*. This idea is that living things can be grouped into increasingly complex units. An analogy might be helpful here. Imagine that you work for a large drug company trying to develop a drug to treat heart disease. Your job is to run chemical analyses on compounds that field agents find in the forests

energy the ability to do work

DNA (deoxyribonucleic acid) the molecule that carries the instructions for life

and jungles of the world. But of course you do not work alone. You are part of a research unit where every person's job is related to heart disease; each week all the people in your unit meet to trade ideas and discuss their work. The heart disease research unit is part of a larger group that includes biologists and medical doctors who will test the potential treatments in animals and in people. The entire heart disease workforce also would include people who might market and sell any treatments developed. And this large heart disease

chemical element a basic kind of matter

atom the smallest unit of an element that has all of the properties of that element

organelle subcellular groups of molecules that have specific functions within cells

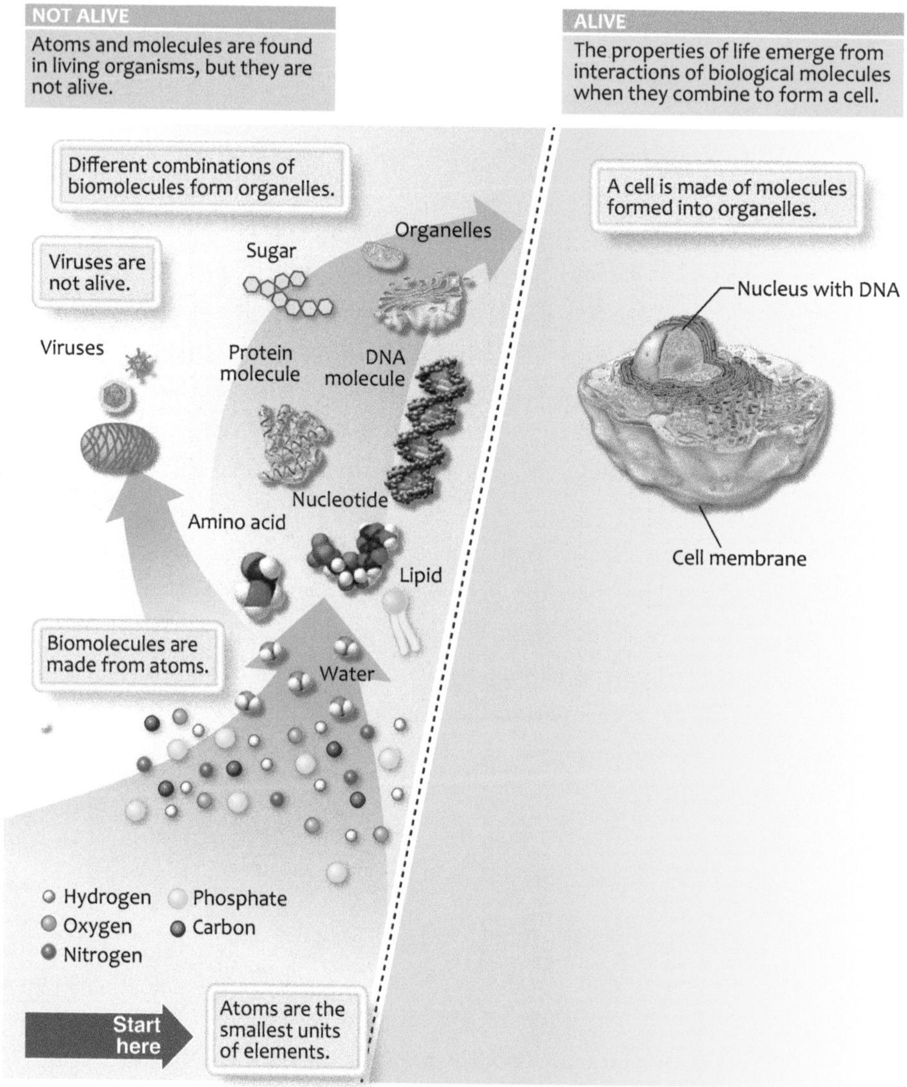

NOT ALIVE
Atoms and molecules are found in living organisms, but they are not alive.

ALIVE
The properties of life emerge from interactions of biological molecules when they combine to form a cell.

Different combinations of biomolecules form organelles.

A cell is made of molecules formed into organelles.

Viruses are not alive.

Organelles

Sugar

Nucleus with DNA

Viruses

Protein molecule

DNA molecule

Amino acid

Nucleotide

Lipid

Cell membrane

Biomolecules are made from atoms.

Water

○ Hydrogen ○ Phosphate
○ Oxygen   ● Carbon
● Nitrogen

Start here

Atoms are the smallest units of elements.

Figure 3.8 From Atoms to a Cell, Life Has Levels of Organization. **Why isn't a DNA molecule alive?**

workforce is just one of many groups in the large drug company. Each level has its own complexity, which builds as you go from one level of organization to the next.

Life is organized in a similar way. The simplest level of organization involves the interactions of the chemicals that make up life. The groupings continue through different types of cells, to the cells that interact within larger organisms, to organisms that interact with one another. The most complex level of organization includes every organism and the nonliving environmental components that support them. There are many levels of organization in between these endpoints.

Individual Organisms Are Made of Chemicals, Cells, Tissues, and Organs

The first level of life is not actually alive but is the foundation on which life is built. Life is made of chemical building blocks called **chemical elements** (**Figure 3.8**). Each element is a basic kind of matter. The smallest unit of an element that has all the properties of that element is an **atom**, and life is composed of just a handful of elements. Hydrogen (H), carbon (C), oxygen (O), and nitrogen (N) are a few examples of elements that are important chemical building blocks of life. Of course, life is more intricate than the atoms of hydrogen or oxygen. Atoms combine to form more complex structures such as *molecules.*

The next level of organization brings us closer to the realm of life (**Figure 3.8**). Molecules and atoms are not by themselves alive, but in the right combinations and under the right chemical and physical conditions they combine to form **organelles**, subcellular groups of molecules that have specific functions within cells. Cells are the basic units of life. Anything less than a cell is not alive. A **virus** is a small structure made of biological molecules, but it is not a cell. A virus cannot independently use chemical energy to build its own structures or carry out life's processes. So a virus is not alive. [...] The point here is that as far as we know, only cells are alive.

Organisms that have just one cell are **unicellular organisms.** Despite their small size, unicellular organisms can have incredible complexity (**Figure 3.9a**). Organisms made of two or more cells are called

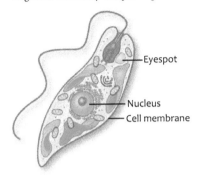

(a) A unicellular organism like *Euglena* has just a single cell with many complex organelles.

Eyespot

Nucleus

Cell membrane

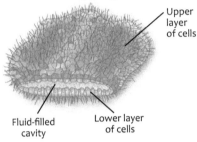

(b) *Trichoplax* is a simple multicellular organism that has many cells arranged around a fluid-filled cavity. Each cell has complex organelles.

Upper layer of cells

Fluid-filled cavity

Lower layer of cells

(c) At its largest, *Trichoplax* is about ten times the size of *Euglena*.

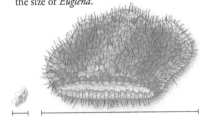

Euglena is 6.8 to 8 micrometers long.

Trichoplax is 700 micrometers at its widest dimension.

Figure 3.9 **A Complex Unicellular Organism and a Simple Multicellular Organism. *Euglena spirogyra* has just one cell with complex organelles. *Trichoplax adhaerens* is one of the simplest multicellular organisms.**

virus a small, nonliving structure that incorporates biological molecules

unicellular organism an organism made of just one cell

multicellular organism an organism made of two or more cells

tissue a group of similar cells gathered together into a unit that performs a specific function

organ a grouping of different types of tissues that work together to perform a specific task

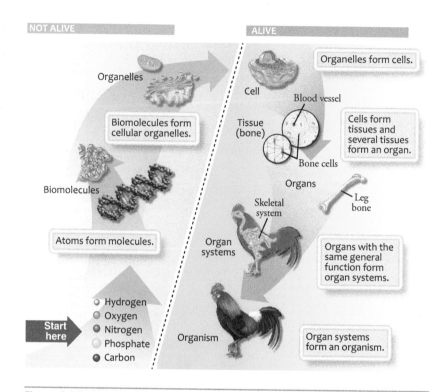

Figure 3.10 Levels of Organization: From Atoms to an Organism.

organ system a group of organs that work together to perform a specific body function

population a group of individuals of one kind of organism living in one geographic locality

multicellular organisms. Just as people in an organization specialize in certain jobs, different cells of multicellular organisms can specialize in certain jobs. Because of this, multicellular organisms can do interesting and complex things that unicellular organisms cannot do. **Figure 3.9b** shows *Trichoplax,* one of the simplest known multicellular organisms. *Trichoplax* has just five types of cells, but they aren't organized into tissues. A **tissue** is a group of similar cells gathered together into a unit that performs a specific function. For instance, blood is a tissue that transports nutrients and water. Muscle is a tissue that contracts and moves body parts.

In more complex multicellular organisms, different kinds of tissues are grouped into **organs** to perform even more complex tasks (**Figure 3.10**). For example, individual bones are organs that are part of the skeletal system. Bones are composite structures that, like all organs, are formed of several kinds of tissues such as connective tissues, blood, blood vessels, and nerves. Connective tissue binds the bone to the rest of the body, while blood and blood vessels supply nutrients to bone cells and remove wastes. Bone cells secrete deposits of calcium around themselves, forming patterns of concentric rings. Just as atoms are not alive by themselves, tissues and organs are not by themselves whole

Table 3.2 Major Human Organ Systems and Their Functions.

ORGAN SYSTEM	MAJOR COMPONENTS	FUNCTION
Integumentary	Skin, hair, nails	Protection from water loss, mechanical injury, and infection
Muscular	Skeletal muscles	Movements of body parts and of whole body
Skeletal	Bones, ligaments, tendons	Support of body and protection of internal organs
Digestive	Mouth, pharynx, esophagus, stomach, intestines, liver, pancreas, gallbladder, anus	Digestion and absorption of food, and elimination of food wastes
Circulatory	Heart, blood vessels, blood	Movement of substances to and from individual cells
Respiratory	Trachea, breathing tubes, lungs	Gas exchange: obtaining oxygen and releasing carbon dioxide
Lymphatic and immune	Lymphatic vessels, lymph nodes, lymph, immune cells, bone marrow, thymus, spleen, white blood cells	Defense against infection and cleanup of dead cells
Excretory	Kidneys, ureters, bladder, urethra	Elimination of metabolic wastes and regulation of chemistry of blood
Endocrine	Pituitary, thyroid, pancreas, ovaries, testes, and other glands that secrete hormones	Coordination of body functions by hormones
Nervous	Brain, spinal cord, nerves, sense organs	Sensing internal and external stimuli and coordination of entire body's functions
Reproductive	Ovaries, testes, and related organs	Reproduction

organisms. Organs that perform related functions are grouped into an **organ system** that accomplishes a major body function. For instance, all of the bones in the body are all part of the skeletal system, which has the job of supporting and protecting the body's soft tissues. **Table 3.2** lists the major organ systems of the human body. Finally, an organism consists of the whole body of a living thing, so you are an organism and a rooster, a *Euglena*, a *Trichoplax*, an oak tree, a bacterium, and a mosquito are organisms too.

Figure 3.11 Leaf Cutter Ants. (Arpingstone)

Individual Organisms Interact as Part of One or Several Groups

If you took a careful census of the organisms that live in your backyard, you would probably discover thousands of different kinds, most of them small, and many of them insects. Not only are there lots of different organisms, but they can be viewed as components of larger interacting biological systems. Let's consider some of the interactions in the lives of one such insect, a leaf cutter ant that lives in rain forests in Central and South America (**Figure 3.11**). Ants interact with each other, with other kinds of organisms like the plants whose leaves they gather, and with the nonliving parts of their environment like soil, water, and air. A group of individuals of one kind of organism living in one geographic locality is called a **population.** All of the populations of a single kind of organism form a *species*. All individuals of a species have similar characteristics that help define them as one species.

One of the important lessons from modern biology is that individual organisms do not exist in isolation. Instead, every individual depends on others for its survival. Leaf cutter ants are part of a colony whose members accomplish different tasks and support each other. Worker ants use their sharp-edged jaws to snip off bits of plants and carry these back to the colony. There the raw plant matter is chewed and the mulch is added to the colony's underground garden of fungus that provides food for the colony. The tiniest workers tend the fungus garden. As a whole the colony enriches the soil it lives in, and so it has an impact on other organisms that live there. As the ants dig their colony into the soil, they bring up and distribute soil that has a higher mineral content than surface soil. The ants, in turn, are food for other animals like anteaters, armadillos, and some birds.

Interactions between individuals and their environment produce more complex organizations. Because of limits set by geography, an individual usually interacts only with a small subset of its own species. In many cases a population is the most important group when considering the interactions between individuals. For instance, while all the populations of *Atta cephalotes* leaf cutter ants form one species, populations of leaf cutters in widely separated geographic regions are not likely to interact. In contrast, populations of *different* species can interact to form a larger unit called a **community.** In the case of the ants, the community includes the plants they snip to grow their fungus gardens, the fungi they eat, and animals that prey on and parasitize them. Communities interact with other nearby communities, forming larger units that impact one another around the globe. An **ecosystem** is a larger unit that consists of communities plus their nonliving environments. In turn, ecosystems are grouped into larger regional ecosystems called **biomes** that are controlled by broad climatic patterns and characterized by typical forms of vegetation and by animals with distinctive adaptations to these environments. Leaf cutter ants are part of an ecosystem, the tropical rain forest biome, and the biosphere. Finally, all biomes are included in the **biosphere.**

Interactions at Each Level of Organization Produce the Complexities of the Next Higher Level

Living things do so many unique and amazing things that it may be hard to grasp the idea that life is controlled by the same rules as the rest of the universe. Nevertheless, the same universal laws that govern the interactions of chemicals in stars, power plants, and test tubes also govern chemical interactions within living organisms. How is it that life appears to be so different from chemical compounds found in jars and bottles on a chemist's shelf? The answer lies in the principle of **emergent properties**: the concept that simple components can interact to produce something that is much more complex.

You experience emergent properties in your daily life. Think of the many parts of a car, as shown in **Figure 3.12**: engine, brakes, steering wheel, and so on. At a basic level a car is made of parts manufactured from steel, plastic, aluminum, rubber, and glass. By themselves these parts don't do much, but they are shaped and assembled into the car's component systems. For instance, your car has an engine, an electrical system, and a set of wheels associated with other parts that form a steering system. Each of the car's systems has interesting properties, but again, they are not too useful until they are combined and are working together. By itself, none of the parts could produce a vehicle that moves at high speeds, carries passengers, and can stop on demand. But together these individual component systems interact to make a car that does all of these things. The properties of a car emerge when all of its components interact. With this analogy in mind, let's return to the various levels of life's organization.

Just as unassembled auto parts do not have the properties of an intact car, by themselves the chemicals and molecules inside a cell do not have the properties of life. As you saw in **Figure 3.10**, life emerges from the interactions of atoms and molecules within a cell. Similarly, individual cells of a multicellular organism cannot do all of the things the whole organism can do. For instance, a single cell of your body cannot grasp a tool, watch an ant, or write a song. It takes the entire body to produce these complex behaviors. Repeating the same theme, new properties emerge when individuals interact within populations and when different populations interact within communities. While a single tree can

The properties of a car become evident only when its component parts are correctly assembled.

Figure 3.12 The Concept of Emergent Properties.

community interacting populations of different species that live in a local area

ecosystem communities and the nonliving aspects of their environments

biome a geographic region dominated by distinctive climate patterns and distinctive vegetation

biosphere all of Earth's ecosystems and biomes

emergent properties the principle that simple components interact to produce more complex systems with more complex traits and behaviors

Quick Check   3.3

List the levels of organization of life, starting with atoms and ending with the biosphere.

In what ways does a car show emergent properties?

produce shade, a grove of trees has a broad, leafy canopy that provides shelter and protection for the community that lives on, within, and beneath the canopy. Similarly, a single chimpanzee can defend itself from a predator, but a troop of chimpanzees can cooperatively defend an expansive territory. Individuals within the troop can specialize in more complex tasks such as mating or raising young. The ecosystem that the community of the leaf cutter ant colony belongs to has its own properties. The ecosystem influences the characteristics of the soil. It has characteristic patterns of sunlight, temperature, moisture, and rainfall, and provides nutrients, shelter, and other complex services for the organisms that live within the ecosystem.

3.4
EVOLUTION AND NATURAL SELECTION HAVE PRODUCED LIFE'S DIVERSE FORMS

The study of modern biology has revealed many astounding things about the living world and one of them is the incredible diversity of life. Each day scientists discover new kinds of life that thrive in the most amazing places. Living things are small, large, soft, hard, colorful, drab, and have diverse adaptations that help them to survive. Even at the level of individuals there is diversity. Every human is unique, and this also is true of every other living thing. Diversity is fundamental to the nature of life. Yet, diverse organisms solve the problems of staying alive in a limited number of ways. This is a critical insight. Life is diverse—and at the same time life is unified by shared chemicals, processes, and structures.

These two themes—unity and diversity—characterize living organisms, but how can living things be so different and yet so similar? The idea of evolution provides the answer. The name most associated with evolution is Charles Darwin. He understood that **evolution** is a change in a species over generations. Because evolutionary changes lead to new species, evolution produces biological diversity.

One of the most convincing ways to see evolution is to trace the history of life on Earth (**Figure 3.13**). Notice that different kinds of organisms emerged gradually over time, and that the transitions from one general group of organisms to another make sense. The earliest living things—probably formed about 3.8 billion years ago—were unicellular organisms with lots of biochemical diversity but not very much structural diversity. Later, about 3 billion years ago, unicellular organisms became more complex with intricate internal and

evolution a change in a species over generations

natural selection the effects of environmental factors that allow some individuals in a population to survive and produce offspring, while others do not

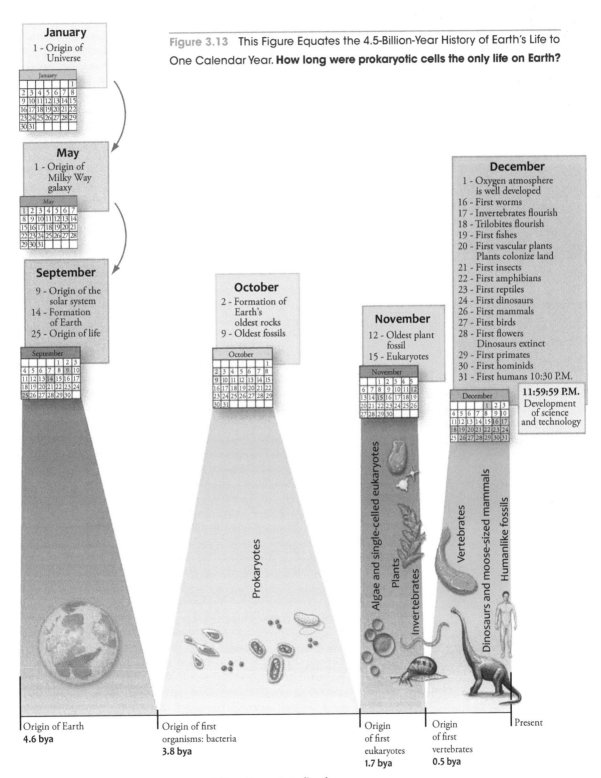

Figure 3.13 This Figure Equates the 4.5-Billion-Year History of Earth's Life to One Calendar Year. **How long were prokaryotic cells the only life on Earth?**

January
1 - Origin of Universe

May
1 - Origin of Milky Way galaxy

September
9 - Origin of the solar system
14 - Formation of Earth
25 - Origin of life

October
2 - Formation of Earth's oldest rocks
9 - Oldest fossils

November
12 - Oldest plant fossil
15 - Eukaryotes

December
1 - Oxygen atmosphere is well developed
16 - First worms
17 - Invertebrates flourish
18 - Trilobites flourish
19 - First fishes
20 - First vascular plants Plants colonize land
21 - First insects
22 - First amphibians
23 - First reptiles
24 - First dinosaurs
26 - First mammals
27 - First birds
28 - First flowers Dinosaurs extinct
29 - First primates
30 - First hominids
31 - First humans 10:30 P.M.

11:59:59 P.M.
Development of science and technology

Prokaryotes

Algae and single-celled eukaryotes

Plants

Invertebrates

Vertebrates

Dinosaurs and moose-sized mammals

Humanlike fossils

Origin of Earth
4.6 bya

Origin of first organisms: bacteria
3.8 bya

Origin of first eukaryotes
1.7 bya

Origin of first vertebrates
0.5 bya

Present

Billion Years Ago (bya)

Figure 3.14

An Unfriendly World. Weather; availability of food, shelter, and water; predators; and disease are all natural agents that can select for or against an individual's survival. (Alnus)

external structures. The first multicellular organisms were not zebras or pine trees. Instead they were fairly simple organisms not too different from the green algae that grow on the sides of your fish tank. The earliest animals had soft bodies, were small, and did not have limbs. Later more complex animals and plants evolved, and by half a billion years ago there were lots of complex lifeforms.

To this point all life was still restricted to the oceans, rivers, and lakes of the world, but there were invertebrate animals, vertebrate animals, and highly structured aquatic plants. Around this time organisms moved out of the water and colonized land, where new species evolved. Vertebrates with limbs, invertebrates with complex social organizations, plants with intricate life cycles, and many other diverse species evolved even more biological diversity.

How did this tremendous diversity of species come about? How does evolution happen? One answer is found in the concept of evolution by means of **natural selection.** The idea is simple, yet enormously powerful. In the process of evolution by means of natural selection, the traits of species change over time (or evolve) because in each generation only some individuals survive to reproduce the next generation. Therefore, those individuals that survive to produce offspring determine the traits of the next generation. In natural selection the qualities of nature—meaning various aspects of an individual's environment—are the factors that govern who survives to reproduce and pass on their DNA to the next generation (**Figure 3.14**).

One thing to note about this history of life is that life does not get *better* over time, but it does get more complex and more diverse. It would be a stretch to say that humans are in any way better organisms than bacteria. After all, bacteria can survive in harsh environments that quickly would kill a person. In addition, bacteria and other small, simple organisms will probably be around long after humans are extinct. But it is fair to say that humans are more complex than bacteria. Evolution has produced more complexity over time.

The modern understanding that evolution has produced Earth's incredible biological diversity is the cornerstone of all modern biology. Why?

Quick Check   3.4

What are the two biological themes that characterize living organisms?

How does natural selection produce evolution?

Because of this important insight: everything we know about biology says that *all organisms are genetically related.* Think about what that statement means. You know what it means genealogically to find a long-lost cousin: you are related to that cousin because you share a common ancestor. The same is true for all living things, alive or extinct. This conclusion that all living things are genetically related is supported by biological knowledge that has been accumulated over the past 200 years.

BIOLOGY APPLIES THE METHODS OF SCIENCE TO THE STUDY OF LIFE

Life can be understood by the same means used to reveal how the rest of the universe works—the methods of science. Simply put, science is a way to answer questions about the world around us. People have always asked questions, tried to understand their surroundings, and attempted to predict what will happen. Modern science is a more formal expression of these shared approaches to knowledge.

Art, music, philosophy, literature, ethics, and religion are also ways in which people ask questions and look for answers about life, but they are different from science. The central feature of a scientific statement is that it must be tied to an *observation of the real world*. Because the aim of science is to understand the world around us, science requires that ideas be tested against the world to find out if they are correct. More than just making observations, though, science reflects the human tendency to explain observations. In science explanations are given in terms of natural causes—other things that can be observed and described. These seemingly obvious comments about science have important implications, so let's consider them in greater detail.

Much scientific research is focused on getting a thorough description of the things and events in the world. To do this you must accept that there is a real world that can be studied. More importantly, you must understand that the nature of the world is independent of a person's beliefs. For example, no matter how firmly you believe that the Earth is flat or round, your belief would have no impact on whether the Earth is flat or round. Science is much more than just a description of the world, though.

The real motivation behind doing science is to use knowledge to predict what will happen tomorrow.

For instance, farmers want to predict the cycles of floods and droughts; governments want to predict storms and other possibly harmful natural events; parents want to predict the health of their children.

In short, humans want some advantage in the face of an uncertain future—and the predictive power of science is the best way to get that advantage. A full description of events sometimes can be used to predict what will happen next, but the real predictive power of science comes from understanding the causes of events—in other words to understand how and why things happen. Where do scientists look for causes? An important assumption in science is that all observable events can be explained by other observable events. If an explanation for an event relies on something supernatural, or something that can never be observed, or can be observed only by people with certain beliefs, then it is not a scientific explanation.

Scientific Statements Reflect the Variation in the Universe

You may have experienced frustration when a newspaper article declares that science has discovered some fact, only to find three years later that this "fact" is not so reliable. What is going on here?

Isn't a "scientific fact" something that is always true? The problem is that while there are reliable principles, causes, and events in the world, there also is variation. Because almost everything that is interesting

Table 3.3 The Probability Game.

This jar contains 15 tickets. If you agree to play the game, you will have a chance to draw a ticket. You must abide by the directive on the ticket. Will you play the game?
No? Well, it may help if you know what is on the tickets. Here are their messages:
You win $1,000!
A month's worth of food is donated to the family of your choice.
You must pay $1.
For one week you must do the laundry for everyone in your house.
For one week you must stop talking to your best friend.
Now, will you play the game?
Is it likely that you will get a good message on one draw? What are the chances? Would it help if you know how the messages are distributed on the tickets?
One ticket reads: You win $1,000!
Two tickets read: A month's worth of food is donated to the family of your choice.
Two tickets read: You must pay $1.
Five tickets read: For one week you must do the laundry for everyone in your house.
Five tickets read: For one week you must stop talking to your best friend.
Now will you play the game? Is there any more information to give you? No.
No one can predict the future, but you can calculate your chances of success or failure. As you see from this game, when you know more about what is in the jar, you know more about the odds of success. This is the kind of information that science provides. It tells you more about what is in the jar—or in the world around you.

to study has many dimensions and multiple causes, discovering the consistencies can be difficult. Consider, for example, the simple finding that smoking cigarettes causes lung cancer, one of the most reliable observations in modern medicine, yet this cause-and-effect relationship is not 100% certain. Not everyone who smokes gets lung cancer, and not everyone who does not smoke remains free of lung cancer. This is because lung cancer is a complex event affected by many different factors, one of which is cigarette smoke.

Probability is another way to describe the chances that something will happen. Probability is a statement of the likelihood of an event and ranges from zero to 1.0. The probability game in **Table 3.3** will help you to understand how science helps to predict the likelihood of something happening.

An event with a 0.0 probability will never happen, while an event with 1.0 probability will definitely happen and has a 100% certainty. Some statements in science such as the speed of light or the structure of a hydrogen atom have close to a 1.0 probability. Other statements such as "the Earth is the center of the solar system" are known to be false and so have a probability of just about zero. Many of the statements in science, especially in biology, have a probability somewhere in between 0.0 and 1.0. This does *not* mean that science is a flawed way of looking at the world.

Rather, it means that the world is a complex place, and nearly every event can have multiple causes.

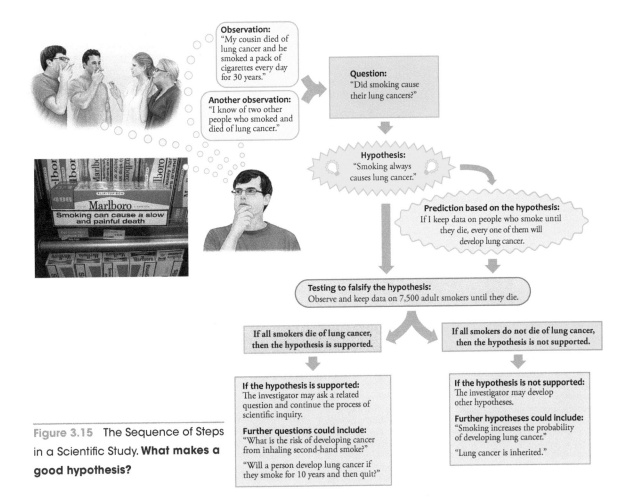

Figure 3.15 The Sequence of Steps in a Scientific Study. **What makes a good hypothesis?**

Observation:
"My cousin died of lung cancer and he smoked a pack of cigarettes every day for 30 years."

Another observation:
"I know of two other people who smoked and died of lung cancer."

Question:
"Did smoking cause their lung cancers?"

Hypothesis:
"Smoking always causes lung cancer."

Prediction based on the hypothesis:
If I keep data on people who smoke until they die, every one of them will develop lung cancer.

Testing to falsify the hypothesis:
Observe and keep data on 7,500 adult smokers until they die.

If all smokers die of lung cancer, then the hypothesis is supported.

If all smokers do not die of lung cancer, then the hypothesis is not supported.

If the hypothesis is supported:
The investigator may ask a related question and continue the process of scientific inquiry.

Further questions could include:
"What is the risk of developing cancer from inhaling second-hand smoke?"

"Will a person develop lung cancer if they smoke for 10 years and then quit?"

If the hypothesis is not supported:
The investigator may develop other hypotheses.

Further hypotheses could include:
"Smoking increases the probability of developing lung cancer."

"Lung cancer is inherited."

Smoking can cause a slow and painful death

Repeated and verified scientific studies on a subject allow you to base your choices in life on the chances that certain events will follow those choices. The choice to smoke or not to smoke cigarettes is just one example.

Events or groups of events that can be expected to happen with near 1.0 probability and with mathematical precision can be expressed as **scientific laws.** A law can be formulated when the events in question can be given precise numbers, and these numbers can be used instead of words to describe what is happening. In some cases laws apply universally—as far as we know—such as the speed of light and its relationship to mass in Albert Einstein's famous equation $E = mc^2$. Sometimes laws apply only in some situations, but still are reliable.

For instance, while Newton's laws of gravity do not apply precisely in all situations, they do describe the movement of objects with a great deal of accuracy.

scientific law a reliable and precise mathematical description of an event or set of events

hypothesis a possible explanation of an event or an answer to a scientific question that can be tested by formal studies or experiments

Science Involves a Disciplined Way of Studying the Universe

Now it's time to consider how scientists ensure that scientific conclusions accurately reflect the world. There are two important aspects to consider: the processes of science and the culture of science. First, the processes of science usually involve thoughtful, careful observations or experiments.

Second, the culture of science includes a set of expectations for behavior that increases the probability that scientific statements reflect the truth about the universe. Let's look more deeply at each of these aspects of science, starting with the sequence of steps involved in a scientific study. **Figure 3.15** uses the example of studying the relationship between tobacco smoking and cancer to show how the scientific method works.

- A *question* or an *observation* often sparks a scientific study.
- Additional *observations* lead to a preliminary answer to the question.
- The preliminary answer is formalized as an **hypothesis**, a statement that the researcher thinks explains the phenomenon or answers the question.
- The investigator uses the hypothesis to make a prediction that then will be tested by further observations and experiments.
- The investigator will test the *prediction* in a formal study or experiment, trying hard to disprove or *falsify* the hypothesis.
- The results of the test will be used to reject, modify, or support the hypothesis. This usually leads to a restatement of the hypothesis or the statement of a new hypothesis.
- The modified or new hypothesis is tested by a new round of observations.

Science often starts with observations and questions that lead to a hypothesis. You might develop your own questions after observing living things, or by thinking while you sit in your chair, or from a discussion with a friend. Your questions become science when you actually try to resolve them by testing them. But before you can even try to find an answer, you must clearly and precisely state your question and your plan for finding an answer, so that there is no confusion about what you mean. Initially your questions may be vague and uncertain, such as "Why did my aunt die of lung cancer?" As your thoughts get more organized, you can state your hypothesis more clearly and start to think of some answers. The question about your aunt might then be turned into this statement: "My aunt died from lung cancer because she smoked a pack of cigarettes a day for 30 years." When you state your proposed answer clearly in a way that can be tested, you have developed a hypothesis.

Once your question and hypothesis have been clearly stated, you must think of a way to test them. Sometimes you must devise specific situations and use special instruments to determine if your hypothesis is likely to be correct. Even more important, to be sure that you are not just fooling yourself, you must try hard to show that your hypothesis is *wrong*. This probably sounds strange. But if you try hard to show that your hypothesis is wrong—and it is wrong—you actually have learned something valuable. Alternatively, if you diligently try to show that your hypothesis is wrong and it seems to be right, you can have more confidence in this conclusion. In the case of your aunt, you would search for other possible reasons why she might have died from lung cancer. For instance, was she exposed to toxic chemicals or radiation? Did she have a history of associated lung diseases? These other reasons would be stated as hypotheses and tested along with the hypothesis that exposure to cigarette smoke did cause her cancer.

The scientific studies of a question rarely stop with the initial answers. Scientific conclusions go through stages. As more studies are done that support a hypothesis—and do not cause it to be rejected—the conclusions become more reliable and are more likely to be correct. As experiments continue, the hypothesis may become broader, and apply to more situations. Once a set of related hypotheses are strongly supported and apply broadly, eventually the explanation is called a **theory**. You probably do not think of the word *theory* in this way, but to science a theory is a well-tested explanation. The theory of continental drift in geology is an example, as is the theory of evolution by the process of natural selection in biology. So when you hear someone say, "That is just a theory," if they

theory a scientific explanation that is strongly supported by a large body of scientific research and is a highly likely explanation of a broad set of related events

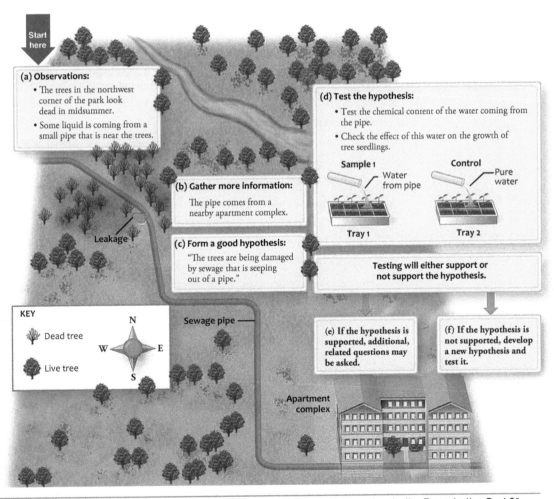

Figure 3.16 A Scientific Investigation of the Question: "What Is Happening to the Trees in the Park?"

are talking about a scientific theory, then the idea is something you can count on as being supported by years of scientific research and the best explanation that is available.

Most science is done at the level of formulating and testing a hypothesis, so before leaving the topic of how science is done, let's use an example to make the development of a hypothesis less abstract. Let's assume that the trees in the northwest corner of your local park are covered with withered leaves in the middle of the summer (**Figure 3.16**). You are worried that these trees might be dying, so you team up with your local park service scientists to answer the question: "What is happening to the trees?"

Your investigation begins with careful observations. You note what kinds of trees are involved. You examine the area in their immediate vicinity and compare it with the rest of the park. You note how much sunlight the withered trees get and examine the soil beneath them. You try to notice any animals that are around them. To this point your observations are not guided by any ideas; instead you are just gathering as much information as possible. As your information comes together, you realize that the only notable difference between the withered trees and those in the rest of the park seems to be a small wet area of ground in the midst of the withered trees where there are a number of dead young trees (**Figure 3.16a**).

Aha! Now you have an idea. Perhaps there is something leaking underground—maybe a sewage pipe? This idea is the *beginning* of a hypothesis, but you need more information to make your hypothesis more precise. From architectural drawings in the local library, you find that there *is* a sewage pipe from a nearby apartment complex (**Figure 3.16b**). Now you can make your hypothesis more precise. It becomes: "The trees are being damaged or killed by something that is seeping out of this pipe" (**Figure 3.16c**).

The next step is to devise experiments that will test the hypothesis. For instance, your hypothesis predicts that the pipe is actually leaking a harmful substance, so you must test for that. You also might grow a patch of seedlings using water from the pipe to see if it causes them harm (**Figure 3.16d**). You might think of other ways to test your predictions and your hypothesis, but the critical point is that a hypothesis must be tested, and each test will help support or reject your hypothesis (**Figure 3.16e**). For instance, if tests reveal that the water in the pipe contains no harmful chemicals, or if experiments show that the contaminated water does not harm the growth of tree seedlings, then you either will have to revise your hypothesis or reject it and form another one (**Figure 3.16f**). Once you are reasonably confident of your results, you will share them with other people, perhaps through a town meeting or even publication in the local paper. In this way your work may have a positive impact on your local park and could probably help other scientists to understand stresses on trees in other urban environments.

Science Uses Different Kinds of Studies

Three kinds of studies commonly used by biologists include observational studies, correlational studies, and controlled experiments. Let's take a closer look at each of these. **Observational studies** are descriptions of organisms and the real problems they solve in their natural environments. Scientific observations may involve sophisticated viewing and recording strategies and are more rigorous than casual or untrained observations. The field worker must be highly observant and careful not to interfere with the organisms under study. A scientific observer must take care to be objective and not influence his or her own observations. This is true whether the organisms are birds, mammals, plants, or even bacteria. To return to the example of the withered trees in the park, the initial careful observations of the trees and their surroundings are observational studies that provide a wealth of useful descriptive information that can be followed by other kinds of research.

observational study

a thoughtful, planned examination of organisms in their natural environment

The results of observational studies often are used to form a hypothesis and make a prediction. By zeroing in on specific information they help the investigator to begin to try to falsify the hypothesis. If you found sewage leaking from the pipe, you then could conclude that the sewage and the withered trees go together in space and time. By searching for other possible contaminants in the leakage, you might be able to conclude that excess metals or industrial pollutants were not present and therefore did not go together with the withered trees. This is good and necessary information. Based on this kind of study, however, you could not conclude that the leaking sewage *caused* the leaves to wither. The sort of finding that merely demonstrates that events occur together in space and time is called a **correlation.** Finding a correlation between two events is not enough to conclude that one event causes another.

To conclude that there is a causal relationship between two events, you must perform a **controlled experiment.** In this type of study you expose some experimental subjects—trees or mice or people, for example—to the factor you suspect is a cause and withhold exposure from another identical group of subjects. In the withered trees example you would grow a group of young trees with exposure to the fluid leaking from the pipe, while another group of young trees would have no exposure to it. The second group is treated exactly the same as the

correlation when two events reliably happen together in space and time

controlled experiment a scientific study in which some subjects (the experimental subjects) are assigned to experience a specific experimental condition, while similar subjects (the controls) do not experience the experimental conditions

control group any group or condition that is included in a study to rule out other interpretations

pseudoscience a statement that sounds scientific but is based on faulty or incomplete evidence

first, except it receives none of the leaking fluid. The second group serves as the **control group** and demonstrates what happens in the absence of the factor being investigated. Only a controlled experiment can allow you to conclude that the leaking fluid actually causes the withered leaves. Finally, just a single controlled experiment is not enough to support or refute a hypothesis. The controlled experiment must be repeated several times to make sure that the results are reliable.

The Culture of Science Maintains Scientific Integrity

This discussion of the process of science gives you hints about the culture of science. Scientists follow some fairly strict rules and practices to ensure that science is reliable and trustworthy. First, they must strive to be objective and must try to prove themselves wrong. This may be difficult, especially when jobs and careers depend on successful research, but all well-trained scientists strive to be skeptical of their own or others' ideas. Any scientific finding is given intense review and criticism, and it is common for a finding or a study to be repeated before it can be published in a scientific journal. Nearly all findings are repeated by other scientists as they try to build on published knowledge. This is part of the reason that some "findings" reported in the newspapers are contradicted several months or years later.

Scientists must be honest about the results of their studies. While it is true that a false report is not likely to survive if other scientists try to repeat it and fail, the whole enterprise of science rests on the assumption that scientists honestly report the results of their studies. All scientists are trained in this code of honesty. The rare scientist who fakes data is seen as a threat to the entire enterprise. There have been cases of federal agents seizing lab notebooks and prosecuting scientists who faked results. Because of the way that new scientific research builds on previous experiments, frauds eventually are discovered and discredited. Fraudulent work leads to loss of respect, funding, and employment.

Science Versus Pseudoscience

Sometimes it is hard to tell if something is science or just ideas masquerading as science. **Pseudoscience** is not easy to define but could be viewed as a statement that sounds scientific—but on closer examination is found to be based on faulty or incomplete scientific evidence. In addition, pseudoscience is more likely to push a particular idea rather than try to find out what the world is really like. Examples of pseudoscience are common, but it is often hard to see them without doing some background investigation. Many of the health claims for products sold on the Internet may be based on pseudoscience. One way to investigate the validity of these claims is to turn to the actual research literature and read the scientific studies that the claims are based on. Information also can be found on the Websites of research universities, government organizations, and well-established private organizations. The American Cancer Society, for example, has information on alternative therapies for cancer that can be helpful. Often you will find that one or two studies make a suggestion that then is touted to sell a product. In some cases you will find some evidence to support the claims, but it may be incomplete. Science cannot keep up with the willingness of people to latch onto beliefs, so you will not always find a scientific answer to whether a particular claim is pseudoscience. Especially where health is concerned you certainly want to have as much information as possible before deciding on treatment options.

Biologists Use Special Techniques and Tools in Their Study of Life

Like other modern scientific fields, biology relies on special techniques and tools. It is not possible to describe them all, but here a few examples will give you a feel for the range of available tools.

Mathematical Tools Are an Important Foundation of All Sciences

Many of the observations of the universe involve counting or measuring, so the results must be expressed in numbers. Sometimes it is useful to examine, graph, or categorize the numbers obtained from your measurements, but often simply reporting the numerical results of a study can be confusing and difficult to interpret. If you make the same measurement on many different subjects or samples you will not get the exact same number each time. Human body weight is a simple example (**Figure 3.17**). If you measure the mass of 50 adults to the nearest kilogram, you will get a wide range of results. People have difficulty interpreting long lists of numbers, so they use mathematical tools to summarize them. The **mean**, or average of a group of numbers, is one example of a mathematical summary statistic. It is easier to grasp that one group of people has an average mass of 70 kilograms (150 pounds) than it is to look at list of 100 measurements and draw conclusions about the mass of the people in the group.

Mathematical tools also can help you to interpret the results of a study. Interpretation is necessary when you want to know if two

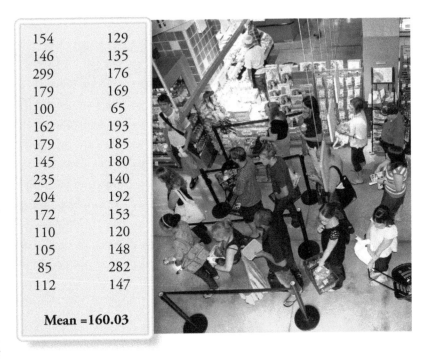

154	129
146	135
299	176
179	169
100	65
162	193
179	185
145	180
235	140
204	192
172	153
110	120
105	148
85	282
112	147

Mean =160.03

Figure 3.17 Summary Statistics Like the Mean Make Long Lists of Data Easier to Understand. (David Shankbone)

mean *the average of a group of numbers; to calculate the mean you divide the sum by the total number of values*

inferential statistics *mathematical tools that can determine the probability that results of a study are real or just chance differences*

groups of subjects are the same or different on some measurement. Suppose you want to know if average heights for men and women differ. Of course, you cannot measure the height of every human alive, so you might go into a local football stadium during a game and measure the heights of 300 men and 300 women. You find that your sample of men is on average taller than your sample of women. But is this the correct interpretation of your finding? Because every individual, human or otherwise, is different from every other individual, there is always some chance that differences between groups are just a reflection of random individual variation. By chance you may have sampled a lot of short women and a lot of tall men. The mathematical tools called **inferential statistics** can help you to judge the validity of your results. With inferential statistics you can calculate the probability that two averages or two other measurements of a group represent two different populations, rather than being two samples taken from the same population or group. You may not realize that ads often use results of studies analyzed with inferential statistics, but the next time you encounter a claim that is something like "eating a low-fat diet *significantly* reduces the risk of heart disease," you can know that inferential statistics were used. In this case inferential statistics help determine that a low-fat diet is highly likely to have a real and measurable effect on your probability of having heart disease.

Chemical Tools Are Used to Identify and Analyze Biological Chemicals

A variety of tools and techniques can tell you about the chemicals present in a biological sample, and some chemical tests are quite simple. For example, some chemicals will change color when they react with other chemicals. Starches—complex molecules that are plentiful in potatoes and pasta—will turn a dark color when mixed with iodine. So you can test a sample with iodine, and if it turns dark, there is starch in the sample. Other chemical techniques are more complex. For example, a sophisticated group of techniques and tools can be used to identify and analyze the DNA in an organism's cells. Collectively called **molecular biology techniques**, these procedures can detect even tiny differences in the DNA taken from two people and determine if they may be genetically closely related.

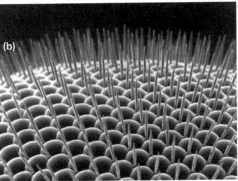

Fruit fly

2 mm ⌣
actual size

Figure 3.18 Different Microscopes Reveal Different Images of the Eye of a Fruit Fly.
(a) A fruit fly photographed through a compound microscope. (b) This high magnification scanning electron micrograph of the eye of a fruit fly reveals the hundreds of lenses that compose it. (a: Paul Reynolds; b: Dartmouth College). **What are the advantages and disadvantages of each kind of microscope?**

Microscopes Reveal Worlds That Are Unseen by the Naked Eye

Most living organisms are quite small, and the structures within cells are too tiny to be seen with the unaided eye. For example, a human blood cell is 7.5 micrometers in diameter. A micrometer is one-millionth of a meter. The period at the end of this sentence is about 500 micrometers, or half a millimeter in diameter—and about 67 red blood cells could line up across its middle. Microscopes of various sorts allow you to see tiny objects. Since the early 1600s, when it began to be developed, the microscope has allowed biologists to investigate forms of life and living structures too small to be seen by the unaided eye. Microscopes are some of the most influential and important tools of modern biology.

The **compound microscope**, or **light microscope**, is the oldest and most familiar kind of microscope. The compound microscope comes in many forms, but in all of them the system of internal lenses accomplishes the same thing—the lenses bend light rays in a way that mimics bringing an object closer to your eye. This makes the object appear larger, and allows you to see more detail (**Figure 3.18a**).

molecular biology techniques tools and procedures used to isolate and identify the DNA in a sample of cells

compound microscope, or light microscope a scientific instrument that uses lenses to bend light rays in a way that makes objects appear closer to your eye and therefore larger

electron microscope (EM) a scientific instrument that uses a beam of electrons to give greater magnification than can be obtained with a light microscope

Quick Check   3.5

What is probability?

What is the difference
between a hypothesis and a
scientific theory?

Compound microscopes can magnify objects up to 1,200 times. At higher magnifications the image gets larger, but it is not possible to see greater details. For instance, cells can be seen easily with a compound microscope, but many of their small internal structures are not visible. Other types of microscopes make subcellular details visible. One of the most useful is the **electron microscope (EM)**, which uses a beam of electrons instead of light rays to produce an image. With a magnification of up to 80,000 to 100,000 times, electron microscopes produce black-and-white photographs that show the internal or external details of cells or other objects. Electron microscopes come in two kinds. A transmission electron microscope (TEM) magnifies thin slices of objects by passing an electron beam through the slice. A scanning electron microscope (SEM) bounces a beam of electrons off the surface of a small object, which reveals remarkably fine surface details (**Figure 3.18b**).

What Causes Four Corners Disease?

In this chapter you have seen that science uses a set of organized steps to answer questions about the world. The organized steps are not a dogmatic list of requirements: They are a set of guidelines that must be adapted to fit each new situation. Let's return to the chapter-opening problem concerning Four Corners disease and see how scientific methods helped to solve it. While this disease scare happened many years ago, the detailed methods used to find the answer are applied to disease outbreaks whenever they occur. Similar approaches have been used to figure out recent diseases such as severe acute respiratory syndrome (SARS), bird flu, and Ebola hemorrhagic fever.

Scientific solutions to questions usually start with careful observations, and investigation of Four Corners disease followed this pattern. Hospital workers were stunned and puzzled when they saw the first case of this mysterious illness in May 1993. They had no immediate hypotheses but ran many tests on the sick young man, hoping to find evidence of a known disease that they could work to cure. They did not find the answer in these first rounds of tests, but the results did give the researchers enough evidence to develop some ideas about what was going on. When the young man died, the health professionals involved became more determined to find out what killed him.

One of their priorities was to find out if this was an isolated case or if there were other people who showed similar symptoms. His specific symptoms had been documented, and workers searched for others with the same symptoms. Not only did they find that his fiancée had died in a similar fashion, in a short time they also found others in the same region with a similar disease. Hospital researchers assembled a detailed description of the common symptoms. They kept records of how this mysterious disease progressed, noting symptoms as well as who recovered and who died. These detailed observations formed the base of the studies that isolated the cause of Four Corners disease.

Armed with this background information, some researchers were ready to state a specific hypothesis. Others in the region made wild guesses, but the health officials and scientists involved kept their hypotheses tied to known information. The first and most important hypothesis was that a virus caused the disease. A study of published records showed that a family of viruses called hantaviruses had caused similar disease symptoms in other locations around the world, but a hantavirus had never been isolated in the United States. So rather than suspect a new and unusual possibility, researchers began with the most likely hypothesis and predicted that a hantavirus would turn out

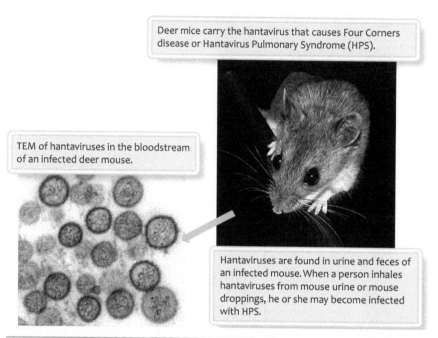

Deer mice carry the hantavirus that causes Four Corners disease or Hantavirus Pulmonary Syndrome (HPS).

TEM of hantaviruses in the bloodstream of an infected deer mouse.

Hantaviruses are found in urine and feces of an infected mouse. When a person inhales hantaviruses from mouse urine or mouse droppings, he or she may become infected with HPS.

Figure 3.19 The Connection Between Hantaviruses, Deer Mice, Humans, and HPS. (Mouse: © iStockphoto LP; TEM: Centers for Disease Control and prevention)

to be the culprit. To test this hypothesis they examined tissue samples using chemical tests that would reveal whether the victims had been exposed to any hantavirus. But they also tested for exposure to many other kinds of viruses as well—and in so doing, they tried to prove themselves wrong. The results showed that the only viral exposure that all victims shared was to a hantavirus.

Another important test of the hantavirus hypothesis was the connection to rats, mice, and other rodents. In other known cases rodents carried this virus, so if a hantavirus was the culprit, rats or mice also should be involved. To determine if this prediction was correct, researchers looked for signs of rodent infestation in households with infected inhabitants. But this would not be enough evidence to support the hypothesis. They also had to search for signs of rodent infestation in control houses—neighboring households where there was no disease. For example, if all houses in the Four Corners area had mice or rats, then it would be less likely that rodents were the disease carriers. Signs of deer mouse infestation were found exclusively in infected households (**Figure 3.19**).

Modern health workers were not the only ones to make careful observations and hypotheses to explain Four Corners disease. The Navajo people who live in the Four Corners area had long recognized this disease, and scientists used Navajo oral histories to better understand why hantavirus disease appeared at some times but not at others. Navajo oral history documents outbreaks of the disease in 1918 and 1933, when wet weather had allowed local mouse populations to increase. Navajo traditions admonished people to keep deer mice out of their homes and to keep food supplies clean of mouse contamination.

Scientists strive to provide explanations that cut across different disciplines and levels of explanation. This relates back to the point made earlier that all of the disciplines in science describe the same universe. The investigation of Four Corners disease is no different. For example, scientists wanted to know why this hantavirus disease erupted at this particular time. Why were there so many deer mice in the spring of 1993? Here the search for the cause of this outbreak of deadly hantavirus in the Four Corners region becomes related to broader environmental factors. Every 3 to 7 years a warm current of water develops in the Pacific Ocean and affects weather patterns in all of the Americas. Because the current often coincides with the Christmas holidays, it is called *El Niño*. Environmental biologists and meteorologists confirmed that during the winter of 1992 El Niño produced abundant snow and rain in the desert Southwest. That meant a lush growth of green plants in a place that usually is arid, and consequently it meant lots of food for young deer mice. The wet weather produced by El Niño (**Figure 3.20**) resulted in a rapid increase in the deer mouse population. Consequently, more deer mice invaded human houses, and human exposure to hantavirus in mouse droppings and dried urine was more widespread. **Table 3.4** summarizes the

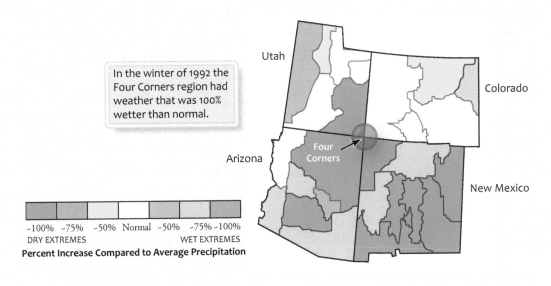

In the winter of 1992 the Four Corners region had weather that was 100% wetter than normal.

Utah

Colorado

Arizona

Four Corners

New Mexico

~100%   ~75%   ~50%   Normal   ~50%   ~75% ~100%
DRY EXTREMES   WET EXTREMES
Percent Increase Compared to Average Precipitation

Figure 3.20   During El Niño Years the Four Corners Region had Extremely Wet Weather.

steps that helped confirm the hantavirus hypothesis and relates them to what you have learned about scientific procedures.

Table 3.4   Steps That Solved the Mystery of Four Corners Disease and How They Relate to the Scientific Process.

DATE IN 1993	EVENTS	EFFECT IN THE SCIENTIFIC PROCESS
May 14	Unexplained death and autopsy of first patients: a young Navajo man, his fiancée, and four others who died of respiratory illness	Careful observation revealed that this illness was not routine and was linked to other unexplained deaths. Routine tests ruled out common disorders. First hypothesis: these deaths could be explained by tests for several well known diseases.
Late May	Indian Health Service (IHS) investigation into poisons as alternative cause of the deaths	*Second hypothesis:* poison, not a pathogen, caused the deaths. Visits to homes of victims showed no evidence of any exposure to poisons. Poison hypothesis rejected.
May	CDC is alerted to the presence of a mysterious, fatal disease in the Four Corners region and joins the investigation	*Third hypothesis:* a known but rare virus is responsible for the deaths. Chemical tests revealed whether a person had been exposed to a particular virus. Most tests were negative. Tests of hantavirus strains showed a weak positive result.
June	CDC critically evaluates hantavirus hypothesis	*Fourth hypothesis:* hantavirus carried by local rodents causes Four Corners disease. Hantavirus is always associated with rodents. This hypothesis is tested by investigating role of local rodents in disease.
Summer	Even before the hypothesis was confirmed, U.S. State Health Departments notify doctors of this threat to health and warn people to avoid rodents	Practical public health action protects public safety.
November	CDC Special Pathogens Unit continues to work on the case	Attempts to characterize virus: 1. Matches to known hantavirus with antibody tests give only weak matches. 2. Attempts to grow and characterize viruses isolated from Four Corners rodents in laboratory fail. 3. Molecular biology techniques copy viral DNA and identify virus as new form of hantavirus. *The rodent-hantavirus hypothesis is supported.*
Late in 1993	Investigators look further to support the hypothesis, investigating local rodent population patterns and tissues from victims of disease	Records from local Navajo tribes and from local university researchers confirm that the disease increases when local rodent populations increase and is associated with certain warm weather patterns. Further tests of tissues from victims of Four Corners disease confirm that they are infected with a local strain of hantavirus. The rodent-hantavirus hypothesis is further supported.
	Public health alerts slow the outbreak of disease	While no cure has been found for hantavirus, public health information allows people to prevent the disease by avoiding rodent habitats.

The study of the hantavirus and all of its ramifications did not stop in 1993 because wherever deer mice and certain other rodents are common, people continue to be infected. The number of people infected each year is low, but infected people still can get quite sick. Even with current treatments there are no medicines to kill the virus, and nearly half of infected people still die. This ongoing problem means that scientists will continue to study the hantavirus, trying to find a way to treat the disease it causes. If you search a medical database, you will find that scientists continue to learn more about this virus and how it causes disease, now called HPS (short for hantavirus pulmonary syndrome). Scientific studies almost never end when the immediate question is answered. The curiosity of individual scientists and the need for answers drive the search for deeper explanations.

Quick Check   3.6

What infectious agent was the cause of Four Corners disease?

Why did researchers suspect that Four Corners disease might be spread by rats and mice?

NOW YOU CAN UNDERSTAND

[We have] introduced you to three general foundations of the science of biology. First, you considered an overview of the breadth of biological science. Second, you learned a bit about what science is and how it differs from other intellectual disciplines. Third, you discovered some of the important tools that biologists use as they seek to understand the living world. You can use the insights gained here to better understand some of the events and debates taking place around you. [...]

Risk factors—what do they mean?

Almost every newspaper or Web news summary has information about risk factors. Often these risk factors refer to common human diseases, such as heart disease, diabetes, and cancer. Risk factors are characteristics that give a higher or lower probability of succumbing to a disease or condition. To be useful risk factors must be evaluated realistically. For example, a recent study showed that eating a "Mediterranean diet" reduces your risk of dying from heart disease by over 70%, compared with people who eat a "regular" American diet. That is a dramatic effect. The risk of dying from heart disease or other complication is quite high if you eat a diet rich in animal fats and simple starches and if you are overweight and do not exercise. In comparison, the risk of dying from eating apples sprayed with pesticides is quite low. This does not mean that you should not worry about pesticides in your food or that eating pesticides might not make you sick. Rather, you should be sensitive to the actual level of risk that you face in various aspects of your life.

Antibiotic Resistance

You may have heard much about antibiotic resistance in the news, but now you can understand antibiotic resistance as a variant of natural selection. Because human intervention is involved, it is a form of unintentional human-induced selection. When you take antibiotics to cure a bacterial infection, like strep throat or tuberculosis, the drug may not kill some of the germs. Bacteria that resist the drug's effects survive and multiply. They pass their trait of resistance to the antibiotic on to their offspring. If antibiotics are overused, large populations of resistant bacteria evolve, leaving people with no effective treatments when they do get sick. This growing problem reflects how some agent of selection—in this case the antibiotic—can produce a change in a population of bacteria—in this case resistance to the lethal effects of that antibiotic. This is an excellent example of how evolution works.

WHAT DO *YOU* THINK?

Mental Telepathy

Science provides a way to increase the chances that your beliefs about the world reflect what the world actually is like. Yet most people continue to hang on to some personal beliefs about the world, even in the face of strong scientific evidence to the contrary. Mental telepathy is an example. Many scientific studies have investigated whether mental telepathy can be demonstrated. There are some weak positive results in some special circumstances, but most studies find no evidence for mental telepathy. Yet many people firmly believe that mental telepathy is real, and many believe they have experienced it.

Here is an exercise to give you a perspective on your personal beliefs. First, think about and write down some of the strong beliefs you hold but which you suspect or know do not have scientific support. Second, over the next few weeks talk to your friends and colleagues about some of the things they believe in. When you find that your friends have beliefs that you do not hold, do you treat your own beliefs differently than those of your friends? Are your beliefs more or less credible if someone else shares them? What do you think?

CHAPTER REVIEW

Chapter Summary

3.1 Biology Touches Every Aspect of Your Life
Biology has profound impacts on your daily life. The biological themes of emergent properties, unity and diversity of life, evolution by means of natural selection, and the processes of science weave through all biological knowledge.

biology **23**

organism **24**

3.2 Life Is Defined by a Set of Features That All Living Things Share
Organisms are complex, organized, cellular, homeostatic entities that respond to and interact with their environments. Organisms use energy to power their internal processes and use the instructions in DNA to conduct these processes and to reproduce.

cell **25**
cell membrane **25**
DNA (deoxyribonucleic acid) **29**

energy **29**
homeostasis **28**

3.3 Levels of Organization Are Characteristic of Life
Cells, tissues, organs, organ systems, and organisms form one set of biological levels. Above the level of individual organism are population, community, ecosystem, biome, and biosphere.

atom **30**
biome **35**

biosphere **35**
chemical element **30**

community **35**

ecosystem **35**

emergent properties **35**

multicellular organism **32**

organ **32**

organelle **32**

organ system **32**

population **32**

tissue **32**

unicellular organism **32**

virus **32**

3.4   Evolution and Natural Selection Have Produced Life's Diverse Forms

All life is related. Earth's diverse forms of life have resulted from the process of evolution by means of natural selection.

evolution **36**

natural selection **36**

3.5   Biology Applies the Methods of Science to the Study of Life

Scientists follow a disciplined path toward gathering knowledge. Their methods involve thoughtful observations, reference to the scientific literature, and careful stating and testing of hypotheses using controlled experiments. A scientific theory has been tested time and again and has been substantiated. Biologists use mathematical and physical tools to gather and process information. Different microscope technologies reveal aspects of life that are invisible to the unaided eye.

compound (*or* light) microscope **49**

control group **46**

controlled experiment **46**

correlation **46**

electron microscope (EM) **49**

hypothesis **41**

inferential statistics **48**

mean **48**

molecular biology techniques **49**

observational study **45**

probability **40**

pseudoscience **46**

scientific law **41**

theory **43**

3.6   Weaving Life's Tapestry: What Causes Four Corners Disease?

In a relatively short period of time, investigators were able to use the methods of science to trace Four Corners disease to a hantavirus transmitted to humans from deer mice and to tie the outbreak of hantavirus to wider environmental events.

Review Questions

TRUE or FALSE
If a statement is false, rewrite it to make it true.

1. Because every living organism is unique, it is not possible to discover common principles in the study of life.

2. The levels of biological organization, from simplest to most complex, are atom, molecule, cell, tissue, organ, organ system, organism, population, community, ecosystem, and biosphere.

3. The major chemical elements needed by all living things include silicon, hydrogen, oxygen, and nitrogen.

4. All the individuals of a single kind of organism living in one geographic area form a population.

5. A compound microscope uses lenses to bend light and magnify tiny objects.

MULTIPLE CHOICE
Choose the best answer of those provided.

6. Which of the following is *not* a theme in the study of biology that you were introduced to in this chapter?

    a. heat, cold, acidity are the fundamental determinants of life

    b. atoms combine to form molecules, which combine to form cells

    c. emergent properties, unity and diversity, evolution through natural selection

    d. scientific method, forming hypotheses that are testable, careful measurements, statistical analysis

    e. populations form a community; communities form an ecosystem; ecosystems form a biome; biomes form the biosphere

7. You are observing a burning candle. As you watch the flame, you wonder how someone who didn't know better could demonstrate whether the flame is alive. Which of the following is a characteristic of life that is not a characteristic of fire?

    a. The flame responds to and interacts with the environment.

    b. The flame uses energy to power itself.

    c. The flame can grow.

    d. The flame is made up of one or more cells.

    e. The flame can reproduce.

8. What is the role of the cell membrane?

    a. energy production and cellular instructions

    b. protection from the environment and communication with the environment

    c. cellular reproduction and cellular longevity

    d. protection from the environment and energy production

    e. none of the above

9. One example of homeostasis is that you

    a. eat food because it tastes good.

    b. shiver because you are cold.

    c. stay well because you take antibiotics.

    d. get sick because you are invaded by pathogenic bacteria.

    e. eat more and you gain weight.

10. Which of the following carries instructions for the processes of life?

    a. energy

    b. the cell membrane

    c. proteins

    d. individual atoms

    e. DNA

11. What is an atom?

    a. the nucleus of a cell that has DNA

    b. a complex molecule that carries information

    c. an organelle that is made of molecules

    d. the smallest unit of an element that has all the properties of that element

    e. the largest unit of a molecule that has all the properties of that molecule

12. What is one important feature of a virus?

    a. It is the same as a cell.

    b. It is larger than a cell.

    c. It is a small nonliving structure made of biological molecules.

    d. It is a small living structure made of biological molecules.

    e. It is a small structure that has internal organelles and carries out all of the processes of life.

13. Which of the following is a species of ants?

    a. all of the individuals of a particular kind of ant

    b. all of the ants that live in a particular location

    c. all of the ants that live in a particular environment

    d. only the ants that meet one another in daily interactions

    e. all of the above

14. What is one distinguishing feature of ecosystems?

    a. An ecosystem includes just the living organisms in an individual's environment.

    b. An ecosystem contains all of the biomes in the biosphere.

    c. Biomes are smaller than ecosystems.

    d. Ecosystems are all living systems outside the biosphere.

    e. Ecosystems include living communities and their nonliving environmental components.

15. Which of the following is not an important concept related to the evolution of life?

    a. All life is genetically related.

    b. Living organisms are diverse.

    c. Life evolves by the process of natural selection.

    d. The diversity of life emerged gradually over the history of the Earth.

    e. Every individual within a species is identical.

16. Central features of science are
    a. belief systems.

    b. observations of the real world.

    c. intuitions about the real word.

    d. well-worded philosophical arguments.

    e. statements that rely on authority figures in science.

17. A testable explanation or prediction is called
    a. a hypothesis.

    b. a theory.

    c. a correlation.

    d. a fact.

    e. none of the above.

18. Which of these statements is true?
    Control groups usually
    a. receive exactly the same treatment as experimental groups.

    b. are quite small.

    c. are quite large.

    d. are unnecessary.

    e. demonstrate the effect of no experimental treatment.

19. What are inferential statistics?
    a. mathematics that allow people to infer their own conclusions from the results of experiments

    b. mathematics that summarize a large set of numbers

    c. the misuse of statistics to promote erroneous conclusions

    d. mathematical tools to determine the probability that given results happened by chance

    e. mathematical tools to determine if certain patterns of numbers happened in the past

20. Hantaviruses have always been associated with

   a. hot climates and deserts.

   b. cold winters.

   c. poor food sanitation.

   d. antibiotic overuse.

   e. mice and rats.

Connecting Key Concepts

1. What are the properties of life that all cells share?

2. Outline a scientific process you might use to determine if taking vitamin C can prevent people from catching colds.

Quantitative Query

Calculate the mean of this set of numbers:

10 15 2 30 25 1 1 35 2 2 45 4 3 35

Is the mean a good representation of this set of numbers? Why or why not? What would be a better summary of these numbers?

Thinking Critically

1. A few years ago newspapers reported that people feared living near high-tension power lines because they thought it increased their chances of getting cancer. Imagine you are a member of your local county commission. Many families that live near power lines have stories about illness in their families. Angry and fearful residents are demanding that high-tension power lines be restructured and moved away from their houses. As a council member you must decide whether the county should undertake this expensive project, which will decrease funding for schools and other community projects. How will you decide whether to support the power line restructuring project?

2. Study the experiment presented in **Table 3.5**. What hypothesis is the experiment testing? Explain the way in which this hypothesis relates to the reason the person gives for using the supplement. What is wrong with the design of the experiment? Given the way that the experiment was carried out, are the experimenter's conclusions verified? Develop a hypothesis that will lead to a more useful experiment. Design a study that will answer the experimenter's question about the effectiveness of the supplement.

TABLE 3.5	WHAT IS WRONG WITH THIS EXPERIMENT?

Your friend is using a nutritional supplement that he hopes will improve his performance at martial arts. As a curious scientist you ask him why he thinks this supplement will improve his agility, stamina, and speed—all essential goals of the serious martial arts student.

Your friend replies that he has found the following study on a Website for a distributor of this product. It has convinced him that the product is worthwhile. In this study:

- Five volunteers offered to take the supplement for 6 weeks.
- Their ability to perform a weight lifting routine was measured at the beginning and end of the study.
- At the end of the study every participant had improved in both the amount of weight they could lift and in the number of repetitions they could do with each weight.
- Your friend believes that this is dramatic proof of the supplement's effectiveness. Is your friend getting a good bargain with this nutritional "short cut"? Or is he wasting his money?

3. What is meant by the term *emergent properties*? Define the term, and then give an example that is not in the text—for instance, baking a loaf of bread.

Additional Reading

Glaberson, William, "Court Stories: Death of a Young Navajo Casts the Spotlight on a Rare Virus," *New York Times,* April 23, 2001. Accessed September 22, 2010.

Eight years after hantavirus was identified as the cause of Four Corners disease, people still died from it because their illnesses were misdiagnosed.

Janovy, John. "The Practice of Biology." In *Becoming a Biologist*, 39–75. New York: Harper & Row, 1985.

A professional biologist examines how biology actually is done and provides several surprising insights. Don't be daunted by the thirty-six pages of this chapter—this is a small-sized book and Janovy's writing will keep you turning pages.

Kauffman, Stuart. "Order for Free." In *At Home in the Universe*, 23–28. New York: Oxford University Press, 1995.

Kauffman explores the theory of complexity now known as "emergent properties," in which self-organization of small entities results in higher levels of order and ultimately produces new living systems. This excerpt presents this idea in a nutshell.

Schulte, Bruce A. "Scientific Writing & the Scientific Method: Parallel 'Hourglass' Structure in Form & Content." *The American Biology Teacher* 65, no. 11 (2003): 591–94.

Scientific writing differs from regular prose. This article relates the scientific method to scientific writing. Once you've read it, both will become much clearer.

Steinbeck, John. *The Log from the Sea of Cortez.* New York: Penguin Books, 1941.

Think of this as your next summer's beach read. Steinbeck was great friends with California biologist Ed Ricketts. This book chronicles their 4,000-mile collecting voyage around the Baja peninsula and combines the best of Steinbeck, the novelist; Steinbeck, the biologist; Steinbeck, the hell-raiser; and Steinbeck, the student of life. A keeper.

Yates, Terry L., James N. Mills, Cheryl A. Parmenter, Thomas G. Ksiazek, Robert R. Parmenter, John R. Vande Castle, Charles H. Calisher et al. "The Ecology and Evolutionary History of an Emergent Disease: Hantavirus Pulmonary Syndrome." *Bioscience* 52, no. 11 (2002): 989–98.

This scholarly article discusses Hantavirus Pulmonary Syndrome (HPS) and predicts future risks of humans contracting the disease.

CREDITS

Chapter opener: Copyright © 2009 iStockphoto/ monkeybusinessimages

Figure 3.1A: Copyright in the Public Domain.

Figure 3.1B: Copyright © kaibara87 (CC by 2.0) at http://commons.wikimedia.org/wiki/File: Onion_cells_without_any_staining.jpg

Figure 3.1C: Copyright in the Public Domain.

Figure 3.1D: Copyright © Rolf Dieter Mueller (CC by 3.0) at http://commons.wikimedia.org/wiki/File:Hypericum_perforatum_stem_cross_section.jpg

Figure 3.2: Copyright © Masur (CC by 3.0) at http://commons.wikimedia.org/wiki/File:Yeast membrane proteins.jpg

Figure 3.5: Copyright © Thomas Shahan (CC by 2.0) at http://commons.wikimedia.org/wiki/File:Robber_Fly_(Triorla_interrupta)_with_Dragonfly_(Plathemis_lydia).jpg

Figure 3.6: Copyright © Lxowle (CC by 3.0) at http://commons.wikimedia.org/wiki/File:Cat_and_mouse.jpg

Figure 3.11: Copyright in the Public Domain.

Figure 3.14: Copyright © Alnus (CC by 3.0) at http://commons.wikimedia.org/wiki/File:Charadrius_dubius_P4223391.jpg

Figure 3.15: Copyright © (CC by 3.0) at http://commons.wikimedia.org/wiki/File:Marlboro_warning_death.jpg

Figure 3.17: Copyright © David Shankbone (CC by 3.0) at http://commons.wikimedia.org/wiki/File:Waiting_in_line_at_a_food_store.JPG

Figure 3.18A: Copyright © Paul Reynolds (CC by 2.5) at http://commons.wikimedia.org/wiki/File: White-eyed_Drosophila.jpg

Figure 3.18B: Copyright in the Public Domain.

Figure 3.19: Copyright © iStockphoto

Figure 3.19: Copyright in the Public Domain.

ECOSYSTEMS AND BIOMES

BY JOELLE PRESSON AND JAN JENNER

5 States to Confer With Federal Aides on Lake Erie Pollution

August 1, 1965

Cleveland, Ohio in 1937. This vintage aerial photo of shows one of the basic causes of the pollution of Lake Erie. The Cuyahoga River winds through the heavily industrialized "flats" region of Cleveland, gathering sewage and pollution along the way and emptying it into the waters of Lake Erie. Eventually the river was so choked with oil and industrial pollutants that in 1969 the Cuyahoga caught on fire.

Navigating the Renaissance of an Ohio River that Once Caught Fire

January 23, 2000

The Death and Life of Lake Erie

Lake Erie in the 1960s and 1970s was the most badly polluted of the five Great Lakes. Parents did not allow their children to run along Lake Erie's beach because it stank of dead fish and overgrown algae. And of course, you would never *eat* anything that came out of Lake Erie because everyone knew that the fish were loaded with toxins. As if all of this were not bad enough, in Ohio in 1969 the Cuyahoga River, which empties into Lake Erie, actually caught fire, burned, and set fire to a bridge **(see chapter opening photo).** The Cuyahoga was so choked with oil and other pollutants that a tossed match set it aflame. Johnny Carson, then the renowned host of the *Tonight Show,* quipped, "Lake Erie is where fish go to die."

At the time all the Great Lakes were polluted ghosts of their former glory, but Lake Erie was dead. It was ugly. Plain and simple. Kids no longer splashed in Lake Erie's waves, tried to catch fishes, built sand castles, or raced along the shore. Idyllic summer days at Lake Erie's beaches were just a memory.

But conditions weren't always so bleak. The enormous Great Lakes, which contain 20% of the world's freshwater, were once clean and beautiful. When European settlers first arrived at the shores of Lake Michigan, they thought they had reached the Pacific Ocean, but then realized that the water wasn't salty. Native Americans called the Great Lakes "sweetwater seas." For generations the lakes were unpolluted and filled with life. Fishing fleets netted big fishes like pike, sturgeon, salmon, and herring. The Great Lakes were a jewel of North America's natural heritage and should have been cherished and protected for future generations to enjoy. Yet by the 1960s or 1970s all of the Great Lakes were a mess, and Lake Erie was the worst of them.

What has happened to Lake Erie since the 1970s? At the end of this chapter you will refocus your attention on Lake Erie and read about its current state. First you will explore the subject of this chapter—larger ecological units: ecosystems, biomes, and the biosphere.

4.1

AN ECOSYSTEM IS THE FUNCTIONAL ECOLOGICAL UNIT

ecosystem all of the biotic and abiotic factors in a defined area

abiotic nonliving components of the environment

Living organisms interact with one another to form *ecological communities* [...], and they also interact with the nonliving environment. An **ecosystem** is an ecological community plus the **abiotic** or nonliving features of its environment—such as water, soil and soil nutrients, rocks, and atmospheric gases.

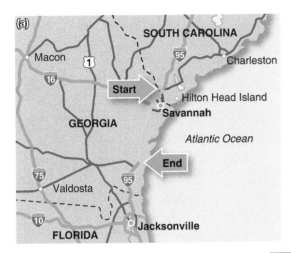

Figure 4.1 Two Different Ecosystems.
(a) Route of the 50-mile-long drive from Jasper County, South Carolina to the Atlantic Coast. Two of the ecosystems you would see on this trip are (b) longleaf pine flatwoods, and (c) dunes of the Atlantic coast

The concept of an ecosystem may be easier to understand if you compare it to a town. The people, animals, plants, and other organisms that live in this town are its biotic components; the buildings, streets, roadways, soil, rocky landscape, and atmosphere are some of its abiotic components. So are its electrical supply, water and sewage facilities, and landfill. Just as the town cannot function without people, the town cannot function without the buildings and utilities. *Ecology* concentrates on the interactions between organisms and their environments. The interdependent biotic communities of an ecosystem rely on, and are affected by, the abiotic environment. In ecosystems populations affect one another in immediate or distant ways as they obtain energy and use and/or recycle the chemical elements essential to life.

Each geographic region has many ecosystems, and you can see a variety of ecosystems even within a relatively short distance. As examples, consider just two different ecosystems that you would see on a 50-mile drive from Jasper County, South Carolina, across the Georgia state line and east to the Atlantic coast (**Figure 4.1a**).

In Jasper County you would travel through longleaf pine flatwoods: a distinctive forest ecosystem where tall, longleaf pine trees grow in soil with a thick layer of clay beneath it (**Figure 4.1b**). You might see a fox squirrel scramble up the trunk of a tree, or hear the call of a red-bellied woodpecker. The thin, sandy soil of the forest floor is littered with fallen pine needles and pine cones. You notice deer and turkey tracks and watch your step because diamondback rattlesnakes also live in flatwoods. Here and there are openings in the pines where sunny, wet meadows are dotted with carnivorous plants that live only in the acidic bogs associated with the pine flatwoods ecosystem.

Next you drive about 50 miles (80 kilometers) east to the Atlantic coast to an entirely different ecosystem—the coastal dunes. The grass-tufted dunes that front the beach are the dominant feature of this ecosystem—that of the sand dunes near the ocean. Here the wind and salt spray blown off the ocean shape the vegetation (**Figure 4.1c**). Behind the dunes ground-hugging shrubs and trees grow in low, wind-twisted groves. These plants have small, tough leaves and can withstand windblown salt spray, scouring by sand, and extremely dry conditions. You see the tracks of mice, rabbits, and foxes and hear the cries of gulls.

4.2

ENERGY MOVES THROUGH ECOSYSTEMS, AND CHEMICALS CYCLE WITHIN ECOSYSTEMS

QUICK CHECK   4.1

What are the biotic and abiotic components of the ecosystem that surrounds you right now?

Ecosystems characterized by the movement of energy and chemicals. Natural processes and ecological relationships move energy and chemicals between and among abiotic and biotic components of an ecosystem. The movement of chemicals through and between ecosystems is different from the movement of energy. Any given chemical—either an atom or a molecule—can be indefinitely cycled through ecosystems. Although chemicals are changed as they move from one part of an ecosystem to another, chemicals are re-used. The Sun's energy also is passed from one organism to another, but unlike chemicals, energy is not recycled indefinitely. Let's consider how energy moves through ecosystems, and then see how chemicals are cycled and recycled.

Energy Is Lost at Each Link in a Food Chain

The Sun's energy flows in a one-way direction through an ecosystem: from the Sun to producers to various levels of consumers (**Figure 4.2a**). Producers capture the energy in sunlight and convert it to energy stored in the bonds of biological molecules. Some of the energy in the molecules of producers is used by the consumers that eat them. When the producers and consumers die, some of their chemical energy is taken up and used by detritivores such as fungi and bacteria. It may sound like energy is recycled in this food chain, but at each link energy is lost to the environment as heat. Eventually none of the solar energy captured by a given producer is available for other organisms to use. This is why life requires a constant supply of energy from an external source, such as the Sun.

Photosynthesis carried out by producers captures and uses *less than 2%* of the solar energy that reaches Earth's surface. Nevertheless, once it has been captured, transformed by photosynthesis, and fixed in the carbon-to-carbon bonds of glucose molecules, this tiny fraction of solar energy supports nearly all life. As this energy is transferred from one link in a food chain to another, energy is lost. Because it costs energy to

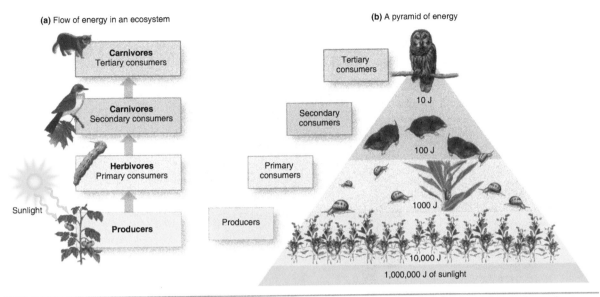

(a) Flow of energy in an ecosystem

Carnivores
Tertiary consumers

Carnivores
Secondary consumers

Herbivores
Primary consumers

Sunlight

Producers

(b) A pyramid of energy

Tertiary
consumers

Secondary
consumers

Primary
consumers

Producers

10 J

100 J

1000 J

10,000 J

1,000,000 J of sunlight

Figure 4.2 **Energy Flow in an Ecosystem.** (a) Energy flows in a one way direction from producers to various levels of consumers. (b) Because on average only 10% of energy available to an organism is stored in its tissues, pyramids of energy are typical of organisms that are linked in food chains. J stands for Joule, a unit of energy.

run an organism's metabolism and life activities, about 90% of the energy that an average organism takes in is used up. Only about 10% of the energy is stored in the chemical bonds in an organism's tissues. So, a snail that eats a plant does not have access to all of the solar energy that the plant absorbed. (**Figure 4.2b**). This *rule of 10%* continues up the food chain. For instance, the shrew that eats the snail gets only about 10% of the energy that the snail got from the leaves it ate. The metabolic processes and activities of the hawk also have a high energy cost. Again, about 90% of the energy that the hawk takes in is used up, and only about 10% is stored in its tissues. This drastic loss of energy at each link in a food chain is the reason that there are few terrestrial food chains with more than three or four links. *Pyramids of energy* show the energy available to each link in a food chain. They demonstrate the loss of energy in metabolic costs as energy flows through a food chain.

As you move up the links of a food chain, the number of individuals in each population decreases. A *pyramid of numbers* counts the individuals at each level or link in a food chain (**Figure 4.3**). In any ecosystem there are many more individual producer organisms than individual primary consumers. Similarly, there are more primary consumers than secondary consumers and more secondary consumers than top consumers. As you move up the links of a food chain, the number of individuals in each population decreases. The loss of energy at each link of a food chain restricts the amount of energy available to higher-level consumers—which is why you'll see mostly producers when you look at a landscape. There are fewer primary consumers and even fewer top consumers.

Tertiary consumers

Secondary consumers

Primary consumers

Producers

Number of individuals →

Figure 4.3 Numbers of Organisms Reflect Available Energy. Because more energy is available to lower links of a food chain, in any community there are more individual producers than primary consumers, more primary consumers than secondary consumers, and more secondary consumers than tertiary consumers.

biogeochemical cycle
the circulation of a chemical as it passes through biotic and abiotic components of the biosphere

Natural Processes Recycle Chemical Elements

Although the energy for Earth's life comes primarily from the Sun, everything else that life must have to survive must be obtained here on Earth. The chemical elements necessary for life, notably C, H, N, O, P, S, Ca, and K plus many more were available to the first cells that evolved nearly 4 billion years ago; they still are required by living cells. But because chemicals are recycled, many living cells, including some of the cells in your body, contain the *exact same* atoms and molecules that were present billions of years ago! For instance, although some water molecules are broken down and re-formed during metabolism, many water molecules pass unchanged from one cell to another or from one organism to another. Furthermore, water in rivers and streams as well as the water that comes out of the kitchen faucet contains some of the same water molecules that dinosaurs and other prehistoric animals drank and excreted millions of years ago.

Biogeochemical cycles move chemicals through the biosphere, passing them through organisms and abiotic components of the biosphere such as atmosphere, oceans and freshwaters, soils, and rocks. Like a wheel with no beginning and no end, a cycle is a continual process of transformations. The basic components of a cycle may be used over and over in slightly different forms, but they always return to the original form to begin the cycle again.

Each living organism is a part of many different biogeochemical cycles. Although the details of these cycles differ, they follow similar patterns. First, biogeochemical cycles are driven by energy from the Sun that powers biological and physical processes such as photosynthesis, evaporation, condensation, and precipitation. Second, each biogeochemical cycle involves *reservoirs* where chemicals are stored or concentrated for long or short periods of time. Reservoirs of various chemicals can be within the bodies of organisms, or within abiotic components of the environment. Third, biogeochemical cycles function on both local and global levels, linking distant ecosystems. Earth has many biogeochemical cycles, and they demonstrate that Earth is a closed system. Elements are recycled, not replenished from some outside source. This recycling of materials is one reason that environmentalists often call our planet Spaceship Earth. Biogeochemical cycles demonstrate how apt this name actually is.

Physical and Chemical Processes Cycle Water

Life must have water. All of the biochemical interactions required for life take place in a watery environment. You might think that because water covers three-quarters of Earth's surface, getting water would not be a problem for organisms, but you would be wrong. Ocean water is called salt water because it has high concentrations of dissolved sodium, potassium, chloride, and other chemicals. In contrast, freshwater has low levels of these chemicals. While ocean water is fine for the species adapted to live in it, terrestrial or freshwater species lack adaptations necessary to tolerate salt water. About 97% of the water on Earth is salty; only 3% is fresh. In the water cycle freshwater is continually purified by evaporation and recycled by other natural processes.

Let's begin the water cycle with all that salty ocean water, the largest reservoir in the water cycle (**Figure 4.4**). Even though the oceans are salty, they are the

Figure 4.4

The Water Cycle. Water that evaporates from the ocean falls as precipitation over land, and flows through lakes, rivers, and aquifers back to the ocean.

What two processes of the water cycle purify water?

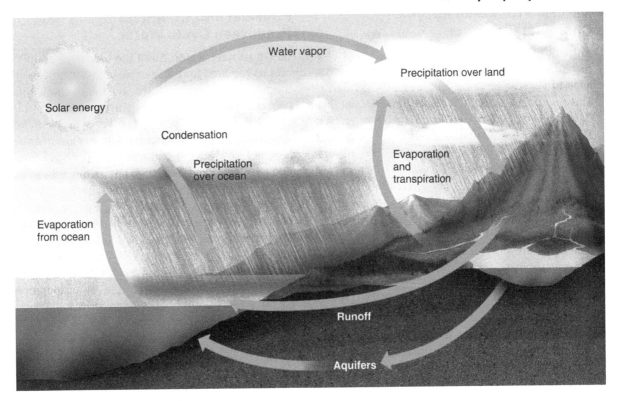

evaporation the process in which molecules of liquid water are transformed into water vapor

condensation the process in which water molecules come close together, form hydrogen bonds, and turn into liquid water or ice

precipitation water that falls from the atmosphere to Earth in the form of rain, snow, sleet, or ice

aquifer a porous layer of underground rock or sand that holds large quantities of water

primary source of freshwater on Earth. The heat of the Sun causes ocean water to evaporate into the atmosphere. The process of **evaporation** transforms liquid water molecules into *water vapor,* the gaseous form of water. As ocean water evaporates, the dissolved salts are left behind. This means that water evaporated out of the ocean is freshwater. Evaporation from the oceans contributes to atmospheric freshwater that can come down on land as rain, sleet, hail, or snow. Water molecules in water vapor are spread out because the hydrogen bonds that once held them together have been broken. If these diffuse water molecules are to come down as rain, snow, sleet, or hail, they must get closer together; in other words, they must *condense.* In the process of condensation molecules in water vapor get close enough together that hydrogen bonds form, resulting in liquid water or solid ice. **Condensation** can occur when a mass of warm air holding water vapor hits a mass of colder air. At the interface between warm and cold air, water vapor condenses, forming drops of rain. If the temperature is above freezing, rain will fall. If it is freezing or close to it, hail, sleet, or snow will fall. These forms of water that fall from the sky are grouped under the technical term, **precipitation**. All solid forms of precipitation can melt into liquid water that can run off into lakes, rivers, and oceans, and seep into the ground, accumulating in **aquifers**. These are porous layers of underground rock or sand that hold large quantities of water. Runoff also is taken up by plants and animals. The process of *transpiration* in plants also contributes water vapor to the water cycle as water passes through the bodies of plants and evaporates from leaves [...]. Because Earth is a closed system, precipitation eventually returns to its starting point in the oceans.

Most of the water vapor that evaporates from the ocean falls right back into it as precipitation, but wind drives some clouds over land, and so precipitation reaches Earth's continents. Some precipitation is absorbed into the soil. There it may stay or collect in aquifers. Other rainwater flows over the land, perhaps finding its way to creeks, lakes, or rivers.

Photosynthesis and Respiration Cycle Carbon

Carbon is the central element in all biological molecules. Biological carbon is found in molecules such as sugars, lipids, amino acids, and nucleotides. Other carbon molecules associated with organisms include carbon dioxide (CO_2) in the atmosphere and calcium carbonate ($CaCO_3$) in *limestone* rocks. Carbon cycles among five major compartments in the environment (**Figure 4.5**): dissolved carbon dioxide in water reservoirs such as oceans, lakes, and rivers; carbon dioxide in the atmosphere; carbon compounds in tissues of living organisms; carbon compounds in limestone

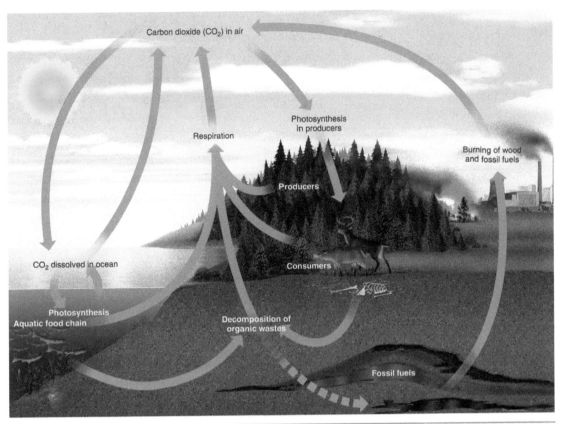

Figure 4.5 **The Carbon Cycle.** Carbon dioxide in the atmosphere and in bodies of water is taken up by photosynthesizers and used to make carbon-based biological molecules. Consumers eat photosynthetic organisms, and eat each other, and make their own carbon-based biological molecules. Cellular respiration burns glucose and other biological molecules and so returns carbon dioxide to the atmosphere and to oceans, rivers, and lakes. Human burning of fossil fuels also returns carbon dioxide to the atmosphere.

and other rocks; and carbon compounds in deposits of fossil fuels produced from the remains of living organisms. Notice that only one of these compartments is biotic. Although fossils contain mineralized remains of organisms, they are not currently alive, and so are not biotic. Exchanges between the biotic and abiotic compartments of the carbon cycle result from several processes.

The largest reservoirs of carbon are the carbon dioxide in the ocean and in the atmosphere. Biotic and abiotic processes add or subtract carbon dioxide from these reservoirs. For instance, occasional volcanic eruptions contribute 3% of the carbon dioxide in the atmosphere. Biotic processes move a large amount of carbon dioxide into and out of the atmosphere and oceans. Aerobic respiration returns carbon dioxide to the environment, while photosynthesis removes carbon dioxide from the environment and uses it to form carbon-based biological molecules. The metabolic processes of photosynthesis and respiration keep carbon rapidly cycling to and from reservoirs in waters and the atmosphere.

Other metabolic processes store carbon compounds in tissues of living organisms for longer periods. For example, the glycogen and fat deposits in animals and the starch deposits in plants remain for long-term use and are not rapidly metabolized to carbon dioxide. When energy is needed, stored carbon compounds can be broken down, and carbon dioxide is released in the process. Carbon-based compounds are incorporated into chitin and calcium carbonate in exoskeletons, bones, shells, and coral skeletons. When marine and freshwater organisms die, their calcium carbonate shells settle to the bottom of a body of water. Over eons this sediment accumulates, forming limestone rocks that are extremely long-term storage for carbon dioxide. It may be millions or even billions of years before chemical reactions move some of the stored carbonates back to the atmosphere as carbon dioxide.

Decomposers are crucial parts of biogeochemical cycles. In the carbon cycle decomposers extract energy from the carbon molecules of dead organisms and release carbon dioxide. Biological molecules not immediately degraded may enter other long-term storage compartments of the carbon cycle, where physical and chemical processes may transform them into fossil fuels such as peat, coal, oil, or natural gas. Peat is compressed organic matter that forms over centuries. Coal, oil, and natural gas are incompletely decomposed deposits of organic material that have been compressed to form substances composed largely of hydrocarbons. It takes millions of years to form deposits of coal, oil, and natural gas.

When fossil fuels are burned, their carbon-to-carbon bonds are broken. This releases energy and returns carbon to the atmosphere as carbon dioxide. Burning fossil fuels adds other greenhouse gases to the atmosphere and contributes to global warming. It also adds acidic compounds to the atmosphere and can contribute to acid precipitation and smog. Levels of carbon dioxide in the atmosphere have fluctuated over geologic history, reflecting geological processes and biological events. In the last 200 years or so, however, levels of atmospheric carbon dioxide have increased dramatically. The overwhelming scientific consensus is that increased levels of carbon dioxide and other greenhouse gases are heating up Earth's atmosphere. Most scientists are convinced that global climate change is real. Although no one is certain what all of the effects of global climate change will be, high-altitude glaciers, ice caps, and ice sheets are melting at record rates, global temperatures have risen by an average of 0.3 to 0.6°C (0.5 to 1.0°F), and biological seasons are shifting.

Prokaryotes Are Key Players in the Nitrogen Cycle

Nitrogen is a critical component of nucleic acids and proteins, and each day organisms require fresh supplies of these biomolecules. Because nitrogen is the most abundant gas in Earth's atmosphere, obtaining nitrogen could be as simple as breathing. But most organisms cannot use nitrogen gas directly from the atmosphere. Only certain bacteria can split molecules of atmospheric nitrogen (N_2) into single atoms of nitrogen for use in their own metabolic processes. Directly or indirectly, most other organisms depend on these bacteria to incorporate atmospheric nitrogen into compounds like nitrates (NO_3) and ammonia (NH_3) that contain single nitrogen atoms. Bacteria that can do this include cyanobacteria and certain soil bacteria that are the focus of the nitrogen cycle.

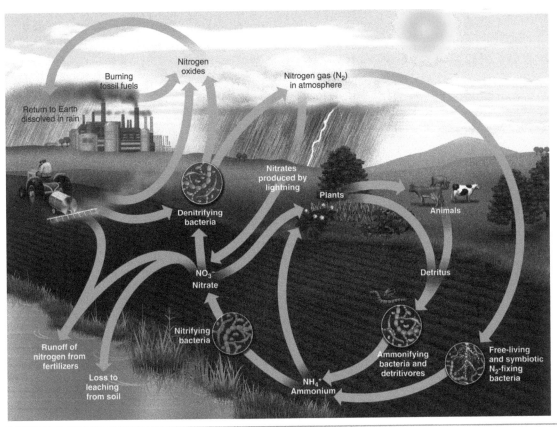

Figure 4.6 **The Nitrogen Cycle.** Atmospheric nitrogen cannot be directly used by living organisms, but some soil bacteria can convert nitrogen to useable compounds. Nitrogen fixing bacteria convert atmospheric nitrogen to ammonia and other compounds. Nitrifying bacteria convert ammonia to nitrate compounds that can be used by plants, animals, fungi, and other organisms. Denitrifying bacteria return nitrogen to the atmosphere.

The technical term for incorporating an atom into a chemical form suitable for cycling through living organisms is *fixing*. For example, some bacteria called **nitrogen-fixing bacteria** take in molecules of atmospheric nitrogen and fix the nitrogen into ammonia molecules that are released into the soil (**Figure 4.6**). While many nitrogen-fixing bacteria live in soil and water, swellings on the roots of some plants contain colonies of nitrogen-fixing bacteria. This is a mutualistic relationship: the plant receives a supply of ammonia, while the bacteria have a sheltered environment and direct access to small carbon-based molecules to use as sources of energy and building materials. Plants in the legume family such as peas and clover commonly have swellings on their roots that contain nitrogen-fixing bacteria, and other plants also have them.

Many eukaryotes cannot use ammonia as a nitrogen source and need another form of nitrogen as the basis for their biological molecules. They get these other

nitrogen-fixing bacteria soil bacteria that incorporate atmospheric nitrogen into nitrogen-containing compounds that other organisms can use

forms of nitrogen from metabolic processes in bacteria. Some bacteria convert ammonia (NH_3) to nitrites (NO_2) that are released into the soil. Still other bacteria take up nitrites and convert them to nitrates (NO_3). Plant roots take up nitrates and can use this form of nitrogen in the synthesis of amino acids, which are then used to make plant proteins. Animals get most of their nitrogen in the form of amino acids from plants. Some animals eat plants and use plant amino acids to build their own proteins. These animals are food for yet other animals.

Through these biogeochemical transformations of nitrogen from one molecule to another, atmospheric nitrogen becomes available to different lifeforms. In this half of the nitrogen cycle, different kinds of bacteria remove nitrogen from the atmosphere and transform it into nitrogen-containing compounds that organisms use. The remaining half of the nitrogen cycle is completed by other organisms *returning* nitrogen gas to the atmosphere. Although there is an enormous volume of nitrogen in Earth's atmosphere, if nitrogen were continually drained from it, drastic chemical changes eventually would occur. Chemical processing within a different sort of bacteria returns nitrogen to the atmosphere. These bacteria live in mud or other anaerobic environments. They take in nitrates, nitrites, and other compounds that contain nitrogen and oxygen, use the oxygen in their own cellular processes, and release nitrogen back to the atmosphere as a waste product. Because these bacteria *remove* nitrates and nitrites from soil, they are called **denitrifying bacteria**. Notice that bacteria do most of the recycling of nitrogen. Also notice that if one component of the nitrogen cycle is missing, the nitrogen cycle cannot operate.

The Phosphorus Cycle Has No Atmospheric Component

Phosphorus is an essential component of nucleic acids, ATP, and the phospholipids that form cell membranes. The phosphorus cycle has no atmospheric component and takes place within food chains on land and in water. Rocks and soils are important reservoirs of phosphorus (**Figure 4.7**), but until rocks erode, phosphate ions are locked up within them and are unavailable to organisms. When rocks and sediments erode, phosphates are released. Plants must have phosphates to grow well. Mycorrhizae absorb phosphates and pass them on to plants. Because phosphates are not very soluble in water and are not found in all rocks, lack of phosphates limits plant growth. Once phosphates are incorporated into plant tissues, they enter food chains and are passed from organism to organism. When organisms die, decomposers return phosphorus to soil and water. From there geological processes incorporate phosphorus into soils, rocks, and water.

denitrifying bacteria
bacteria that transform nitrites and nitrates and release nitrogen to the atmosphere

Quick check   4.2

Make a chart that compares the long and short-term processes of the carbon cycle, nitrogen cycle, water cycle, and the phosphorus cycle.

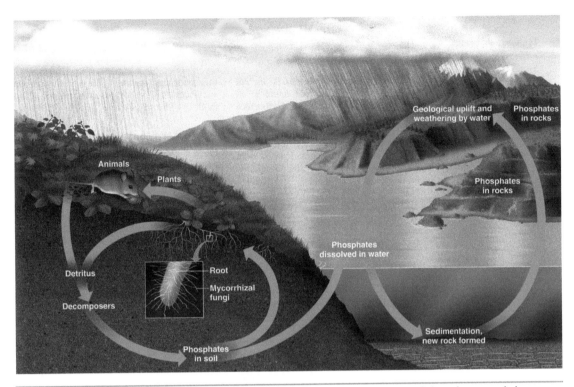

Figure 4.7 **The Phosphorus Cycle.** Phosphorus in rocks dissolves in oceans, lakes, rivers, and streams. Dissolved phosphorous is taken up by photosynthetic organisms. Animals and fungi gain phosphorous by digesting photosynthetic organisms.

4.3
OCEAN LIFE IS INFLUENCED BY FOOD, LIGHT, CURRENTS, AND PRESSURE

To see the most varied forms of life, you've got to go to sea. Some animal phyla have no representatives that live in freshwater or on land. For instance, echinoderms such as sea stars, sand dollars, and sea cucumbers live only in the oceans. Other animal phyla are mostly marine but have a few freshwater representatives. For example, the flamboyant diversity of marine sponges and cnidarians makes the few freshwater species of each phylum seem pale by comparison. Still other animal phyla such as mollusks live in oceans, in freshwater, and on land—but are wildly diverse in the oceans. While there are snails and slugs on land and clams and snails in freshwater, mollusks like chitons, nudibranchs, octopi, and various species of nautilus live only in the oceans. And the comparatively few species of land and freshwater mollusks cannot rival the spectacular diversity of oceanic clams and snails.

Insects are one major terrestrial group that is not found in the oceans. Instead, crustaceans like crabs, lobsters, copepods, and barnacles are common and varied in oceans. Ocean vertebrates include sharks, rays, skates, bony fishes, snakes, crocodiles, turtles, penguins, shore birds, seals, walruses, and whales. Why should more animal phyla live in the oceans than in other environments? One reason is that life first

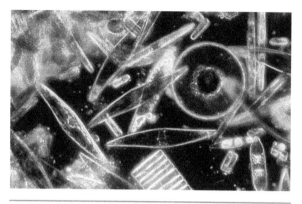

Figure 4.8 Phytoplankton. Free-floating microscopic algae such as these diatoms are at the base of ocean food chains.

evolved in the oceans. The transition to life in freshwater came later, and the move to dry land happened even later. So the oceans are life's earliest home, and some forms of life never have left. Although the oceans are home to the greatest *variety* of animals, the oceans do not have the greatest *number* of animal species. Insects and seed plants evolved on land and proliferated into many species there; later they made the transition to life in freshwater. Only a few species of seed plants or insects are adapted to life in the oceans.

Phytoplankton Are the Basis of Ocean Food Chains

Another way that life in water is different from life on land concerns the organization of food chains. Plants are the producers in land-based food chains. In the oceans the major producers are free-floating microscopic algae called *phytoplankton* (**Figure 4.8**). Since the 1950s scientists have documented that phytoplankton are not uniformly distributed in the oceans but are infinitely more numerous along coastlines of continents and in high latitudes, such as waters off of the Newfoundland coast and in Arctic and Antarctic oceans.

Food chains in oceans begin with tiny organisms called *nano-plankton* and *ultraplankton* that are thought to be responsible for 50 to 70% of photosynthesis in the oceans (**Figure 4.9**). Other types of plankton eat these tiny organisms. Small fishes eat plankton and are eaten by larger fishes, which are eaten by larger animals such as marine mammals.

Bacteriovores are another level of ocean food chains that are especially important. While bacteriovores are found in terrestrial ecosystems, they often are ignored because they are microscopic or small in size. Bacteriovores include marine single-celled eukaryotes such as ciliates, foraminiferans, radiolarians, and flagellates that eat bacteria. In turn, these microscopic single-celled eukaryotes are eaten by *zooplankton,* organisms large enough to be seen with the

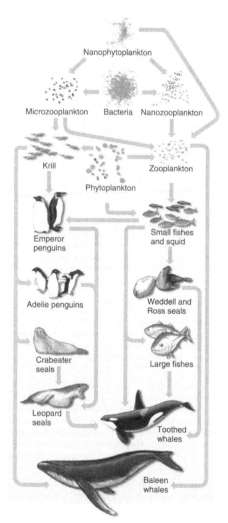

Figure 4.9 A Marine Food Web is Based on Microbes and Various Sizes of Phytoplankton. **What do leopard seals eat? What do baleen whales eat?**

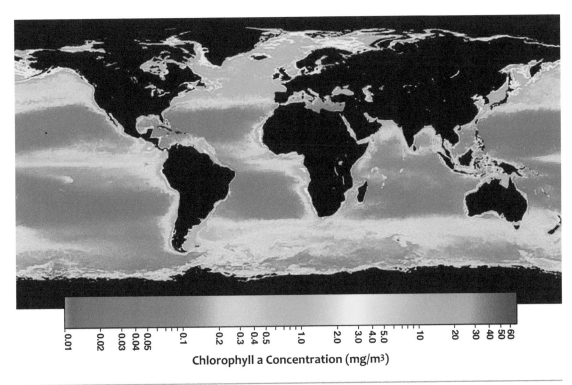

Figure 4.10 **Distribution of Phytoplankton.** Phytoplankton populations shown in green are dense around continents and sparse in the open ocean. (NASA)

naked eye. Zooplankton include larvae of many kinds of marine invertebrates, as well as small crustaceans. Most zooplankton have independent movement and are large enough to swim against the current. The shrimp-like *krill* that swarm in huge clouds in cold ocean waters are important zooplankton.

More recently, satellites have monitored concentrations of chlorophyll in the oceans, allowing us to view global distributions of phytoplankton (**Figure 4.10**). These satellite images have substantiated the pattern of huge populations of phytoplankton around continents and in high latitudes, north and south, and sparse populations of phytoplankton in the open oceans. Satellite imaging also enables scientists to see seasonal changes in phytoplankton populations.

Why are phytoplankton thickly distributed along coastlines and in high latitudes? Two factors are involved. First, runoff from land carries nutrients that allow dense populations of phytoplankton to bloom in the waters near coastlines. Second, at the edges of continents ocean currents collide with the solid continental shelf. Water is forced upward, and this *upwelling* brings nutrients up into surface waters. Ocean waters lack some of the metal ions such as iron that plants require. When open ocean waters that lacked phytoplankton were experimentally seeded with iron, blooms of phytoplankton resulted.

Oceans Contain a Variety of Habitats and Ecosystems

Marine environments are the largest portion of the biosphere and contain about 97% of its habitats. Because many ocean environments are inaccessible to humans without special gear, life in many marine ecosystems is much less well known than is life on land. Nevertheless, biologists have identified different ocean zones differentiated by depth, presence of light, and distance from land. The amount of nutrients, temperature, and currents—rather than moisture and precipitation—influence the distribution and abundance of ocean life. Most photosynthetic activity happens near the ocean's surface where sunlight is most intense. Sunlight fades as water gets deeper. More than 100 feet (about 30 meters) below the surface it is dark and difficult to see. Below 1,000 feet (about 300 meters), it is so dark that you cannot see your hand in front of your eyes. Sporadic lights come from fascinating, often nightmarish, *bioluminescent* creatures.

Oceans can be subdivided into horizontal and vertical zones. The *littoral zone* is located between the high tide and low tide lines. The *neritic zone* is the portion of the ocean above the continental shelf. The neritic zone receives abundant sunlight as well as nutrients from the coasts. So the neritic zone has vast populations of photosynthesizers and supports abundant marine life. Beyond the continental shelf is the *pelagic zone* or oceanic zone that includes deeper ocean waters. The upper, sunlit portion of the pelagic zone is the *photic zone*. The *oceanic zone* is the portion of the ocean over deep water. While its upper portions have abundant light, the pelagic zone has less life because it is farther from shoreline nutrient sources. Pelagic zones can be like deserts, with sparse populations of photosynthesizers and other organisms. Larger organisms like jellyfish and larvae of shrimps that can swim against the current make several daily *vertical migrations* that carry them downward and upward in the water. As these organisms move up and down in the water, they bring food and nutrients to other species that live at different levels. Dead organisms and wastes from swarms of krill drift down to the seafloor, and bring nutrients to the lower zones. As ocean water gets deeper, light and temperature decrease, leading to vertically arranged life zones that have characteristic organisms. The deepest parts of the ocean are the *hadal zone;* above this is the *abyssal zone.* Both are dark, cold, high-pressure waters with few nutrients.

As you might expect, ocean temperatures in regions near the equator are higher than are temperatures in regions closer to the poles, and surface waters are warmer than deeper waters. There also are seasonal changes in ocean water temperatures. This distribution of temperatures is complicated by the flow of major ocean currents (**Figure 4.11**). For example, warm water that originates offshore of Japan crosses the Pacific Ocean and reaches the American Northwest coast, bringing warm water and warmer air with it. This provides the moisture for the foggy Northwest summers that saturate coastal forests with dripping mist. Other currents take colder water to more equatorial regions. The icy Humboldt Current wells up along the coast of South America, bringing cold, nutrient-rich water from Antarctica. Ocean currents offset the effects of local temperatures and make some northern regions warmer, and more biologically productive, than they otherwise would be.

Just like their counterparts on dry land, the ocean's photosynthesizers require phosphorus, nitrogen, potassium, and other nutrients. So life in oceans also is limited by the nutrients available to photosynthesizers. Places where natural nutrient levels are high are the ocean's most productive ecosystems, while places where nutrients are lacking have only sparse life. Life is plentiful along ocean coasts where nutrients enter from land, and waves and currents stir up sediments that contain nutrients. Here water tends to be shallow, and penetrated by light. Coastal areas make up about only about 10% of the ocean, but they are extremely productive and are home to about 90% of ocean life. In the open ocean life is most abundant in the upper sunlit portions where photosynthesis takes place and tends to diminish with depth. In **estuaries**, rivers enter oceans, carrying nutrients from land into oceans. Estuaries and river deltas are generally areas of great biodiversity. Not only do phytoplankton of all sizes bloom in these waters, but also large populations of zooplankton, crustaceans, marine invertebrates, and small fishes provide ample food for birds, fishes, reptiles, and mammals.

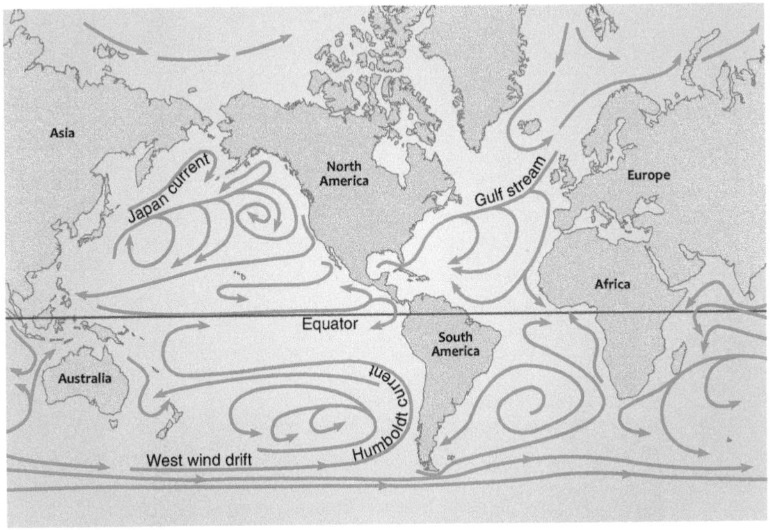

Let's look first at some coastal marine ecosystems and then consider an unusual marine ecosystem located in deeper waters.

Figure 4.11 **Ocean Currents.** The Japan current carries cooler ocean water to the west coast of North America. The Humboldt current carries cooler ocean water to the west coast of South America. The Gulf Stream carries warmer ocean water toward the British Isles and west Africa.

estuary a place where fresh and salt waters mix; generally where rivers enter the oceans

Life in the Littoral Zone Is Adapted to Rough Water and Periods of Dryness and Heat

Consider for a moment how difficult it must be for a barnacle or rock crab to live in the littoral zone (**Figure 4.12**). High tides occur twice a day, about 12½ hours apart, and can involve gentle flooding or vigorous pounding and scouring. Organisms that live here must have ways

Figure 4.12 **Life in the Littoral Zone.** If these seaweeds, sea anemones, and starfish weren't firmly attached to rocks, the pounding and scouring of waves would wash them away.

Figure 4.13 **Salt Marsh.** The roots of *Spartina* grass filter and trap decaying plant and animal tissues from the tidal waters of a salt marsh.

to prevent being damaged and swept away. When the tide is out, they must be able to cope with dry conditions and intensely hot sunlight. Some mollusks have rootlike structures of tough threads that anchor them to rocks. Other mullosks burrow into mud or sand or contract into shells that are clamped to rocks. Sea anemones draw in their tentacles and pull their bodies down to a tough nub. Many types of seaweed grow in the littoral zone, including kelps with hold-fasts that cling to rocks. Kelp beds are home to a wide variety of marine invertebrates including crabs, worms, sea anemones, and starfish.

Estuaries and Mangrove Swamps Are Nurseries for Ocean Life

You may know estuaries as tidal marshes or salt marshes. These are extremely productive environments that occur on tide-covered flat land where freshwater from a river empties into an ocean (**Figure 4.13**). Tidal marshes are washed daily by high tides. The presence of freshwater dilutes ocean water, forming less salty, **brackish water** that allows salt marsh grasses and other plants to gain a foothold and thrive. Cyanobacteria cover the surface of the mud of a salt marsh. Because these prokaryotes can fix atmospheric nitrogen into nitrogen-containing compounds, the nitrogen cycle is especially active in salt marshes. Water continuously filters through the matted plant roots, and organic materials that have been carried into the marsh settle out and decompose. All of this provides abundant nutrients for food chains of detritivores as well as for photosynthetic algae and protists. These form the base of food chains that include shrimp, lobsters, horseshoe crabs, and the young of many other kinds of crustaceans and ocean fishes. In essence, estuaries are muddy, nutrient-rich traps for organic matter that become nurseries for marine invertebrates and vertebrates. Salt marshes also are critical environments for migratory birds and a huge variety of shorebirds.

Mangroves are tropical trees that look like they are walking on stilts. *Mangrove* is an umbrella term for more than 40 species of trees and shrubs that can live in shallow, tidal, salty water and can form huge, often impenetrable swamps around coastlines (**Figure 4.14**). Their "stilts" actually are aerial roots.

brackish water a mixture of salt water and freshwater that occurs in an estuary

Like the roots of grasses in a salt marsh, the roots of mangrove plants trap nutrients. Submerged roots provide shelter for diverse populations of marine invertebrates, algae, and small fishes, while aerial roots provide habitats for other kinds of animals. Many birds, lizards, snails, insects, and snakes live in the understory and canopy of the mangrove swamps where alligators and crocodiles also find shelter. Mangrove trees are sensitive to disturbance. Once they have been cut down, mangroves seldom regrow. This is because other plants move into the area, outcompete the mangroves, and replace them. Mangroves are keystone species, and when the mangroves are gone, many of the populations that they shelter also disappear. Both salt marshes and mangrove swamps occupy prime coastal real estate, so these wetlands are perennially in danger of disappearing as human seaside communities are developed.

Figure 4.14 Mangrove Swamp. The interlaced roots of these mangroves make a mangrove swamp impenetrable to humans, but gives shelter to many organisms that make their homes in mangrove swamps.

Coral Reefs Shelter Organisms and Coastlines

Coral reefs are spectacularly diverse, wildly colorful ecosystems found in shallow, clear, tropical waters (**Figure 4.15**). The reef itself is made of the intricate, calcium carbonate exoskeletons grown by coral polyps. In addition to the coral polyps, however, many other species contribute to the complex ecosystem of a coral reef. For example, the individual corals often are cemented together by *corraline algae*. Coral polyps are carnivores that feed on

Figure 4.15 Coral Reef. Corals, sponges, sea fans, snails, crabs, shrimp, and fishes are just a sample of the diverse life of a coral reef.

smaller organisms and organic particles suspended in the water. Mutualistic single-celled algae live within their tissues and provide the polyps with an additional food source. The resident algae photosynthesize and produce sugars making corals the primary producers in coral reef ecosystems, even though they are animals. Sponges, squid, snails, and crustaceans are just a few of the organisms that live within the crevices of a coral reef. Fishes of all sizes and colors dart about the corals, and schools of other fishes wheel as shifting walls of living silver. Sharks, sea turtles, rays, and skates glide about, all looking for food. Coral reefs are one of Earth's most productive and diverse ecosystems. Coral reefs also shelter shorelines from pounding waves. This is especially important during hurricanes, typhoons, and other violent storms.

Coral reefs are important in the ecology of tropical oceans. Yet they are threatened. For example, when tropical forests are cut, silt washes into rivers and creeks. When these empty into the oceans, silt eventually accumulates on coral reefs. The mutualistic algae within coral animals must have clear water for efficient photosynthesis. If a deposit of silt blocks light, it can reduce photosynthesis and may kill the corals. Collectors hack out corals from reefs, and some divers hunt fishes and invertebrates in coral reefs. Corals are damaged by boats and anchors. Corals are subject to *coral bleaching,* a worrisome phenomenon in which corals lose their beautiful colors and turn completely white. When this happens, the symbiotic algae have abandoned the tissues of the coral polyps. Coral bleaching is a response to environmental stress, and if the corals are not recolonized by symbiotic algae, they may die. While the exact causes of coral bleaching are being investigated, coral bleaching has been linked to global climate change or increased ultraviolet radiation caused by the thinning of Earth's ozone layer. Coral reefs also are threatened by the increase in the amount of carbon dioxide in the atmosphere. Research has shown that corals do not grow well when atmospheric carbon dioxide levels are high, as they are now due to the burning of fossil fuels.

The Ocean Floor Is Rich in Diversity

You may think of the ocean as an expanse of water, but the geography of the ocean floor is as varied as that of land. Valleys, plains, and mountains provide a landscape for life, and some undersea mountains are higher than any found on Earth's dry surface. Volcanoes erupt under the oceans. Some regions of the ocean floor are muddy, some are sandy, and some are rocky. Life on the ocean floor varies with depth. Although life is most plentiful in shallow ocean floor environments, life also flourishes on the floor of the deepest part of the ocean.

Many ocean species live suspended or swimming in the water like the birds and butterflies of life on land. On the ocean floor organisms settle, walk, slither, and crawl much as they do on land. Lobsters, sea anemones, oysters, and starfish inhabit shallow waters, while animals of deeper ocean floors have adaptations to cold, dark waters where physical pressures are enormous. Many are found nowhere else, and if they are brought to the surface their delicate bodies will become physically distorted. Because humans can visit the deep ocean floor only in specially designed submarines and cannot stay for long periods of time, the ocean depths are the least known of any of Earth's ecosystems.

Until just a few years ago it was thought that only glass sponges, brittle stars, and odd kinds of bioluminescent shrimp, squid, and fishes survived in the ocean's depths, as scavengers on the remains of fallen organisms. Thanks to deep-sea submarines it is now clear that the alien realm of the ocean floor is marked by pockets of remarkable life-forms.

Exploring the abyss of one of the ocean's deepest trenches, in the deep-sea submarine *Alvin,* investigators discovered a place where the water was filled with what looked like a black plume of smoke. External sensors showed that the temperature within the plume was 270° to 380°C (518° to 716°F), while typical ocean floor waters are close to freezing. Gradually, the explorers realized that the plume of the "black smoker" was seawater rich with minerals superheated by the hot magma from below Earth's crust (**Figure 4.16**). The heat and nutrients dramatically altered conditions on the barren seafloor, creating a dense ecosystem of unexpected life. The explorers saw enormous red-lipped worms that turned out to belong to a completely new phylum. These worms have no mouths or digestive systems, and cells of the lipstick-red "lips" that protrude from tough chitinous tubes contain hemoglobin. Later studies revealed that these worms have mutualistic colonies of chemosynthetic prokaryotes living within their bodies. Their chemosynthetic bacteria harvest minerals from the black smoker and provide the tube worms with food that allows them to grow quickly. The 9-foot-tall tube worms are among Earth's fastest-growing invertebrates and can grow nearly 6 feet (2 meters) a year. The tube worms were not the only life at the black smoker. An entirely new ecosystem was found in deep ocean trenches. White crabs scuttled away from *Alvin's* lights, and there were many filter feeders, including mussels, clams, and feather duster worms. Scavengers like octopi and fishes are part of the *hydrothermal vent communities,* as are about 500 other species.

Figure 4.16 **Black Smoker.** Superheated sea water rich in minerals from hot magma spews into the frigid, lightless waters of the ocean floor. **What hydrothermal vent organisms can you see in this photo? What basic hydrothermal vent organisms can you not see in this photo?**

How does life survive without light for photosynthesis? The unusual hydrothermal vent organisms have evolved to take advantage of the ability of chemosynthetic bacteria to use hydrogen sulfide (H_2S) to produce glucose. These bacteria produce organic compounds that pass directly to the worms' tissues. Hydrothermal vent communities often are limited in life span. In one or two years the vents can become exhausted, or can close, cutting off the source of energy. Then the organisms die, leaving a ghost community for scientists to study. Some offspring of organisms that live at hydrothermal vents may by chance drift off. A few will find another hydrothermal vent where new populations will form.

QUICK CHECK   **4.3**

Explain how life in ocean ecosystems is influenced by the presence of light and nutrients.

4.4

FRESHWATER ECOSYSTEMS LINK MARINE AND TERRESTRIAL ECOSYSTEMS

Freshwater ecosystems have components found at sea and on land, and they bridge the two. Aquatic invertebrates include diverse forms of insects and insect larvae, worms that belong to several phyla, and a wide variety of mollusks. All groups of vertebrates—including amphibians that are absent from the oceans—live in aquatic ecosystems. In addition to ferns, mosses, and liverworts, many aquatic seed plants are adapted to life in freshwater ecosystems. As in ocean waters, many of the major producers in freshwater systems include phytoplankton of various sizes. Detritivores and food chains based on bacteria are common and important in freshwater ecosystems. Beyond these biotic factors, freshwater ecosystems are influenced by differences in water temperature, water movement, and levels of oxygen. Freshwater ecosystems are broadly divided into *still water,* or lakes and ponds, and *flowing water,* or brooks, creeks, streams, and rivers.

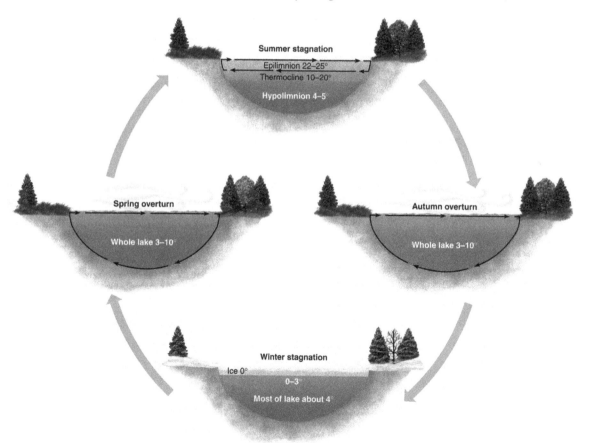

Figure 4.17   **Seasonal Cycle of a Freshwater Pond.** The small black arrows show movements of water at different seasons. These movements are related to the temperature and density of water and are influenced by winds.

Life in Lakes and Ponds Can Suffocate

Oxygen is critical for eukaryotes and when oxygen levels are too low, plants, animals, and other eukaryotes will die. Massive die-offs can occur in lakes that become depleted of oxygen. How does this happen? Sometimes it depends on temperature. Because the temperature of water influences its density, deep lakes and ponds tend to form layers that have different temperatures. In summer a lake is heated by sunlight, and its upper layers grow warm and become less dense than deeper, colder, lower waters. At the bottom of the lake is the coldest, most dense layer of water (**Figure 4.17**). The upper layers have abundant light, so photosynthesizers are active. Thus the warmer layers have lots of oxygen. As the phytoplankton in the lake die, they settle to the bottom of the lake. There aerobic bacteria begin to decompose them and use much oxygen in the process. There is little or no mixing of the layers of a lake, so in summer the lower layers can become oxygen depleted, while the upper layers can become depleted of nutrients by phytoplankton. As seasons turn colder, water temperatures fall. Soon the distinct layers of temperatures disappear, and from top to bottom the lake water reaches about 4°C (39.2°F), the temperature at which water is most dense. Winds blow across the surface and cause the water to *overturn*. The overturn moves nutrients up from the bottom of the lake and moves oxygenated waters down to the bottom. As temperatures continue to fall, water at the top of the lake freezes. This traps slightly warmer and denser water below it. Aquatic organisms live through the winter beneath the ice. Some burrow down into the mud and continue life at a low ebb, while others remain active through the winter but generally do not feed. Ice melts in spring. When water warms to 4°C, it is at its densest. Once again, pushed by winds, the lake water overturns. Again, nutrients are brought up from the bottom, setting the stage for blooms of phytoplankton. Population increases of zooplankton and other members of aquatic food chains typically follow the spring overturn.

In summer the upper, warmer layer of water can become depleted of oxygen, producing die-offs of fishes. Summer stagnation and "summer kills" are typical of many ponds and lakes. This natural **eutrophication,** the process of a body of water developing an overabundance of nutrients, can be worsened by nutrients that originate from human activities. In winter a different sort of die-off can occur. A heavy cover of snow over winter ice can block light so that photosynthesis slows or even stops. Under these conditions winter lakes can become oxygen depleted, and a "winter kill" of fishes and other aquatic organisms can occur.

Just as light is a critical factor that influences the distribution of life in ocean waters, light also influences the distribution of life in still-water ecosystems.

eutrophication

the process in which a body of water becomes enriched with nutrients

Lakes and ponds have littoral zones in which plants grow (**Figure 4.18**). Cattails and rushes are part of the *emergent vegetation* that protrudes above the water. So are leaves and flowers of water lilies and other plants that float on the water's surface. A feature of still freshwater that is absent or minimally exploited in still salt water is the water's *surface film*. Water striders, mosquito larvae, whirligigs, water boatmen, and other aquatic arthropods use the water's surface film as a habitat. Farther out from the shoreline is the limonitic zone, which is penetrated by light. The *profundal zone* is at the bottom of the lake where like deep oceans, it is darker and colder, and there is little or no photosynthesis. Each of these zones has typical life-forms.

Figure 4.18 **Freshwater Ecosystem.** Cattails and are some of the emergent vegetation in this northern pond.

Creeks, Streams, and Rivers Contain Life Adapted to Moving Water

Creeks, brooks, and streams are small bodies of flowing water, while rivers are larger, generally 3 meters or more wide. Creeks, brooks, and streams can flow all year or can be intermittent, flowing only seasonally or after heavy rains, while rivers are more permanent ecosystems. Streams have two basic habitats: *pools* of deeper water and *riffles* where water is shallow and flows rapidly over pebbles or rocks. Water in riffles has a high oxygen content and relatively few planktonic photosynthesizers.

In moving water life must be able to resist the currents or be swept downstream. Some animals that live in these turbulent waters hide beneath pebbles and stay out of the current. Mayfly larvae and salamander larvae use this strategy. Others like trout or dace are strong swimmers that can make headway against the current. Still other riffle organisms have holdfasts that allow them to hang on as the water moves past them. Caddisfly larvae cement grains of sand, twigs, and pebbles into protective cases. Life in pools includes crayfish, fishes, various kinds of burrowing worms, and insect larvae. Frogs, salamanders, and turtles also may be present in freshwater pools.

Flowing-water ecosystems merge into one another as creeks grow wider, become rivers, and empty into the sea. Along this continuum there is a corresponding shift in the physical characteristics and organisms that live in flowing waters. Oxygen levels, water clarity, amount of nutrients, water temperature, and speed of flow all shift as a creek widens into a river that flows to the ocean. Oxygen levels are highest in colder, rapidly moving water upstream and lower in warmer, slowly moving river water. Streams usually are clear, while rivers are murky. Stream fishes usually strike their prey after they have seen it, while scent and taste are much more important to river fishes. Streams have relatively few nutrients when compared to rivers that have abundant populations of photosynthesizers and receive many nutrients from runoff and from all of the streams that enter them.

Flowing water is greatly influenced by organic matter that enters the water from the surrounding environments. Part of this ecological phenomenon in rivers is fishes like salmon and alewives that spend much of their lives in the oceans and "run upstream" to breed. Although some of the adults make the return trip downstream back to the ocean and live for other years, many of these fishes die upstream. As they move upstream, their wastes and dead bodies enrich the stream (**Figure 4.19**).

They also draw foraging land-based carnivores like bears and scavengers like bald eagles. Eventually, these animals enrich the surrounding terrestrial biomes with wastes that originated as the flesh of oceangoing fishes.

Figure 4.19 **Spent Salmon.** Having migrated from the ocean to the stream where they hatched, these salmon have spawned and died. The nutrients in their decaying tissues enrich the freshwater ecosystem and the surrounding biome.

Quick Check	4.4

Compare the factors that shape life in still water as opposed to flowing water.

4.5
BIOMES ARE CHARACTERIZED BY TYPICAL VEGETATION

In broad terms the kinds of life found in a region on land are related to the climate, and similar climates have similar kinds of life. For instance, the Australian outback, the plains and prairies of North America, the pampas of Argentina, and the African plains are primarily grasslands. They have similar climates and plants and animals with similar adaptations, even though the plant and animal species differ. Terrestrial ecosystems like grasslands that cover large geographical areas and share similar climates are called **biomes**. You will read about six major biomes here. **Figure 4.20** shows the distribution of arctic tundra, taiga, temperate deciduous forest, grassland, desert, and tropical rain forest. Notice that each biome can be found in more than just one geographic region. Three features largely define a terrestrial biome: availability of freshwater, temperature, and dominant plant species. Because these features greatly influence natural selection in a region, they influence the kinds of plant and animal adaptations found in each biome. **Figure 4.21** shows the distribution of temperature and rainfall in relationship to biomes. Let's start in high northern latitudes with arctic tundra and work toward the equator and tropical rain forests.

biome a major kind of ecosystem that covers a large geographical region and has a similar climate

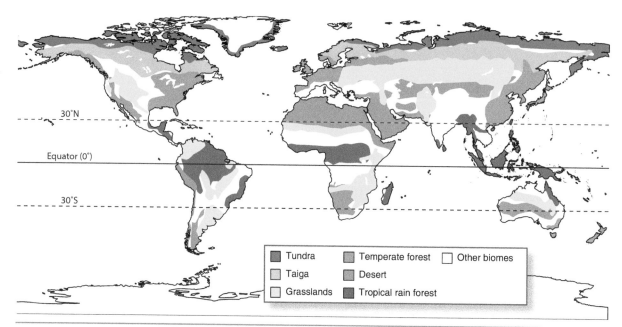

Figure 4.20 Distribution of Biomes.

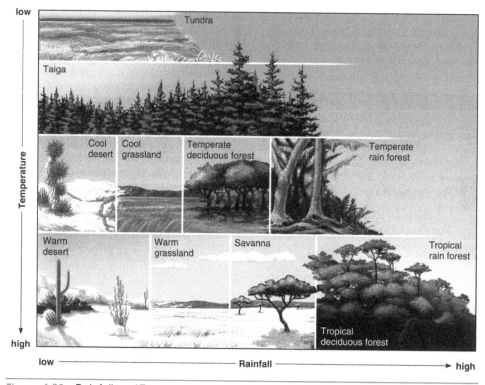

Figure 4.21 Rainfall and Temperature Influence the Distribution of Biomes.

Arctic Tundra Has Short Summers and Permanently Frozen Subsoil

Arctic tundra (Figure 4.22) is a northern biome that can be quite dry but terribly cold. Arctic tundra covers regions close to the Arctic Circle, where temperatures are almost always below freezing, and six months of sunshine are followed by six months of near to total darkness. Because the tundra is so cold, even in summer the subsoil about 3 feet (about 1 meter) from the surface is permanently frozen and is called **permafrost**. The long summer days and the presence of permafrost have a profound impact on the patterns of life in the tundra. For one thing, there are no tall trees. Instead, flowers, small bushes, shrubs, lichens, and mosses carpet the landscape. Why are the plants so short? A combination of permafrost and strong winds is responsible. Because roots cannot penetrate permafrost, root systems are forced to be shallow. Tall trees must have deep roots to stabilize them, and so the combination of permafrost and fierce winds eliminates tall trees from the tundra.

arctic tundra a northern biome characterized by extremely cold temperatures, restricted precipitation, permafrost, short summers with extremely long days, and low, ground-hugging vegetation primarily composed of mosses, lichens, and grasses

permafrost tundra subsoil that is permanently frozen

Figure 4.22 **Tundra**. Permafrost, cold, snowy winters, short summers that can have 24 hours of daylight, low plant growth, and populations of animals that seasonally migrate are characteristic of tundra.

While the tundra is generally dry, if you visit the tundra during its two-month-long summer, it looks extremely wet. In the warm summer months the snow and ice on the surface melts, but water cannot seep down through the permafrost. As a result pools and bogs form, and a few species of insects such as mosquitoes, deer flies, and black flies multiply rapidly and swarm in huge numbers.

Rates of photosynthesis are high during the long summer days, and reproduction is fast. Flocks of birds that have spent the winter in southern latitudes migrate north to mate and raise their young on the tundra. Parents feed their young on an accelerated schedule, and the young grow rapidly. After the brief summer months, juvenile and adult birds gather into flocks and fly south before winter sets in. When the winter darkness returns, the tundra's permanent residents must have enough stored energy to last the long winter. Tundra mammals typically gorge during the summer and then either migrate or stay active beneath the snow during the winter. Few tundra animals hibernate because the permafrost limits deep underground refuges from the cold. Small mammals dig burrows beneath the snow where they shelter from the bitter temperatures and fierce winds. Mammals like brown bears, caribou, and musk oxen grow thick coats of fur. The coats of some mammals like lemmings, hares, and wolves change color to match the snow.

The future of the arctic tundra biome is uncertain. As global temperature change warms the atmosphere, the permafrost across the Arctic is thawing, and warmer temperatures are creating a more humid and moderate climate. Already whole villages that were built on solid permafrost have had to be relocated because the permafrost is melting beneath them. Landscapes that once were covered by only short, thin vegetation are now growing larger shrubs. As permafrost melts, organic matter contained within it also thaws and becomes accessible to bacterial decomposers. Most of these decomposers produce methane as a by-product of their metabolism. For example, since 1950 in parts of Sweden methane release from permafrost regions has increased anywhere from 20 to 60%. Methane is an even *more* powerful greenhouse gas than is carbon dioxide, and it is likely that melting permafrost will intensify the global warming.

Another concern is human exploitation of resources in the tundra. Beneath the Alaskan tundra is a large, economically valuable oilfield, and its development is a concern to ecologists. Arctic haze is a weather phenomenon that carries air pollutants northward to the Arctic, depositing them thousands of miles from their U.S. origins. The tundra also experiences *bioaccumulation,* the phenomenon in which environmental toxins accumulate in the tissues of organisms and move upward in food chains. Carnivores are most vulnerable to bioaccumulation of toxins in their fat deposits. Humans are directly affected when they eat animal fat that contains toxins. Fat is a food source that traditionally is prized by many northern people.

Taiga Is Northern Coniferous Forest

South of the tundra are large regions of coniferous forests, which are among Earth's most common forests (**Figure 4.23**). Recall that conifers are trees such as pines and firs that produce their seeds within cones. **Taiga** is the Russian word for this biome. It also is called *boreal forest*. Winter in the taiga is long, snowy, and extremely cold, and the cool summer growing season is short—typically less than 130 days. There is a bit more water in the taiga than in the arctic tundra, and this combined with the absence of permafrost means that trees have the resources to grow tall. In the taiga one or two species of conifers like spruces and firs cover acre after acre, giving the taiga a uniform appearance. Because these trees are so tall, they block out much of the sunlight, and beneath the trees there is little underbrush and few shrubs. A walk through mature taiga can be a meditative experience: there is plenty of space between trees and the forest floor is quiet and dim. There also are few signs of birds or small mammals, and footsteps are muffled by a thick layer of fallen needles. Caribou, minks, beavers, and arctic hares are typical taiga mammals.

Taiga is the largest biome, and although it is not heavily inhabited, humans are beginning to have a negative impact on it. Large tracts of taiga have been opened to logging, especially in northern Russia. Scientists are concerned about loss of this unique biome and about the contribution to global environmental problems if this vast northern forest is lost.

Figure 4.23 **Taiga.** Dense forests of a few species of conifers are typical of taigas that have cold, snowy winters, but no permafrost.

Trees of Temperate Deciduous Forests Drop Their Leaves in Fall

Temperate deciduous forests (Figure 4.24) are found in the eastern United States, across much of Europe, and in China, Japan, the eastern coast of Australia, and New Zealand. Although some conifers are present, most of the trees in this biome have broad, flat leaves that die and drop from the tree when the cool temperatures and short days of fall and winter arrive. Before they die, the leaves of deciduous trees reveal the colors of their accessory photosynthetic pigments, giving a glorious show of color in autumn. Having deciduous leaves is an adaptation to a strongly seasonal climate, allowing a tree to conserve energy and prevent heat loss by dropping its leaves. In winter the groundwater of a deciduous forest is frozen. To avoid damage from the formation of ice crystals within its water

taiga a northern biome characterized by cold, snowy winters, cool summers, moderate precipitation, and conifer forests

temperate deciduous forest a mid-latitude biome where moisture falls about equally all year; distinct warm and cold seasons favor trees that drop their leaves and go dormant in winter

canopy the tops or crown layer of forest trees

understory a layer of forest growth that is higher than the tallest shrubs but does not reach into the heights of the canopy

Figure 4.24 **Temperate Deciduous Forest.** Autumn displays of colored leaves are typical of temperate deciduous forests.

transport system, a deciduous tree withdraws liquids and useful chemicals from its shoots and stores them in its roots. After a leaf drops, a tough scale forms over the place where the leaf was attached. In spring, as temperatures grow warm, liquids rise within the water transport systems of the trees. Photosynthesis and growth begin again. Buds at the tips of branches that have been protected from freezing by tough, waxy *bud scales* begin to expand. Soon the tree blossoms, and fresh green leaves unfurl on its branches.

Temperate deciduous forests have stratified layers. The **canopy** is the covering formed by the crowns of trees. Below this is an **understory** formed by younger trees growing up into the canopy as well as smaller species of trees that do not grow as high as the canopy trees. Closer to the ground is the *shrub layer,* and farther down are layers of *herbs, grasses,* and *mosses.* Sunlight can reach the forest floor in the spring and fall before the canopy has leafed out and after leaves have fallen; at these seasons wildflowers bloom on the forest floor. There usually is a deep layer of rotting leaves. As these decay, they enrich the forest soil.

Many animals of temperate deciduous forests have adaptations for life in trees. For instance, tree frogs have adhesive discs on their toes, flying squirrels have flaps of skin for gliding from perches, opossums and mice have grasping tails. Because dense leaves of canopy and understory block vision, animals that live in trees tend to have keen hearing, and their voices and calls are important adaptations. In temperate deciduous forests many animals like chipmunks hibernate during the winter to avoid food shortages. Migratory birds are typical of temperate deciduous forests. Nectar-sipping hummingbirds, insect-eating warblers, and caterpillar-eating tanagers migrate to warmer climates when their young are independent. They return to raise their young in temperate deciduous forests in the spring.

From a human perspective the temperate forests have provided a wealth of resources. Northern Europe and North America once were largely covered by temperate forests of one kind or another, but much of this forest was cut down and used for building materials as well as a source of energy. You certainly are aware of worldwide efforts to save rain forests in other parts of the world, but American forests were largely cut down in the first 300 years after the Europeans arrived. A similar loss of forests was seen in Europe as far back as the 1700s and 1800s. Today, efforts at conservation and restoration of forests are being increased, but forests are still being cleared for housing developments and shopping malls. As forest acreage is lost or fragmented, habitats are disrupted and species become locally extinct.

Savannas, Pampas, Prairies, Veldt, and the Outback Are Grasslands

Grasslands are biomes that have only a bit more rainfall than deserts—enough to grow a ground cover of different species of grasses and wildflowers (**Figure 4.25**). Because there is relatively modest water, grasslands usually have no trees except along river or creek banks. The 10 to 30 inches (25 to 75 centimeters) of rain that does fall on grasslands is seasonal, and much of the year grasslands are dry. Grasses are adapted to these arid conditions. Their long, thin leaves minimize evaporation, and grasses have dense, matted root systems that quickly absorb any rainfall. Grasses provide food and moisture for large populations of insects as well as for herds of grazing mammals. Grasses have adaptations that allow them to be gnawed right down to the ground and still survive. As long as the roots and the base of the plant are intact, a grass can grow again. Periodic fires are an important feature of life in grasslands. Fires that usually are started by lightning burn grasses down to the soil. After rains, scattered seeds and roots will sprout a new cover of fresh grasses. Many young deciduous shrubs and trees are not able to withstand regular fires, and fire quickly eliminates most windblown or animal-transported seeds of trees that sprout.

grassland a biome characterized by wet and dry seasons, hot summers and cold winters, and year-round cover of grasses

Figure 4.25 **Grasslands.** Landscapes of grasses and wildflowers make up the North American prairies.

Grasslands usually are found in the interior of a continent. The Australian outback, the South American pampas, the African veldt or savanna, the Russian steppe, and the North American plains and prairies are all grasslands. Early settlers who crossed the United States in large covered wagons called "prairie schooners" described vast seas of grasses, with mile after mile of 3to 5-foot-high grasses swaying in the breeze. The enormous herds of bison that once roamed North America lived on these prairies. Animals that live on grasslands have adaptations that include traveling in herds or large flocks, teeth specialized for grazing, use of burrows, and life cycles that feature adaptations to help them escape from cold or dry seasons. Grassland animals hibernate, migrate, and *estivate,* the term for becoming inactive or dormant in hot and dry conditions.

Grasslands have deep, rich soils, and they are extremely valuable for agriculture. Today, farms have replaced prairies and plains across most of the United States. One consequence of the loss of the original North American prairie is the loss of biodiversity. The diversity of grass species in the prairies maintains the richness of the soil as diverse grasses die back in winter and are decomposed by bacteria and fungi. Modern ecologists and farmers have a lot to learn from the prairies, and conservation focuses on replanting native prairie grasses and reestablishing small pockets of the biome. Little native prairie remains in the United States and Canada.

Deserts Can Be Hot or Cold, But They Are Always Dry

Deserts are some of the most extreme environments on Earth. While some deserts are hot and others are cold, all deserts are dry. To better define this environmental quality, ecologists classify a **desert** as any area that receives less than about 10 inches (25 centimeters) of rainfall a year (**Figure 4.26**). Major deserts are found on all continents, usually about midway between the equator and the poles (30° N and S). Deserts are not dry all year long. In most deserts rain may fall abundantly in some seasons, but in other seasons there is no rainfall. When you think of a desert, you probably imagine camels and sand dunes or cacti and burning hot sunlight, but many deserts don't follow this pattern. For instance, the interior of Antarctica is a desert

Figure 12.26 **Desert.** Scarce rainfall in a desert influences the water-conserving adaptations of desert plants like these saguaro cacti.

where the temperature can drop to nearly −100°C (−148°F). There is lots of water, but because it is frozen, it is unavailable to life.

Extremes of temperature variations are characteristic of deserts. Sunlight raises daytime temperatures, but at night temperatures fall dramatically, sometimes dropping as much as 10°C (50°F). Temperatures fluctuate widely because at night there is little water vapor in the air to retain the Sun's heat. The heat of the day is quickly lost to space.

These conditions of scarce water and fluctuations of temperature limit the kinds of life that can survive in a desert. Instead of broad leaves, most desert plants have thorns or spines that conserve water. Desert plants that do have leaves tend to lose them during dry seasons. Another adaptation of desert plants is that their stems usually are green. The chloroplasts that normally would be found in leaves of other plants are located in the outer tissue layer of modified stems of desert plants. In addition, desert plants have a thick, tough, waxy cuticle and stomata sunken into pits. Both of these adaptations limit water loss. Many desert *succulents* have thickened leaves, stems, or roots where water is stored. These and other adaptations help desert plants conserve water and survive in places where only a little rain falls.

Desert animals also have adaptations that allow them to take advantage of water in wet times and to survive on sparse water in dry times. One example is the kangaroo rat that lives in the Southwest desert of the United States. These small rodents have silky, sand-colored fur that matches the soils where they live. Like other desert animals, kangaroo rats are nocturnal. By day they sleep in cool, moist underground burrows and avoid high temperatures and hot sunlight. They are active at night, when it is cooler. Like most nocturnal mammals, kangaroo

desert a biome characterized by sparse moisture, great daily fluctuations in temperature, poor soils, and sparse vegetation with adaptations to conserve water

rats have large, dark eyes. Like pet hamsters, kangaroo rats have large, fur-lined cheek pouches. The kangaroo rats stuff these pouches full of seeds that they carry down into food caches within their underground burrows. Unlike many other desert rodents, kangaroo rats do not hibernate.

Although it seems unbelievable, kangaroo rats *never* drink water or eat green plant tissue that contains water. Instead they get water as a by-product of the metabolism of their food. Kangaroo rats have several adaptations that preserve their metabolic water, so they do not have to drink. For example, kangaroo rats have highly specialized kidneys that resorb most of the water in their urine. They produce almost no sweat. During the day kangaroo rats block the many entrances to their burrows with soil. This helps retain the cooler, more humid atmosphere in their burrows. Kangaroo rats cannot avoid losing water vapor as they breathe, but while they are within their burrows their exhalations are trapped underground, adding moisture to the air they breathe.

No matter how highly adapted desert animals and plants are to their arid homes, they cannot survive long when humans move in and change the ecological equation. Many U.S. desert regions are under pressure because they have become desirable places to live; towns and cities are expanding into desert regions. Along with an increased human population comes an increased demand for water. Expanding communities divert water from rivers. This leaves less water for human populations that are downriver and creates bitter disputes about who "owns" rivers and has the right to their waters. Most of the migrants to U.S. desert areas come from other places in the United States, Canada, and Mexico, where they are accustomed to having plentiful water. So many of these new residents are not as sensitive to the need for water conservation in their new desert homes. As humans move into desert areas, habitats are fragmented, and wild species are displaced. Increased human presence in deserts has other associated problems including herds of livestock that are released to freely graze on desert vegetation, use of off-road vehicles that damage deserts, and the introduction of alien and invasive species of plants that replace native perennial grasses. Cheatgrass brome is an invasive alien grass. It outcompetes native grasses, reduces the natural biodiversity of desert environments, and creates fire hazards.

Figure 4.27

Tropical Rain Forest. Tropical rain forests have abundant rainfall and plants grow luxuriously. Most of the animals live in the tree canopy. The tropical rain forests have the highest diversity of organisms of any terrestrial biome.

Tropical Rain Forests Have the Greatest Biodiversity of Any Biome

The most lush and productive terrestrial biome is the **tropical rain forest (Figure 4.27)**. Here water and warmth combine to produce an explosion of plant growth and an enormous number of species. Tropical rain forests are distributed in a belt that encircles Earth at the equator. Parts of Central America, South America, western Africa, Indonesia, and Australia all have tropical rain forests. Here the climate is warm to hot, a great deal of rain falls—80 inches (200 cm) or more each year—and it is extremely humid. Because of their equatorial position, tropical rain forests have remarkable uniformity of climate and day length. The temperature is usually about 27°C (80°F) and days and nights are generally 12 hours long, all year long.

Tropical rain forests are extremely active biologically. The vegetation removes a huge amount of carbon dioxide from the air and releases an equally large amount of oxygen. The number of plant species is astounding. In the tropical rain forest neighboring trees are usually different species, and you might have to search for *a mile or two* before you would find another tree of the *same* species. This is markedly different from taiga, where acre after acre will have only one or a few species of conifers. It is also different from temperate deciduous forests, where there will be a few dominant species, with perhaps a dozen to 20 other species present. Water is plentiful in tropical rain forests, so trees can grow very tall, and many have expanded bases that stabilize their tall trunks.

With so much growth, though, there is great competition for sunlight. Tall trees monopolize sunlight, and shorter trees are adapted to use the reduced light that filters through the canopy. In tropical rain forests the canopy is nearly continuous. It blocks light, and the forest floor is dim. Understory plants often have adaptations that maximize the use of whatever sunlight they get. These include large, broad, dark green leaves that have lots of chloroplasts. *Vines* are common in the tropical rain forests but are less common in other biomes. Tropical rainforest vines snake up tree trunks, growing toward the sunlit canopy. *Epiphytes,* plants that grow on other plants, are another unusual feature of the canopy, where tall trees, vines, and epiphytes compete for a place in the Sun. In tropical rain forests entire aerial gardens grow on tree limbs. Researchers have learned that epiphytes may provide a source of nourishment for their host trees. It long was thought that epiphytes sent their roots into the transport tissues of their host plants. Now it seems as though the reverse is true: the supporting plants send accessory roots out of their limbs and into tissues of epiphytes. Because they serve as homes for whole communities of animals within the treetops, and because they trap leaves and other debris, epiphytes are an aerial source of nutrients for trees.

tropical rain forest
the most productive terrestrial biome, characterized by warm to hot year-round temperatures, extreme humidity, large amounts of rainfall, and highly varied vegetation

Although the luxuriant vegetation might make you think that soil beneath a tropical rain forest is Earth's most fertile soil, this is a misconception. Tropical rain forest soils are some of the poorest and *least* fertile soils. These red-orange soils are little more than oxidized clay, and they contain few of the mineral nutrients that plants need. Tropical rain forest soils contribute little to a plant's growth other than stabilizing it and providing water. Most of the nutrients in a tropical rain forest are within the shoots and roots of plants and in the living bodies of other organisms. The soil beneath a tropical rain forest has a scanty covering of dead leaves because dead organic matter decays quickly in the warm, humid climate, and the carbon and nitrogen cycles turn quickly. The forest floor has fewer species of understory trees than does the temperate deciduous forest. It is nothing like the "tropical jungle" that you might imagine. A jungle actually is a place where the canopy has been broken and light streams down to the forest floor. Plants respond with thick, often impenetrable growth. Jungle usually develops along riverbanks, in wind breaks where old trees have fallen, or in areas that humans have cleared.

Most of the animals in the rain forest live in the canopy and seldom descend to the forest floor. Many animals have grasping tails, adhesive toes, or other adaptations that make life in the trees easier. There are gliders, leapers, hangers, acrobatic swingers, and of course fliers in tropical rain forests. Although there are many animal species, like the plants the density of each species is low. So there aren't enormous flocks of birds or huge herds of mammals typical of the tundra, taiga, or grasslands. Being hidden among the leaves, animals often have to rely on sound to communicate. This makes the rain forest a noisy place, especially at dawn and dusk. Like animals in deciduous forests, rain forest animals often have keen hearing and sophisticated ways to produce sounds.

Tropical rain forests are rapidly being cut down. It is estimated that an acre of forest is cleared each second, worldwide, and many biologists predict that at this rate of destruction, all tropical rain forests may be gone in 30 to 50 years. This is worrisome for a number of reasons. Tropical rain forests contain more biological diversity than any other region of Earth. Furthermore, unlike deciduous forests or taiga, there is little evidence that intact, complex tropical rain forests with all of their thousands of species can regenerate once a forest has been cut down. Biologists estimate that *over half* of living species are found only in tropical rain forests. Many of these species are plants and insects, but vertebrates also are diverse in tropical rain forests. And most of these species are still unknown, unstudied, and unidentified. As tropical rain forests disappear, the fascinating tropical rain forest animals will dwindle, disappear, and may even go extinct. It is not an exaggeration to state that a major extinction event is now taking place. Unlike other major extinctions in the history of life, this one is caused by human actions.

Quick Check   4.5

Describe important aspects of the tropical rain forest biome. Why is it so extremely productive when other biomes are less productive?

4.6
THE BIOSPHERE ENCOMPASSES ALL OF EARTH'S BIOMES

Experience has taught you that life is prolific. For instance, if you set out a bucket of table scraps on a hot summer afternoon, in several days it will be seething with maggots, the larvae of flies. That zucchini forgotten at the back of the refrigerator soon rots into a squishy blob spotted with fuzzy, black mold. After a soaking rain mushrooms pop out of the lawn and, if you aren't vigilant, in only a few hot summer days the swimming pool can turn a lovely shade of algal green.

You also know that life is resilient—it flourishes in nearly every region and habitat on Earth. Organisms live under rocks, within rocks, and deep in mine shafts. Pale, blind fishes, blind salamanders, and blind crayfishes lurk in pools deep within caves; insects have been netted as high as 1.86 miles (3,000 meters) into the atmosphere. Extremes of cold and heat are not barriers to life either. In the Antarctic Ocean, where temperatures hover close to the freezing mark for much of the year, algae thrive beneath the ice. They provide a banquet for krill that, in turn, are gobbled by hordes of other animals, including penguins, squids, fishes, seals, and whales. In hot, dry deserts if spring rains are plentiful, delicate flowers will carpet sand dunes (**Figure 4.28**). Hosts of tiny organisms spend their entire lives in the spaces between grains of beach sand. This list could go on and on, but the point is clear—Earth is full of prolific, resilient life.

Even though life is prolific and resilient, it is found only on a thin shell at the Earth's surface. Earth has a diameter of 7,926 miles (12,756 kilometers), but all life is confined to a thin surface coating that is only about 12.4 to 15.5 miles (20 to 25 kilometers) thick. This includes prokaryotes that live more than 1 mile (more than 1.5 kilometers) under the Earth's surface. Just for comparison, Mt. Everest, Earth's highest mountain peak, is 5.5 miles (8.8 kilometers) high. Let's put it another way: if Earth were a peach, its fuzzy covering would hold all known life *as well as* all the environments that support life. This veneer of life permeates Earth's waters, soils, rocks, and atmosphere; it extends to the deepest ocean trenches and the lower

Figure 4.28   Desert in Bloom.

Figure 4.29   **Biosphere**. From space the ecological details of different biomes are barely visible and their atmospheric, geological, and living components merge into the biosphere, Earth's largest ecological level.

portion of the atmosphere (**Figure 4.29**). The portion of Earth that includes all life is called the *biosphere,* and it contains all ecological units: populations, communities, ecosystems, and biomes.

Why does life thrive in the biosphere and nowhere else on Earth? Life can flourish only under a limited set of physical conditions. Energy from the Sun must be available for life to use, but harmful ultraviolet solar radiation must be minimized. For at least part of the year temperatures must allow chemical reactions to proceed at a reasonable pace. Earth's atmosphere helps shield the surface of the planet from ultraviolet radiation, and the atmosphere also traps heat. Nearly all forms of life must have oxygen to release chemical energy. In addition, other atoms and molecules must be available at the right levels. Although scientists are actively searching for life on Mars as this book is being written, the biosphere is the only known place where all of these physical conditions are met and where life exists [...].

Quick Check   **4.6**

What is the biosphere?
Can you see it from space?
Explain your answer.

The Death and Life of Lake Erie

The horror stories of polluted Lake Erie and the other Great Lakes that opened this chapter are not exaggerations. Across the globe humans have degraded environments to the point where they are nearly uninhabitable. In Chattanooga, Tennessee during the 1970s air pollution was so bad that the sky was dark by midafternoon and was filled with soot. Alien grasses are choking the life out of the Mediterranean. The marine environment off the mouth of the Mississippi in the Gulf of Mexico

Figure 4.30   Lampreys Attached to a Lake Trout.

is devoid of all life. It is dead because of pollution added to the river by human activities. From the American Midwest to the plains of China to Africa, grasslands are turning into deserts. And, of course, in the early 1970s the popular press declared that Lake Erie was dead. Can anything bring life back to a lifeless, polluted environment? The answer is a qualified "Yes." It takes a great deal of effort, and it is not easy to combat the natural human tendency to foul our surroundings. But the present state of Lake Erie shows that it can be done.

In the 1960s and 1970s many people in five U.S. states and Canada enjoyed Lake Erie and depended on it including fishermen, vacationers, business and industry, and people from all walks of life. So as Lake Erie became more and more polluted, a rare convergence of public and government opinion declared that enough was enough. No one knew if Lake Erie could be saved, but all agreed that it was worth the effort to try. The result shows that, when given a chance, ecosystems are resilient and will recover. But only if given a chance.

What Polluted Lake Erie?

Many of the problems faced by Lake Erie now are familiar to you. Algae were growing rampantly, and schools of fishes were dying. It took years for researchers to figure out the problem. Pollution from many sources entered Lake Erie. In the end excess nutrients were identified as the major culprits, specifically phosphorus. It may be hard for you to grasp that too much phosphorus could cause such devastating effects. This is an example of how one small ecological factor can have profound, global effects. Phosphorus is a nutrient required by photosynthetic organisms, and too much phosphorus in lakes, streams, or oceans causes algae to overgrow. If you have ever been around an algal bloom, you know it can *stink*. Lake Erie did smell bad, but that was the least of its problems. Algae themselves can harm fishes and other large animals, but excess algae can cause even more damage. Dead algae sank to the bottom where bacteria fed on them. These decomposers are aerobic bacteria that use oxygen in their metabolic pathways. The overgrowth of

Figure 4.31 **Lake Erie Today.** Although Lake Erie is still in danger, now that most sources of pollutants have been eliminated, the lake is repairing itself and becoming beautiful once again.

bacteria depleted the oxygen in Lake Erie. Without oxygen other organisms could not survive. Soon larger fish suffocated, and lots of dead fish washed up on the beach. This effect is called *anthropogenic eutrophication,* and it has been repeated in many waters throughout the world. Lake Erie was just one early example. Eutrophication is a normal event in the life of still bodies of freshwater, but this was something different.

Where did the excess nutrients come from? Detergents were one source. Phosphates make for more effective detergents, so phosphate detergents were popular when they first were marketed. But, of course, phosphates in laundry detergents ended up in wastewater, and this eventually fed into lakes and streams. Phosphorus also entered the lakes from wastes of manufacturing plants and in human sewage—treated or not—that was dumped into natural waterways. So many sources added excess phosphorus to Lake Erie. Each helped to kill the lake.

Phosphorus was not the only problem. Mercury, a major toxic pollutant, entered all the Great Lakes from many manufacturing sources. Mercury accumulates in tissues of fishes and can be deadly for humans who eat mercury-tainted fishes. In 1969 mercury levels in Lake Erie's fishes were so high that fishing was banned. Even if the "dead" lake had any life in it, it was deadly life.

As if all this were not enough, pollution of the Great Lakes, especially Lake Erie, also came from imported species. Exotic or alien species introduced from other regions often cause havoc. Of course, it is usually humans that inadvertently do the importing. In 1921 sea lampreys invaded Lake Erie. Lampreys are parasitic eel-like fishes that attach to other fishes and suck nutrients from them. Sea lampreys are aggressive parasites that are not native to the Great Lakes **(Figure 4.30).** They probably swam into Lake Erie after the Erie Canal was completed in 1819, connecting the Atlantic Ocean to Lake Ontario via the Hudson River. By 1946 sea lampreys had moved all the way to Lake Superior, and they flourished in the Great Lakes. Lampreys decimated the populations of many of the species of larger fishes and contributed to the collapse of the Great Lakes fishing industry.

Lake Erie Is Rehabilitated, If Not Recovered

Beginning in the early 1970s many different forms of legislation addressed these problems. The Clean Water Act of 1972 empowered the federal government to force companies to clean up wastewater before dumping it into waterways that eventually fed into Lake Erie. Canada agreed with this approach, and a treaty was signed that committed both nations to keep inputs to the Great Lakes clean. Under pressure from legislation, ships began the practice of emptying their ballast containers far from sensitive waterways. Detergent manufacturers eventually found substitutes for phosphates that satisfied consumers' preference for "whiter than white" laundry. Sewage treatment plants upgraded their facilities to reduce nutrients that flowed into waterways. Manufacturing plants removed mercury from their processes or cleaned mercury from water before it was released into the environment. Certainly not all parties made these changes willingly or enthusiastically, and threats of fines and penalties were needed to prod many to comply with new regulations. In the end, though, Lake Erie has come back to life **(Figure 4.31).** The offensive algae are gone. People can fish again. In 1999 a milestone was reached when mayflies returned to Lake Erie in numbers. These small insects had disappeared from the lake when it was so degraded. People now enjoy Lake Erie, and the bordering states can boast of its attractions to lure tourists and industry.

The result is not complete recovery, though. Many of the large fish species that once made their home in Lake Erie have not come back, or their populations are struggling to return to former levels. And the kinds of fishes that live in Lake Erie have changed too. The lake is much cleaner but not as pristine as it was even 100 years ago. In the last five years fish catches have declined again. Pollutants still enter the lake, notably polychlorinated biphenyls, or PCBs. These chemicals originate in motor oils, pigments, dyes, paints, and adhesives that are dumped into waterways. Although it has been illegal to use or manufacture PCBs in the U.S. since 1979, they do not biodegrade and accumulate in the tissues of animals. They are found in high concentrations in some Lake Erie fishes.

The lake also faces new challenges. Despite efforts to control the release of ballast water from ships, exotic species are still a problem. Zebra mussels are a well-established introduced pest that now carpets the floor of Lake Erie. Because they filter lake water, zebra mussels are credited with helping to clarify Lake Erie so that algae and seaweed now have enough sunlight to flourish. The downside to the population explosion of zebra mussels is their voracious appetite for single-celled eukaryotes. Some ecologists fear that they will deplete Lake Erie of food for fishes and other freshwater life. So the fight for Lake Erie is not over. As with all efforts to take back what we have lost, the fight is never won. Only with a sustained effort will the positive results be maintained.

Quick Check	**4.7**
What three important concepts have you learned from the story of Lake Erie?	

NOW YOU CAN UNDERSTAND

Ecologically, It Is Impossible to Do Just One Thing

Because of the interconnectedness of all of Earth's systems, even if you want to, it is impossible to do just one thing. Two examples will make the point, starting with a simple one. Let's imagine that you want to eat an apple. And, to make the scenario extremely simple, let's assume that you are fortunate enough to have an apple tree in your own backyard, *and* that it is covered with ripe fruit. You walk outside and pluck an apple. In the kitchen you rinse it off and bite into it. Soon all that is left is the core that you throw into the garbage. Sounds like you have done just one thing, but consider the following:

There has been an effect on the tree of having an apple plucked. The tree will have to heal over the raw spot where its living tissues are exposed.

Rinsing the apple will remove a lot of bacteria and yeasts that live on the apple's skin, but it won't remove all of them. By eating them you introduce them into the culture of normal bacteria that live within your mouth and digestive tract. As they mix with your stomach acids, most will die, but some will multiply and add to the bacterial populations whose home world is inside your body.

Rinsing the apple has linked you to the water cycle. Breathing, cellular respiration, and consuming the apple link you to the carbon cycle. Eating the flesh of the apple introduces new chemicals into your mouth that affect the organisms in the biofilm that coats your teeth and tongue. The sugars will feed populations of rapidly multiplying bacteria there. Eating the apple introduces new nutrients into your body and begins the process of digestion that has ripple effects on your own health and on the communities of microorganisms living within your intestines.

An apple core contains five shiny seeds, and each has the potential to grow into a whole, new apple tree. When you throw the apple core into the garbage or compost, you probably are snuffing out the life in these seeds and are reducing the reproductive potential of the parent apple tree.

If the simple act of eating an apple has so many ecological consequences, imagine how they multiply in a complicated action that introduces a new product or a new idea into the marketplace where ecology and economy intersect. Henry Ford had such an idea in 1896 when he hand built his first motor car, the Quadricycle. In 1908 the first Ford Model T was introduced, and in 1913 Ford innovated the first continuously moving assembly line. Ford Motor Company became the largest automobile manufacturer in the world, and the innovations of Henry Ford's company began a series of ecological ripple effects that continue to this day. Global warming is just one of them. Revolutionizing manufacturing and increasing demand for manufactured instead of handmade goods was another. Increased demand for fossil fuels is another. And, of course, because all of Earth's systems are linked in cycles that transform and move chemical elements and compounds, environmental repercussions have continued to follow and have intensified as the human population has increased.

WHAT DO *YOU* THINK?

Wetlands Conservation

The ecological cycles you have learned about here are critical for the health of the biosphere. Nearly all scientists agree on that. Most of the rest of us agree too, in the abstract, but getting support for projects to restore damaged environments is much more difficult when it conflicts with the self-interest of the people involved. Wetlands are a good example. Wetlands are ecosystems such as swamps, marshes, and salt marshes that are adjacent to major oceans, bays, rivers, or lakes. Wetlands filter and purify water as it goes into the larger body of water, and they provide a habitat for a wide variety of species. Wetlands also provide buffer zones that protect areas inland from floods and storms. If the wetlands around New Orleans and along the Mississippi Gulf Coast had been intact, the damage from Hurricane Katrina in 2005 would have been much reduced. Wetlands have many additional beneficial aspects; not only do they clean runoff, they also are nursery grounds for fisheries, and they provide resting places for many migrating birds. Yet it is hard to get localities to approve the establishment of *new* wetlands in areas where they are needed. In Southern California, for example, a project to establish extensive wetlands met strong objections from people who did not want to lose their beach. In areas across the country developers drain wetlands and refuse to abide by orders to stop, citing their right to develop their land as they see fit. These arguments pit one definition of common good against another, and often the wetlands are the losers. Have you encountered any similar debates in your own community? How would you respond? What do *you* think about the need to protect environmental regions such as wetlands versus the rights of people to develop and use land as they choose?

CHAPTER REVIEW

Chapter Summary

4.1 An Ecosystem Is the Functional Ecological Unit

In ecosystems energy moves in the biotic components of the system, and chemicals cycle between the biotic and abiotic components of the ecosystem. Abiotic ecosystem components include air, water, soil, and rocks. Biotic components are the communities of organisms in the area.

abiotic **68**   ecosystem **68**

4.2 Energy Moves Through Ecosystems, and Chemicals Cycle Within Ecosystems

Because of the metabolic processes of organisms, energy is lost at each link in a food chain, leading to pyramids of numbers of organisms in a community and pyramids of energy. Natural processes cycle materials between biotic and abiotic components of ecosystems, and these cycles have long and short-term components. Evaporation, condensation, precipitation, and transpiration are active in the water cycle. Precipitation not absorbed by plants or soil runs off the land or may be stored within aquifers. Photosynthesis, respiration, and metabolism are active short-term processes of the water cycle, while fossilization and formation of deposits of limestone and fossil fuels are long-term storage of carbon. When fossil fuels are burned, carbon reenters the atmosphere as the greenhouse gas, carbon dioxide. The overwhelming evidence is that carbon dioxide has increased in the atmosphere, and that global climate change is under way. Prokaryotes like nitrogen-fixing bacteria are responsible for the transformation of atmospheric nitrogen into nitrogen-containing compounds that can enter food chains. Other bacteria process ammonia into nitrates that plants can absorb. Denitrifying bacteria transform nitrates and release nitrogen back to the atmosphere, completing the nitrogen cycle. The phosphorus cycle takes place within rocks, soil, water, and organisms. Mycorrhizae help plants absorb phosphorus from soil.

aquifer **74**   evaporation **74**
biogeochemical cycle **72**   nitrogen-fixing bacteria **77**
condensation **74**   precipitation **74**
denitrifying bacteria **78**

4.3 Ocean Life Is Influenced by Food, Light, Currents, and Pressure

Distribution of life in oceans is regulated by temperature, availability of nutrients, and availability of light. Most ocean life is in warm waters of the littoral and neritic zones. Ocean currents can bring warm water that is rich in nutrients to waters that are offshore of continents. Organisms that live in the littoral zone must have adaptations that allow them to survive rough waters and daily exposure to extremes of temperature, dryness, and sunlight. Estuaries like salt marshes and mangrove swamps are nurseries for many forms of ocean life that protect coastlines and slowly release trapped nutrients to offshore waters. Coral reefs are biologically active ecosystems created by the mutualistic association of coral polyps and green algae. Chemosynthetic prokaryotes are the keystone species of deep-sea hydrothermal vents, and the communities that develop there are among Earth's most unusual.

brackish water **84**   estuary **83**

4.4 Aquatic Ecosystems Link Marine and Terrestrial Ecosystems

Aquatic ecosystems have some animal groups, notably amphibians and insects, that are missing from oceans. Plants are important photosynthesizers in aquatic ecosystems. Aquatic ecosystems bridge terrestrial and oceanic ecosystems. Water movement, or the lack of it, contributes important characteristics to aquatic ecosystems. Ponds and lakes have seasonal cycles in which their water overturns, enriching upper waters and carrying dissolved oxygen down to the depths. Ponds and lakes are especially sensitive to oxygen depletion that can occur as a natural process of eutrophication. Stream and river organisms must have means that allow them to maintain their position in rapidly moving currents. Flowing-water ecosystems vary in their oxygen levels, temperatures, turbidity, amount of nutrients, and animal and plant adaptations.

eutrophication **89**

4.5 Biomes Are Characterized by Typical Vegetation

Biomes are defined by dominant plant communities and include tundra, taiga, temperate deciduous forest, grassland, tropical rain forest, and desert. Each biome has characteristic organisms, and each biome is threatened by human activities. Habitat fragmentation and species loss are the most prevalent threats to Earth's biomes.

arctic tundra **93**   tropical rain forest **101**
biome **91**   understory **95**
canopy **95**
desert **99**
grassland **97**
permafrost **93**
taiga **95**
temperate deciduous forest **95**

4.6 The Biosphere Encompasses All of Earth's Biomes

The biosphere contains all of Earth's life and the abiotic components of ecosystems.

4.7 An Added Dimension Explained: The Death and Life of Lake Erie

Lake Erie is rehabilitated from the depths of pollution in the 1970s. Introduced alien species continue to be a problem, as does the tendency of some people to weaken or circumvent the legislation that has rehabilitated Lake Erie. Only constant vigilance will keep Lake Erie clean.

REVIEW QUESTIONS

TRUE or FALSE

If a statement is false, rewrite it to make it true.

1. Rocks, soil, atmosphere, nutrient cycling, water, and organisms are characteristic components of ecological communities.

2. A pyramid of energy explains why there are more producers than there are top consumers in an ecological community.

3. The most varied forms of life are found in freshwater ecosystems.

4. Upwelling, coastal run off and abundant light make the pelagic zone highly productive.

5. Tropical rain forests are analogous to the neritic zone of the ocean.

6. Hydrothermal vent communities depend on mycorrhizae.

7. As streams merge into rivers, levels of oxygen increase, while turbidity decreases.

8. If something doesn't drastically change, biologists predict that tropical rain forests may be gone in 30 to 50 years.

9. Most tropical rain forest animals are familiar and well studied.

10. The biosphere is made of all of Earth's biotic features.

MULTIPLE CHOICE

Choose the best answer of those provided.

11. On average, how much of the energy that a swallow gets from the insects that it eats are stored in its tissues?

    a. none   d. 10%

    b. 1%   e. 50%

    c. 2%

12. If a green plant receives 257,000 watts of solar energy in an afternoon, how much will it be able to capture and use in photosynthesis?

    a. all of it

    b. 128,500 watts

    c. half of it

    d. about 2%

    e. about 10%

13. Life in oceans depends on these photosynthesizers:

    a. plants

    b. bacteriovores

    c. phytoplankton and zooplankton

    d. nanophytoplankton, ultraphytoplankton, and phytoplankton

    e. Portuguese men-o'-war

14. In what oceanic zone would bioluminescent organisms be plentiful?

    a. neritic

    b. abyssal

    c. photic

    d. pelagic

    e. littoral

15. Estuaries, mangroves, salt marshes, marshes, and lake bottoms are all rich in

    a. photosynthesizers.

    b. trapped and decomposing nutrients.

    c. light.

    d. top carnivores.

    e. dissolved oxygen.

MATCHING

16–20. Match the columns. (One choice will be used twice.)

16. evaporation, condensation, precipitation
17. soil bacteria
18. erosion, mycorrhizae
19. limestone, coral reefs
20. photosynthesis, respiration, consumption

a. nitrogen cycle
b. carbon cycle
c. phosphorus cycle
d. water cycle

MATCHING

21–26. Match the columns. (One choice will be used more than once.)

21. arctic tundra   a. seasonally colorful leaves, spring and fall wildflowers; migratory birds

22. taiga   b. threatened by human activities

23. temperate deciduous forest   c. permafrost, mosses, lichens, migratory birds, mosquitoes, bioaccumulation

24. grassland   d. pines and firs, boreal forest, long snowy winter, caribou

25. desert   e. uniform climate, epiphytes, infertile soils; calls are important

26. tropical rain forest   f. periodic fires, grazing mammals, hibernators, migrators, estivators

                                        g. succulents, spiny leaves, nocturnal mammals

CONNECTING KEY CONCEPTS

1. Using specific examples, contrast the characteristics of ocean habitats with terrestrial biomes.

2. Living organisms play a key role in the cycling of elements in the biosphere. Choose two examples of cycles and explain the roles of living organisms in each.

QUANTITATIVE QUERY

1. Assume that a square meter of your backyard has received 1,370 watts of energy in the form of sunlight per day. This square meter is covered with vegetation that captures and uses 2% of this energy. Assume the grass has been growing for 100 days. Metabolic processes of grass plants consume 90% of the solar energy that reaches the grass, and only 10% of the available energy is stored in the organic molecules of the plant. A deer comes along and eats all of the vegetation in the square meter.

1. How much energy was available to the vegetation over the 100 days?

2. How much energy did the vegetation capture and use?

3. How much usable energy does the deer get from the vegetation?

THINKING CRITICALLY

1. How would you redesign the way that plants use photosynthesis to allow plants to capture more than about 2% of the Sun's energy? Suggest a few adaptations that would allow plants to capture more light and then refer to Figure 6.2 for an additional answer.

2. Fossil fuels such as gas and oil are hydrocarbons derived from organisms that lived long ago. When fossil fuel is burned, carbon dioxide is returned to the atmosphere. The burning of fossil fuels as a source of energy is increasing the levels of carbon dioxide in the atmosphere and is a major cause of global climate

change. Many people suggest that massive tree-planting efforts could reduce atmospheric carbon dioxide and lessen global climate change. What is the scientific basis for this suggestion? Others suggest that planting lots of trees is only a short term solution to the atmospheric carbon dioxide problem. What is the basis for this argument? Which side do you agree with?

Additional Reading

Bates, M. *The Forest and the Sea*. Alexandria: Time-Life Books, Inc., 1960.

> *Many have written about coral reefs and rain forests, but Marston Bates is most eloquent. His enthusiasm for these biomes is contagious, and reading him is almost as good as a genuine tropical vacation. His entire, highly influential book is worth reading, but the chapters on rain forests and coral reefs are exceptional.*

Little, C. T. S., "The Prolific Afterlife of Whales," *Scientific American*, February 2010, 78–84.

> *Earth's life is far stranger than anyone expected: creepy and unexpected ecosystems exist around and within sunken, decaying carcasses of dead whales. Who knew about "whale fall" or "zombie worms"? Who knew that entire ecosystems exist on the ocean's dark abyssal plains? Read this article and your world will expand.*

Milius, S. "Out of Thin Air," Science News, April 12, 2008, 235–37.

> *Nitrogen-fixing bacteria remove nitrogen from air and fix it into compounds plants use to make proteins. A wide variety of plants house nitrogen-fixing bacteria within their tissues; bacteria and plants have reciprocal biochemical adaptations that allow them to coexist. Genetic engineering of crop plants to allow nitrogen-fixing bacteria to live within their tissues would have tremendous economic benefits and could potentially eliminate the need for applications of chemical fertilizers. Currently, though, this seems out of reach.*

Mitchell, A. W. *The Enchanted Canopy: Secrets From the Rainforest Roof*. Glasgow: Fontana/Collins, 1986.

> *In the 1980s, the public became aware of tropical rainforests. This beautiful book guides you through the world's rainforests. It is well informed, nicely written, and studded with vivid photos.*

National Geographic. "The Water Issue," April 2010.

> *A world tour that explores the status of Earth's fresh water, this issue of National Geographic is glorious. From the introductory essay by Barbara Kingsolver to the factoids tucked between ads, superb photographs and scholarship are splashed about. Refreshing insights and impressive scholarship. Grab it. Chapter opener: Copyright in the Public Domain.*

CREDITS

BIODIVERSITY AND ITS VALUE

BY REED. F. NOSS AND ALLEN COOPERRIDER

The earth never tires:

The earth is rude, silent, incomprehensible at first—Nature is rude and incomprehensible at first;

Be not discouraged—keep on—there are divine things, well enveloped;

I swear to you there are divine things more beautiful than words can tell.

Walt Whitman (1856), Leaves of Grass

[...]The fundamental question of conservation biology is a critical one: how can the variety of life be maintained in perpetuity? How can we help preserve "divine things more beautiful than words can tell"? No one has an answer to these questions. But scientists have learned a few things about how nature works and what kinds of human activities are compatible and incompatible with life on earth. In this chapter, we first define biodiversity and describe its major components, then discuss why diversity has become an issue in the United States. This leads into a discussion of the values of biodiversity and why management of biodiversity has become a regrettable necessity today.

WHAT IS BIODIVERSITY?

In little more than a decade, biodiversity progressed from a short-hand expression for species diversity into a powerful symbol for the full richness of life on earth. Biodiversity is now a major driving force behind efforts to reform land management and development practices worldwide and to establish a more harmonious relationship between people and nature.

Biodiversity. A symbol? An issue? A driving force? It would be easier if biodiversity could be measured by the quantity of bird species in a forest, wildflowers in a meadow, or beetles in a log. But simplicity is not one of the virtues of biodiversity. Ecosystems are more complex than we can imagine. Our most intricate machines—say, a space shuttle and all its ground-control computers—are simple toys compared to an old-growth forest, its myriad known and unknown species, and their intricate genetic codes and ecological interactions. Just identifying and counting species is difficult enough. The almost infinite complexity of nature defies our best efforts to classify, categorize, or even describe.

A common misconception is that biodiversity is equivalent to species diversity—the more species in an area, the greater its biodiversity. However, biodiversity is not just a numbers game. On a global scale, maintaining maximal species richness is a legitimate goal and requires keeping global extinction rates low enough that they are balanced or surpassed by speciation. When we consider species richness at any scale smaller than the biosphere, quality is more important than quantity. It is not so much the number of species that we are interested in, it is their identity. Fragmenting an old-growth forest with clearcuts, for example, would increase species richness at a local scale but would not contribute to species richness at a broader scale if sensitive species were lost from the landscape.

Diversification can all too easily become homogenization. The greatest cause of homogenization worldwide is the introduction of nonnative plants and animals, often called exotics. Exotics are species that have invaded new areas due to accidental or deliberate transport by humans. Although species naturally disperse and colonize new areas, so that floras and faunas change continually over long periods of time, human transport and habitat disturbance have greatly increased the rate and scale of invasions. Many regions have nearly as many exotic as native species today. Introductions of exotics may increase species richness locally or even regionally, but they contribute nothing positive to biodiversity. Rather, they pollute the integrity of regional floras and faunas and often alter fundamental ecological processes, such as fire frequency and intensity, and nutrient cycles. Thus, whole ecosystems are changed. Regions invaded by exotics lose their distinctive characters. Every place begins to look the same. The result is global impoverishment. For these reasons, we emphasize native biodiversity, not diversity per se.

The important task is not to define biodiversity, but rather to determine the components of biodiversity in a region, their distribution and interrelationships, what threatens them, how we measure and monitor them, and what can be done to conserve them. These topics are the subject of this book. But because working definitions are helpful to summarize what we are talking about, we propose the following modification of a definition developed by the Keystone Dialogue (Keystone Center 1991):

Biodiversity is the variety of life and its processes. It includes the variety of living organisms, the genetic differences among them, the communities and ecosystems in which they occur, and the ecological and evolutionary processes that keep them functioning, yet ever changing and adapting.

This definition recognizes variety at several levels of biological organization . Four levels of organization commonly considered are genetic, population/ species, community/ecosystem, and landscape or regional. Each of these levels can be further divided into compositional, structural, and functional components of a nested hierarchy (Noss 1990a), Composition includes the genetic constitution of populations, the identity and relative abundances of species in a natural community, and the kinds of habitats and communities distributed across the landscape. Structure includes the sequence of pools and riffles in a stream, down logs and snags in a forest, the dispersion and vertical layering of plants, and the horizontal patchiness of vegetation at many spatial scales. Function includes the climatic, geological, hydrological, ecological, and evolutionary processes that generate and maintain biodiversity in ever-changing patterns over time.

Why bother with this cumbersome classification? Because nature is infinitely complex. Unless we try to identify and classify the forms of this complexity, we are likely either to miss something or become hopelessly confused, If something falls through the cracks in our conservation programs, it may be lost forever. With each loss biodiversity is diminished. The earth becomes a less interesting place.

Conserving biodiversity, then, involves much more than saving species from extinction. As implied by our characterization of biodiversity, biotic impoverishment can take many forms and occur at several levels of biological organization. Hence, steps must be taken at multiple levels to counteract impoverishment. Below, we review some conservation issues, goals, and problems that can be addressed at each of four major levels of biological organization. We emphasize that a comprehensive conservation strategy must integrate concerns from all levels of the biological hierarchy.

Genetic Level

Genes, sequences of the DNA (deoxyribonucleic acid) molecule, are the functional units of heredity. Species differ from one another and individuals within species vary largely because they have unique combinations of genes. Gene frequencies and genotypes (individual organisms with a particular genetic make-up) within a population change over time as a consequence of both random and deterministic forces. Random changes include mutations that create new genes or sequences of genes, and loss of genes by chance in small populations (called sampling error or genetic drift). Deterministic changes include natural and artificial selection, where some genotypes are more successful reproducers than others. In the long run, genetic change leads to evolutionary change as individuals adapt to different situations and pass on their new traits to offspring. Genetic diversity is fundamental to the variety of life and is the raw material for evolution of new species. [...]

Conservation goals at the genetic level include maintaining genetic variation within and among populations of species, and assuring that processes such as genetic differentiation and gene flow continue at normal rates. Without genetic variation, populations are less adaptable and their extinction more probable, all else being equal. Small, isolated populations are more likely to diverge genetically, having fewer chances for genetic mixing with other populations. But at the same time small, isolated populations are more likely to suffer from inbreeding depression caused by mating between close relatives, which may result in reduced fertility and other problems (Frankel and Soule 1981). Small, isolated populations also are subject to random loss of genes (genetic drift), which restricts their ability to adapt to a dynamic environment.

Conservationists talk much about saving the earths genetic resources. But with the exception of some agricultural crops, commercial tree species, populations of rare vertebrates in zoos, and a handful of wild populations, we know very little about genetic diversity. Land managers seldom think about maintaining biodiversity at the genetic level. If our vision of conservation is long term, however, genetic variation must be better understood for all organisms.

Species Level

The species level of diversity is probably what most people think of when they hear the term biodiversity. Although in some ways species diversity is the best known aspect of biodiversity, we should bear in mind that the vast majority of species in the world are still unknown. Of an estimated 10 to 100 million species on Earth (Wilson 1992), we have named only about 1.8 million (Stork 1992). Known species are dominated by insects, half of them beetles (Fig. 1.1). But many invertebrates, bacteria, and other organisms remain to be discovered, even in the United States. Hundreds of inverte-brate species can be found in one square meter of soil and litter in an old-growth temperate forest (Lattin 1990). Even more amazing, Norwegian microbiologists found between 4000 and 5000 species of bacteria in a single gram of soil from a beech forest. About the same number of species, with little overlap, was found in a gram of sediment from off the coast of Norway (Wilson 1992). These findings raise the question of whether the tropical rainforests really are the most diverse habitats on Earth. We know too little about biodiversity to conclude much with certainty.

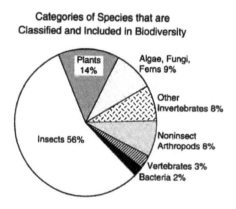

FIGURE 5.1 Taxonomic categories of species that have been named and described (adapted from Office of Technology Assessment 1987). Undescribed species, which outnumber described species by perhaps an order of magnitude, are probably mostly insects, other invertebrates, and bacteria.

Despite the problems and biases of single-species management, many species require individual attention, particularly when they have become so rare that heroic measures are needed to save them In addition, certain kinds of species warrant management emphasis because their protection will conserve more than themselves. Especially important in this regard are keystone species, which play pivotal roles in their ecosystems and upon which a large part of the community depends (Noss 1991a). The importance of a keystone species is often disproportionate to its abundance. The beaver, for instance, creates habitats used by many species and also regulates hydrology and other ecosystem functions (Naiman et al. 1988). If we reduce beaver numbers through heavy trapping, then all else being equal, we impoverish the landscape. The beaver is not an endangered species, but it is greatly reduced or even absent from many regions where it was once abundant. Major declines of keystone species are more important ecologically than the loss of the last few individuals of rare species that play minor roles in their communities. This said, we must recognize that the term keystone species is poorly defined. Instead of a dichotomy of keystones and non-keystones, communities may be better characterized by a wide range of interactions of variable strengths (Mills et al 1993). Because we know so little about the ecological roles of species, each species must be considered important.

Some kinds of species have great pragmatic value for conservation, especially those we can characterize as "umbrellas" or "flagships" (Noss 1991a). To illustrate the umbrella concept, consider a carnivore (such as a grizzly bear or wolf) that requires millions of acres of land to maintain a viable population. If we secure enough wild habitat for these large predators, many other less-demanding species will be carried under the umbrella of protection. Umbrella species are often charismatic, so they also function as flagships or symbols for major conservation efforts. The grizzly bear, for in-stance, is a potent symbol for wilderness preservation in the northern Rocky Mountains. No umbrella is complete, however. Some endemic plant species have very small ranges—perhaps restricted to a single rock outcrop—that might not be protected in an ideal wilderness network established for grizzlies.

Animals and plants that are highly vulnerable to human activity often need to be managed individually, at least until their habitats can be protected by an ecosystem-level approach. Otherwise, biodiversity will continue to diminish with each extinction. Although we might accept the egalitarian notion that all species are ultimately equal, at any given place and time some species thrive on human activity and others suffer. Familiar examples of species that are extremely vulnerable to human activity are the northern spotted owl, threatened by logging of old-growth forests in the Pacific Northwest (Thomas et al 1990); the red-cockaded woodpecker, endangered by logging of longleaf pine forests in the Southeastern Coastal Plain (Jackson 1986); and the desert tortoise, often shot or run over by motorized recreationists, forced to compete with livestock, collected for pets, and now ravaged by disease (U.S. Fish and Wildlife Service 1993) Species declines are signals that the environment is not healthy, but vulnerable species often require intensive care above and beyond immediate protection of their habitat.

Community or Ecosystem Level

In many cases, conservation is most efficient when focused directly on the community or ecosystem. A community is an interacting assemblage of species in an area. Terrestrial communities are usually defined by their dominant plants (for instance, the beech-maple forest), but functional or taxonomic groups of animals (for example, bird communities, lizard communities, herbivore communities) are also recognized. Functional groups of organisms (species that use a set of resources in similar ways, such as bark-gleaning birds) are often called guilds. Similarly, aquatic communities may be taxonomically or functionally defined, for example fish communities or littoral (shoreline) vegetation.

An ecosystem is a biotic community plus its abiotic environment. Ecosystems range in scale from microcosms, such as a vernal pool, to the entire biosphere. Many ecologists equate the terms ecosystem and community, except that ecosystem ecologists emphasize processes more than species and other entities. The Nature Conservancy defines natural communities by their most striking characteristics, whether biotic or abiotic. Thus, coastal plain pond, rich graminoid fen, black spruce-tamarack bog, and rich mesophytic forest are all described communities of New York State (Reschke 1990). These communities might also be called ecosystem "types/' The variable spatial scale of ecosystems confuses the issue sometimes. Although scientists usually think of ecosystems as relatively discrete and existing at the same spatial scale as natural communities, conservationists often use the term ecosystem to encompass many different communities. For example, the Greater Yellowstone Ecosystem covers a diverse region of 14 to 19 million acres (see Chapter 5).

We consider conservation at the community or ecosystem level to complement, not replace, species-level management. The rationale for protecting ecosystems is compelling: if we can maintain intact, ecologically functional examples of each type of ecosystem in a region, then the species that live in these ecosystems will also persist. Representing all native ecosystems in a network of protected areas is the most basic conservation goal at the ecosystem level (see Chapter 4). Opportunities for adequate representation of ecosystems are being rapidly diminished as many of our native vegetation types are being reduced in area and degraded in quality (Noss et al 1994).

Practicing conservation at the community or ecosystem level demands attention to ecological processes. Maintaining processes is not just a way to maintain species. Rather, processes are valuable for their own sake as part of the diversity of life. The processes that are most crucial for ecological health vary from ecosystem to ecosystem. In terrestrial communities some of the most important processes are fire and other natural disturbances, hydrological cycles, nutrient cycling, plant—herbivore interactions, predation, mycorrhizal interactions between tree and shrub roots and fungi, and soil building processes. All of these processes affect biodiversity at several levels and are included within our definition of biodiversity. They must be maintained within normal limits of variation if native biodiversity is to persist. Clearcutting and other intensive forest management may fail to conserve biodiversity because they disrupt nutrient retention and other ecological processes. Livestock grazing that interferes with basic ecological processes will also fail to conserve native biodiversity in rangelands.

LANDSCAPE AND REGIONAL LEVELS

Alpha, Beta, and Gamma Diversity

The variety of species in a defined area is one common measure of biodiversity at the ecosystem level. But to say that more diverse areas are better is misleading because measures of species richness or diversity neglect a most important consideration— the identity of species. One way to consider species diversity while paying close attention to species composition is to note the spatial scale of observation and how composition changes from one scale to another. The collection of species within an area of relatively homogeneous habitat is called alpha diversity or within-habitat diversity (Whittaker 1972, Karr 1976). Each site will have its own characteristic alpha diversity, although physically similar habitats in the same region can be expected to have similar species composition.

As we expand the scale of observation, we encounter variation in the underlying physical environment (environmental gradients). As we move along a gradient, say up-slope, down-slope, or from one soil type to another, we encounter new species adapted to these different conditions. The turnover in species along an environmental gradient is called beta diversity or between-habitat diversity. When we measure the diversity of species across several different habitats in a landscape, we are measuring beta diversity.

At a still broader scale, many environmental gradients are found and geographic replacements of species occur as range boundaries are crossed. Diversity at this regional scale is called gamma diversity. The alpha, beta, and gamma diversity concepts are useful for comparing biodiversity in different regions or in the same region under different management scenarios. Two regions of roughly equivalent gamma diversity may differ greatly in alpha and beta diversity. For example, Region A is mostly lowland forest with high alpha diversity but little habitat diversity. Thus, any site in the region is likely to contain roughly the same set of species. In contrast, Region B is mountainous, with tremendous differences in species composition between habitats but lower diversity within any single habitat. Generally speaking, a landscape in the eastern deciduous forest biome will have higher alpha diversity than many areas in the West. However, western landscapes characteristically have higher beta diversity due to the effects of aridity and topographic variation. Conservationists would have to consider very different scales and factors in planning reserve systems in the two regions. It is prudent to consider the maintenance of alpha and beta diversity within the broader context of gamma (and ultimately global) diversity.

If biodiversity occurs at multiple levels of organization, it is worth protecting at all levels. Forman and Godron (1986) defined a landscape as "a heterogeneous land area composed of a cluster of interacting ecosystems that is repeated in similar form throughout." Similarly, Urban et al (1987) characterized a landscape as "a mosaic of heterogeneous land forms, vegetation types, and land uses." These definitions suggest that landscapes have a pattern and that this pattern consists of repeated habitat components that occur in various shapes, sizes, and spatial interrelationships. In many landscapes, this pattern consists of patches and corridors in a matrix, the matrix being the most common or interconnected habitat in the landscape (Forman and Godron 1986). Other landscapes are mosaics of many habitats, and the pattern is difficult to classify into discrete components.

We use the term region (also bioregion or ecoregion) to refer to large landscapes that can be distinguished from other regions on the basis of climate, physiography, soils, species composition patterns (biogeography), and other variables. Landscape or regional diversity is pattern diversity—the pattern of habitats and species assemblages across a land area of thousands to millions of acres—and can be considered a higher level expression of biodiversity. The pattern of species distributions and communities across a landscape has functional ramifications. Many animals, for example black bears, use more than one habitat type to meet their life history needs. We cannot protect these species by managing different communities in isolation. Bears and other wide-ranging animals are often important in dispersing seeds across a landscape. Disrupting bear movements by fragmenting the landscape may indirectly affect other species.

Adjacent habitats affect each other in many ways, including by microclimatic effects and transfer of nutrients, propagules, and disturbances across edges and ecotones. Because human activities often change landscape patterns, they have impacts on biodiversity that ripple through other levels of organization, affecting species composition and abundances, gene flow, and ecosystem processes. If a forest landscape is fragmented into small patches, those patches may experience a drier microclimate than the original forest, increased susceptibility to windthrow, loss of forest interior species, reduced genetic diversity within remaining populations, and invasion by weedy and exotic species (Burgess and Sharpe 1981, Harris 1984, Franklin and Forman 1987). These problems cannot be solved patch by patch, but only across all patches and their matrix. Hence, the regional landscape is an appropriate scale at which to identify important sites and patterns, and to manage and restore land for conservation purposes (Noss 1983, Turner 1989).

A primary conservation goal at the landscape or regional level is to maintain complete, unfragmented environmental gradients. This extends the representation goal beyond traditional ecosystem boundaries. Species richness and composition are known to vary along environmental gradients. The most commonly studied gradient is elevation. In the western Cascades of Oregon, the number of species of amphibians, reptiles, and mammals declines sharply with increasing elevation (Fig. 1.2). This pre-sents a problem for conservation, because generally speaking, the low-elevation, high-diversity sites are private lands which are often heavily exploited and have few natural areas left. Mid-elevation sites are commodity-production public lands, and large protected areas (such as designated wilderness) occupy the high-elevation, lowest diversity sites. This biased pattern of habitat protection is common throughout the western United States (Davis 1988, Foreman and Wolke 1989, Noss 1990b). By contrast, in southeastern states with abundant wetlands, such as Florida, most wilderness areas are habitats too wet for commercial forestry. Preserving only the most species-rich sites or portions of environmental gradients is no solution, because different species occupy different portions. Alpine wildflowers are not found in the rich lowlands. Conservation programs must strive to maintain natural ecosystems and biodiversity across the full extent of environmental gradients.

The effects of natural disturbance on biodiversity often can be best appreciated at the landscape scale. Disturbances typically create patches in the landscape, of various sizes, that are used by different sets of species (Pickett and White 1985). Disturbance-recovery processes are complex. For example, most forest fires are mosaics of many different fire intensities, with some patches experiencing crown fires, other patches untouched, and a wide range of intensities in between. Recovery after fire varies with intensity (sometimes the soil may be sterilized and succession is slow), seed sources, weather, and other factors. Variability in disturbance regime is responsible for much of the habitat diversity found in natural landscapes. Generally speaking, the more diverse the habitat, the more species can coexist. However, diversification by disturbance has a limit. Actions that diversify habitat locally may reduce diversity at regional and global scales if disturbance-sensitive species are eliminated. Disturbance regimes will be discussed in more detail in Chapter 2.

In landscape ecology, context is just as important as content. Small reserves set aside for their content (for example, to represent plant community types or to protect a remnant population of a rare species) are heavily affected by their context when the surrounding landscape is altered. Eventually, a small reserve or a system of small, isolated reserves may fail to maintain the elements for which they were established. Natural fire regimes, migration of large animals, landform evolution, and hydrological cycles are ecological processes that can be perpetuated only by conservation at land-scape and regional scales. Thus, a biodiversity conservation strategy is complete only when expanded to these scales.

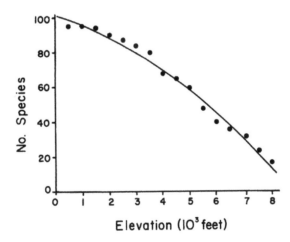

FIGURE 5.2 Relation between elevation and species richness of amphibians, reptiles, and mammals in western Oregon (from Harris 1984). The decline in species richness with increasing elevation is accompanied by a decline in density of individuals of all species combined. Used with permission of the author and University of Chicago Press.

CULTURAL OR SOCIAL DIVERSITY

Have we missed anything in our broad characterization of biodiversity? During the Keystone Dialogue on Biological Diversity and in similar forums, some participants insisted that human cultural or social diversity be included in the definition of biodiversity and in any strategy for its conservation. The Global Biodiversity Strategy (WRI, IUCN, UNEP 1992) makes this point strongly: Human cultural diversity could also be considered part of biodiversity. Like genetic or species diversity, some attributes of human cultures (say, nomadism or shifting cultivation) represent "solutions" to the problems of survival in particular environments. And, like other aspects of biodiversity, cultural diversity helps people adapt to changing conditions. Cultural diversity is manifested by diversity in language, religious beliefs, land-management practices, art, music, social structure, crop selection, diet, and any number of other attributes of human society.

On the face of it, inclusion of social diversity in a definition of biodiversity makes sense. We are fundamentally as much a part of Nature as any other species and share kinship and ecological interactions with all of life. But what would be the practical effect of including diversity of human languages, religious beliefs, behaviors, land management practices, etc., in a biodiversity definition and striving to promote this diversity in conservation strategy? We believe the effect would be to trivialize the concept and make it unworkable, even dangerous. As Kent Redford (personal communication) notes, "This definition allows Manhattan or Sao Paulo to be considered on equal footing with the Great Barrier Reef of Australia and makes impossible any coherent discussion of biodiversity conservation." We are not interested in maintaining social or cultural diversity if it means maintaining Nazis, slave owners, or those who enjoy using desert tortoises for target practice. This [chapter] is about how culture might adapt to nature. We want to conserve all cultural approaches that are compatible with conserving biodiversity. To combine cultural and biological diversity into one definition is to muddle the concept.

WHY HAS BIODIVERSITY BECOME AN ISSUE?

Why has biodiversity become an issue in the United States? Have conventional approaches to conservation failed? Consider the continent of North America 300 years ago. A description from an early explorer in Florida portrays the diversity of life in the Southeastern Coastal Plain, a richness paralleled in many different and glorious ways across the continent:

> We returned, viewing the Land on both sides of the River, and found as good tracts of land, dry, well wooded, pleasant and delightful as we have seen anywhere in the world, with great burthen of Grasse on it. . . the woods stor d with abundance of Deer and Turkies every where . . . also Partridges great store, Cranes abundance, Conies . . . several Wolves howling in the woods, and saw where they had torn a Deer in pieces. Also in the River we saw great store of Ducks, Teile, Widgeon, and in the woods great flocks of Parrakeeto s ... we measured many of the Oaks in several places, which we found to be in bignesse some two, some three, and others almost four fathoms; in height, before you come to boughs or limbs, forty, fifty, sixty foot, and some more

... Also a very tall large Tree of great bignesse, which some do call Cyprus. ... (Hilton 1664, in Salley 1911)

The European explorers' impressions of a vast wilderness continent were accurate enough. All of this country was roadless, unpolluted, rich with wildlife, and incomparably beautiful. But this was not a wilderness "untrammeled by man," in the controversial language of our Wilderness Act of 1964 (Callicott 1991) The North American wilderness was a peopled wilderness, yet peopled sparsely and, for the most part, gently. An estimated 10 million native humans, 3 percent of the present human population, inhabited North America when the first white people arrived. In places the Indians modified their landscape considerably, especially through the use of fire (Day 1953, Pyne 1982). Hunting by their ancestors probably contributed to the extinction of large mammals near the close of the Pleistocene (Martin and Klein 1984). But native cultures occasionally enriched native biodiversity locally and perhaps regionally through diverse agricultural plantings (Nabhan 1982). Although the romantic notion of Indians as the original environmentalists is not entirely accurate (Callicott 1982), in general the native Americans seem to have lived in harmony with the rest of nature. Without such a relationship they would have had trouble persisting here for over 20,000 years. A culture that destroys its environment is suicidal.

The picture changed dramatically after the arrival of European settlers. The biological history of North America since then—a story seldom told in American history classes—has been one of profound impoverishment, particularly in the last 200 years. The slaughter of native Americans by early explorers and colonists is now well known, but the desire of Europeans for subjugation extended to other life forms as well. This subjugation continues today. In the words of Barry Lopez (1992):

> The assumption of an imperial right conferred by God, sanctioned by the state, and enforced by a militia; the assumption of unquestioned superiority over a resident people, based not on morality but on race and cultural comparison . . . the assumption that one is due wealth in North America, reverberates in the journals of people on the Oregon Trail, in the public speeches of nineteenth-century industrialists, and in twentieth-century politicians. You can hear it today in the rhetoric of timber barons ... standing before the last of the old-growth forest, irritated that anyone is saying "enough . . . , it is enough."

European settlers saw the people, wildlife, and land of North America as something to be conquered, tamed, and subjected to their will. A concern for or even knowledge of what was being lost was altogether lacking.

As biologist Larry Harris describes it, "we swept across this continent so quickly . . . that we never really knew what was here" (quoted in Chadwick 1990). The great eastern deciduous forest exists today only as tattered remnants, growing slowly back in some regions, such as parts of the Northeast and southern Piedmont, but still being fragmented and subdivided in others. Cougar are gone from the East with the exception of a tiny population of Florida panthers on the verge of extinction in south Florida, and scattered but questionable reports farther north. The ivory-billed wood-pecker, Carolina parakeet, Labrador duck, heath hen, great auk, and passenger pigeon (the most abundant landbird in the world when Europeans arrived) are gone from the earth, as are Merriam s elk, Audubon bighorn, the buffalo wolf, sea mink, and Caribbean monk seal. The estimated 40 million pronghorn that roamed the West before arrival of the pioneers were quickly reduced to fewer than 20,000. An estimated 60 million bison were reduced to fewer than a thousand by 1890 (Zeveloff 1988). The Boskowitz Hide Company of Chicago shipped more than 34,000 bison hides out of Montana and northern Wyoming in 1880. In 1884 they could get only 529 (Madson 1987).

These megafauna were only the most conspicuous losses. The Nature Conservancy estimates that over 200 full species of plants, plus many more varieties, and 71 species and subspecies of vertebrates have gone extinct in North America north of Mexico since European settlement (The Nature Conservancy 1992, Russell and Morse 1992). Over 750 species of plants and animals in the United States are federally listed as threatened or endangered, thus officially considered close to extinction. Another 3000-plus species are candidates for listing, yet at present rates of listing many of these candidates will be lost before receiving protection under the Endangered Species Act. Only five listed species have recovered enough to be removed from the list (Wilcove et al 1993). The steady erosion of our native biodiversity is a direct consequence of the callous disregard we have shown for our environment and our evolutionary kin. This disregard continues today, ironically despite polls showing that 89 percent of the na-tional public agrees with the statement "humans have an ethical obligation to protect plant and animal species" (Shindler et al 1993).

Opponents of conservation often point out that extinction is natural and not worth worrying about. However, with the exception of a few mass extinction events in ancient geological history, the rate at which new species are created has exceeded the rate of extinction. Therefore, the number of species on Earth seems to have slowly but, with a few punctuations, steadily increased over time. That trend is being reversed today. As explained by Wilson (1985):

No comfort should be drawn from the spurious belief that because extinction is a natural process, humans are merely another Darwinian agent. The rate of extinction is now about 400 times that recorded through recent geological time and is accelerating rapidly. Under the best of conditions, the reduction of diversity seems destined to approach that of the great natural catastrophes at the end of Paleozoic and Mesozoic Eras, in other words, the most extreme for 65 million years. And in at least one respect, this human-made hecatomb is worse than at any time in the geological past. In the earlier mass extinctions, possibly caused by large meteoritic strikes, most of the plant diversity survived; now, for the first time, it is being mostly destroyed. (Knoll 1984)

Recent extinctions and the ever-expanding list of endangered species in North America show that the biodiversity crisis is not just a tropical problem. Although current extinction rates in the tropics, estimated at somewhere between 10,000 and 150,000 species lost per year over the next few decades (Wilson 1988, Diamond 1990), are higher than in the temperate zone due to the apparently greater diversity of tropical systems, some North American ecosystems are more endangered than tropical rainforests and stand to lose as great a proportion of their species. Examples from the United States of natural communities being de-stroyed faster than tropical rainforests include freshwater habitats in California (Moyle and Williams 1990) and old-growth forests of the Pacific Northwest (Norse 1990). In 1992, newspapers throughout the country reported a NASA study showing that the loss of old-growth forests in the Pacific Northwest surpassed in rate and extent the clearing of the Amazon basin. Satellite photographs vividly compared the damage (Fig.

1.3). Earlier, a National Geographic article portrayed the loss of virgin forests in the 48 conterminous states (Findley 1990), which amounts to at least 95 percent of the forests that greeted the first European settlers. Ancient forests have finally captured the publics attention, but they are not the only ecosystems disappearing. Estimates of ecosystem decline throughout the United States are shockingly high (Noss et al 1994). We have already lost far more than most Americans realize.

WHY ARE WE CONCERNED ABOUT BIODIVERSITY?

Aldo Leopold (1953) observed: "The last word in ignorance is the man who says of an animal or plant: 'What good is it?' If the land mechanism as a whole is good, then every part is good, whether we understand it or not. If the biota, in the course of aeons, has built something we like but do not understand, then who but a *fool* would discard seemingly useless pares? To keep every cog and wheel is the first precaution of intelligent tinkering."

FIGURE 5.3 Satellite images from NASA show forest fragmentation more severe in the Mt. Hood National Forest of Oregon (A) than i n the Amazon basin of Brazil (B). Source: NASA/GSFC (1992).

Do people care if species go extinct and natural areas are converted to shopping malls? Public opinion polls in the United States show that Americans are concerned about endangered species. For example, a recent poll of 1000 registered voters spanning the demographic, political, and geographic spectrums of the U.S. showed that 66 percent support the Endangered Species Act and only n percent opposed protecting endangered species (Stolzenburg 1992). Another poll showed that 78 percent of the national public believes that greater protection should be given to fish and wildlife habitats on federal forest lands; 65

percent disagreed with the statement that endangered species laws should be set aside to preserve timber jobs (Shindler *et al.* 1993). Although these polls asked mostly about species, not ecosystems, we can expect chat many people will oppose destruction of natural areas, especially areas near and dear to them.

Are there more fundamental reasons for protecting species and ecosystems, besides public support for such actions? Many texts have examined the values of biodiversity (e.g., Ehrlich and Ehrlich 1981, Prescott-Allen and Prescott-Allen 1983, 1986, Norton 1986, Wilson 1988, World Wildlife Fund 1991). The value of biodiversity is our fundamental assumption. If we did not believe in it, we would not be writing this book. However, it is worth reviewing briefly the types of value that humans ascribe to nature. Often arguments about what is proper management of natural resources can be put in perspective, if not totally resolved, by understanding how people value nature in different ways. The limitations of different value justifications for saving nature also need to be understood. Although we prefer to think that nature has essentially one value-with no necessary distinction between utilitarian and intrinsic-we partition this value below for purposes of discussion.

Direct Utilitarian Values

The kind of value easiest to appreciate, for many people, is the utilitarian or instrumental value of a species or other natural resource. That the "what good is it" question is so often asked suggests that many people value things largely for their direct utility for humans. Though incomplete as a justification for saving biodiversity, such values are real.

The medicinal value of certain plants and invertebrates provides a powerful argument for conservation, as does the value of wild gene pools for agriculture and wild populations for food. Wild species provide an estimated 4.5 percent of the Gross Domestic Product of the United States, worth $87 billion annually in the late 1970s (Prescott-Allen and Prescott Allen 1986). Fisheries contributed 100 million tons of food to people worldwide in 1988 (FAO 1988). One-fourth of all prescription drugs in the United States contain active ingredients extracted from plants, and nearly 3000 antibiotics are derived from microorganisms (WRI, IUCN, UNEP 1992). These statistics suggest that it is in our best interest to prevent extinctions of species that are potentially useful to us. What if the Pacific yew, until recently considered a trash tree and destroyed during clearcutting in the Pacific Northwest, were extinguished before we discovered that it contained taxol, a valuable new drug for treating several forms of cancer? This question is of more than academic interest. By one estimate, only about 5000 (2 percent) of the 250,000 described species of vascular plants have been screened for their chemical compounds (World Wildlife Fund 1991). We are driving species to extinction without even trying to learn what they might contribute to human society.

Arguments based on utility are limited, however. Leopold (1949) observed that "one basic weakness in a conservation system based wholly on economic motives is that most members of the land community have no economic value." Similarly, Ehrenfeld (1988) lamented, "what biologist is willing to find a value-conventional or ecological-for all 600,000-plus species of beetles?" What happens if we thoroughly screen a plant for medicinal compounds and conclude that it has none? Do we then say it is permissible to extinguish that species? Conservationists often fall into the trap of justifying species preservation for utilitarian purposes, thereby sanctioning the humanistic attitude that is responsible for the biodiversity crisis (Ehrenfeld

1978, 1988). The attitude implied by economic valuations is that the worth of a species depends on its direct utility to humans. If a species does not benefit us, it is worthless.

At best, the utilitarian argument for biodiversity conservation is a double-edged sword. Under some circumstances it might help gain public support for protecting species and ecosystems, but in other cases it can be used to justify destruction of seemingly worthless forms. In all cases, it encourages disrespect for species in and of themselves. Thus, we are troubled that current arguments for maintaining international biodiversity, such as those expressed in the Global Biodiversity Strategy produced by the World Resources Institute (WRI), World Conservation Union (IUCN), and United Nations Environment Programme (UNEP) (1992), are thoroughly utilitarian; they hinge almost entirely on presumed benefits to humans. The sustainable development theme of the Global Biodiversity Strategy and related international conservation programs is potentially dangerous. Sustainable development could do more harm than good to biodiversity if strict protection of sensitive areas is not part of the program (Robinson 1993).

Indirect Utilitarian Values

Natural ecosystems and biodiversity also provide benefits to humans that are indirect, yet essential. Paul and Anne Ehrlich (1981) call these benefits "ecosystem services." Every habitat on Earth, including urban and agricultural environments, is an ecosystem that receives and transforms energy, produces and recycles wastes, and relies on complex interactions among species to carry out these functions. But urban and agricultural ecosystems are dependent on natural ecosystems for their sustenance. Solar energy is the basis of virtually all food chains (rare exceptions include chemically based communities in deep-sea vents) and is converted to chemical energy by photosynthetic plants. Plants, including crops, often depend on animals to pollinate their flowers and disperse their seeds, on nitrogen-fixing bacteria to convert molecular nitrogen to a form that can be assembled into proteins, and on microorganisms to convert complex organic compounds into inorganic nutrients that can be taken up by their roots. Animals, fungi, and microbes in an ecosystem have comparable interdependencies. Thus, an ecosystem is a richly interconnected web of relationships greater than the sum of its parts.

But how does a natural ecosystem benefit humans, besides providing pharmaceuticals and other products? An entire book could be written on this subject. Ehrlich and Ehrlich (1981) describe ecosystem services upon which human civilization is entirely dependent, including: (1) maintaining atmospheric quality by regulating gas ratios and filtering dust and pollutants; (2) controlling and ameliorating climate through the carbon cycle and effects of vegetation in stimulating local and regional rainfall; (3) regulating freshwater supplies and controlling flooding (wetlands, for example, can act as giant sponges to soak up moisture during rainy periods and release water slowly during dry periods); (4) generating and maintaining soils through the decomposition of organic matter and the relationships between plant roots and mycorrhizal fungi; (5) disposing of wastes, including domestic sewage and wastes produced by industry and agriculture, and cycling of nutrients; (6) controlling pests and diseases, for example through predation and parasitism on herbivorous insects; and (7) pollinating crops and useful wild plant species by insects, bats, hummingbirds, and other pollinators. The public-service functions of ecosystems remain little known to most people, perhaps because we need to understand ecology in order to appreciate the functional relationships that underlie these services. Our society, by any measure, is ecologically ignorant. The role of biodiversity in supporting ecosystem services is striking, but we cannot easily predict how many or what kinds of species can be lost before ecosystems break down. Because all ecosystems contain some functional redundancy (with different species playing similar roles), we might impoverish an ecosystem substantially before impairing basic ecological processes such as nutrient cycling. From a utilitarian perspective, we don't *need* every species. Some simplified, human-created ecosystems may perform virtually all of the public service functions reviewed above. The danger is that natural ecosystems have evolved their functional relationships over thousands or millions of years, whereas our experiments in manipulating ecosystems are comparatively brief. Who knows when we may lose a species or set of relationships critical to ecosystem function?

Recreational and Aesthetic Values

Probably most people who care about the environment are motivated primarily by their personal appreciation of nature's beauty. John Muir, founder of the Sierra Club and a leading force in the creation of the U.S. national park system, firmly believed that exposure of ordinary people to wild places would foster an attitude to save these places (Fox 1981). Leopold (1949), too, noted that people will behave ethically only toward something they can experience and have faith in. Recreational and esthetic enjoyment of nature often leads directly to appreciation of nature for its own sake, that is, to a spiritual or ethical appreciation of biodiversity. Without people motived by their experiences of wild places, we would arguably have fewer wild areas remaining and the status of biodiversity in North America would be even more precarious.

Despite the critical role of these kinds of human experience in promoting conservation, areas set aside to fulfill recreational or esthetic objectives do not necessarily meet biodiversity conservation goals. Many national parks, wilderness areas, and other large reserves selected on the basis of esthetic criteria are relatively depauperate biologically. The Forest Service evaluates the "need" for wilderness designation on the basis of expected recreational visitor days, not on biological criteria. As a result, most wilderness areas are rock and ice, or other such scenic but not particularly diverse lands.

Many managers of national forests and other public lands, forced to reduce commodity production because such uses were unsustainable and in violation of environmental laws, are turning to recreation as an alternative use of these lands. This trend can be risky to the extent that it emphasizes motorized recreation. Managers justify road-building, leaving logging roads open to the public, and allowing use of off-road vehicles by arguing that the public needs access to these lands. Motorized recreation is almost always destructive of biodiversity. Furthermore, it encourages an attitude of dominance over nature. As Leopold (1949) put it: "It is the expansion of transport without a corresponding growth of perception that threatens us with qualitative bankruptcy of the recreational process. Recreational development is a job not of building roads into lovely country, but of building receptivity into the still unlovely human mind.'

Thus, conservation arguments based on promoting human enjoyment are incomplete, at best. A deeper reason for protecting nature must be found.

Intrinsic, Spiritual, and Ethical Values

The limitations of utilitarian arguments for conserving biodiversity leave an alternative: the appreciation of wild creatures and wild places for themselves. We believe that nature and biodiversity possess *all* the kinds of value reviewed above, but that intrinsic values (or the spiritual and ethical appreciation of nature for its own sake) offer the least biased and ultimately most secure arguments for conservation. Virtually all religious traditions recognize the value of a human being-for example, a newborn baby-as at least partially independent of what that person might do for us. Why shouldn't we feel the same way about other creatures? The acknowledgment that natural objects and processes are valuable in themselves reflects a basic intuition of many people. Science cannot prove or disprove intrinsic value. Yet as scientists, we see no objective reason for believing that humans are fundamentally superior to any other organism. If we have value, then all natural things have value.

The ethical basis for respecting and protecting nature was expressed eloquently by Aldo Leopold (1949) in his famous essay on the land ethic. "A thing is right," Leopold wrote, "when it tends to preserve the integrity, stability, and beauty of the biotic community. It is wrong when it tends otherwise." Ecologists might quibble with Leopold's choice of such imprecise terms as integrity and stability, noting that Nature is instead dynamic and unpredictable (Botkin 1990), and they might wonder how we can objectively measure beauty. But few challenge his primary message that ethical obligations must encompass more than our fellow human beings (Nash 1989, Noss 1992a). Many philosophers have joined Leopold in calling for consideration of all life in our decisions about what is morally right or wrong (Devall and Sessions 1985, Rolston 1988, Naess 1989). To do so is to expand our circle of ethical concern beyond the individual self and ultimately to the ecological self the land as a whole (Fig. 5.4).

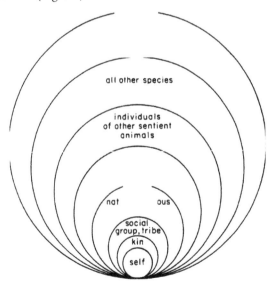

FIGURE 5.4 An ethical sequence, showing circles of moral concern and obligation increasing from the self and immediate family to all other species and the earth as a whole (the ecological self). Concern for higher levels is an extension, not a replacement, of traditional ethical concern for human beings. From Noss (1992a). Used with permission of Routledge, Chapman & Hall.

Without moral consideration of the needs of other creatures, policies for protecting biodiversity remain on shaky ground. Thus, we urge a reaffirmation of the World Charter for Nature, adopted by the United Nations General Assembly in 1982, which stated: "Every form of life is unique, warranting respect regardless of its worth to man, and, to accord other organisms such recognition, man must be guided by a moral code of action."

WHERE HAVE WE FAILED?

The United States has a long and venerable conservation history, with many accomplishments worthy of pride. Our laws, including the National Park Organic Act of 1916, the Wilderness Act of 1964, the Endangered Species Act of 1969 and 1973, and the National Environmental Policy Act of 1969 and 1973, are held up as models for the world to follow. Yet the biodiversity crisis continues to worsen. Our air and water get dirtier, the ozone layer thins, and most significantly for biodiversity, more and more natural habitat is destroyed in the name of progress and jobs. Why have the American people allowed this to happen?

Let us briefly examine the failure of conventional conservation practices and institutions to address the "big picture" (this topic will be explored in more depth in Chapter 3). We have laws, regulations, and agencies set up to protect aspects of the environment, yet none of them has measured up to the challenge of protecting biodiversity as a whole. We have trained four generations of professionals in forestry, wildlife management, fisheries, and range conservation, yet these disciplines remain fragmented and are often narrow. The traditional approach to conservation has been piecemeal: species by species, resource by resource, project by project, threat by threat. The first laws in the United States oriented toward natural resources were game protection laws. Market hunting was big business in the late nineteenth century. After George Perkins Marsh (1864) published *Man and Nature*, wildlife declines became widely recognized. Sportsmen led the fight to enact more laws protecting wildlife, including a bill outlawing bison killing in 1874, pocket-vetoed by President Grant for anti-Indian reasons; the Lacey Act (1900), authorizing the federal government to prohibit interstate transport of illegally taken game and wildlife parts; and the Migratory Bird Treaty with Canada (1916) and Mexico (1936), which protected nongame birds. Meanwhile, the Boone and Crockett Club was established in 1887, largely to promote sport over market hunting, and The Audubon Society was formed in 1886 to combat the fashion of wearing the feathers and skins of birds.

About the same time, Americans began formally protecting places where wildlife and scenery could be enjoyed. The Yellowstone Park Protection Act passed in 1892, twenty years after actual creation of the Park. Yellowstone and other national parks were not established primarily to protect wildlife, but rather "to conserve the scenery and the natural and historic objects and the wild life" within parks, and "to provide for the enjoyment of the same in such manner and by such means as will leave them unimpaired for the enjoyment of future generations" (National Park Organic Act of 1916). Also in 1892, the Sierra Club was founded by John Muir and other mountain hikers (Fox 1981). The first federal wildlife refuge, Pelican Island, Florida, was established by Theodore Roosevelt in 1903 to protect egrets, herons, and brown pelicans from plume hunters. Before leaving office in 1909, Roosevelt created 51 refuges for birds and mammals (Zaslowsky 1986), but he also escalated the war against wolves, bears, puma, and other predators (Worster 1977).

Conservation history in the United States is largely a series of responses to urgent threats against popular species and scenic wonders. Game management rose as a formal science in the United States in the 1930s, with the publication of *The Bobwhite Quail* by Herbert Stoddard (1931), and *Game Management* by Aldo Leopold (1933), and with the founding of The Wildlife Society in 1937. Most of wildlife management since then has been concerned with promoting population surpluses of favored species. Some single-species projects have worked remarkably well. The intended beneficiaries, game species like the wild turkey and endangered species like the peregrine falcon, have made remarkable comebacks as a result of reintroductions and intensive management. But such management has cost millions of dollars per species. Efforts this expensive can hardly be applied to all species. Even if such enormous funds were available, the conflicting needs of different species would make management inefficient and conflict-ridden.

Many biologists now acknowledge that, despite notable successes, single-species management has caused many problems. For instance, game managers traditionally advocated forest harvest patterns that maximized fragmentation of the landscape because many game species thrive where forage and cover areas are interspersed and edges between habitat types are abundant (Leopold 1933). But we now know that while fragmentation may benefit deer and other game, it does not contribute to native biodiversity (Noss 1983). Forest fragmentation has benefited deer so much in the upper Midwest that several conifer species are not regenerating in many areas due to over-browsing (Alverson et al. 1988). Intense herbivory from white-tailed deer threatens many rare plant species throughout the eastern and midwestern United States (Miller et al. 1992). In addition to manipulative habitat management, control of predators for the benefit of game animals and domestic livestock has led to many ecological problems (Dunlap 1988). Amazingly, costly and destructive predator control continues on public lands today.

When wildlife managers expanded their concern beyond game species and began considering nongame and endangered species, the circle of conservation broadened. Leopold (1933) recognized a historical and progressive sequence of wildlife management: (1) restriction of hunting, (2) predator control, (3) reservation of game lands, (4) artificial replenishment, and (5) environmental controls. Environmental control is habitat management and is based on ecological principles and empiricism. As acknowledged by Leopold, this approach has considerable potential for expansion to nonhunted species. But the spectrum of species considered by most conservation programs today remains limited.

Endangered species efforts, by definition, do not worry about life forms until they teeter on the brink of extinction or appear to be rapidly approaching that brink. A recent study found that 39 plant species in the United States were listed only when 10 or fewer individuals were known to exist; a freshwater mussel, *Quadrula fragosa*, was not listed until a single non-reproducing population remained (Wilcove et al. 1993). Because we wait so long to list species, saving them is bound to be expensive and the chances of success are poor. Most of the funding for recovery of listed species has been devoted to a few popular vertebrates (Kohm 1991), and even then recovery targets are usually less than what it would take to restore population viability (Tear et al. 1993).

Endangered species programs, although critical as a safety net to catch imperiled species where other actions fail, are obviously reactive rather than proactive. They make no attempt to identify potentially vulnerable species before they begin the slide toward extinction. They usually fail to recognize opportunities for protecting suites of species, such as those associated with an endangered ecosystem type, in a cost-effective way. They pay no attention to levels of organization beyond species. Although the first stated purpose of the Endangered Species Act of 1973 is "to protect the ecosystems upon which endangered species and threatened species depend," the agencies have never taken this ecosystem protection mandate seriously, and Congress has never told them how they might do so.

Nongame species programs have the potential to be proactive and taxonomically broad, but with very few exceptions (states such as Missouri, which has a portion of its sales tax allocated to conservation) they have received little funding. Furthermore, their focus has usually been on vertebrate groups popular with the public, such as birds, and they have made little attempt to determine the conservation needs of such groups as salamanders, mites, liverworts, or fungi. Because there has been no effective national nongame program, state programs operate without full knowledge of what is going on around them and have little incentive or opportunity to coordinate programs with other states and nations.

The continually expanding list of endangered species and ongoing degradation of entire ecosystems is proof enough that current approaches to conservation are flawed. In the case of the Endangered Species Act, grossly inadequate funding and political interference with listing and recovery actions are much to blame (Bean 1991). But today the Endangered Species Act and other conservation laws are being asked to do more than what they were designed to do. Knowledge of conservation problems and techniques has expanded greatly since these pieces of legislation were enacted. The interdisciplinary field of conservation biology is growing at a phenomenal pace. And, hopefully, our esthetic and ethical appreciation for life has deepened since the early days of American conservation.

Many conservationists now insist that we move beyond game species, endangered species, and other popular organisms, and start inventorying and protecting whole assemblages of species, habitats, and ecosystems before they decline further. What's more, the grassroots members of the "New Conservation Movement" (Foreman 1991) are urging ecological restoration at a massive scale, including removal of roads and developments in many areas and reintroduction of large predators. Dissatisfied with a biologically simplified America, they want back much of what has been lost. And why not? At first glance, a vision of North America with regained wildness and biodiversity seems unrealistic, even utopian. But when we consider that restoration at this scale is a process requiring decades or even centuries, it begins to make sense (Soule 1992). Perhaps recovery is inevitable. The human population cannot grow forever, and must either plateau, decline gradually, or crash. In any case, repairing the damage our culture has done and giving other creatures a fair chance for life is the job of enlightened management today and in the future. This is our chance to pay retribution.

WHY MANAGEMENT?

Throughout this [chapter] we use the term *management*. All land management is biodiversity management, whether intended or not. All land-use decisions-including a decision to designate a reserve, put a fence around it, and leave it alone-are land management decisions with significant consequences for biodiversity. It is much better to manage biodiversity by design rather than by default. As the most powerful species on earth, we can alter biodiversity worldwide and are expressing that capability in a frightening way. Accepting responsibility for our actions means not only that we carefully consider the effects of management on biodiversity, but also that our management programs be designed explicitly to protect and restore native biodiversity.

In some respects, management is an arrogant concept. How can we presume to manage nature if we can't even manage ourselves? What right do we have to manage and manipulate landscapes for human ends, be they conservation or development? Why not let landscapes manage themselves and let organisms fulfill their evolutionary destinies with little human interference? We are sympathetic to these concerns but believe that, for better or worse, humans are now responsible for the continuing or ending of 3.5 billion years of organic evolution. Such power must be wielded carefully and wisely.

Land managers often become overly enthusiastic and manipulate habitats that should be left alone. On the other hand, stopping land management would in many cases be an ecological disaster. In landscapes already fragmented by human activity, the remaining natural areas are vulnerable to all sorts of threats from outside their boundaries, including edge effects. For example, the brown-headed cowbird, a parasite that lays its eggs in the nests of other birds, may need to be controlled if other bird species are to survive in remaining patches of forest. Management of the endangered Kirtland's warbler and black-capped vireo includes trapping and removing cowbirds. Without such intrusive management, these endangered birds cannot reproduce successfully. Exotic plants, such as Japanese and bush honeysuckles in eastern forests and kudzu in the South, often seriously compete with native species and need to be controlled. Without management, invasive exotics overrun many landscapes and eliminate some native species. In all such cases, we have created a dangerous situation-an environment favorable to proliferation of weedy and exotic species-that we must now correct through management or risk losing more biodiversity as sensitive species decline.

Vegetation types that require frequent fire to maintain their native species composition and structure offer some of the strongest arguments for ecologically informed management (see Chapter 2). A small, isolated patch of prairie in a fragmented landscape is not likely to receive lightning strikes often enough to burn regularly and sustain its natural structure. If we do not manage these fire-dependent systems by use of prescribed fire, they will lose their native biodiversity.

The role of management in conservation strategy can be denied only at great risk. But perhaps management is optimally a set of interim measures that will help ecosystems recover their natural values. The ideal future may be one where management is no longer needed because ecosystems are wild and healthy enough to take care of themselves. Even if one does not accept this long-term goal, it cannot be denied that large, essentially self-managing wilderness areas are among the most important reservoirs of native biodiversity today. No one really knows how to manage a natural ecosystem. Thus, "we should at least keep our minds open to the proposition that nature-if given a chance-can still manage land better than we can" (Noss 1991b).

We fear, unfortunately, that letting things be is not a safe option for much of our landscape in the near future, however valuable it may be as a guiding principle for large wilderness areas and possibly for some distant future worldwide. But concerning management, one thing is clear: Traditional approaches have failed to protect biodiversity. A new approach to land conservation, built on what we feel is the best of past and current approaches, is [necessary]. But first, we examine in more detail the forces responsible for evolution of biodiversity in North America and the limitations of past approaches to managing this incredible diversity.

ECOSYSTEMS AND THEIR SERVICES

FROM MILLENNIUM ECOSYSTEM ASSESSMENT REPORT

EXECUTIVE SUMMARY

- An ecosystem is a dynamic complex of plant, animal, and microorganism communities and the nonliving environment, interacting as a functional unit. Humans are an integral part of ecosystems.

- A well-defined ecosystem has strong interactions among its components and weak interactions across its boundaries. A useful ecosystem boundary is the place where a number of discontinuities coincide, for instance in the distribution of organisms, soil types, drainage basins, or depth in a water body. At a larger scale, regional and even globally distributed ecosystems can be evaluated based on a commonality of basic structural units.

- Ecosystem services are the benefits people obtain from ecosystems. These include provisioning services such as food and water; regulating services such as flood and disease control; cultural services such as spiritual, recreational, and cultural benefits; and supporting services, such as nutrient cycling, that maintain the conditions for life on Earth.

- Biodiversity is the variability among living organisms. It includes diversity within and among species and diversity within and among ecosystems. Biodiversity is the source of many ecosystem goods, such as food and genetic resources, and changes in biodiversity can influence the supply of ecosystem services.

- People seek many services from ecosystems and thus perceive the condition of an ecosystem in relation to its ability to provide desired services. The ability of ecosystems to deliver services can be assessed by a variety of qualitative and quantitative methods.
- An assessment of the condition of ecosystems, the provision of services, and their relation to human well-being requires an integrated approach. This enables a decision process to determine which service or set of services is valued most highly and how to develop approaches to maintain services by managing the system sustainably.

Introduction

Millions of species populate Earth. The vast majority gain energy to support their metabolism either directly from the sun, in the case of plants, or, in the case of animals and microbes, from other organisms through feeding on plants, predation, parasitism, or decomposition. In the pursuit of life and through their capacity to reproduce, organisms use energy, water, and nutrients. Terrestrial plants obtain water principally from soil, while animals get it mainly from free-standing water in the environment or from their food. Plants obtain most of their nutrients from the soil or water, while animals tend to derive their nutrients from other organisms. Microorganisms are the most versatile, obtaining nutrients from soil, water, their food, or other organisms. Organisms interact with one another in many ways, including competitive, predatory, parasitic, and facilitative ways, such as pollination, seed dispersal, and the provision of habitat.

These fundamental linkages among organisms and their physical and biological environment constitute an interacting and ever-changing system that is known as an ecosystem. Humans are a component of these ecosystems. Indeed, in many regions they are the dominant organism. Whether dominant or not, however, humans depend on ecosystem properties and on the network of interactions among organisms and within and among ecosystems for sustenance, just like all other species.

As organisms interact with each other and their physical environment, they produce, acquire, or decompose biomass and the carbon-based or organic compounds associated with it. They also move minerals from the water, sediment, and soil into and among organisms, and back again into the physical environment. Terrestrial plants also transport water from the soil into the atmosphere. In performing these functions, they provide materials to humans in the form of food, fiber, and building materials and they contribute to the regulation of soil, air, and water quality.

These relationships sound simple in general outline, but they are in fact enormously complex, since each species has unique requirements for life and each species interacts with both the physical and the biological environment. Recent perturbations, driven principally by human activities, have added even greater complexity by changing, to a large degree, the nature of those environments.

Ecosystem Boundaries and Categories

Although the notion of an ecosystem is ancient, ecosystems first became a unit of study less than a century ago, when Arthur Tansley provided an initial scientific conceptualization in 1935 (Tansley 1935) and

Box 6.1 The Ecosystem Approach: A Bridge Between the Environment and Human Well-being

The concept of an ecosystem provides a valuable framework for analyzing and acting on the linkages between people and their environment. For that reason, the ecosystem approach has been endorsed by the Convention on Biological Diversity (CBD) and the Millennium Ecosystem Assessment (MA) conceptual framework is entirely consistent with this approach. The CBD defines the ecosystem approach as follows:

The Ecosystem Approach is a strategy for the integrated management of land, water and living resources that promotes conservation and sustainable use in an equitable way. Thus, the application of the ecosystem approach will help to reach a balance of the three objectives of the Convention: conservation; sustainable use; and the fair and equitable sharing of the benefits arising out of the utilization of genetic resources. An ecosystem approach is based on the application of appropriate scientific methodologies focused on levels of biological organization, which encompass the essential structure, processes, functions and interactions among organisms and their environment. It recognizes that humans, with their cultural diversity, are an integral component of many ecosystems.

According to the CBD, the term ecosystem can refer to any functioning unit at any scale. This approach requires adaptive management to deal with the complex and dynamic nature of ecosystems and the absence of complete knowledge or understanding of their functioning. It does not preclude other management and conservation approaches, such as biosphere reserves, protected areas, and single-species conservation programs, or other approaches carried out under existing national policy and legislative frameworks; rather, it could integrate all these approaches and other methodologies to deal with complex situations. As described in the CBD, there is no single way to implement the ecosystem approach, as it depends on local, provincial, national, regional, and global conditions.

The conceptual framework of the MA provides a useful assessment structure that can contribute to the implementation of the CBD's ecosystem approach. By way of analogy, decision-makers would not make a decision about financial policy in a country without examining the condition of the economic system, since information on the economy of a single sector such as manufacturing would be insufficient. The same applies to ecological systems or ecosystems. Decisions can be improved by considering the interactions among the parts of the system. For instance, the draining of wetlands may increase food production, but sound decisions also require information on whether the potential added costs associated with the increased risk of downstream flooding or other changes in ecosystem services might outweigh those benefits.

Raymond Lindeman did the first quantitative study in an ecosystem context in the early 1940s (Lindeman 1942). The first textbook built on the ecosystem concept, written by Eugene Odum, was published in 1953 (Odum 1953). Thus the ecosystem concept, so central to understanding the nature of life on Earth, is actually a relatively new research and management approach.

Tansley's formulation of an ecosystem included "not only the organism-complex, but also the whole complex of physical factors forming what we call the environment" (Tansley 1935:299). He noted that ecosystems "are of the most varied kinds and sizes." The main identifying feature of an ecosystem is that it is indeed a system; its location or size is important, but secondary.

Following Tansley and subsequent developments, we chose to use the definition of an ecosystem adopted by the Convention on Biological Diversity (CBD): "a dynamic complex of plant, animal and microorganism communities and their nonliving environment interacting as a functional unit" (United Nations 1992: Article 2).

Biodiversity and ecosystems are closely related concepts. Biodiversity is defined by the CBD as "the variability among living organisms from all sources including, *inter alia,* terrestrial, marine and other aquatic ecosystems and the ecological complexes of which they are part; this includes diversity within species, between species and of ecosystems" (United Nations 1992: Article 2). Diversity thus is a structural feature of ecosystems, and the variability among ecosystems is an element of biodiversity. The parties to the convention have endorsed the "ecosystem approach" as their primary framework for action. (See Box 6.1.)

For analysis and assessment, it is important to adopt a pragmatic view of ecosystem boundaries, depending on the questions being asked. In one sense, the entire biosphere of Earth is an ecosystem since the elements interact. At a smaller scale, the guiding principle is that a well-defined ecosystem has strong interactions among its components and weak interactions across its boundaries. (See also Chapter 5.) A practical approach to the spatial delimitation of an ecosystem is to build up a series of overlays of significant factors, mapping the location of discontinuities, such as in the distribution of organisms, the biophysical environment (soil types, drainage basins, depth in a water body), and spatial interactions (home ranges, migration patterns, fluxes of matter). A useful ecosystem boundary is the place where a number of these relative discontinuities coincide. At a larger scale, regional and even globally distributed ecosystems can be evaluated based on the commonality of basic structural units. We use such a framework in the MA for the global analysis of ecosystem properties and changes.

The global assessment being undertaken by the MA is based on 10 categories: marine, coastal, inland water, forest, dryland, island, mountain, polar, cultivated, and urban. (See Box 6.2.) These categories are not ecosystems themselves, but each contains a number of ecosystems. The MA reporting categories are not mutually exclusive: their boundaries can and do overlap. Ecosystems within each category share a suite of biological, climatic, and social factors that tend to differ across categories. More specifically, there generally is greater similarity within than between each category in:

- climatic conditions;
- geophysical conditions;
- dominant use by humans;

- surface cover (based on type of vegetative cover in terrestrial ecosystems or on fresh water, brackish water, or salt water in aquatic ecosystems);
- species composition; and
- resource management systems and institutions.

The factors characterizing ecosystems in each category are highly interrelated. Thus, for example, grasslands are found in many areas where potential evaporation exceeds precipitation. Grasslands, in turn, tend to be used by humans either as rangeland or for agricultural purposes. The areas used for rangeland tend to have pastoral, sometimes nomadic, resource management systems. Thus these factors—high potential evaporation relative to precipitation, grassland cover, use for livestock, and pastoral or nomadic management systems—tend to be found together. (This is typical of the dryland system category in Box 6.2.)

Box 6.2 Reporting Categories Used in the Millennium Ecosystem Assessment

Social and ecological systems can be categorized in an infinite number of ways. For the purposes of reporting the global Millennium Ecosystem Assessment (MA) findings, we have developed a practical, tractable, sufficiently rich classification based on 10 systems. Thus, for example, the MA will report on "forest systems," defined to be areas with at least 40 percent canopy (tree) cover. Using this approach, a forest system will contain a variety of different types of ecosystems, such as freshwater ecosystems, agroecosystems, and so forth. But all areas within the boundaries of the forest system as defined here will tend to share a suite of biological, climatic, and social factors, so the system categories provide a useful framework for analyzing the consequences of ecosystem change for human well-being. Because the boundaries of these reporting categories overlap, any place on Earth may fall into more than one category. Thus a wetland ecosystem in a coastal region, for instance, may be examined both in the MA analysis of "coastal systems" as well as in the analysis of "inland water systems."

The following table lists the basic boundary definitions that will be used in the global MA analysis. In a number of cases the MA will also examine conditions and changes in ecosystems with reference to more than one boundary definition. For example, although we use a boundary of 40 percent tree (canopy) cover as our basic definition of the forest category, another widely accepted definition of "forests" is at least 10 percent canopy cover.

MILLENNIUM ECOSYSTEM ASSESSMENT REPORTING CATEGORIES		
CATEGORY	CENTRAL CONCEPT	BOUNDARY LIMITS FOR MAPPING
Marine	Ocean, with fishing typically a major driver of change	Marine areas where the sea is deeper than 50 meters.
Coastal	Interface between ocean and land, extending seawards to about the middle of the continental shelf and inland to include all areas strongly influenced by the proximity to the ocean	Area between 50 meters below mean sea level and 50 meters above the high tide level or extending landward to a distance 100 kilometers from shore. Includes coral reefs, intertidal zones, estuaries, coastal aquaculture, and seagrass communities.
Inland water	Permanent water bodies inland from the coastal zone, and areas whose ecology and use are dominated by the permanent, seasonal, or intermittent occurrence of flooded conditions	Rivers, lakes, floodplains, reservoirs, and wetlands; includes inland saline systems. Note that the Ramsar Convention considers "wetlands" to include both inland water and coastal categories.
Forest	Lands dominated by trees; often used for timber, fuelwood, and non-timber forest products	A canopy cover of at least 40 percent by woody plants taller than 5 meters. The existence of many other definitions is acknowledged, and other limits (such as crown cover greater than 10 percent, as used by the Food and Agriculture Organization of the United Nations) will also be reported. Includes temporarily cut-over forests and plantations; excludes orchards and agroforests where the main products are food crops.
Dryland	Lands where plant production is limited by water availability; the dominant uses are large mammal herbivory, including livestock grazing, and cultivation	Drylands as defined by the Convention to Combat Desertification, namely lands where annual precipitation is less than two thirds of potential evaporation, from dry subhumid areas (ratio ranges 0.50–0.65), through semiarid, arid, and hyper-arid (ratio <0.05), but excluding polar areas; drylands include cultivated lands, scrublands, shrublands, grasslands, semi-deserts, and true deserts.
Island	Lands isolated by surrounding water, with a high proportion of coast to hinterland	As defined by the Alliance of Small Island States
Mountain	Steep and high lands	As defined by Mountain Watch using criteria based on elevation alone, and at lower elevation, on a combination of elevation, slope, and local elevation range. Specifically, elevation >2,500 meters, elevation 1,500–2,500 meters and slope >2 degrees, elevation 1,000–1,500 meters and slope >5 degrees or local elevation range (7 kilometers radius) >300 meters, elevation 300–1,000 meters and local elevation range (7 kilometers radius) >300 meters, isolated inner basins and plateaus less than 25 square kilometers extent that are surrounded by mountains.
Polar	High-latitude systems frozen for most of the year	Includes ice caps, areas underlain by permafrost, tundra, polar deserts, and polar coastal areas. Excludes high-altitude cold systems in low latitudes.

MILLENNIUM ECOSYSTEM ASSESSMENT REPORTING CATEGORIES		
CATEGORY	CENTRAL CONCEPT	BOUNDARY LIMITS FOR MAPPING
Cultivated	Lands dominated by domesticated plant species, used for and substantially changed by crop, agroforestry, or aquaculture production	Areas in which at least 30 percent of the landscape comes under cultivation in any particular year. Includes orchards, agroforestry, and integrated agriculture-aquaculture systems.
Urban	Built environments with a high human density	Known human settlements with a population of 5,000 or more, with boundaries delineated by observing persistent night-time lights or by inferring areal extent in the cases where such observations are absent.

We use overlapping categories in the global MA analysis because this better reflects real-world biological, geophysical, social, and economic interactions, particularly at these relatively large scales. For example, an important issue for ecosystems and human well-being in forested regions relates to the impact of forest harvest or conversion on the timing, quantity, and quality of water runoff. Given the importance of this interaction, it is helpful to analyze an area dominated by forest land cover as a single ecosystem even if it contains some freshwater and agricultural areas within it, rather than analyzing the forest, agriculture, and freshwater ecosystems separately, since this allows for a more holistic analysis of these interactions.

Ecosystem Services

Ecosystem services are the benefits people obtain from ecosystems. This definition is derived from two other commonly referenced and representative definitions:

> Ecosystem services are the conditions and processes through which natural ecosystems, and the species that make them up, sustain and fulfill human life. They maintain biodiversity and the production of ecosystem goods, such as seafood, forage timber, biomass fuels, natural fiber, and many pharmaceuticals, industrial products, and their precursors (Daily 1997b:3).

> Ecosystem goods (such as food) and services (such as waste assimilation) represent the benefits human populations derive, directly or indirectly, from ecosystem functions (Costanza et al. 1997:253).

The MA definition follows Costanza and his colleagues in including both natural and human-modified ecosystems as sources of ecosystem services, and it follows Daily in using the term "services" to encompass both the tangible and the intangible benefits humans obtain from ecosystems, which are sometimes separated into "goods" and "services" respectively.

Like the term ecosystem itself, the concept of ecosystem services is relatively recent—it was first used in the late 1960s (e.g., King 1966; Helliwell 1969). Research on ecosystem services has grown dramatically within the last decade (e.g., Costanza et al. 1997; Daily 1997a; Daily et al. 2000; de Groot et al. 2002).

It is common practice in economics both to refer to goods and services separately and to include the two concepts under the term services. Although "goods," "services," and "cultural services" are often treated separately for ease of understanding, for the MA we consider all these benefits together as "ecosystem services" because it is sometimes difficult to determine whether a benefit provided by an ecosystem is a "good" or a "service." Also, when people refer to "ecosystem goods and services," cultural values and other intangible benefits are sometimes forgotten.

Ecosystem services have been categorized in a number of different ways, including by:

- functional groupings, such as regulation, carrier, habitat, production, and information services (Lobo 2001; de Groot et al. 2002);
- organizational groupings, such as services that are associated with certain species, that regulate some exogenous input, or that are related to the organization of biotic entities (Norberg 1999); and
- descriptive groupings, such as renewable resource goods, nonrenewable resource goods, physical structure services, biotic services, biogeochemical services, information services, and social and cultural services (Moberg and Folke 1999).

For operational purposes, we will classify ecosystem services along functional lines within the MA, using categories of provisioning, regulating, cultural, and supporting services. (See Figure 6.1.) We recognize that some of the categories overlap.

Provisioning Services

These are the products obtained from ecosystems, including:

- *Food and fiber.* This includes the vast range of food products derived from plants, animals, and microbes, as well as materials such as wood, jute, hemp, silk, and many other products derived from ecosystems.
- *Fuel.* Wood, dung, and other biological materials serve as sources of energy.
- *Genetic resources.* This includes the genes and genetic information used for animal and plant breeding and biotechnology.
- *Biochemicals, natural medicines, and pharmaceuticals.* Many medicines, biocides, food additives such as alginates, and biological materials are derived from ecosystems.
- *Ornamental resources.* Animal products, such as skins and shells, and flowers are used as ornaments, although the value of these resources is often culturally determined. This is an example of linkages between the categories of ecosystem services.
- *Fresh water.* Fresh water is another example of linkages between categories—in this case, between provisioning and regulating services.

Regulating Services

These are the benefits obtained from the regulation of ecosystem processes, including:

Ecosystem services are the benefits people obtain from ecosystems. These include provisioning, regulating, and cultural services that directly affect people and supporting services needed to maintain the other services.

PROVISIONING SERVICES	REGULATING SERVICES	CULTURAL SERVICES
Products obtained from ecosystems	Benefits obtained from regulation of ecosystem processes	Nonmaterial benefits obtained from ecosystems
• Food • Fresh water • Fuelwood • Fiber • Biochemicals • Genetic resources	• Climate regulation • Disease regulation • Water regulation • Water purification • Pollination	• Spiritual and religious • Recreation and ecotourism • Aesthetic • Inspirational • Educational • Sense of place • Cultural heritage
Supporting Services Services necessary for the production of all other ecosystem services • Soil formation • Nutrient cycling • Primary production		

Figure 6.1 Ecosystem Services.

- *Air quality maintenance.* Ecosystems both contribute chemicals to and extract chemicals from the atmosphere, influencing many aspects of air quality.
- *Climate regulation.* Ecosystems influence climate both locally and globally. For example, at a local scale, changes in land cover can affect both temperature and precipitation. At the global scale, ecosystems play an important role in climate by either sequestering or emitting greenhouse gases.
- *Water regulation.* The timing and magnitude of runoff, flooding, and aquifer recharge can be strongly influenced by changes in land cover, including, in particular, alterations that change the water storage potential of the system, such as the conversion of wetlands or the replacement of forests with croplands or croplands with urban areas.
- *Erosion control.* Vegetative cover plays an important role in soil retention and the prevention of landslides.
- *Water purification and waste treatment.* Ecosystems can be a source of impurities in fresh water but also can help to filter out and decompose organic wastes introduced into inland waters and coastal and marine ecosystems.
- *Regulation of human diseases.* Changes in ecosystems can directly change the abundance of human pathogens, such as cholera, and can alter the abundance of disease vectors, such as mosquitoes.
- *Biological control.* Ecosystem changes affect the prevalence of crop and livestock pests and diseases.
- *Pollination.* Ecosystem changes affect the distribution, abundance, and effectiveness of pollinators.
- *Storm protection.* The presence of coastal ecosystems such as mangroves and coral reefs can dramatically reduce the damage caused by hurricanes or large waves.

Cultural Services

These are the nonmaterial benefits people obtain from ecosystems through spiritual enrichment, cognitive development, reflection, recreation, and aesthetic experiences, including:

- *Cultural diversity.* The diversity of ecosystems is one factor influencing the diversity of cultures.
- *Spiritual and religious values.* Many religions attach spiritual and religious values to ecosystems or their components.
- *Knowledge systems* (traditional and formal). ecosystems influence the types of knowledge systems developed by different cultures.
- *Educational values.* Ecosystems and their components and processes provide the basis for both formal and informal education in many societies.
- *Inspiration.* Ecosystems provide a rich source of inspiration for art, folklore, national symbols, architecture, and advertising.
- *Aesthetic values.* Many people find beauty or aesthetic value in various aspects of ecosystems, as reflected in the support for parks, "scenic drives," and the selection of housing locations.
- *Social relations.* Ecosystems influence the types of social relations that are established in particular cultures. Fishing societies, for example, differ in many respects in their social relations from nomadic herding or agricultural societies.
- *Sense of place.* Many people value the "sense of place" that is associated with recognized features of their environment, including aspects of the ecosystem.
- *Cultural heritage values.* Many societies place high value on the maintenance of either historically important landscapes ("cultural landscapes") or culturally significant species.
- *Recreation and ecotourism.* People often choose where to spend their leisure time based in part on the characteristics of the natural or cultivated landscapes in a particular area.

Cultural services are tightly bound to human values and behavior, as well as to human institutions and patterns of social, economic, and political organization. Thus perceptions of cultural services are more likely to differ among individuals and communities than, say, perceptions of the importance of food production. The issue of valuing ecosystem services is addressed in Chapter 6.

Supporting Services

Supporting services are those that are necessary for the production of all other ecosystem services. They differ from provisioning, regulating, and cultural services in that their impacts on people are either indirect or occur over a very long time, whereas changes in the other categories have relatively direct and short-term impacts on people. (Some services, like erosion control, can be categorized as both a supporting and a regulating service, depending on the time scale and immediacy of their impact on people.) For example, humans do not directly use soil formation services, although changes in this would indirectly affect people through the impact on the provisioning service of food production. Similarly, climate regulation is categorized as a regulating service since ecosystem changes can have an impact on local or global climate over time scales relevant to human decision-making (decades or centuries), whereas the production of oxygen gas (through photosynthesis) is categorized as a supporting service since any impacts on the concentration of oxygen in the atmosphere would only occur over an extremely long time. Some other examples of supporting services are primary production, production of atmospheric oxygen, soil formation and retention, nutrient cycling, water cycling, and provisioning of habitat.

A Multisectoral Approach

Every part of Earth produces a bundle of ecosystem services. (See Box 6.3.) Human interventions can increase some services, though often at the expense of other ones. Thus human interventions have dramatically increased food provisioning services through the spread of agricultural technologies, although this has resulted in changes to other services such as water regulation. For this reason, a multisectoral approach is essential to fully evaluate changes in ecosystem services and their impacts on people. The multisectoral approach examines the supply and condition of each ecosystem service as well as the interactions among them. The MA has adopted just such an approach.

When assessing ecosystem services, it is often convenient to bound the analysis spatially and temporally with reference to the ecosystem service or services being examined. Thus a river basin is often the most valuable ecosystem scale for examining changes in water services, while a particular agroecological zone may be more appropriate for assessing changes in crop production. When looking at interactions among services, the combination of services provided by an ecosystem, or the variety of services drawn on by a society, the question of boundaries becomes more complex.

Biodiversity and Ecosystem Services

Habitat modification, invasion, and many other factors are leading to changes in biodiversity across many taxa within most ecosystems. Recently, theoretical and empirical work has identified linkages between changes in biodiversity and the way ecosystems function (Schulze and Mooney 1993; Loreau et al. 2002). The MA will address how ecosystem services are affected by such linkages.

Among the most important factors identified is the degree of functional redundancy found within an ecosystem. This indicates the substi-tutability of species within functional groups in an ecosystem such that the impact created by the loss of one or more species is compensated for by others (Naeem 1998). For example, in many ecosystems there are several species that fix nitrogen (known as a functional group of species). If the loss of any one of them is compensated for by the growth of others and there is no overall loss in nitrogen fixation, then there is functional redundancy in that ecosystem.

Some species make unique or singular contributions to ecosystem functioning, however, and therefore their loss is of greater concern (Walker 1992). Small changes in the biodiversity of diverse systems may lead to only small changes in the functioning of an ecosystem, including its production of services, providing no species with unique roles are lost (Jones et al. 1994; Power et al. 1996). But the possibility of significant losses of function increases as more species are lost and as redundancy is reduced—that is, there

Box 6.3 Analysis of Ecosystem Services

Any region of Earth produces a set of services that in turn influences human well-being. It also receives flows of energy, water, organisms, pollutants, and other materials from adjacent regions and releases similar materials into those regions. Various strategies and interventions influence the quantity and quality of the services provided.

An ecosystem is typically composed of a number of different regions, such as forest, agriculture, and urban areas, each of which produces a different bundle of services. In an ecosystem assessment, both the production of services from each area and the flows of materials between areas must be assessed.

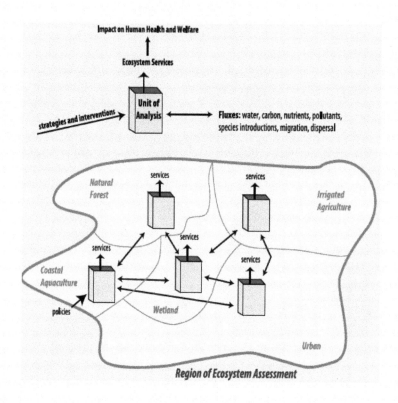

is an asymptotic relationship between biodiversity and ecosystem functioning. For example, the high diversity of South African fynbos ecosystems ensures steady rates of production because many plant species can compensate for losses by growing when others cannot (Cowling et al. 1994). Greater redundancy represents greater insurance that an ecosystem will continue to provide both higher and more predictable levels of services (Yachi and Loreau 1999).

The MA will seek to evaluate biodiversity and potential declines in biodiversity for different ecosystems under a set of different scenarios for plausible changes in driving forces. This work will extend previous studies that developed scenarios for biodiversity change (Sala et al. 2000). For provisioning and supporting services, the MA will identify which ecosystem functions are associated with these services and link their response to declining biodiversity, using the fundamental asymptotic relationship between biodiversity and ecosystem functioning. Both magnitudes and stability responses to biodiversity loss can be considered using this fundamental relationship.

Ecosystem Condition and Sustainable Use

People seek multiple and different services from ecosystems and thus perceive the condition of an ecosystem in relation to its ability to provide the services desired. The ability of ecosystems to deliver particular services can be assessed separately with various methods and measures. An adequate assessment of the condition of ecosystems, the provision of services, and their implications for human well-being (see Chapter 3) requires an integrated approach. With such an assessment in hand, a decision process (see Chapter 8) can then determine which set of services are valued most highly (see Chapter 6) and can manage the system in a sustainable way.

In a narrow sense, the sustainability of the production of a particular ecosystem service can refer simply to whether the biological potential of the ecosystem to sustain the yield of that service (such as food production) is being maintained. Thus a fish provision service is sustainable if the surplus but not the resource base is harvested, and if the fish's habitat is not degraded by human activities. In the MA, we use the term "sustained yield management" to refer to the management and yield of an individual resource or ecosystem service.

More generally, however, sustainability is used in the context of "sustainable development" to refer to a pattern of development that meets current needs without diminishing prospects for future generations. We use sustainability, and sustainable management, to refer to this goal of ensuring that a wide range of services from a particular ecosystem is sustained.

The MA will consider criteria and methods to provide an integrated approach to ecosystem assessment. The condition and sustainability of each category of ecosystem services is evaluated in somewhat different ways, although in general a full assessment of any service requires considerations of stocks, flows, and resilience.

Condition of Provisioning Services

The flows of provisioning services do not accurately reflect their condition, since a given flow may or may not be sustainable over the long term. The flow is typically measured in terms of biophysical production, such as kilograms of maize per hectare or tons of tuna landings. The provisioning of ecological goods such as food, fuelwood, or fiber, depends both on the flow and the "stock" of the good, just as is the case with manufactured goods. (In economics, "stock" refers to the total merchandise kept on hand by a merchant; in this section, we use "stock" in its economic sense to show how considerations of ecosystem goods can be incorporated into the economic framework of stocks and flows.) The quantity of goods sold by a manufacturer (the flow), for example, is an incomplete measure of a factory's productivity, since it could come from either the production of new goods or the depletion of built-up stocks. Indeed, production of biological resources has often been maintained in the short term at a higher rate than its sustainable yield. In the long term, the production of overharvested resources will fall.

Marine fisheries provide examples of an ecosystem service being degraded even while output has been temporarily maintained or increased by more intensive harvesting. Numerous fisheries around the world have been overharvested, exhibiting a general pattern of rapid growth in landings (production) followed by the eventual collapse of the fishery. (See Box 6.4.) Similar patterns can be found with virtually all other provisioning services.

Agricultural production, for example, can be maintained through the addition of fertilizers and through new crop varieties even while the productive potential of the ecosystem is degraded through soil erosion. Some 40 percent of agricultural land has been strongly or very strongly degraded in the past 50 years by erosion, salinization, compaction, nutrient depletion, biological degradation, or pollution even while overall global food production has increased (WRI et al. 2000). So long as manufactured capital can compensate for losses of the natural capital of the ecosystem, agricultural production can be maintained. In this case, however, manufactured and natural capital are not perfectly substitutable, and once a critical level of soil degradation is reached, agricultural output will decline. A complete accounting of the condition of food production would reveal that it has been degraded because the underlying capability of the ecosystem to maintain production has been degraded.

Historically, it has not been common for environmental or resource assessments to include measures of the productive potential of biological resources when monitoring the condition of the resource. Thus although all countries have considerable information on the production of grain, fisheries, and timber, relatively little is known about the actual condition of these services since the productive potential of the resource has rarely been evaluated. The Pilot Analysis of Global Ecosystems, which was prepared by the World Resources Institute and the International Food Policy Research Institute to assist in the MA design, attempted to provide a more complete assessment of the condition of ecosystem services along these lines (Matthews et al. 2000; Revenga et al. 2000; White et al. 2000; Wood et al. 2000).

Condition of Regulating, Cultural, and Supporting Services

In the case of regulating services, as opposed to provisioning services, the level of "production" is generally not relevant. Instead the condition of the service depends more on whether the ecosystem's capability to regulate a particular service has been enhanced or diminished. Thus if forest clearance in a region has resulted in decreased precipitation and this has had harmful consequences for people, the condition of that regulatory service has been degraded.

The evaluation of the condition of cultural services is more difficult. Some cultural services are linked to a provisioning service (such as recreational fishing or hunting) that can serve as a proxy measure of the cultural service. But in most cases no such proxy exists. Moreover, unlike provisioning or regulating services, assessing the condition of cultural services depends heavily on either direct or indirect human use of the service. For

Box 6.4   Collapse of the Atlantic Cod Fishery

The Atlantic cod stocks off the east coast of Newfoundland collapsed in 1992, forcing the closure of the fishery after hundreds of years of exploitation. Until the late 1950s, the fishery was exploited by migratory seasonal fleets and resident inshore small-scale fishers. From the late 1950s, offshore bottom trawlers began exploiting the deeper part of the stock, leading to a large catch increase and a strong decline in the underlying biomass. Internationally agreed quotas in the early 1970s and, following the declaration by Canada of an Exclusive Fishing Zone in 1977, national quota systems ultimately failed to arrest and reverse the decline.

Two factors that contributed to the collapse of the cod stock were the shift to heavy fishing off-shore and the use of fishery assessment methods that relied too much on scientific sampling and models based on the relatively limited time series and geographical coverage of the offshore part of the fish stocks. Traditional inshore fishers, whose landings account for one third to one half of the total, had noticed the decline in landings even before the mid-1980s, ahead of the scientists involved in fisheries assessment work but these observations could not be used in stock assessments because of technical difficulties in converting the catches into a suitable form. Finlayson (1994) noted that "science will confer the status of 'valid' only on very specific forms of data presented in a very specialized format."

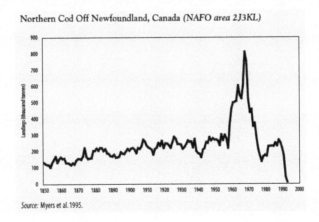

Northern Cod Off Newfoundland, Canada (NAFO *area* 2J3KL)

Source: Myers et al. 1995.

example, the condition of a regulating service such as water quality might be high even if humans are not using the clean water produced, but an ecosystem provides cultural services only if there are people who value the cultural heritage associated with it.

Information about the condition of cultural services can be obtained by identifying the specific features of the ecosystem that are of cultural, spiritual, or aesthetic significance and then examining trends in those

Box 6.5   Dynamics and Stability in Ecosystem Services

This figure illustrates the level of provisioning of an ecosystem service that has been perturbed twice. Hypothetically, such a service exhibits stochastic (random or uncontrolled) and inherent variability (fluctuations above and below the two horizontal lines, which represent different system states). The system recovers after the first perturbation, with its resilience being measured by the duration of the recovery phase or return time to its first state. Note that crossing the threshold of the second state does not cause a shift when in the first state. The second perturbation causes the service to cross the second threshold, which leads to a regime shift or catastrophic change to an alternative stable state. The long dashed lines illustrate two thresholds. Only when a system crosses a threshold does it switch to an alternate state.

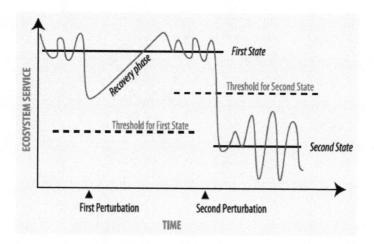

features. For example, salmon are a totemic or revered species in almost all parts of the world where they are found, and thus the degradation of wild salmon stocks represents degradation of a cultural service provided by the ecosystem. But cultural service information such as this would be difficult to obtain and to quantify: tigers, for instance, remain totemic species even in areas where they have been extinct for decades. Recognizing that the concept of cultural services is relatively new, the MA will explore methods for evaluating the condition and value of these services.

Supporting services maintain the conditions for life on Earth but may affect people only indirectly (by supporting the production of another service, as soil formation supports food production) or over very long time periods (such as the role of ecosystems in producing oxygen). Because the link to human benefits is indirect, as opposed to the other ecosystem services just discussed, a normative scale for assessing the condition of a service is not always practical. For example, primary production is a fundamental supporting service, since life requires the production of organic compounds. But if global primary production were to increase by 5 percent over the next century, it would be difficult to categorize the change as an enhancement or degradation of the service, though it certainly would be a significant change. In such cases the MA will report on the current biophysical state (production, flux, and stocks) of the supporting service.

Variability, Resilience, and Thresholds in Services

Whenever possible, individuals and governments generally invest in various types of insurance that can buffer human welfare against natural variability. Such investments may be as basic as establishing limited stores of food, medicine, and potable water for disaster relief to more elaborate investments such as building dams, levies, and canals to guard against 100-year floods. How, when, and where to invest in such insurance requires assessing not just mean levels of stocks and flows of ecosystem services but also their dynamics or, more specifically, their variability and stability.

Three characteristics of ecosystem services are important in such an assessment: ecosystem variability, resilience, and thresholds. (See Box 6.5.) There are many other properties of stability in dynamic systems (such as resistance, sensitivity, persistence, reliability, predictability, and so forth), but the MA will limit its focus to these three important and well-studied stability properties.

Variability in ecosystem services consists of changes in stocks or flows over time due to stochastic, intrinsic, and extrinsic factors, all of which must be disentangled to understand system behavior properly. Stochastic variability is due to random or uncontrolled factors creating variability that is often considered background or "white" noise in system behavior. In contrast, intrinsic (inherent) variability is due to the structural properties of an ecosystem, such as oscillations in systems where predation or disease regulate the number of animals. Examples of extrinsic variability, due to forces outside the system, include seasonality in temperate systems and longer-term climate systems such as El Niño-La Nina cycles.

Resilience is most often considered a measure of the ability of a system to return to its original state after a perturbation—a deviation in conditions that is outside the range experienced over a decade or more, such as a large-scale fire or an unusually severe drought. When the duration of the recovery phase is short in comparison to other systems, the system is considered to be more resilient than the others.

Thresholds or breakpoints in ecosystems represent dramatic, usually sudden (less than a decade) deviations from average system behavior. Such dramatic shifts—also known as regime shifts, catastrophic change, or entering alternative stable states—are often primed by a steady change in internal or external conditions that increases a system's susceptibility to being triggered to enter an alternative state (Scheffer et al. 2001; Carpenter 2003). For example, on a global scale, small, steady increases in global warming may lead to a sudden reorganization of Earth's ocean circulation patterns (Broecker 1997). On a local scale, the increase in grazing animals by ranchers or herders may be responsible for shifts in steppe (grass-dominated) to tundra (moss-dominated) ecosystems (Zimov et al. 1995).

While management goals are often conceived in terms of stocks and flows, reducing system variability and improving predictability are often key parts of management strategies. Examples of such interventions include irrigating crops during droughts, using biocides during pest outbreaks, controlled burning to prevent catastrophic fires, and culling herds to prevent a population explosion. Maintaining forests to prevent erosion or coral reefs to prevent wave impacts in the face of severe storms are examples of managing ecosystems for their insurance value. Ecosystem variability is often addressed through a variety of methods, but management aimed at maintaining ecosystem resilience and avoiding thresholds is sometimes overlooked. In part this is because the mechanisms responsible for such behavior are seldom known, so it is difficult to design management that can deal with resilience or thresholds. In addition, there are no accurate assessments of the probability of perturbations, and the time frame over which such events occur is too long.

The costs to human welfare of ecosystem deviation from its norms of behavior, however, are often severe, thus its inclusion in assessments and management is important. The MA will examine not only magnitudes of ecosystem stocks and flows as they are related to ecosystem goods and services, but also their stability properties. Much of this will be done by extrapolation from expert assessment of paleo records (for instance, climate records derived from ice cores) and historical records (such as long-term fisheries, forestry, or agricultural records) to obtain guidelines on the norms of system variability, resilience, known thresholds, and the environmental stresses that cause ecosystems to be triggered by perturbations to enter into alternative states.

Ecosystem Health and Other Related Concepts

Ecosystem health is a concept that has often been applied to the evaluation of ecosystems (Rapport et al. 1995). This has become a subdiscipline in the life sciences, with its own journals and professional organizations, such as the International Society for Ecosystem Health (ISEH) and the Aquatic Ecosystem Health and Management Society. The term is used sometimes to mean the links between ecosystems and human health. For example, the mission of ISEH is to "encourage the understanding of the critical linkages between human activity, ecological change and human health" (Rapport et al. 1999:83). It is also used to refer to the health of the ecosystem itself: "an ecological system is healthy ... if it is stable and sustainable—that is, if it is active and maintains its organization and autonomy over time and is resilient to stress" (Costanza et al. 1992:9).

This concept has generated debate and alternative approaches within the scientific literature (e.g., Reid 1996; de Leo and Levin 1997). One method measures health as a departure from some preferred (often "natural") state. Another, which is consistent with the approach used in the MA to examine the condition of ecosystem services, relates health to the ability of an ecosystem within its surrounding landscape to continue to provide a particular set of services. This considers whether the ecosystem and its external inputs (such as energy or fertilizer) are sustainable in the long term as well as whether the ecosystem can withstand or recover from perturbations (resistance and resilience, respectively) and similar issues.

The concept of ecosystem health is important both within the research community and as a means of communicating information about ecosystems to the general public. Although the MA has not adopted ecosystem health as its primary organizational framework, the concept could be usefully applied within an assessment that used the MA framework.

Several other concepts will also inform the MA without being adopted as organizational frameworks. For instance, ecosystem integrity has been defined as "the maintenance of the community structure and function characteristic of a particular locale or deemed satisfactory to society" (Cairns 1977: 56) or "the capability of supporting and maintaining a balanced, integrated, adaptive community of organisms having species composition, diversity, and functional organization comparable to that of natural habitats of the region" (Karr and Dudley 1981:171). Another example is the "ecological footprint," which expresses the impact of human activity on ecosystems in terms of areas required to provide the services used by an individual or community.

Substitution of Services

Substitutes are available for some ecosystem services, although often the cost of a technological substitution will be high and it may not replace all the services lost. For example, water treatment plants can now substitute for ecosystems in providing clean drinking water, although this may be expensive and will not overcome the impacts of water pollution on other components of the ecosystem and the services they provide. Another outcome of substitution is that often the individuals gaining the benefits are not those who originally benefited from the ecosystem services. For example, local coastal fish production can be replaced by shrimp aquaculture in tropical regions, but the individuals making a living from capture fisheries are not those who would profit from the new shrimp aquaculture facilities.

Therefore, a full assessment of ecosystems and their services must consider:

- information on the cost of a substitute,
- the opportunity cost of maintaining the service,
- cross-service costs and impacts, and
- the distributional impacts of any substitution.

Sustainable Approaches and Case Studies

PART
2

THE EVOLVING HUMAN RELATIONSHIP WITH THE ENVIRONMENT

Traditional Landscape Management

BY MARY MYERS

Humans have had a dependent and enduring relationship with the environment over the millennia. For nearly our entire existence, people have been hunter-gatherer societies, relying directly upon the environment for food and shelter. Knowledge of plants and animals was necessary for survival. But local environments could support only a limited number of each species, including humans. This led to dispersal throughout the world, with humans adjusting to more and more difficult places and climates. Adjustment was facilitated by our powers of observation; ability to make connections between different realms of knowledge; and capacity to project into the future. People have adapted to extreme places from the tropics to the polar regions without the use of sophisticated technologies. Some hunter-gatherer societies persisted into the 20th century but very few remain today due to their assimilation into dominant cultures. This chapter covers some of the land-management practices of traditional peoples because those practices have relevance today. Aboriginal peoples are the original sustainable designers because their practices worked within nature's cycles.

THE INNU: POPULATION LIMITS IN A HUNTING SOCIETY

Figure 7.1. Inuit Woman and infant. The Inuit and Innu tribes both live in the northern part of North America and are related.

One hunter-gatherer society, the Innu of northern Labrador, was studied by anthropologist Georg Henriksen. He traveled to the northern Labrador coast to conduct field research in the mid 1960's, at a time when the Innu population still migrated by dog sleds to the interior (called the "barrens") to hunt caribou in winter. The barrens is a landscape of open plains, lakes, and rivers with small patches of conifers, where the Innu pitched their tents. Henriksen described it as an arctic environment where winter temperatures can range from minus 40° to minus 80°C (Henriksen, p. 8). Henriksen camped with the Innu and recorded conversations with them, describing their way of life, hunting approaches, and eventual settlement in permanent coastal villages.

For centuries the tribe had survived, as most hunter-gatherer peoples have, by moving with the herd. Caribou were the staple of the Innu diet, supplemented by bear, porcupine, fish, and ptarmigan. Most important, Henriksen points out, "(t)he caribou played a pivotal role in the culture and social life…It was through hunting, lavish sharing of meat and hides, and the making of beautiful moccasins, snowshoes and other products that men and women gained prestige and renown" (Henriksen, p. 9).

Additionally, although the Innu territory was vast, it did not provide enough food resources for a large human population. The Innu were limited in what they could hunt and store. They were aware that over-hunting one season could cause starvation the next. Weather conditions effecting food supply, predation, and disease cause natural fluctuation in all animal species. Thus the caribou population varied from year to year. The Innu tried to adjust their own population "to the bottom level of the caribou cycle, that is when the number of animals was at its lowest" (Henriksen, p. 11). They acknowledged that the environment is not inexhaustible and that human welfare is directly related to that of other species.

Other native peoples such as the Lenni Lenape (or Delaware) also practiced population control. In addition, they actively stewarded and managed natural resources. Wild plants were harvested at particular frequencies and animal herds culled at specific intensities.

MANAGING THE LANDSCAPE FOR FOOD AND BASKETRY

Figure 7.2. A basket woven by Californian Miwok-Mono Paiute Native American named Lucy Telles shows the craft and beauty of basketry. Note the birds, plants, butterflies, and other insects incorporated in the pattern.

Much of what we consider wilderness today was in fact shaped by Indian burning, harvesting, tilling, pruning, sowing and tending.... (Anderson, p. 8)

Ethnobotanists use a variety of techniques to understand how traditional peoples managed land. They compare historic records with current plant distribution, and look at plant remains from archaeological sites to understand if plants are local or were introduced through trade (Lepofsky and Lertzman, p. 133).

Indigenous tribes of Northwest North America lived in a region extending from Alaska to southern Oregon and into the Pacific Coast regions. There is evidence that people managed the northwest landscape for at least 2,400 years through selecting and planting vigorous plants, and conducting prescribed forest burns. For example, to increase hardy root vegetables, people selected and planted the largest tubers and bulbs. To increase their favorite foods, they are thought to have collected and scattered seed. Prescribed forest burns were used to benefit certain plants, such as *Vaccinium sp.*, blueberries. Evidence indicates that the burns were of relatively brief duration in relatively small areas. Then, as now, the burns were probably managed by specialists to ensure that they did not get out of control and do unwanted damage.

Field research in the Northwest has also uncovered high concentrations of fruit-bearing plants, such as *Rubus spectabilis*, salmonberries; *Amelanchior alnifolia*, Saskatoon berries; and *Malus fusco*, Pacific crabapples, found in specific locations. The plants have similar, preferred characteristics of berry color and taste and "suggest that (they) were particularly tended, or even transplanted to these locations" (Lepofsky and Lertzman, p. 132).

Indigenous peoples developed and used many types of objects and tools in daily life. Anderson (2005) documented the native Californians' use and creation of baskets. Baskets were an important feature of everyday life. They were vessels used to transport objects and to collect and store foodstuffs. Many different types and sizes were crafted. The Californian tribes sought out and probably assisted plants that exhibited qualities of flexibility, straightness, and pleasing bark color without blemishes. "Basketmakers adhered to the strict practice of using only young (first, second, or third year) growth for making baskets" (Anderson, 1999, p. 83).

Like other peoples, the California tribes prized the craft and aesthetic aspect of baskets, as well as their function. Anderson identifies the plants most widely used for California baskets: *Cercis* (redbud); *Ceanothus* (wild lilac); Corylus (hazelnut); *Rhus* (sumac); and *Salix* (willow). She also explains that these plants do well with disturbance, such as fire or heavy pruning, which benefit adaptive traits, such as flexibility and straightness" (Anderson, 1999, p. 82). The interest in how native peoples used the landscape sustainably is driving more research into their land-management practices. Understanding the practices and the underlying approach and relationship with the land can help to guide contemporary practice.

MENOMINEE FOREST STEWARDSHIP

The needs of the forest drive the production and marketing processes at Menominee Tribal Enterprises. Manufacturing and marketing do not drive the forest harvest. (Menominee Tribal Enterprises MTE, p. 19)

Nurturing and managing woodland plants is a practice that continues today among the Menominee tribe of southern Wisconsin. Their cultural beliefs have guided decisions related to forest management on their lands. They are now recognized as producing very high-quality timber products within a sustainable framework. Menominee practices are studied by other tribes and businesses.

Cultural Values and Planning Process

Figure 7.3. Menominee spear fishing at night. The tribe obtained all its needs from the environment, subsisting on fish, deer, and other animals, cranberries, blueberries, maple sugar, and wild rice. Trees were harvested for birchbark canoes and wigwams and teepees. Paul Kane.

The Menominee describe themselves as "woodland people" who are deeply connected with the "spirit" of the forest, and all of the animals and plants within the forest. They have lived in this particular place for about 5,000 years and are very attached to it. Concern for forest health has guided Menominee timbering decisions during the past two centuries. In fact, sustained yield was written into the tribe's constitution. The reservation land is not owned by individuals but by the entire community. Decisions are made by consensus—that is, by unanimous vote. This form of decision making is also practiced by certain religious groups, such as the Society of Friends (Quakers).

Interestingly, consensus-oriented groups have tended to make positive decisions related to sustainability and the environment. In the Philadelphia area, the Quakers have led in developing buildings and landscapes that express their values of environmental stewardship.

During the late 1800's and mid-1900's, the Menominee fought federal and state policy changes that would have damaged or destroyed their forest. The first of these was the notion that reservation land that is timbered should be agricultural. The tribe rejected this idea knowing that the land was not suited for farming but for sustained-yield forestry. The second policy change was a legislation that put the community-owned land into the hands of private individuals. Such a policy was in direct conflict with the tribe's communal principles. This act was fought through litigation and eventually overturned.

The Menominee Reservation is composed of 235,000 acres with about 233,000 acres in trust status. Of this, about 217,000 acres are commercial forested acres, the majority of which is under active forest management (http://www.mtewood.com/Forestry/Forest). The reservation land also includes 123 lakes and 400 miles of rivers and streams (MTE "The Forest Keepers," 1997. P.10). The clarity and overall water quality of the lakes and streams is valued by the tribe. While a lumber mill has been operating on the reservation since the 1800's, it was understood that timbering actions would affect water and soil quality. A policy followed the general principles of one of their great chiefs:

> *Start with the rising sun and work toward the setting sun. But take only the mature trees, the sick trees and the trees that have fallen. When you reach the end of the reservation, turn and cut from the setting sun to the rising sun and the trees will last forever.* (Attributed to Chief Oshkosh, around 1860)

Scientific principles and advice from expert foresters help guide the forest harvesting plan, which extends out 150 years. This long time span is roughly the planning window espoused by the Iroquois nation, who suggested that leaders should consider the effects of their decisions on their children seven generations hence. The Menominee 150-year span is broken into ten segments, or fifteen-year cycles. Each cycle is "determined through scientific processes used to ascertain harvesting schedules and provide optimum conditions for forest health, diversity, productivity and quality" (MTE, p. 19).

Figure 7.4. Menominee woods showing dense mixed forest on both sides of the road.

Menominee land is located at the intersection of two plant zones. The forest is diverse because it includes coniferous trees common in the northern part of the state and deciduous trees found in the southern part of the region. In total thirty-three different tree species are found on the reservation, twenty-five of which are used for timber. "The Menominee reservation contains 11 of the 16 major types of forest habitat in Wisconsin...All species originally found on the reservation continue to persist there, with the exception of the elm" (Landis).

Table 7.1

MENOMINEE FOREST COVER TYPE	PERCENTAGE OF OVERALL FOREST
Northern Hardwoods	32%
White Pine	16%
Swamp Conifers	10%
Aspen	9%
Mid-Tolerant Hardwoods	7%
Red Oak	6%

Source: (http://www.mtewood.com/Forestry/Forest) overview: accessed January 5, 2013."

Management strategies focus on maintaining diversity of tree type and age of stand. While there are mature, stately 200-year-old trees, there are also young sprouts found in shelterwood zones, and the pioneer aspen and birch species found in clearcut areas.

The Menominee Tribal Enterprises 1997 Report lays out the practices used for harvesting the trees: selective cutting, shelterwood cutting, and clear cutting. The selective cutting follows Chief Oshkosh's principle of taking mature, sick, and fallen trees. Trees past maturity, of poor quality, or that are not likely to survive until the next cutting are harvested. Selective cutting does not thin the canopy, so the understory continues to flourish within approximately the same conditions as prior to the cut. Trees such as hemlock, beech, sugar maple, and basswood benefit from this approach because they need dense shade to regenerate. "Selection cutting works best for species that can regenerate in full shade like sugar maple, beech, hemlock and basswood. The selection method results in a forest of all classes of trees" (MBE, p. 13). This method also results in trees that are older, bigger, and have highly valued wood when they are felled. So the quality of the lumber is better, along with the quality of the living forest. In 2004, well-known architect Frank Gehry chose to use Menominee sugar maple for his prize-winning furniture. Not only was the maple sustainably harvested, it produced beautiful chairs that won awards for their unique design.

Certain tree species, such as oak, require sunlight for regeneration. The shelterwood harvesting technique supports those species by removing a tree stand gradually over time. Fifty to sixty percent of the mature trees are cut, allowing sunlight in for sprouting of new seedlings. Eventually all but a few large trees, are removed to transition the forest to a new, younger forest where the trees have ample sunlight to grow quickly. The old trees that remain provide sources of seed for the new trees and habitat for certain animals. As the name implies, trees not cut serve as shelter and Downs, et al. (2011) studied the effect of the shelterwood approach on oak regeneration in Ohio forests. They found that it was successful in regenerating new trees although competing vegetation might pose a problem. They proposed prescribed burns for managing competing species. The Menominee use controlled burns as part of their forest-management strategy.

Clear cutting removes all of the trees in a particular area. The Menominee use clear cutting to regenerate species such as red pine, jack pine, and aspen, which need full light. Raspberries and blackberries frequently come into clearcut areas, providing food for wildlife such as bear and birds. Although it is a legitimate approach to developing an early successional landscape, of which there are few on the reservation, it is still controversial among the tribe. Clear cuts are a means of developing a different ecosystem type and of increasing diversity of ecosystems. However, they are unsightly things initially. On other state and federal lands, clearcut sites are frequently hidden from view, but not here. The effects of forest management decisions are out in the open for the public to see and discuss (Landis). This aspect of the Menominee management is quite interesting. It infers that since the land is owned by everyone, all forms of management should be visible. This allows practices to be commented upon, criticized, and perhaps improved or changed. It is quite a different approach from the standard American view that private landowners have the right to do what they wish with their own property even if it damages the land or reduces its ecological integrity.

Aldo Leopold's *Land Ethic*, found in a later chapter of this book, promotes a different approach, suggesting that the land has integrity in its own right and that it should not be viewed as a chattel. His view corresponds more closely with that of many traditional peoples. The Menominee, Innu, California, and Northwest peoples share a view of landscape management grounded in a philosophy emphasizing long-term ecological integrity of the land. The role of humans is to manage and steward the land sustainably in order to "meet current needs without compromising those of future generations." Perhaps we should be looking to traditional or ancient practices as a basis for sustainable design, agriculture, and land management.

QUESTIONS

1. How do politics affect sustainability?
2. How do economics affect sustainability?
3. The Innu approach to population control was based upon what? How does this relate to sustainability?
4. What traditional land management practices or attitudes might you use in setting up an urban farm?
5. Identify a benefit and challenge for using Native American approaches to land management.
6. In 1997, the Menominee tribe noted:

   During the last 140 years we have harvested more than 2.5 billion board foot of lumber from our land. That is the equivalent of cutting all the standing timber on the reservation almost twice over. Yet, the saw timber volume now standing is greater than that which was here in 1854 when the Wolf River Treaty defined the Reservation.... (MTE, p. 19)

   This means that although a significant amount of timber has been cut, the forest has increased. How has this happened?

REFERENCES

Anderson, M. Kat. 1999. "The Fire, Pruning, and Coppice Management of Temperate Ecosystems for Basketry Material by California Indian Tribes." *Human Ecology.* 27:1: 79–113.

Anderson, M. Kat. 2005. *Tending the Wild: Native American Knowledge and the Management of California's Natural Resources.* Berkeley and Los Angeles: University of California Press.

Downs, James D., Roger A. Williams, and Joni A. Downs. 2011. "The Effects of Shelterwood Harvesting on Oak Regeneration Two Years After Harvest in Southern Ohio." Proceedings, *17th Central Hardwood Forest Conference;* 2010 April 5–7; Lexington, KY; Gen. Tech. Rep. NRS-P-78. Newtown Square, PA: U.S. Department of Agriculture, Forest Service, Northern Research Station: 262–269.

Henriksen, Georg. 2009. *I Dreamed the Animals, Kaniuekutat: The Life of an Innu Hunter.* New York: Berghahn Books. (http://www.mtewood.com/Forestry/Forest) overview: accessed January 5, 2013.

Landis, Scott. 1992. "Seventh-Generation Forestry: Wisconsin Menominee Indians Set the Standard for Sustainable Forest Management." *Harrowsmith Country Life*, November, 1992.

Lepofsky, Dana and Ken Lertzman. 2008. "Documenting Ancient Plant Management in the Northwest of North America." *Botany.* 86: 129–145.

"Menominee Tribal Enterprises: The Forest Keepers." 1997. The Menominee Forest Based Sustainable Development Tradition. (http://www.epa.gov/ecopage/upland/menominee/forestkeepers.pdf).

Trosper, Ronald L. 2007. "Indigenous Influence on Forest Management on the Menominee Indian Reservation" *Forest Ecology and Management* 249 134–139.

CREDITS

ENDURING DESIGN

BY MARY MYERS

More than half of the world currently lives in cities. This trend is likely to continue as population increases. Future cities are likely to include both historic and new buildings and many different scales of green space with multiple functions. Projects should integrate sustainability, function, and beauty. Beautiful design inspires people's care, or stewardship, ensuring that it will persist for many decades or centuries. Longevity is a feature of sustainability because it conserves matter and energy.

Humans use art and design to acknowledge, record, and celebrate their relationship with the world around them. Art is defined as: "a visual object or experience consciously created through an expression of skill or imagination" (http://www.merriam-webster.com/dictionary/art). Design is defined as the modification of a place, object, or process with intention or purpose. While design usually has a clear, functional purpose, it can also be artful and express imaginative and aesthetic ideas. Objects such as, textiles, vessels, clothing, and furniture can be so thoughtfully designed that they are admired for their beautiful form, finish, execution, and skill. Likewise, some buildings such as

Figure 8.1. Functional objects, such as shields, headdresses, baskets, and other vessels can have an aesthetic dimension that seems to cross the threshold of design and art.

Figure 8.2. Standing stones at Avebury, Wiltshire, England. The stone circle, built and altered between 2850 B.C. and 2200 B.C., encloses nearly 300 acres. Like many other Bronze and Iron age sites in Britain, this is thought to be a sacred site or monument. Its origins are mysterious but its beauty speaks across the ages.

Figure 8.3. Uffington Horse, Berkshire Downs, England.

the Roman Pantheon, and landscape designs such as Central Park, are considered works of art.

Ancient peoples, long dead, communicate with modern peoples through artifacts. Sometimes modern people are left to guess at the meaning or purpose of a particular work of art, such as the standing stones at Avebury or Stonehenge where huge stones were quarried and shaped with a purpose (Jellicoe and Jellicoe, p. 19). They were positioned as sculpture in the landscape, forming a sacred place. The purpose of the monumental circles is mysterious but seems to have been linked to worship and commemoration of the seasonal cycles.

The Uffington White Horse has been cared for since it originated in about 100 A.D. Jellicoe and Jellicoe (1982) write that Celtic people carved the 400-foot-long horse into the chalk-based soil. It is engraved into the ground and situated at the base of a steep hillside where it can be viewed from above. The horse is thought to be a symbol of the Celtic horse goddess Epona, representing fertility, healing, and death. It has a curvilinear Celtic design motif and a distinctly abstract and timeless style. For 2,000 years, people have maintained the Uffington horse, scraping plants and weeds away from the chalk and ensuring that nothing has been built on top of or too close to the engraving. This care indicates the appreciation people have for its timeless beauty. Timelessness is a distinctive characteristic of enduring design. When an object, landscape, or building is considered to be beautiful by many people, that appreciation can span generations. The object, building, or place is judged to be worthy of passing down to future generations. Its beauty is cared for through government protection and funding, or through private endowment or grassroots efforts.

Affection for and stewardship of beauty can play a pivotal role in protection of buildings and places. For example, the Pantheon in Rome has endured, changing from a Roman Temple to Christian Church. Visitors are struck with reverie as they gaze at the light beaming in from a single, round opening (oculus) in the ceiling that originated as an opening through which the gods could fly.

The earth is becoming increasingly populated and managed by humans, which means we will need to focus on conservation, restoration, and beautification. Landscapes, cities, and buildings will become more multifunctional—serving multiple purposes including an *aesthetic* purpose. (In traditional hunter-gatherer societies, landscapes were probably always viewed that way.)

In cities of the future, well-built and beautiful buildings and open space of all sizes will become more precious. Such places connect us with the past, allowing us to reflect on the beauty created and stewarded by former generations. While some new, large parks may be created, there are likely to be many small green spaces, including converted vacant lots or rail corridors, garden plots, rain gardens at the edges of streets, and linear greenways. Abandoned industrial zones of cities will be reclaimed and reinvented as valued green space capable of storing and cleaning stormwater, and converting carbon dioxide to oxygen. If designed with *beauty as a fundamental attribute*, the new urban landscape will contribute to the aesthetic pleasure and well-being of the city's inhabitants. This pleasure and appreciation can establish a cycle of human and landscape health—each contributing to the health and longevity of the other.

Figure 8.4. Painting of the interior of the Pantheon, Rome by Giovanni Panini (1692–1755) shows people conversing and marveling, as well as, praying. The single source of natural light is the oculus in the center of the roof, creating a powerful and ever-changing effect during the course of a day and season.

QUESTIONS

1. Recall and describe an ancient place, building, or artifact that you have seen. How do you think it was created and for what purpose?
2. Why do you think it has endured to the present day? What special features does it have?
3. What steps were necessary to protect it?

4. How does it relate to sustainability? What biogeochemical cycles (if any), or matter and energy laws does it support?

REFERENCES

Jellicoe, Geoffrey and Susan Jellicoe. 1975. *The Landscape of Man: Shaping the Environment from Prehistory to the Present Day.* Thames and Hudson Ltd., London.

(http://www.merriam-webster.com/dictionary/art). Accessed June 20, 2013.

Nassauer, Joan Iverson. 1997. "Cultural Sustainability: Aligning Aesthetics and Ecology" in *Placing Nature: Culture and Landscape Ecology.* Island Press: Washington, D.C.

CREDITS

WASTE EQUALS FOOD

BY WILLIAM MCDONOUGH AND MICHAEL BRAUNGART

Nature operates according to a system of nutrients and metabolisms in which there is no such thing as waste. A cherry tree makes many blossoms and fruit to (perhaps) germinate and grow. That is why the tree blooms. But the extra blossoms are far from useless. They fall to the ground, decompose, feed various organisms and microorganisms, and enrich the soil. Around the world, animals and humans exhale carbon dioxide, which plants take in and use for their own growth. Nitrogen from wastes is transformed into protein by microorganisms, animals, and plants. Horses eat grass and produce dung, which provides both nest and nourishment for the larvae of flies. The Earth's major nutrients—carbon, hydrogen, oxygen, nitrogen—are cycled and recycled. Waste equals food.

This cyclical, cradle-to-cradle biological system has nourished a planet of thriving, diverse abundance for millions of years. Until very recently in the Earth's history, it was the only system, and every living thing on the planet belonged to it. Growth was good. It meant more trees, more species, greater diversity, and more complex, resilient ecosystems. Then came industry, which altered the natural equilibrium of materials on the planet. Humans took substances from the Earth's crust and concentrated, altered, and synthesized them into vast quantities of material that cannot safely be returned to soil. Now material flows can be divided into two categories: biological mass and technical—that is, industrial—mass.

From our perspective, these two kinds of material flows on the planet are just *biological and technical nutrients*. Biological nutrients are useful to the biosphere, while technical nutrients are useful for what we call the *technosphere,* the systems of industrial processes. Yet somehow we have evolved an industrial infrastructure that ignores the existence of nutrients of either kind.

FROM CRADLE-TO-CRADLE TO CRADLE-TO-GRAVE: A BRIEF HISTORY OF NUTRIENT FLOWS

Long before the rise of agriculture, nomadic cultures wandered from place to place searching for food. They needed to travel light, so their possessions were few—some jewelry and a few tools, bags or clothes made of animal skins, baskets for roots and seeds. Assembled from local materials, these things, when their use was over, could easily decompose and be "consumed" by nature. The more durable objects, such as weapons of stone and flint, might be discarded. Sanitation was not a problem because the nomads were constantly moving. They could leave their biological wastes behind to replenish soil. For these people, there truly was an "away."

Early agricultural communities continued to return biological wastes to the soil, replacing nutrients. Farmers rotated crops, letting fields lie fallow in turn until nature made them fertile again. Over time new agricultural tools and techniques led to quicker food production. Populations swelled, and many communities began to take more resources and nutrients than could be naturally restored. With people more tightly packed, sanitation became a problem. Societies began to find ways to get rid of their wastes. They also began to take more and more nutrients from the soil and to eat up resources (such as trees) without replacing them at an equal rate.

There is an old Roman saying, *Pecunia non olet:* "Money doesn't stink." In Imperial Rome service people took wastes away frompublic spaces and the toilets of the wealthy and piled them outside the city. Agriculture and tree-felling drained soils of nutrients and led to erosion, and the landscape became drier and more arid, with less fertile cropland. Rome's imperialism—and imperialism in general—emerged in part in response to nutrient losses, the center expanding to support its vast needs with timber, food, and other resources elsewhere. (Tellingly, as the city's resources shrank and conquests grew, Rome's agricultural deity, Mars, became the god of war.)

William Cronon chronicles a similar relationship between a city and its natural environment in *Nature's Metropolis.* He points out that the great rural areas around Chicago, America's "breadbasket," were actually organized over time to provide services for that city; the settlement of the surrounding frontier did not happen in isolation from Chicago but was inextricably bound to the city and fueled by its needs. "The central story of the nineteenth-century West is that of an expanding metropolitan economy creating ever more elaborate and intimate linkages between city and country," Cronon observes. Thus the history of a city "must also be the history of its human countryside, and of the natural world within which city and country are both located."

As they swelled and grew, the great cities placed incredible pressure on the environment around them, sucking materials and resources from farther and farther away, as the land was stripped and resources taken.

For example, as the forests of Minnesota disappeared, logging moved on to British Columbia. (Such expansions affected native people; the Mandans of the upper Missouri were wiped out by smallpox, in a chain of events resulting from settlers staking homesteads.)

Over time cities all over the world built up an infrastructure for transferring nutrients from place to place. Cultures went into conflict with other cultures for resources, land, and food. In the nineteenth and early twentieth centuries, synthetic fertilizers were developed, laying the ground for the massively intensified production of industrialized agriculture. Soils now yield more crops than they naturally could, but with some severe effects: they are eroding at an unprecedented rate, and they are drained of nutrient-rich humus. Very few small farmers return local biological wastes to the soil as a primary source of nutrients any longer, and industrialized farming almost never does. Moreover, the synthetic fertilizers were often heavily contaminated with cadmium and radioactive elements from phosphate rocks, a hazard of which farmers and residents were generally unaware.

Yet certain traditional cultures have well understood the value of nutrient flows. For centuries in Egypt, the Nile River overflowed its banks each year, leaving a rich layer of silt across the valleys when waters withdrew. Beginning about 3200 B.C., farmers in Egypt structured a series of irrigation ditches that channeled the Nile's fertile waters to their fields.

They also learned to store food surpluses for periods of drought. The Egyptians maximized these nutrient flows for centuries without overtaxing them. Gradually, as British and French engineers entered the country during the nineteenth century, Egypt's agriculture shifted to Western methods. Since the completion of the Aswan High Dam in 1971, the silt that enriched Egypt for centuries now accumulates behind concrete, and people in Egypt build housing on once fertile areas originally reserved for crops. Houses and roads compete dramatically for space with agriculture. Egypt produces less than 50 percent of its own food and depends on imports from Europe and the United States.

Over thousands of years, the Chinese perfected a system that prevents pathogens from contaminating the food chain, and fertilized rice paddies with biological wastes, including sewage. Even today some rural households expect dinner guests to "return" nutrients in this way before they leave, and it is a common practice for farmers to pay households to fill boxes with their bodily wastes. But today the Chinese, too, have turned to systems based on the Western model. And, like Egypt, they are growing more dependent on imported foods.

Humans are the only species that takes from the soil vast quantities of nutrients needed for biological processes but rarely puts them back in a usable form. Our systems are no longer designed to return nutrients in this way, except on small, local levels. Harvesting methods like clear-cutting precipitate soil erosion, and chemical processes used in both agriculture and manufacture often lead to salinization and acidification, helping to deplete more than twenty times as much soil each year as nature creates. It can take approximately five hundred years for soil to build up an inch of its rich layers of microorganisms and nutrient flows, and right now we are losing five thousand times more soil than is being made.

In preindustrial culture, people did consume things. Most products would safely biodegrade once they were thrown away, buried, or burned. Metals were the exception: these were seen as highly valuable and were melted down and reused. (They were actually what we call early technical nutrients.) But as industrialization advanced, the consumption mode persisted, even though most manufactured items could no longer actually be consumed. In times of scarcity, a recognition of the value of technical materials would flare up; people who grew up during the Great Depression, for example, were careful about reusing jars, jugs, and aluminum foil, and during World War II, people saved rubber bands, aluminum foil, steel, and other materials to feed industrial needs. But as cheaper materials and new synthetics flooded the postwar market, it became less expensive for industries to make a new aluminum, plastic, or glass bottle or package at a central plant and ship it out than to build up local infrastructures for collecting, transporting, cleaning, and processing things for reuse. Similarly, in the early decades of industrialization, people might pass down, repair, or sell old service products like ovens, refrigerators, and phones to junk dealers. Today most so-called durables are tossed. (Who on Earth would repair a cheap toaster today? It is much easier to buy a new one than it is to send the parts back to the manufacturer or track down someone to repair it locally.) Throwaway products have become the norm.

There is no way, for example, that you are going to consume your car; and although it is made of valuable technical materials, you can't do anything with them once you finish with it (unless you are a junk artist). As we have mentioned, these materials are lost or degraded even in "recycling" because cars are not designed from the beginning for effective, optimal recycling as technical nutrients. Indeed, industries design products with built-in obsolescence—that is, to last until approximately the time customers typically want to replace them. Even things with a real consumable potential, such as packaging materials, are often deliberately designed not to break down under natural conditions. In fact, packaging may last far longer than the product it protected. In places where resources are hard to get, people still creatively reuse materials to make new products (such as using old tire rubber to make sandals) and even energy (burning synthetic materials for fuel). Such creativity is natural and adaptive and can be a vital part of material cycles. But as long as these uses are ignored by current industrial design and manufacturing, which typically refrain from embracing any vision of a product's further life, such reuse will often be unsafe, even lethal.

MONSTROUS HYBRIDS

Mountains of waste rising in landfills are a growing concern, but the quantity of these wastes—the space they take up—is not the major problem of cradle-to-grave designs. Of greater concern are the nutrients—valuable "food" for both industry and nature—that are contaminated, wasted, or lost. They are lost not only for lack of adequate systems of retrieval; they are lost also because many products are what we jokingly refer to as "Frankenstein products" or (with apologies to Jane Jacobs) "monstrous hybrids"— mixtures of materials both technical and biological, neither of which can be salvaged after their current lives.

A conventional leather shoe is a monstrous hybrid. At one time, shoes were tanned with vegetable chemicals, which were relatively safe, so the wastes from their manufacture posed no real problem. The shoe could biodegrade after its useful life or be safely burned. But vegetable tanning required that trees be harvested for their tannins. As a result, shoes took a long time to make, and they were expensive. In the past forty years, vegetable tanning has been replaced with chromium tanning, which is faster and cheaper. But chromium is rare and valuable for industries, and in some forms it is carcinogenic. Today shoes are often tanned in developing countries where few if any precautions are taken to protect people and ecosystems from chromium exposure; manufacturing wastes may be dumped into nearby bodies of water or incinerated, either of which distributes toxins (often disproportionately in low-income areas). Conventional rubber shoe soles, moreover, usually contain lead and plastics. As the shoe is worn, particles of it degrade into the atmosphere and soil. It cannot be safely consumed, either by you or by the environment. After use, its valuable materials, both biological and technical, are usually lost in a landfill.

A CONFUSION OF FLOWS

There may be no more potent image of disagreeable waste than sewage. It is a kind of waste people are happy to get "away" from. Before modern sewage systems, people in cities would dump their wastes outside (which might mean out the window), bury them, slop them into cesspools at the bottom of a house, or dispose of them in bodies of water, sometimes upstream from drinking sources. It wasn't until the late nineteenth century that people began to make the connection between sanitation and public health, which provided the impetus for more sophisticated sewage treatment. Engineers saw pipes taking storm water to rivers and realized this would be a convenient way to remove waterborne sewage. But that didn't end the problem. From time to time the disposal of raw sewage in rivers close to home became unbearable; during the Great Stink of London in 1858, for example, the reek of raw sewage in the nearby Thames disrupted sittings of the House of Commons. Eventually, sewage treatment plants were built to treat effluents and sized to accommodate waterborne sewage combined with added storm water during major rains.

The original idea was to take relatively active biologically based sewage, principally from humans (urine and excrement, the kind of waste that has interacted with the natural world for millennia), and render it harmless. Sewage treatment was a process of microbial and bacterial digestion. The solids were removed as sludge, and the remaining liquid, which had brought the sewage to treatment in the first place, could be released essentially as water. That was the original strategy. But once the volume of sewage overwhelmed the waterways into which it flowed, harsh chemical, treatments like chlorination were added to manage the process. At the same time, new products were being marketed for household use that were never designed with sewage treatment plants (or aquatic ecosystems) in mind. In addition to biological wastes, people began to pour all kinds of things down the drain: cans of paint, harsh chemicals to unclog pipes, bleach, paint thinners, nail-polish removers. And the waste itself now carried antibiotics and even estrogens from birth control pills. Add the various industrial wastes, cleaners, chemicals, and other substances that will join household wastes, and you have highly complex mixtures of chemical and biological substances that still go by the name of sewage. Antimicrobial products—like many soaps currently marketed for bathroom use—may sound desirable, but they are a problematic addition to a system that relies on microbes to be effective. Combine them with antibiotics and other antibacterial ingredients, and you may even set in motion a program to create hyperresistant superbacteria.

Recent studies have found hormones, endocrine disrupters, and other dangerous compounds in bodies of water that receive "treated" sewage effluents. These substances can contaminate natural systems and drinking-water supplies and, as we have noted, can lead to mutations of aquatic and animal life. Nor have the sewage pipes themselves been designed for biological systems; they contain materials and coatings that could degrade and contaminate effluents. As a result, even efforts to reuse sewage sludge for fertilizer have been hampered by farmers' concern over toxification of the soil.

If we are going to design systems of effluents that go bad into the environment, then perhaps we ought to move back up stream and think of all the things that are designed to go into such systems as part of nutrient flows. For example, the mineral phosphate is used as a fertilizer for crops around the world Typical fertilizer uses phosphate that is mined from rock, however, and extracting it is extremely destructive to the environment. But phosphate also occurs naturally in sewage sludge and other organic wastes. In fact, in European sewage sludge which is often landfilled, phosphate occurs in higher concentrations than it does in some phosphate rock in China, where much of it is mined to devastating effect on local ecosystems. What if we could design a system that safely captured the phosphate already in circulation, rather than discarding it as sludge?

FROM CRADLE-TO-GRAVE TO CRADLE-TO-CRADLE

People involved in industry, design, environmentalism, and related fields often refer to a product's "life cycle." Of course, very few products are actually living, but in a sense we project our vitality—and our mortality—onto them. They are something like family members to us. We want them to live with us, to belong to us. In Western society, people have graves, and so do products. We enjoy the idea of ourselves as powerful, unique individuals; and we like to buy things that are brand-new, made of materials that are "virgin." Opening a new product is a kind of metaphorical defloration: "This virgin product is mine, for the very first time. When I am finished with it (special, unique person that I am), everyone is. It is, history." Industries design and plan according to this mind-set.

We recognize and understand the value of feeling special, even unique. But with materials, it makes sense to celebrate the sameness and commonality that permit us to enjoy them—in special, even unique, products—more than once. What would have happened, we sometimes wonder, if the Industrial Revolution had taken place in societies that emphasize the community over the individual, and where people believed not in a cradle-to-grave life cycle but in reincarnation?

A WORLD OF TWO METABOLISMS

The overarching design framework we exist within has two essential elements: mass (the Earth) and energy (the sun). Nothing goes in or out of the planetary system except for heat and the occasional meteorite. Otherwise, for our practical purposes, the system is closed, and its basic elements are valuable and finite. Whatever is naturally here is all we have. Whatever humans make does not go "away."

If our systems contaminate Earth's biological mass and continue to throw away technical materials (such as metals) or render them useless, we will indeed live in a world of limits, where production and consumption are restrained, and the Earth will literally become a grave.

If humans are truly going to prosper, we will have to learn to imitate nature's highly effective cradle-to-cradle system of nutrient flow and metabolism, in which the very concept of waste does not exist. *To eliminate the concept of waste means to design things—products, packaging, and systems—from the very beginning on the understanding that waste does not exist.* It means that the valuable nutrients contained in the materials shape and determine the design: form follows evolution, not just function. We think this is a more robust prospect than the current way of making things.

As we have indicated, there are two discrete metabolisms on the planet. The first is the biological metabolism, or the biosphere—the cycles of nature. The second is the technical metabolism, or the technosphere—the cycles of industry, including the harvesting of technical materials from natural places. With the right design, all of the products and materials manufactured by industry will safely feed these two metabolisms, providing nourishment for something new.

Products can be composed either of materials that biodegrade and become food for *biological cycles,* or of technical materials that stay, in closed-loop *technical cycles,* in which they continually circulate as valuable nutrients for industry. In order for these two metabolisms to remain healthy, valuable, and successful, great care must be taken to avoid contaminating one with the other. Things that go into the organic metabolism must not contain mutagens, carcinogens, persistent toxins, or other substances that accumulate in natural systems to damaging effect. (Some materials that would damage the biological metabolism, however, could be safely handled by the technical metabolism.) By the same token, biological nutrients are not designed to be fed into the technical metabolism, where they would not only be lost to the biosphere but would weaken the quality of technical materials or make their retrieval and reuse more complicated.

THE BIOLOGICAL METABOLISM

A *biological nutrient* is a material or product that is designed to return to the biological cycle—it is literally consumed by microorganisms in the soil and by other animals. Most packaging (which makes up about 50 percent of the volume of the municipal solid waste stream) can be designed as biological nutrients, what we call *products of consumption.* The idea is to compose these products of materials that can be tossed on the ground or compost heap to safely biodegrade after use—literally to be consumed. There is no need for shampoo bottles, toothpaste tubes, yogurt and ice-cream cartons, juice containers, and other packaging to last decades (or even centuries) longer than what came inside them. Why should individuals and communities be burdened with downcycling or landfilling such material? Worry-free packaging could safely decompose, or be gathered and used as fertilizer, bringing nutrients back to the soil. Shoe soles could degrade to enrich the environment. Soaps and other liquid cleaning products could be designed as biological nutrients as well; that way, when they wash down the drain, pass through a wetland, and end up in a lake or river, they support the balance of the ecosystem.

In the early 1990s the two of us were asked by DesignTex, a division of Steelcase, to conceive and create a compostable upholstery fabric, working with the Swiss textile mill Röhner. We were asked to focus on creating an aesthetically unique fabric that was also environmentally intelligent. DesignTex first proposed that we consider cotton combined with PET (polyethylene terephthalate) fibers from recycled soda bottles. What could be better for the environment, they thought, than a product that combined a "natural" material with a "recycled" one? Such hybrid material had the additional apparent advantages of being readily available, market-tested, durable, and cheap.

But when we looked carefully at the potential long-terra design legacy, we discovered some disturbing facts. First, as we have mentioned, upholstery abrades during normal use, and so our design had to allow for the possibility that particles might be inhaled or swallowed. PET is covered with synthetic dyes and chemicals and contains other questionable substances— not exactly what you want to breathe or eat. Furthermore, the fabric would not be able to continue after its useful life as either a technical or a biological nutrient. The PET (from the plastic bottles) would not go back to the soil safely, and the cotton could not be circulated in industrial cycles. The combination would be yet another monstrous hybrid, adding junk to a landfill, and it might also be dangerous. This was not a product worth making.

We made clear to our client our intention to create a product that would enter either the biological or the technical metabolism, and the challenge crystallized for both of us. The team decided to design a fabric that would be safe enough to eat: it would not harm people who breathed it in, and it would not harm natural systems after its disposal. In fact, as a biological nutrient, it would nourish nature.

The textile mill that was chosen to produce the fabric was quite clean by accepted environmental standards, one of the best in Europe, yet it had an interesting dilemma. Although the mill's director, Albin Kaelin, had been diligent about reducing levels of dangerous emissions, government regulators had recently defined the mill's fabric trimmings as hazardous waste. The director had been told that he could no longer bury or burn these trimmings in hazardous-waste incinerators in Switzerland but had to export them to Spain for disposal. (Note the paradoxes here: the trimmings of a fabric are not to be buried or disposed of without expensive precaution, or must be exported "safely" to another location, but the material itself can still be sold as safe for installation in an office or home.) We hoped for a different fate, for our trimmings: to provide mulch for the local garden club, with the help of sun, water, and hungry microorganisms.

The mill interviewed people living in wheelchairs and discovered that their most important needs in seating fabric were that it be strong and that it "breathe." The team decided on a mixture of safe, pesticide-free plant and animal fibers for the fabric: wool, which provides insulation in winter and summer, and ramie, which wicks moisture away. Together these fibers would make for a strong and comfortable fabric. Then we began working on the most difficult aspect of the design: the finishes, dyes, and other process chemicals. Instead of filtering out mutagens, carcinogens, endocrine disrupters, persistent toxins, and bioaccumulative substances at the end of the process, we would filter them out at the beginning. In fact, we would go beyond designing a fabric that would do no harm; we would design one that was nutritious.

Sixty chemical companies declined the invitation to join the project, uncomfortable at the idea of exposing their chemistry to the kind of scrutiny it would require. Finally one European company agreed to join. With its help, we eliminated from consideration almost eight thousand chemicals that are commonly used in the textile industry; we also thereby eliminated the need for additives and corrective processes. Not using a given dye, for example, removed the need for additional toxic chemicals and processes to ensure ultraviolet-light stabilization (that is, colorfastness). Then we looked for ingredients that had *positive* qualities. We ended up selecting only thirty-eight of them, from which we created the entire fabric line. What might seem like an expensive and laborious research process turned out to solve multiple problems and to contribute to a higher-quality product that was ultimately more economical.

The fabric went into production. The factory director later told us that when regulators came on their rounds and tested the effluent (the water coming out of the factory), they thought their instruments were broken. They could not identify any pollutants, not even elements they knew were in the water when it came into the factory. To confirm that their testing equipment was actually in working order, they checked the influent from the town's water mains. The equipment was fine; it was simply that by most parameters the water coming out of the factory was as clean as—or even cleaner than—the water going in. When a factory's effluent is cleaner than its-influent, it might well prefer to use its effluent as influent. Being designed into the manufacturing process, this dividend is free and requires no enforcement to continue or to exploit. Not only did our new design process bypass the traditional responses to environmental problems (reduce, reuse, recycle), it also eliminated the need for regulation, something that any businessperson will appreciate as extremely valuable.

The process had additional positive side effects. Employees began to use, for recreation and additional work space, rooms that were previously reserved for hazardous-chemical storage. Regulatory paperwork was eliminated. Workers stopped wearing the gloves and masks that had given them a thin veil of protection against workplace toxins. The mill's products became so successful that it faced a new problem: financial success, just the kind of problem businesses want to have.

As a biological nutrient, the fabric embodied the kind of fecundity we find in nature's work. After customers finished using it, they could simply tear the fabric off the chair frame and throw it onto the soil or compost heap without feeling bad—even, perhaps, with a kind of relish. Throwing something away can be fun, let's admit it; and giving a guilt-free gift to the natural world is an incomparable pleasure.

THE TECHNICAL METABOLISM

A *technical nutrient* is a material or product that is designed to go back into the technical cycle, into the industrial metabolism from which it came. The average television we analyzed, for example, was made of 4,360 chemicals. Some of them are toxic, but others are valuable nutrients, for industry that are wasted when the television ends up in a landfill. Isolating them from biological nutrients allows them to be *upcycled* rather than recycled—to retain their high quality in a closed-loop industrial cycle. Thus a sturdy plastic computer case, for example, will continually circulate as a sturdy plastic computer case—or as some other high-quality product, like a car part or a medical device—instead of being downcycled into soundproof barriers and flowerpots.

Henry Ford practiced an early form of upcycling when he had Model A trucks shipped in crates that became the vehicle's floorboards when it reached its destination. We are initiating a similar practice that is a modest beginning: Korean rice husks used as packing for stereo components and electronics sent to Europe, then reused there as a material for making bricks. (Rice husks contain a high percentage of silica.) The packing material is nontoxic (rice husks are safer than recycled newspapers, which contain toxic inks and particles that contaminate indoor air); its shipping is inclusive in the freight costs the electronic goods would incur anyway; and the concept of waste is eliminated.

Industrial mass can be specifically designed to retain its high quality for multiple uses. Currently, when an automobile is discarded, its component steel is recycled as an amalgam of all its steel parts, along with the various steel alloys of other products. The car is crushed, pressed, and processed so that high-ductile steel from the body and stainless steels are smelted together with various other scrap steels and materials, compromising their high quality and drastically restricting their further use. (It can't, for example, be used to make car bodies again.) The copper in its cables is melded into a general compound and lost to specific technical purposes—it can no longer be used as a copper cable. A more prosperous design would allow the car to be used the way Native Americans used a buffalo carcass, optimizing every element, from tongue to tail. Metals would be smelted only with like metals, to retain their high quality; likewise for plastics.

In order for such a scenario to be practical, however, we have to introduce a concept that goes hand in hand with the notion of a technical nutrient: the concept of *a product of service*. Instead of assuming that all products are to be bought, owned, and disposed of by "consumers," products containing valuable technical nutrients—cars, televisions, carpeting, computers, and refrigerators, for example—would be reconceived as *services* people want to enjoy. In this scenario, customers (a more apt term for the users of these products) would effectively purchase the service of such a product for a *defined user period*—say, ten thousand hours of television viewing, rather than the television itself. They would not be paying for complex materials that they won't be able to use after a product's current life. When they finish with the product, or are simply ready to upgrade to a newer version, the manufacturer replaces it, taking the old model back, breaking it down, and using its complex materials as food for new products. The customers would receive the services they need for as long as they need them and could upgrade as often as desired; manufacturers would continue to grow and develop while retaining ownership of their materials.

A number of years ago we worked on a "rent-a-solvent" concept for a chemical company. A solvent is a chemical that is used to remove grease, for example, from machine parts. Companies ordinarily buy the cheapest degreasing solvent available, even if it comes from halfway around the globe. After its use, the waste solvent is either evaporated or entered into a waste treatment flow, to be handled by a sewage treatment plant. The idea behind rent-a-solvent was to provide a degreasing service using high-quality solvents available to customers without selling the solvent itself; the provider would recapture the emissions and separate the solvent from the grease so that it would be available for continuous reuse. Under these circumstances, the company had incentive to use high-quality solvents {how else to retain customers?) and to reuse it, with the important side effect of keeping toxic materials out of waste flows. Dow Chemical has experimented with this concept in Europe, and DuPont is taking up this idea vigorously.

This scenario has tremendous implications for industry's material wealth. When customers finish with a traditional carpet, for example, they must pay to have it removed. At that point its materials are a liability, not an asset—they are a heap of petrochemicals and other potentially toxic substances that must be toted to a landfill. This linear, cradle-to-grave life cycle has several negative consequences for both people and industry. The energy, effort, and materials that were put into manufacturing the carpet are lost to the manufacturer once the customer purchases it. Millions of pounds of potential nutrients for the carpet industry alone are wasted each year, and new raw materials must continually be extracted. Customers who decide they want or need new carpeting are inconvenienced, financially burdened with a new purchase (the cost of the unrecoverable materials must be built into the price), and, if they are environmentally concerned, taxed with guilt as well about disposing of the old and purchasing the new.

Carpet companies have been among the first industries to adopt our product-of-service or "eco-leasing" concepts, but so far they have applied them to conventionally designed products. An average commercial carpet consists of nylon fibers backed with fiberglass and PVC. After the product's useful life, a manufacturer typically downcycles it—shaves off some of the nylon material for further use and discards the leftover material "soup." Alternately, the manufacturer may chop up the whole thing, remelt it, and use it to make more carpet backing. Such a carpet was not originally designed to be recycled and is being forced into another cycle for which it is not ideally suited. But carpeting designed as a true technical nutrient would be made of safe materials designed to be truly recycled as raw material for fresh carpeting, and the delivery system for its service would cost the same as or less than buying it. One of our ideas for a new design would combine a durable bottom layer with a detachable top. When a customer wants to replace the carpeting, the manufacturer simply removes the top, snaps down a fresh one in the desired color, and takes the old one back as food for further carpeting.

Under this scenario, people could indulge their hunger for new-products as often as they wish, without guilt, and industry could encourage them to do so with impunity, knowing that both sides are supporting the technical metabolism in the process. Automobile manufacturers would *want* people to turn in their old cars in order to regain valuable industrial nutrients. Instead of waving industrial resources good-bye as the customer drives off in a new car, never to enter the dealership again, automobile companies could develop lasting and valuable relationships that enhance customers' quality of life for many decades and that continually enrich the industry itself with industrial "food."

Designing products as products of service means designing them to be disassembled. Industry need not design what it makes to be durable beyond a certain amount of time, any more than nature does. The durability of many current products could even be seen as a kind of intergenerational tyranny. Maybe we want our things to live forever, but what do future generations want? What about their right to the pursuit of life, liberty, and happiness, to a celebration of their own abundance of nutrients, of materials, of delight? Manufacturers would, however, have permanent responsibility for storing and, if it is possible to do so safely, reusing whatever potentially hazardous materials their products contain. What better incentive to evolve a design that does without the hazardous materials entirely?

The advantages of this system, when fully implemented, would be threefold: it would produce no useless and potentially dangerous waste; it would save manufacturers billions of dollars in valuable materials over time; and, because nutrients for new products are constantly circulated, it would diminish the extraction of raw materials (such as petrochemicals) and the manufacture of potentially disruptive materials, such as PVC, and eventually phase them out, resulting in more savings to the manufacturer and enormous benefit to the environment.

A number of products are already being designed as biological and technical nutrients. But for the foreseeable future, many products will still not fit either category, a potentially dangerous situation. In addition, certain products cannot be confined to one metabolism exclusively because of the way they are used in the world. These products demand special attention.

WHEN WORLDS COLLIDE

If a product must, for the time being, remain a "monstrous hybrid," it may take extra ingenuity to design and market it to have positive consequences for both the biological and technical metabolisms. Consider the unintended design legacy of the average pair of running shoes, something many of us own. While you are going for your walk or run, an activity that supposedly contributes to your health and well-being, each pounding of your shoes releases into the environment tiny particles containing chemicals that may be teratogens, carcinogens, or other substances that can reduce fertility and inhibit the oxidizing properties of cells. The next rain will wash these particles into the plants and soil around the road, (If the soles of your athletic shoes contain a special bubble filled with gases for cushioning—some of which were recently discovered factors in global warming—you may also be contributing to climate change.) Running shoes can be redesigned so that their soles are biological nutrients. Then when they breaks down under pounding feet, they will nourish the organic metabolism instead of poisoning it. As long as the uppers remain technical nutrients, however, the shoes would be designed for easy disassembly in order to be safely recirculated in both cycles (with the technical materials to be retrieved by the manufacturer). Retrieving technical nutrients from the shoes of famous athletes—and advertising the fact—could give an athletic-gear company a competitive edge.

Some materials do not fit into either the organic or technical metabolism because they contain materials that are hazardous. We call them *unmarketables,* and until technological ways of detoxifying them—or doing without them—have been developed, they also require creative measures. They can be stored in "parking lots"—safe repositories that the producer of the material either maintains or pays a storage fee to use. Current unmarketables can be recalled for safe storage, until they can be detoxified and returned as valuable molecules to a safe human use. Nuclear waste is clearly an unmarketable; in a pure sense, the definition should also include materials known to have hazardous components. PVC is one such example: instead of being incinerated or landfilled, it might instead be safely "parked" until cost-effective detoxification technologies have evolved. As currently made, PET, with its antimony content, is another unmarketable: with some technological ingenuity, items that contain PET, such as soda bottles, might even be upcycled to remove the antimony residues and to create a clean polymer ready for continuous, safe reuse.

Companies might undertake a *waste phaseout,* in which unmarketables—problematic wastes and nutrients—are removed from the current waste stream. Certain polyesters now on the market could be gathered and their problematic antimony removed. This would be preferable to leaving them in textiles, where they will eventually be disposed of or incinerated, perhaps therefore to enter natural systems and nutrient flows. The materials in certain monstrous hybrids could be similarly gathered and separated. Cotton could be composted out of polyester-cotton textile blends, and the polyester then returned to technical cycles. Shoe companies might recover chromium from shoes. Other industries might retrieve parts of television sets and other service products from landfills. Making a successful transition requires leadership in these areas as well as creative owning up.

Should manufacturers of existing products feel guilty about their complicity in this heretofore destructive agenda? Yes. No. It doesn't matter. Insanity has been defined as doing the same thing over and over and expecting a different outcome. Negligence is described as doing the same thing over and over even though you know it is dangerous, stupid, or wrong. Now that we know, it's time for a change. Negligence starts tomorrow.

GREEN FABRIC

BY CYNTHIA GIRLING AND RON KELLETT

Trees are the oldest and largest living things on the earth, and they are a good measure of the health and quality of our environment. Trees are the original multi-taskers. [They] provide social, ecological, and economic benefits. Their beauty inspires writers and artists, while their leaves and roots clean the air we breathe and the water we drink.

American Forests Web site, http://www.americanforests.org (2005)

The term "green fabric" refers to a city's vegetated lands. It is everywhere that plants grow. Unlike the gray fabric, the green fabric exists throughout the city—crossing the borders of green and gray, networks and fabric (Figure 10.1). Much of it, especially trees, grows along streets and even on buildings, traversing a continuum from natural to highly managed. Along the green networks, it often exists in its most natural state, whereas on rooftops, balconies, and along downtown streets, it is in its most cultured state. Green fabric also crosses public-private boundaries, from public streets and parks to private gardens. As a whole, it creates a unique ecosystem, one in which people have a heavy hand. Green fabric is synonymous with the broadest definitions of urban forest.

While the term "urban forest" is often used to refer only to the city's trees, it is much more, encompassing all of the trees and related woody vegetation in a city.[1] Just as rural forests are understood to be ecosystems—some highly managed, some much less so—urban forests are also ecosystems,

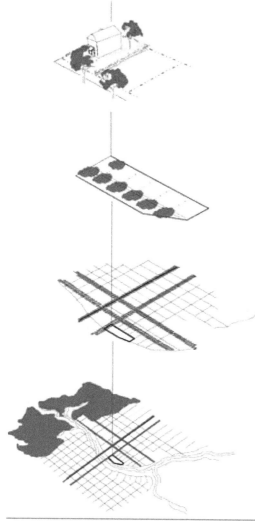

Figure 10.1 Green fabric shown across scales.

composed not only of all urban vegetation but also of soils and related microorganisms, insects, wildlife, and humans.[2] Urban forest ecosystems are unique in the degree to which they reside in a built environment and are controlled by people; as such, they are perhaps closer to a garden than to a forest. The urban forest is a vast area of cultured trees, shrubs, and herbaceous plants, interspersed with tiny remnants of natural landscapes. Even as a heavily managed resource, it provides important environmental services to the city.

While cities grow in population and extent, their environmental impacts amplify even more. The total ecological footprint, or impact, of the average Canadian was estimated in 1991 to be 10.6 acres, the average American's was 12.6 acres, and the average footprint of a person in India was 1 acre. For an American city of 2 million people, the footprint would be 25.2 million acres, an area the size of Kentucky.[3] Yet, as cities grow, their forest canopy typically declines. American Forests has documented losses of forest canopies over twenty to thirty-year spans. In 1998, the tree canopy cover of Dade County, Florida, for example, was estimated to be only 10 percent. That of Milwaukee, Wisconsin, was estimated at 16 percent. Between 1972 and 1996 in the Puget Sound region, areas with greater than 50 percent canopy cover decreased by 37 percent, from 1.64 million acres to 1.04 million acres. The lost value in air pollution mitigation for the Puget Sound region was estimated to be $95 million.[4] Between 1972 and 2000, in the Willamette/Lower Columbia regions of Oregon and Washington, average tree cover in the region's urban areas dropped from 21 percent to 12 percent, and the lost value for stormwater mitigation for that region was estimated to be $2.4 billion.[5]

Urban forests, the environmental workhorses of cities, have the potential to vastly diminish the negative environmental impacts of urbanization while serving many other important functions. Urban populations are probably most cognizant of the greening and shading roles of trees. Through day-to-day experience, most residents recognize the invaluable capacity of trees to ameliorate extreme climate conditions. Trees provide shade in hot weather and a temporary respite from rain. Hedges and hedgerows block the wind. Most urban populations also place a high value on the aesthetic contributions of urban vegetation (Figure 10.2). The dominant green color is the presence of—and, perhaps more important, symbolizes—nature in the city.[6] For most people, vegetation softens the brutality of the built environment, emphasizing the changing seasons and representing our undeniable relationship to nature. Researchers, including Stephen and Rachael Kaplan and Roger Ulrich, have clearly established the important psychological benefits of vegetation and views of "nature" for urban populations.[7] Donald Appleyard writes: "Apart from the sky, and sometimes water, trees are the primary and last representatives of nature in the city. In this sense, they are a constant reminder, not only of the world out there beyond the city, but of our distant past."[8]

The urban forest plays a well-known role in mitigating air pollution. Trees absorb gaseous pollutants, intercept particulates, reduce ozone, and sequester carbon dioxide.[9] The process of photo: to filter and sequester carbon and polluting gases as Some research estimates that a street lined with hea as 7,000 particles per liter of air.[10] The larger the tr canopy in older areas of Sacramento, for example, st 69 tons per acre), whereas smaller trees in the subur per acre).[11]

Healthy urban forests can reduce urban energy blocking, the sun's radiation. Heavy canopy trees car buildings and parking lots helps to reduce the no helps to keep air temperatures lower in urban areas (Figure 10.3). Three well-placed shade trees around a house can cut air-conditioning energy needs by 10 to 50 percent. Conversely,

Figure 10.2 Trees in Quincy Market in Boston, Massachusetts.

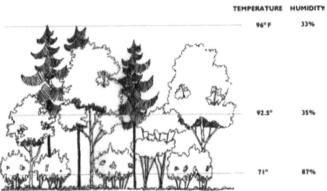

Figure 10.3 Temperature drops and humidity increases under a forest canopy.

well-placed trees can also reduce wind speeds and thus moderate heating needs in cold climates.[12] Trees also reduce urban temperatures through evapotranspiration. The process by which plants release water vapor, evapotranspiration utilizes heat energy, increases humidity, and results in a net heat loss throughout the day.[13] This process consumes solar energy that might otherwise heat the air. A single tree can transpire up to 100 gallons of water a day during the growing season. Because each gallon transpired consumes heat energy, this has the same effect as running five average air conditioners for twenty hours.[14]

Urban forests also provide ecological benefits, such as providing wildlife habitat, conserving soil, and enhancing biodiversity.[15] Trees provide habitat for urban wildlife, including insects, birds, and small mammals. They supply food, nesting sites, and safe havens for these creatures. Although virtually all of the urban forest supports urban wildlife, remnant forests and wetlands, left over from predevelopment landscapes, likely provide the most intact, valuable habitat for native species in urbanized areas. The more linked these patches of habitat are, the healthier an urban ecosystem is assumed to be and the more likely it is to support a diversity of plant and animal species.[16] Yet, even in the most developed contexts, a continuous canopy of trees can provide airborne travel corridors for some creatures, keeping them out of harm's way.

URBAN FOREST AS GREEN INFRASTRUCTURE

Urban foresters were among the first natural resource professionals to use the term "green infrastructure" to refer to the important environmental work that the urban forest performs for the city.[17] Whereas urban forestry prior to the 1990s focused on managing the city's public trees, contemporary urban forestry is taking a more ecologically based approach, in which the forest is managed for both human and ecological functions. Using green infrastructure as a concept aligns the forest with other urban infrastructure, such as water and sewer systems. The concept recognizes that urban forests can and should perform environmental services—that they should contribute to the urban ecosystem. The green infrastructure concept holds that the urban forest should be managed as a healthy ecosystem, using concepts of process and change, biodiversity, interconnectedness, and economy of means as the basis for environmental health.[18] Understood as green infrastructure, the urban forest is a interwoven system of landscapes performing multiple human and natural functions.

Trees are the canopy layer, or umbrella, of the urban ecosystem. They exist as part of the city's natural ecosystems but also extend into the most artificial areas of the city. Trees are the layer of the urban forest that clearly steps out of natural contexts, such as greenways and parks, and across the developed areas. In downtown or industrial areas, shopping centers, and strip malls, to name a few, trees are the only enduring landscape elements— stepping stones across and through built-up areas. Trees and their landscaped understory (where it exists) must perform environmental services in the most developed areas of cities. They play multiple roles in this context, one of the most important being to mitigate stormwater runoff.

Research is now emerging that quantifies the role trees play in detaining and filtering stormwater runoff, encouraging infiltration, and dissipating rainfall. Tree canopies intercept rainfall, allowing some to re-evaporate while drips are absorbed into the root system (Figure 10.4).[19] The higher the percentage of forest, trees, and other permeable surfaces, the less runoff that reaches piped drainage systems, reducing erosion and flooding. Thus, treed areas act as detention ponds, slowing the rate at which urban runoff enters streams.[20] In a study in Sacramento, California, a mature, mixed-forest canopy intercepted 36 percent of summer rainfall at the canopy level.[21] A study of a proposed development in Eugene, Oregon, found that when the proposed trees mature, producing a canopy that covers 58 percent of the site, the trees will reduce stormwater peak flows by more than 25 percent in leaf-on conditions.[22]

Root systems and their associated microbes act as sediment filters to trap and break down many stormwater pollutants. Pesticides, fertilizers, petroleum products, and suspended solids all can be either stabilized or taken up by plants. The science of phytoremediation, a biological method of cleaning up toxic lands, has taught us that biological processes occurring in the root zones of plants can remove or neutralize toxins, metals, sediments, minerals, salts, and other pollutants.[23] Plants also stabilize slopes and soils and help prevent construction-and storm-related erosion. For example, in the Gunpowder Falls Basin in the Chesapeake Bay area, forested areas released 50 tons of sediment per square mile per year to the local waters, whereas suburban areas contributed up to twice that amount. Land stripped for construction released 25,000 to 50,000 tons of sediment, or five hundred to one thousand times as much as the forest.[24]

The percentage of land covered by tree canopies can help indicate development impacts. American Forests has developed methods for evaluating general environmental impacts of losing tree canopy area to development. They have also been able to quantify the monetary value to cities of increases or decreases of tree canopy cover relative to cities' requirements to mitigate air and water pollution

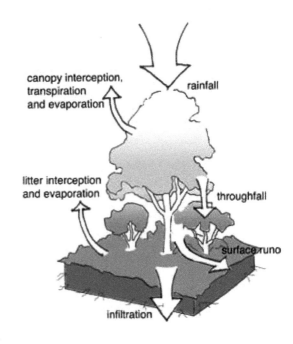

Figure 10.4 Net rainfall entering the soil under a heavy tree canopy. (Source: derived from Bureau of Environmental Services Clean River Plan)

and stormwater runoff. Based on many analyses of urban ecosystems, American Forests recommends that cities establish targets for tree canopy cover. For cities east of the Mississippi and in the Pacific Northwest they recommend an overall average canopy cover of 40 percent of the land area. For downtown areas, they recommend 15 percent cover; for urban residential areas, 25 percent cover; and for suburban residential areas, 50 percent cover. Lower goals are recommended for cities in the Southwest and the dry West.[25]

PLANTING GREEN STREETS

The urban forest as broadly defined is the primary tool to be used in restoring a natural urban hydrology. In natural stormwater management practices urban plants and their roots systems are being called on to absorb and filter stormwater runoff in the same way as plants and soils in natural landscapes. Many jurisdictions have implemented new stormwater management codes and standards that require some form of mitigation for impervious surfaces, while some charge stormwater fees based on areas of impervious surfaces. Many stormwater management departments are planning more naturally based approaches to replace or supplement underground piped drainage. Some are running up against street and landscape design standards that essentially prohibit innovative stormwater design. For example, most urban areas require 6-inch curbs along

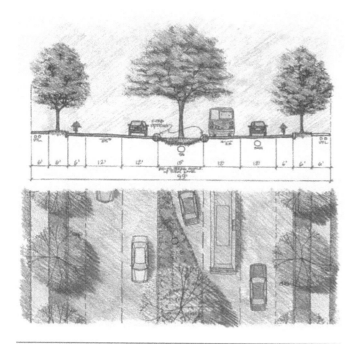

Figure 10.5 Green street with stormwater filtration/infiltration in the center median (cross section and plan views). (Source: Metro, Trees for Green Streets)

streets for safety reasons. This makes it very difficult to direct water from the street to a roadside swale (gentle ditch) for draining stormwater. Such conflicts are requiring new collaborations to rethink the details of standard urban design.[26]

Metro, the regional planning and policy district for Portland, Oregon, developed a Green Streets program and related guidebook (also see Chapter 4), designed to protect the natural resources being acquired under its regional open spaces program, to adhere to federal and state environmental laws, and to provide education and guidance to the twenty-seven jurisdictions in its metropolitan area. Intended to help public agencies and developers design and build streets that incorporate stormwater treatment and infiltration within the right-of-way, the techniques promoted in the guidebook include reducing the impervious surfaces associated with streets, planting trees (particularly large-canopy trees) to cover much of the paved areas, and using trees, planting strips, and center medians along streets to control and filter runoff (Figure 10.5). For each stormwater-related problem, a range of solutions is provided. For example, the guidebook explains many drainage swale types and illustrates several choices of curb types that allow water to run into roadside swales. Tree planting along and within streets is emphasized, as are street designs that provide adequate space and growing conditions for large-canopy trees and multiple rows of trees. Stormwater treatment medians include trees interspersed with planted stormwater gardens (planted detention basins). A compendium document, *Trees for Green Streets,* details the functions of and selection and planting details for trees intended for use in green streets or other stormwater mitigation efforts.[27] Green streets that manage their own runoff are clearly an essential component of designing green neighborhoods, and trees are essential components of these streets.

Villebois, in the Portland metropolitan area (see the case study in Chapter 2), uses green streets as part of a broader rainwater management plan, which is designed to not only reduce the impacts of its development but also restore the groundwater system damaged by the former occupant, a state mental hospital. After the citizens of Wilsonville, Oregon, successfully defeated a proposal for a new prison on the property, the state agreed to collaborate with the city and developers on a new mixed-use development for the land. In their successful bid for the project, the developers proposed a smart growth community that would incorporate "cutting edge green development practices and rainwater management techniques."[28] The plan for this 482-acre community includes 154 acres (31 percent of the site) in parks and open spaces. Restoring the pre-development hydrology of the site was a primary objective, in part to assist the goals of ecological restoration and in part to address a water shortage in the city that had previously required a construction moratorium. The Coffee Lake wetlands (71 acres), an extension of Metro-owned land to the north, and two significant forested areas were mandated for protection. Set aside as preserves, they form key habitat patches in an interconnected system of on-site open spaces. The greenway loops through the developed areas following a historic streambed. It also provides stormwater management and recreation and is the primary green corridor, ranging from 150 to 400 feet

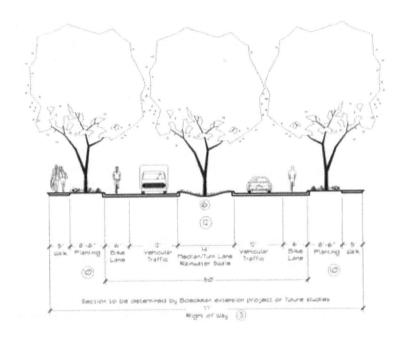

Figure 10.6 Villebois: minor arterial street with a rainwater swale in the center median (cross section view). (Source: Walker Macy et al., Villebois, vol. 4)

wide. Set aside first in the planning process, historic wetlands, creeks, and remnant forests largely structured the plan of the community. All three creeks on the site, buried by the former occupants, are to be restored.[29]

Extensive natural landscapes and a rainwater management system are two components of the Villebois greenway system. Several boulevards on the proposed development will include biofiltration swales in center medians (Figure 10.6). A sitewide rainwater management standard requires retention, infiltration, and treatment of 90 percent of the typical winter's rainstorms— drizzle that typically produces a quarter inch of rain or less in twenty-four hours. For these drizzle events, rainfall must be directed to bioretention areas, rainwater gardens, rainwater planters, and vegetated swales. These systems capture the rainfall from all drizzle events and filter 70 percent of suspended solids and 65 percent of phosphorous, a particularly problematic stormwater pollutant in the region. A backup piped system will handle runoff from larger rainfalls, which occur on average once every two to one hundred years.[30]

Trees will be an integral part of these systems. Mitigation for impervious surfaces is required at Villebois, and because trees slow, absorb, and filter runoff, they factor into the stormwater system design. Based on conservative figures (used because trees take time to grow), each deciduous tree, leafless during the rainy season, would mitigate 100 square feet of impervious surface, and each evergreen tree would mitigate 200 square feet. Builders will select their trees from an extensive list provided by the developer and preapproved by the city.[31] A tree-planting plan designates where green streets will be and where the largest trees are required (Figure 10.13).

This encoding of trees as viable components of stormwater management systems not only recognizes their true contribution but also will encourage more extensive planting of trees in the future.

DEFINING NEIGHBORHOOD SPACE

Figure 10.7 Tree-lined streets radiating from the Arc de Triomphe in Paris.

Beyond helping to define a street, separating the pedestrian realm from vehicles, and providing shade, what makes trees so special is their movement; the constant movement of their branches and leaves, and the ever-changing light that plays on, through, and around them.

A. B. Jacobs, *Great Streets*

Urban trees are the principal aesthetic elements of urban outdoor spaces. Many of the world's most famous urban streets and spaces are made memorable by their trees. Around the world, many parks, gardens, campuses, boulevards, streets, and urban spaces receive their defining character from the placement, type, and size of their trees (Figure 10.7). In Paris, the Champs Elysees, the most famous street in the world according to author Allan Jacobs, is a boulevard that is defined by its trees (particularly between Rond-Point and the Place de la Concorde).[32] London plane trees line the street edge; further back, double rows of elms form a bosk that marks the outside edge of a spacious public realm. In Beijing, China, multiple rows of trees, each row a different species and often a different age, line the edges of streets to create both a grand scale and layered edges. Many of Beijing's streets exhibit very close spacing of trees, creating a fully canopied character.[33] Some American streets distinctive for their trees include Benjamin Franklin Parkway in Philadelphia, Royal Palm Way in Palm Beach, Florida, and innumerable residential streets, such as those in old Savannah, Georgia. Certain urban spaces, including Bryant Park and Paley Park in New York, are also made captivating by their trees.[34]

In all of these memorable urban spaces, trees complement built structures in creating and defining outdoor rooms and corridors. Trees subtly establish spatial boundaries (e.g., edges and canopies), create rhythms to heighten outdoor experience, and give urban spaces a sense of scale. They express the seasons with their leaves and flowers and record time by their growth.[35] The orderly qualities of deciduous trees or what we have come to know as "street" trees—tall, columnar trunks topped by spreading canopies—makes them exemplary complements to built structure in the urban environment. They mitigate a transition between the order of building interiors and the ill-defined out-of-doors. By emphasizing and extending the geometry of buildings and of the street system in the city, trees create a comfortable vestibule between interior and outdoor environments. They define and subdivide space by enclosing rooms within larger spaces or simply creating subspaces under their canopies, and they connect spaces by creating corridors along parks, plazas, or street edges (Figure 10.8).[36]

Beyond the urban core of most North American cities, the size and density of buildings diminish, and these buildings do little to define street and pedestrian spaces. Particularly in low-density areas, where buildings are eclectic in design, widely spaced, and set back from the street, trees and other landscape elements (e.g., hedges) become the primary tools for defining and subdividing public space.[37] In fact, in the residential environment, a street lined with majestic, full-canopied trees is a quintessential image of a "good" neighborhood. Examples exist in virtually any North American city; a few notable examples include the streets of Riverside near Chicago, Monument Avenue in Richmond, Virginia, and Orange Grove Boulevard in Pasadena, California.[38] Of Riverside, designer Frederick Law Olmsted wrote: "A tasteful and convenient disposition of shade trees, and other plantings along the road-sides and public places, will, in a few years, cause the whole locality . . . to possess, not only the attraction of neatness and convenience, and the charm of refined sylvan beauty and grateful umbrageousness, but an aspect of secluded peacefulness and tranquility."[39]

In the residential environment, trees and the adjacent sidewalk are what declare the street to be public space and what subdivide it into a series of corridor-like rooms—with the smaller, edge spaces under the tree canopy and along the sidewalk for pedestrians and the larger space along the road for vehicles. Even young trees planted in lines, with relatively close and consistent spacing, begin to define the street space. With maturity, they will make the street a gracious outdoor room. To subdivide the street right-of-way into zones or rooms effectively or (to use a building metaphor) to line the street with a colonnade (of trees), street trees must be spaced closely. Similarly, to provide a canopy of branches and leaves to walk under, the trees have to be planted closely (Figure 10.9). According to urban designers, such as Allan Jacobs and Henry Arnold, trees lose their visual effectiveness and can fail at the job of spatial definition when they are planted more than 30 feet apart.[40] This, in turn, demands that the street design include adequate space and growing conditions to nurture healthy trees and that urban forest design be an early, proactive component of neighborhood design.

Figure 10.8 Trees define a sitting area at Battery Park City, New York, New York.

Figure 10.9 A pedestrian corridor created by closely spaced red maples on Robson Street in Vancouver, British Columbia, designed by Cornelia Hahn Oberlander.

Figure 10.10 Garrison Woods: a renovated street with many preserved trees.

New or redeveloped neighborhoods are our modern-day opportunity to create great twenty-first-century streets. In new communities, the street system, the open space system, and parks are designed in advance. The opportunity exists to design the street with trees playing a major space-defining role from the outset. The heavy emphasis in smart growth and new urbanist communities on creating positive, comfortable pedestrian streets establishes a major role for trees. They appear prominently in many illustrations of these communities and are a requirement in the design standards of most. In a few new communities, trees play an even larger role related to neighborhood identity and way finding. Garrison Woods and Villebois are two redevelopment projects that deserve specific mention for their extraordinary efforts to preserve existing trees and to feature trees as significant components of urban design.

Garrison Woods is an inner-city redevelopment of a Canadian Forces base in Calgary, Alberta. The developers, Canada Lands, worked closely with the City of Calgary and surrounding neighborhoods to design a new neighborhood that would knit into the surrounding areas, preserve and restore housing stock from the base, and also preserve some of the existing landscape, particularly the trees. At the same time, it would create a new neighborhood of much higher density, with schools, parks, and neighborhood commercial services. Garrison Woods was sited on a primarily residential portion of the former base, a neighborhood composed of two-story duplex officers' housing. The need to increase density while creating single-family home sites made it impossible to keep all streets in their prior location. However, efforts were made to align some new streets with previous ones to retain mature trees. Some of the most notable trees on the private lots were protected as well (Figure 10.10). Grand Boulevard, the main street through the neighborhood, was the most significant effort and success in tree protection. City of Calgary staff in parks planning and urban forestry worked hard on behalf of the developers to convince the city's engineering staff to modify street design standards. The result was a skinny street with parking that is occasionally interrupted by sidewalks that meander to avoid large trees. Put together with renovated older homes and traditionally styled new homes, the street provided an immediate feeling of an established neighborhood the summer it was completed.

Designers of Villebois, in Wilsonville, Oregon, had an even grander scheme for the development's urban forest. In addition to the significant efforts at habitat preservation (discussed earlier in this chapter), designers conceived the urban forest early in the design process as contributing strongly to the identity of "the village near the woods," as promotional literature dubs it.[41] Intended to address the three core principles of the Villebois concept— connectivity, diversity, and sustainability—a tree plan was created in the earliest phases of design. Both existing and newly planted trees play a significant urban design role in the project.[42]

The Dammasch hospital, the original site of Villebois, was constructed in 1958. Most of the hospital site was landscaped in turf, ornamental trees, and shrubs. These forty-five-year-old trees were recognized as a valuable resource by the city, who encouraged the developers of the project to preserve as much of

Figure 10.11 Villebois: trees that will be preserved in the redevelopment of the site.

the existing urban forest on the site as possible.[43] Costa Pacific and their designers embraced the idea of maximizing tree preservation. A detailed tree survey was completed, locating all existing trees on the site and describing and evaluating them for size, species, health, and structure as well as factoring in their historical importance. Throughout the design and construction process, efforts were made to preserve most of the "important" or "good" trees (Figure 10.11). For example, in refining the neighborhood plan, parks and other open spaces were sited around significant trees. Two streets in the new development were aligned with old ones to preserve the street trees, and the Village Center was sited to take advantage of some particularly majestic trees

Figure 10.12 Villebois: the Village Center plaza, sited around magnificent mature trees. (Source: Fletcher Farr Ayotte)

(Figures 10.12 and 10.13). The greenway was enlarged to include several clusters of mature trees, including some native Oregon white oaks. Hilltop Park was located on a historic homestead site, which contained a massive bigleaf maple, English walnuts, and the original hedgerow of Douglas fir and cedar. On private lands, trees will be protected under the city's stringent tree protection standards, which require a tree protection plan for each component of the development and oversight throughout the construction process by a certified arborist.[44]

The plan addressed Metro's green streets guidelines by including bioswales along several major streets and by emphasizing the use of large canopy trees. To provide continuity, such preferred trees as oak, elm, beech, and plane trees were selected for each of the major streets leading into and around the community. For example, the Loop Road, which aligns the greenway and two parks, will be lined with tulip trees, whereas the arterials that cross through the middle of the site will be lined with Accolade elm. Designers addressed diversity by establishing a list of more than twenty-two tree species (with several varieties of each to avoid monocultures) and by encouraging the use of native plants and those that would provide habitat.[45]

Figure 10.13 Villebois: street tree plan. (Source: Walker Macy et al., Villebois, vol. 4)

The efforts made to preserve natural areas and trees, and to establish a substantial tree canopy cover over time, addressed sustainability in terms of the significant role the trees would eventually play in both stormwater and air quality mitigation. Taken together, the attention to landscape preservation, stormwater management geared toward repairing site hydrology, and an intentionally designed urban forest, Villebois provides a clear example of landscape as green infrastructure.

Set within the context of Portland's Metropolitan Greenspaces plan and the related green streets guidelines, Villebois demonstrates how the urban forest can play significant green infrastructure and urban design roles concurrently in new community design. The multifunctional role for the urban forest was conceived at the earliest stages of visualizing the development and, in fact, shaped the plan. No less important was the context of a long-range regional program of green networks and strong local tree preservation laws. The intentional and early design of the urban forest for multiple functions is a key component of green neighborhood design.

GREEN FABRIC STRATEGIES

- Plant, grow, and nurture a healthy, sustainable urban forest, one that contributes to civic beauty and to a healthy urban ecosystem.
- Plan the urban forest as a keystone component of green networks.
- Preserve remnant forests and mature trees.
- Set a goal of 40 percent tree canopy cover.
- Use the urban forest to help conserve, clean, and manage urban water.
- Use trees to structure memorable, distinctive urban spaces.
- Give high priority to street trees; design the new urban forest early and for longevity.

NOTES

1. *Grey and Deneke,* Urban Forestry; *TreePeople,* Second Nature.
2. *U.S. Department of Agriculture Forest Service,* An Ecosystem Approach to Urban and Community Forestry.
3. *Wackernagel and Rees,* Our Ecological Footprint.
4. *American Forests,* Regional Ecosystem Analysis Puget Sound Metropolitan Area.
5. *American Forests,* Regional Ecosystem Analysis for the Willamette/Lower Columbia Region.

6. R. Kaplan, "The Green Experience."

7. Kaplan and Kaplan, *The Experience of Nature;* Ulrich, "The Role of Trees in Human Well-being and Health"; S. Kaplan, "The Restorative Environment"; Ulrich, "Benefits of Urban Greening for Human Well-being"; R. Kaplan, "The Nature of the View from Home."

8. Appleyard, "Urban Trees, Urban Forests."

9. Nowak, Crane, and Dwyer, "Compensatory Value of Urban Trees in the United States."

10. U.S. Environmental Protection Agency, *Cooling Our Communities.*

11. McPherson, "Atmospheric Carbon Dioxide Reduction by Sacramento's Urban Forest."

12. U.S. Environmental Protection Agency, *Cooling Our Communities.*

13. *Spirn,* The Granite Garden.

14. U.S. Environmental Protection Agency, *Cooling Our Communities.*

15. Nowak and Dwyer, "Understanding the Benefits and Costs of Urban Forest Ecosystems."

16. Dramstad, Olson, and Forman, *Landscape Ecology Principles.*

17. U.S. Department of Agriculture Forest Service, *An Ecosystem Approach to Urban and Community* Forestry.; Wolf, "From Tree to Forest."

18. *Hough,* Cities and Natural Process.

19. Xiao et al., "Rainfall Interception by Sacramento's Urban Forest"; Nowak and Dwyer, "Understanding the Benefits and Costs of Urban Forest Ecosystems."

20. Dwyer, McPherson, et al., "Assessing the Benefits and Costs of the Urban Forest."

21. Xiao et al., "Rainfall Interception by Sacramento's Urban Forest."

22. Girling and Lamb, "Comparing Alternative Urban Forestry Scenarios for the Royal Avenue Specific Plan in Eugene, OR."

23. Great Plains/Rocky Mountain Hazardous Substance Research Center, "Phytoremediation."

24. Moll and Ebenreck, eds., *Shading Our Cities.*

25. *American Forests,* Regional Ecosystem Analysis Puget Sound Metropolitan Area; *American Forests,* Regional Ecosystem Analysis for the Willamette/Lower Columbia Region.

26. Tunney, "Innovative Stormwater Design."

27. *Metro,* Green Streets; Trees for Green Streets.

28. Costa Pacific Homes, "Villebois to Feature Cutting Edge Rainwater Management and 'Green' Development Practices."

29. David Aulwes of Walker Macy, personal communication, February 17, 2004.

30. Alpha Engineering Inc. et al., *Villebois,* vol. 4.

31. Alpha Engineering Inc. et al., *Villebois,* vol. 4.

32. A. B. Jacobs, *Great Streets.*

33. A. B. Jacobs, *Great Streets.*

34. *Arnold,* Trees in Urban Design.

35. *Arnold,* Trees in Urban Design.

36. A. B. Jacobs, *Great Streets;* Strom, "Urban and Community Forestry."

37. Ellis, "The Spatial Structure of Streets."

38. Girling and Helphand, *Yard, Street, Park;* A. B. Jacobs, *Great Streets.*

39. Schuyler et al., eds., *The Papers of Frederick Law Olmsted,* vol. 6, p. 286.

40. *Arnold,* Trees in Urban Design; *A. B. Jacobs,* Great Streets.

41. Costa Pacific Homes,"Villebois to Feature Cutting Edge Rainwater Management and 'Green' Development Practices."

42. Walker Macy et al., *Villebois,* vol. 4.

43. David Aulwes, personal communication, February 17, 2004.

44. City of Wilsonville,"Tree Preservation and Protection";Walker Macy et al., *Villebois,* vol. 4.

45. Walker Macy et al., *Villebois,* vol. 4.

CH.11

THE HYDROLOGIC CYCLE

Case Studies

BY MARY MYERS

The biogeochemical cycles, powered by the sun, are "vast global recycling systems" that cycle the nutrients necessary for life. The five major biogeochemical cycles are carbon, oxygen, nitrogen, phosphorus, and hydrologic (water). The terms "bio" (living), "geo" (earth), and "chemical" indicate that the nutrient atoms are cycled between air, water, soil, rock, and living organisms (Miller 2005, p. 76). Nutrients may be changed from one form to another, as in the hydrologic (water) cycle where liquid water is transformed to vapor, then back to liquid.

201

HYDROLOGIC CYCLE

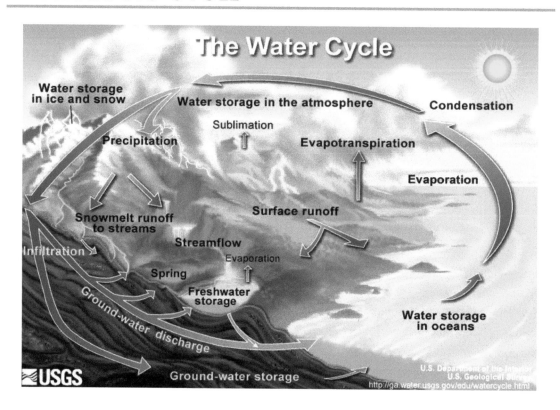

Figure 11.1 The hydrologic cycle "collects, purifies, distributes and recycles the earth's fixed supply of water." The hydrologic cycle purifies water through the evaporation process, which distills and removes impurities. Decomposer bacteria in soil also remove impurities (Miller, 2005, pp. 76–77).

The sun heats the surface water of oceans, lakes, ponds, rivers, and streams, transforming it from liquid to vapor form.[1] The vapor rises, forming clouds in the atmosphere. When temperatures drop, the vapor condenses, and gravity then returns the water molecules as precipitation to the earth. According to Miller (2005) about 10% of the precipitation falling to earth becomes locked up in glaciers. The precipitation that falls on land surfaces becomes surface runoff that flows to streams and lakes and rivers. Some of the precipitation infiltrates into soil where it either: is taken up by plant roots and eventually transpired by plant leaves into the air; or percolates downward to replenish aquifers (groundwater storage areas).

---

1 About 84% of atmospheric water vapor comes from oceans; the rest is from land sources (Miller 2005, p. 77).

DESIGN IMPLICATIONS

Climate change is causing warmer temperatures that are projected to result in increased precipitation and surface runoff in Pennsylvania and the eastern USA.[2] Unmanaged and un-infiltrated surface runoff can cause flooding, soil erosion, and other problems.

Although the eastern USA is expected to receive more water, parts of the western USA and other countries will receive less water. Increased human population will also impact water resources. More water will be used for drinking, washing, cooling of machinery including nuclear power plants, and other purposes. Infiltration of surface runoff will be reduced with construction of impermeable buildings, parking lots, and roads. Reduced infiltration accelerates stormwater runoff into streams and rivers. The runoff quality is often poor due to oils, other pollutants, and debris.

Designers, planners, and the public need to respond to these trends and to develop strategies for conserving potable (drinking) water and for managing the increased run off. Buildings should be designed to conserve and recycle water. Landscapes will be designed to hold and store stormwater so that local streams and rivers are not overburdened with excess runoff caused by the impermeable surfaces of buildings and roads. Understanding and responding to the hydrologic cycle will benefit sustainable design. Knowing the roles of solar energy, gravity, vegetation, and decomposer bacteria can be useful in designing sanitary and stormwater systems. For example, living machines purify sanitary sewage water through filtration by plants and decomposer bacteria. These machines are small-scale, simplified replicas of the large-scale global hydrologic cycle.

---

2   Climate change projections for Pennsylvania forecast a continuing trend of increased rainfall. "Average precipitation for the state rose from just under 38 inches in the early part of the twentieth century to nearly 44 inches by its end. Projections show this trend continuing under both higher- and lower-emissions futures…Should the state follow the regional trend, extreme rainfall events would be expected to produce more flash flooding, which threatens lives, property, and water-supply infrastructure" (Union of Concerned Scientists 2008, 11).

Figure 11.2 Living Machine at Ethel M Botanical Cactus Garden, Las Vegas, Nevada (Stan Shebs)

Green roofs replace impermeable rooftops with plants that transpire precipitation back into the atmosphere, contributing in a positive way to the hydrologic cycle. Water-saving features, such as low-flow toilets and faucets, waterless urinals, and low-water-use washing machines conserve water. Grey water (water that has been used but does not contain human biological wastes) can be used for flushing toilets and other uses that do not require potable water. In areas where there is little water, such as the southwestern USA, landscaping can use plants that are adapted to drought conditions. In areas where there is plenty of, or even too much, water, native plants can also be used to conserve irrigation water and to help store and transpire stormwater. Native plants are adapted to a particular climate and soil. They thrive in those settings and many are adaptable to changing conditions (such as increased rainfall).

Floodplains are low-lying land areas adjacent to rivers that can store and absorb storm water. Flood plains should not be built upon because this reduces their capacity to retain water, increasing the volume and velocity of water flowing downstream. In other words, building on floodplains increases environmental and economic damage.

The cost of flood damage has risen dramatically, from approximately "$5.6 billion per year in the 1990's to nearly $10 billion per year in the 2000's, with some years much more than that" (ASFM, March 1, 2013). According to the Association of State Floodplain Managers (2013), the combined cost to US federal taxpayers of Hurricane Sandy and Hurricane Katrina will exceed $200 billion. "Trends indicate that the Federal taxpayer is paying a greater share of disaster costs than any time in history. A recent analysis shows that from 1989 to 2004, Federal aid as a percentage of all economic costs from major hurricane events averaged 26%.

Since 2005, the Federal aid proportion jumped dramatically to 69%" (J. David Cummings, 2010 in ASFM Report March 1, 2013, p. 4).

Increased rainfall (for PA and the eastern USA) is associated with climate change. Mitigation techniques include:

1. "identifying and managing flood prone areas through land use policy
2. prohibiting certain types of building or activities in high risk flood zones
3. elevating and flood proofing pre-existing buildings that are allowed to remain" (Miller 2005, p. 329)
4. restoring flood plains and wetlands to stream edges
5. restoring natural curvature and stream characteristics to slow peak flows
6. using technologies, such as flood gates, in flood-prone cities

CASE STUDIES

The following case studies were undertaken as part of research conducted for the Landscape Architecture Foundation (LAF) in 2011 and 2012.[3] Both demonstrate sensitivity to stormwater conditions and healthy functioning of the hydrologic cycle. The case studies here can be explored in greater detail at: (http://www.lafoundation.org/research/landscape-performance-series/).

Black Rock Sanctuary in Phoenixville, PA, is a county park adjacent to the Schuylkill River that restores flood plain, creates bird habitat, and provides for education and recreation. It is a model for environmental clean-up and flood protection. Black Rock uses native plants to create and support habitat for rare and endangered birds along the Eastern Flyway. It is an example of floodplain restoration through wetland creation. Additional consideration was given to the habitat needs of amphibian and bird species and recreational/educational needs of humans.

The Salvation Army Kroc Community Center (SAKCC) is located in north Philadelphia, PA. It stores and infiltrates nearly all of its stormwater on site, keeping it from entering the antiquated city combined sewer system. SAKCC uses a chain of treatment, which includes a cistern where roof water is stored for irrigation, and seven rain gardens. The rain gardens provide a visual connection to stormwater (and the hydrologic cycle) that is typically invisible to urbanites because it is hidden below ground in pipes.

BLACK ROCK SANCTUARY

Black Rock Sanctuary is a 121-acre park located in Chester County, PA, adjacent to the Schuylkill River, the eastern bird migratory flyway. The site is associated with the region's manufacturing heyday when discovery

---

3   The purpose of the LAF case study investigation is to assess landscape performance based upon quantification of environmental, social, and economic benefits. I was assisted in the research by Temple University Master of Landscape Architecture students Andrew Hayes and Allison Arnold.

of coal in the counties north of Philadelphia triggered industrial development. A slack water canal system was built in 1815 to bring coal by barge from Schuylkill County to Philadelphia along the Schuylkill River. "By 1900, waste from upstream coal operations was contributing over 3,000,000 tons of silt to the river annually. By 1930 so much silt had built up behind the dams and in the river that navigation ceased, flooding increased, recreation use came to an end, and the river's value as a water supply was being threatened" (Spencer, p. 54). In 1945, dredging operations began to remove the silt "to strategically located basins." The basins were located behind long earthen berms (linear mounds). At Black Rock, an 80-acre silt basin was placed behind a berm that is 20-foot-high, 8,000-foot-long, adjacent to the Schuylkill River. In 1990, the PA Bureau of Mines sold the site to Chester County for recreational use.

The Black Rock site remained untouched until 1999, when the first of a series of grants funded the creation of a bird sanctuary and park. Triggered by the site's location on the Eastern Flyway, the project goal was to reclaim and create a series of high-quality wetland habitat areas for rare or endangered migratory waterfowl species to breed and nest. A second goal was to educate the public about wetland environments through an interpretive trail and environmental programming.

The project team was led by landscape architect Carl Keleman of KMS Design Group and included Normandeau Consultants, wetland scientists. The design responded to the scientific evidence associated with wetland habitats necessary for bird mating and nesting.

HABITAT AREAS

Forty-seven acres of new wetland area was created, including emergent, mound and pool, forested, deep water, and vernal pool habitats. Creation involved topography changes, clearing of invasive plant species, and planting of native species. Some branch clumps were retained for use in deep-water environments as fish refuges.

Figure 11.3 Deep-water pool can be viewed from interpretative trail, which is located on the top of the 20′ high berm. Photo by Allison Arnold.

Over ten acres of upland wildflower, warm season grass, and meadow habitat was created. Twelve thousand cubic yards of coal silt in the basin was sold to a recycling company for reuse as charcoal briquettes or power plant fuel. All stormwater entering the site is controlled on site. The design also included outdoor exhibits to educate the public and was especially directed toward middle school children. Educational exhibits included: vernal pools to demonstrate the delicate balance in maintaining a healthy amphibian population; adaptations of waterfowl species; an interactive display to demonstrate watersheds; and a biofilter to demonstrate the difficulties of dealing with surface water runoff and chemical pollution. Exhibits also present the basic needs of wildlife survival such as habitat, food, and water.

Figure 11.4 "Bird's Nest" Interpretative Feature, Black Rock Sanctuary uses discarded Ailanthus branches to create a human-scale nest. The nest is large enough to accommodate a class (25–30 students). It is located just off the interpretive trail, about 20 feet above grade, giving a feeling of being up high in a tree with views out. Photo by Allison Arnold.

MEASURABLE BENEFIT

Bird counts at Black Rock Sanctuary tripled over a seven-year period, increasing from 262 observations in 2004 to 907 observations in 2011.

Additionally, the number of bird species increased by 63% from 70 species sighted in 2003-04 to 110 species sighted in 2015-16. Species present now that were not present in 2004 include the following:

Table 11.1

Acadian Flycatcher	Fish Crow	Rock Pigeon
American Black Duck	Fox Sparrow	Ruby-crowned Kinglet
American Redstart	Golden-crowned Kinglet	Ruby-throated Hummingbird

Bald Eagle	Hairy Woodpecker	Rusty Blackbird
Black-throated Blue Warbler	Hermit Thrush	Scarlet Tanager
Blue-gray Gnatcatcher	Louisiana Waterthrush	Snow Goose
Brown Creeper	Magnolia Warbler	Spotted Sandpiper
Brown Thrasher	Nashville Warbler	Swamp Sparrow
Canada Warbler	Northern Parula	Tundra Swan
Chipping Sparrow	Osprey	Wood Duck
Common Nighthawk	Pileated Woodpecker	Yellow-billed Cuckoo
Eastern Phoebe	Pine Warbler	
Eastern Wood-Pewee	Ring-necked Duck	

The data are based upon observations that have been collected since 2003 by birders. The observations were entered into *eBird*, a program launched in 2002 by the Cornell Lab of Ornithology and National Audubon Society.[4] We decided to use 2004 as the "start" year because it was the first year for which all 12 months of observation were recorded. Bird observations in 2004 totaled 262 and have steadily increased to a total of 907 birds in 2011. Observations are maintained by local partner conservation organizations. The increase in birds is an indication that the design's goal of creating habitat for mating and nesting has been successful.

SALVATION ARMY KROC COMMUNITY CENTER CASE STUDY

Salvation Army Kroc Community Center (SAKCC) is a 12.43-acre former brown field. The site was used to manufacture pulleys by Budd Corporation, a large manufacturer of train cars and automobile bodies (1915–2002). At its peak, Budd had about 10,000 employees in north Philadelphia. When the company relocated its operations to Detroit in 2002, SAKCC was used as a city parking impoundment site (Spaulding, 1990, p. 1). In October 2010, the site reopened as a neighborhood center whose purpose is to serve the community through social, educational, recreational, and spiritual programs. Landscape architect Andropogon Associates, Ltd. and civil engineers Duffield Associates, worked jointly to develop the site and stormwater approach for SAKCC.

---

4   Background of ebird methodology:
eBird is a program that allows birders to enter observations into an online computer software program. Data gathered include bird species, date of observation, and location of observation. Volunteers are educated in the methodology behind the program prior to using it. The goal of the creators is to help develop baseline data related to birds in order to develop predictions, which could help shape landscape use. Their aim is to "develop spatially and temporally explicit models of species occurrence by relating environmental features that are important to a species (e.g., habitat, climate, elevation) to observational data. Once related, statistical models can make predictions at unsampled locations and times" (Sullivan, et al. 2011). Sullivan, B.L., C.L. Wood, M.J. Iliff, R.E. Bonney, D. Fink, and S. Kelling. 2009. eBird: a citizen-based bird observation network in the biological sciences. *Biological Conservation* 142: 2282–2292.

STORMWATER MITIGATION ON SITE

Philadelphia, like some other aging cities, has an antiquated combined sewer system. During heavy rains, storm water flushes sanitation waste into creeks and rivers. In June 2011, Philadelphia signed an agreement with the Pennsylvania Department of Environmental Protection to reduce outflows into local creeks and rivers. (The Delaware River provides a substantial portion of the city's drinking water.) Philadelphia now requires that post-construction stormwater be designed to recharge the groundwater table (Philadelphia Stormwater Regulations, June 2011, p. 132). This requirement, which promotes green infrastructure, stipulates that the first inch of rainfall be infiltrated on site and held back from the city's system. Although SAKCC was designed and built prior to the new law, it meets and exceeds the standard.

The first step in reducing discharge is to reduce impervious surfaces (buildings, walkways, and parking lots). At SAKCC, impervious surfaces were reduced by 43%, from 9.26 acres to 5.30 acres. The stormwater associated with the 5.30 acres (130,000-sq.ft. building, concrete patio, and sidewalks) is treated with a series of green infrastructure solutions. The first inch (1") of stormwater runoff is captured, reused, and infiltrated on site using a combination of cisterns, bioswales, rain gardens, porous pavements, and engineered soil mixes.

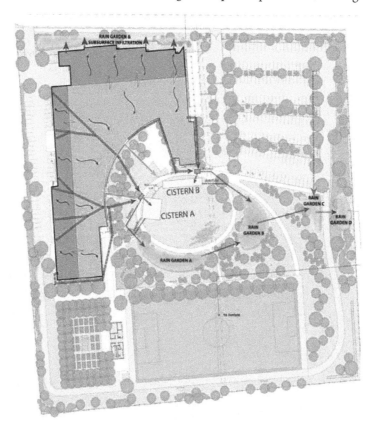

Figure 11.5 Stormwater diagram by Andropogon Associates, Ltd. The rain gardens are designed as a linked series to filter and infiltrate stormwater runoff from the building and porous parking lot.

The velocity and volume of stormwater runoff were significantly reduced through the conversion of impermeable surface to permeable, planted areas. The plantings and porous soils provide a filtering function for the stormwater. Equally important, the rain gardens detain the water through surface ponding (Duffield Associates).

Table 11.2

RATE OF STORMWATER RUN OFF	2 YEAR STORM	10 YEAR STORM	100 YEAR STORM
PRE-DEVELOPMENT	42.2 cu.ft./sec.	70.9 cu.ft./sec.	119.0 cu.ft./sec
POST-DEVELOPMENT	0.8 cu.ft./sec.	2.2 cu.ft./sec.	43.5 cu.ft./sec.
PERCENT REDUCTION	98%	97%	64%

Source: Calculations by Andrew Hayes, P.E. based upon Duffield Associates Report

All of the 2.98-acre building's stormwater is collected and stored on site in a rain garden and underground cistern. Condensate from the building's air conditioning system is also directed to the cistern whose water is used to irrigate the site's landscape.

STORMWATER AESTHETICS

Figure 11.6 Rain Garden edged by lawn, regularly spaced shade trees, and path. Photo by: KD Carrington.

The rain gardens are designed as plant communities and therefore have diverse textures, heights, and colors. These gardens look "organic" and informal. However, they are bounded by clipped lawn areas, which contrast with their informality. The lawns sets off the areas as something rather special, like a jewel nested in its setting. The contrast "works" for both elements because too much lawn is boring and sterile, while too many diverse plants might seem overwhelming to some visitors. Nassauer (2012) and others point out that lawns suggest human care and maintenance and thus may lend an aura of deliberate aesthetic purpose to a setting.

Figure 11.7A-B Granite runnel detail on left shows stormwater route. Narrow, polished stones in the center channel create a dry stream effect. The rough edges of stones above hearken to a natural stream edge, although the runnel is clearly manmade with its rectangular form and cut stone. Note detail of metal grate allowing walkways to pass over runnel, affording interaction with the stormwater. Photos by K. Daryl Carrington

Another aspect of stormwater aesthetics is the expression of stormwater traveling from the building to the cisterns via granite runnels. The runnels are cleverly detailed to link the building to the site. Storm grates allow walkways to pass over them. Stone benches terminate the runnels where they go underground to the cisterns.

SITING THE BUILDING TO MAXIMIZE OPEN SPACE

Choosing the best situation for a building is critical to the landscape. The two can work together, as at SAKCC, or the building can be sited in a way that compromises site opportunities. The SAKCC building is located in the northern quadrant of the site. The close frontal location along Wissahickon Avenue adds to the street context, whereas a large set-back (which might have included parking lots), would not. The "pushing" of the building to the street allows enough space behind to create a small park with multiple rain gardens and recreational amenities. From a biodiversity standpoint, maximizing open space is desirable. SAKCC's landscape includes many native plant species whose seeds may disperse to other parts of the city.

Collectively, such spaces are important because they are fragments of "nature" within the urban environment, which may have an aggregate benefit (Hopkins, et al., p. 8). More information about SAKCC is found in "Multivalent Landscape: The Salvation Army Kroc Community Center" in *Landscape Journal* fall 2013 issue.

G. Tyler Miller adds an important comment about floods: "Sooner or later the river, or ocean, always wins" (Miller, 2005, p. 76). Sustainable design acknowledges this and works to keep water on site where it can nourish ground water or plants and then be evapo-transpired to the atmosphere.

QUESTIONS

1. The transformation of H_2O molecules from liquid to vapor is an expression of which Law?
2. What are the design and political ramifications of water shortages?
3. What role does gravity play in the water cycle?
4. What, if any, land-use policy changes should result from hurricanes, such as Hurricane Irene (Louisiana) and Hurricane Sandy (New Jersey)?
5. Name two design strategies that you could put into effect to reduce your water footprint.
6. What methods could be used to track the presence of amphibians at Black Rock Sanctuary?
7. Why is it important to restore natural flood plains?
8. What design feature could be added to the storm water system at SAKCC that is not present now?

REFERENCES

Association of State Floodplain Managers, March 1, 2013. "Flood Mapping for the Nation: A Cost Analysis for the Nation's Flood Map Inventory." (http://www.floods.org/acefiles/documentlibrary/2012_NFIP_Reform/Flood_Mapping_for_the_Nation_ASFPM_Report_3-1-2013.pdf). Accessed: June 17, 2013.

Fink, Daniel, Marshall Iliff, Steve Kelling, Brian Sullivan, and Chris Wood. 2011. "eBird: Engaging Birders in Science and Conservation." PLoS Biology. 9.12 (Dec. 2011). (http://dx.doi.org/10.1371/journal.pbio.1001220).

Hopkins, JJ, HM Allison, CA Walmsley, M Gaywood, and G. Thurgate. 2007. Conserving Biodiversity in a Changing Climate: Guidance on Building Capacity to Adapt. Department for Environment, Food and Rural Affairs, UK. (http://www.lafoundation.org/research/landscape-performance-series/).

Miller, G. Tyler, Jr. 2005. Living in the Environment. Fourteenth Edition. Brooks Cole/Thomson Pub: Pacific Grove, CA.

Nassauer, Joan. 2012. "The Appearance of Ecological Systems as a Matter of Policy." Landscape Ecology. 6(4): 239–250.

October 19, 2010. "New Salvation Army Kroc Center Dedicated in Philadelphia." (http://www.use.salvationarmy.org/use/ www_use_Philadelphiakroc.nsf).

Nelson, Glenn, Chester County Parks Naturalist, May 2012. Interview with Mary Myers and Allison Arnold.

Spaulding, Harold E. 1990. Workshop of the World. Oliver Evans Press.

Spencer, John, Chester County Parks Ranger. 2010. "Black Rock Sanctuary Interpretive Trail, Chester County, PA."

Union of Concerned Scientists. October 2008. Climate Change in Pennsylvania: Impacts and Solutions for the Keystone State. UCS Publications: Cambridge, MA.

CREDITS

CLOSING STREETS AND ROADS

BY PETER HARNIK

In every city there are hundreds of acres of streets and roadways potentially available as park and recreational facilities. While parks make up about 20 percent of New York City's total area, streets make up about 30 percent. In Chicago, 26 percent of the land is devoted to streets compared with only 8 percent for parks. Converting some street capacity for recreational activity—either full-time or part-time—is an underrealized opportunity.

Wresting space away from automobiles is never easy, but if any opportunities constitute "low-hanging fruit" they are the hundreds of miles of roads within city parks. Naturally, all large parks need some streets for access to facilities as well as to allow motorists to get from one side to the other, but most city parks have a surfeit of auto corridors. The National Mall in Washington, D.C., formerly had four parallel drives running for about a mile between the U.S. Capitol and the Washington Monument. Not only was the green Mall thoroughly intersected every few dozen yards by asphalt, but the drives themselves were permanently clogged with tourists (and government workers) looking for parking spaces. In 1976, just in time for the national bicentennial celebration, Assistant Interior Secretary Nathaniel Reed decided to abolish the two central roads and replace them with pebble-covered walkways reminiscent of those in Paris parks. The aggregate amount of space—about 4 acres—was relatively small, but the impact on park usability, ambience, safety, and air quality was monumental. Similarly, in Atlanta, following a raft of crime and nuisance issues that were negatively affecting Piedmont Park, Parks Commissioner Ted Mastroianni and Mayor Maynard Jackson announced test weekend road closures. Despite protests, the results led to dramatic increases in other uses of the park, such as running, walking, and cycling, and, in 1983 the closures were made total and permanent. (Piedmont Park is today the most car-free major city park in the United States.)

Other examples abound (see table 24.1). San Francisco's longtime Sunday closure of 2 miles of John F. Kennedy Drive in Golden Gate Park was extended in 2007 to Saturdays as well. The program, which makes available one of the only hard, flat, safe areas for children in the entire hilly city, according to the San Francisco Bike Coalition, effectively added about 12 acres of parkland without any acquisition or construction costs. Park usage during car-free hours is about double that of when cars are around. Even cities that are thoroughly oriented to cars are finding an enthusiastic constituent response to park road closures. Kansas City, Missouri, bans automobiles on beautiful Cliff Drive within Kessler Park from Friday noon until Monday morning during the summer. San Antonio permanently closed Brackenridge Park's Wilderness Road and Parfun Way in 2004. And Los Angeles has permanently closed 10 miles of Via del Valle and Mt. Hollywood Drive in Griffith Park to protect wildlife, reduce the risk of fire, and provide a safe, quiet venue for walkers, runners, and cyclists.

It's not just large parks. Many small parks that were disfigured by roads can be regreened, too. New York City's Washington Square, famous as a Greenwich Village movie set and also for street theater, rallies, and as a de facto quad for New York University, had been bisected by Fifth Avenue until 1964. Ironically, a proposal to expand that avenue into a freeway led to the uproar that made the park entirely car-free—and a much more successful space. In Washington, D.C., Thomas Circle had gradually been sliced down in size almost to the diameter of the statue of General George Henry Thomas and his horse, with traffic consuming the entire area. In 2007 the National Park Service and the District of Columbia reinstituted the original circle and rebuilt pedestrian walkways to allow people to use it. Earlier, a similar project reunified 2.5-acre Logan Circle and helped ignite a renewal of its neighborhood.

In 2007 Houston got itself a park addition by trading away a street. It happened in Hidalgo Park, a venerable 12-acre greenspace in the city's hard-bitten East End, near the Turning Basin on Buffalo Bayou where Houston started. When a small sliver between the park and the bayou came up for sale, the city secured federal funds to buy it through an obscure federal program called Coastal and Estuarine Land Conservation. The sliver had two drawbacks: It was separated from Hildago Park by a street, plus there is a federal requirement that coastal funds be matched one-to-one by nonfederal dollars. Park Director Joe Turner took a tour of the site and had a "Eureka!" moment—why not close the street, have it transferred from the Public Works Department to Parks and Recreation, and use its land value as the local match for the federal grant? The politics and geography happened to be perfect: There were no houses on the street, it had no through access, and the one industrial user at the far end had another plant entrance it could use. And since no one before Joe Turner had ever offered to use the value of a street as a local match, the federal bureaucrats were surprised enough to say yes. (They've since rethought it and forbidden the maneuver, but the Houston handshake was grandfathered in.) Today Hidalgo Park is a much- improved 14 acres with unbroken access to the channel and views of the enormous ships coming up to the Turning Basin.

Table 12.1 Do Not Enter: Park Roads that Have Been Closed to Automobiles, Selected Parks

PARK	CITY	ROAD NAME	MILEAGE	CLOSURE TIME	YEAR FIRST CLOSED
Golden Gate Park	San Francisco	John F. Kennedy Dr.	2	P	1965
Central Park	New York	Central Park Dr.	6	P	1966
Prospect Park	Brooklyn, N.Y.	Prospect Park Dr.	3.5	P	1966
Gwynns Falls Trail	Baltimore	Ellicott Drive/Wetheredsville Rd.	6	F	1972
The National Mall	Washington, D.C.	Washington Dr. & Adams Dr.	2	F	1976
Audubon Park	New Orleans	Audubon Jogging Path	3.1	F	1980
Rock Creek Park	Washington, D.C.	Beach Dr.	4	P	1981
Fairmount Park	Philadelphia	Martin Luther King Dr.	4	P	1982
Piedmont Park	Atlanta	Piedmont Park Drive	2.9	F	1983
Washington Park	Denver	Marion Pkwy/Humboldt Dr.	2	F	1985
Overton Park	Memphis	Interior Rd.	2	F	1987
Griffith Park	Los Angeles	Mt. Hollywood Dr. & Vista del Valle	10	F	1991
Memorial Park	Houston	Picnic Loop	1.2	P	1994
Garden of the Gods	Colorado Springs	Gateway Road	0.25	F	1996
Brackenridge Park	San Antonio	Wilderness Rd. & Parfun Way	1	F	2004
Fair Park	Dallas	First Ave.	0.25	F	2004
Pope Park	Hartford, Conn.	Pope Park Dr.	0.2	F	2005
Franklin Mountains State Pk	El Paso	Scenic Drive	3	P	2008
Kessler Park	Kansas City, Mo.	Cliff Drive	2.6	P	2008
Hampton Park	Charleston, S.C.	Mary Murray Drive	1.5	P	n.a.

F—full-time; P—part-time; n.a.—not available

Source: Center for City Park Excellence, Trust for Public Land, 2008

Closing and beautifying streets that are not in parks is more difficult. Many cities, including Boston, Santa Monica, and New Orleans, have turned one of their key downtown streets into a car-free zone, although in nearly all cases the motivation is less for casual, free recreation and clean air than for upscale shopping and dining. Portland, Oregon, however, did pull off a famous and extraordinarily successful "road-to-park" conversion. It involved the 1974 elimination of four-lane Harbor Drive, an expressway along the Willamette River that had been rendered redundant by a new interstate highway. Most cities would have given in to the strenuous remonstrances of their traffic engineers and kept highways along both sides of their river, but under the leadership of Mayor (later Governor) Tom McCall the old roadway was dug up and replaced by 37-acre Waterfront Park. The park opened in 1978, exactly three-quarters of a century after the concept was first proposed by planner and landscape architect Frederick Law Olmsted, Jr., in his plan for Portland. Built for about $8.5 million, the park in its very first year was credited with stimulating an estimated $385 million in retail, office, hotel, and residential development in the vicinity. Later named after the visionary governor, Tom McCall Waterfront Park has since become Portland's focal point for all kinds of activities and festivals.

Some cities, including Baltimore, El Paso, Chicago, New York, and Miami, have recently begun experimenting with the idea of once-a-summer or once-a-month road closures on regular city streets, following the example of the "ciclovias" that have become immensely popular in Bogota, Colombia; Quito, Ecuador; and several other Latin American cities. Called such things as "Summer Streets," "Scenic Sundays," "Walk and Roll," and "Bike Days Miami," the events often take place on cities' most park-like streets (Park Avenue in New York, Scenic Drive in El Paso) and bring forth tens of thousands of people in an electrifying, community atmosphere in a domain normally dominated by cars. (The events are often initially organized and promoted by bicyclists but soon become so congested that they evolve into street festivals.)

Cities can permanently convert streets into park-like "Woonerfs," a Dutch concept for neighborhood ways where pedestrians, bicyclists, and children are given priority over cars. (The name translates to "Home Zone," which is what it is called in Great Britain.) While the concept has yet to fully establish itself in the United States, variants have surfaced. On downtown Asheville, North Carolina's, Wall Street, the city installed brick pavers, bollards, benches, and lights so intertwined that they become an obstacle course that greatly reduces automobile speeds. Seattle is doing similar traffic calming in certain neighborhoods and is also adding numerous pervious areas and water-capturing features to add ecological benefits to these "street-parks."

CONJOINED NATURE IN BUILDINGS

BY K. DARYL CARRINGTON, PHD, AIA

"In Nature we never see anything isolated, but everything in connection with something else which is before it, beside it, under it, and over it."

Johann Wolfgang von Goethe

This essay explores using "conjoined nature" to simultaneously enhance building performance and environmental carrying capacity. Conjoined nature is *nature within, upon, and adjacent to buildings that simultaneously provides building service(s) and ecological service(s)*. Conjoined nature has the potential to reduce the environmental impacts of building and to enhance the environmental quality of our cities.

Conjoined nature is proposed as a way to reduce energy and waste associated with buildings and to enhance their overall sustainability. In the United States, buildings consume 36 percent of the total energy used; 30 percent of raw materials; 12 percent of potable water consumption; and are responsible for 30 percent of waste output (136 million tons annually) (US Green Building Council). We must reduce these outputs in order to address growing population needs as well as declining environmental carrying capacity. Some very interesting design solutions are emerging that consider ways to reduce or even eliminate building energy use and waste: conjoined nature.

UNDERSTANDING THE PROBLEM

Ehrlich and Holdren's (1971) I=PAT formula (Human Impact = Population x Affluence x Technology) provides a metric that informs the fundamental conflict between human impacts on the planet and its ability to support life. Population growth will not slow in the near future, nor will our desire for affluence and technology. This indicates the carrying capacity of the planet needs to expand to provide food and shelter. But it cannot, because creating shelter and providing for increased population removes land from ecosystems, thereby reducing the carrying capacity of the planet.

To better understand this dilemma, imagine you are looking at a digital image of Earth from outer space. The planet is composed of millions and millions of pixels. They are each part of the whole, providing habitat and contributing to supporting life through the ecological services they provide. These individual pixels include where you live and where I live. To planners, architects, and landscape architects—who are responsible for our built environment—each of the pixels is a site or potential place to build. Now, zoom to the pixel that is a building or a parking lot. These are parts of the whole that do not provide ecological services and do not contribute to the carrying capacity of the planet. It is anticipated that cities will grow to accommodate 50–75 percent of the rapidly growing world population and cover more land with buildings, roads, and parking lots. The earth's carrying capacity will continue to diminish unless a way can be found to prevent it.

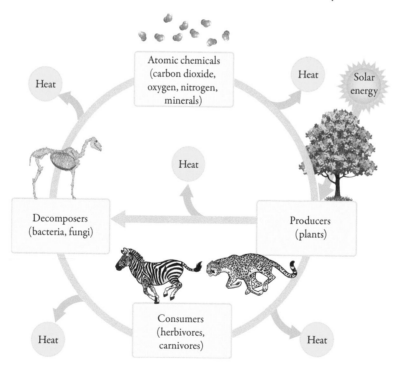

Figure 13.1 Matter and Energy Flows in Ecosystems from Living in then Environment

The impact of buildings upon ecosystems is clear in the attached diagram of matter and energy flows in ecosystems (Miller). Historically, building diminishes biodiversity, disrupts the biogeochemical cycles, kills the producers and decomposers, and reduces, bifurcates, and removes habitat for the consumers. It is possible to use conjoined nature to minimize the impacts of building and restore many of the damaged ecological services.

CONJOINED NATURE AS A MEANS OF ADDRESSING THE PROBLEM

The term *conjoined nature* is used to describe designs for natural systems, comprised of producers and decomposers joined to an engineered interface, intended to enhance the performance or replace engineered building systems. Nature provides ecological services, including supporting, provisioning, regulating, and cultural services. Ecological services can be harnessed to partially or fully offset the need for building services normally provided by engineered and mechanical systems. Conjoined nature might also be described as a "natural/engineered system." The engineered setting is designed to enhance particular performance characteristics such as storm water management for a green roof. The growing medium and drainage have been engineered. The plants provide the ecological service of keeping rainwater in the hydrologic cycle, which is also the storm water management building service. The plants also support other biogeochemical cycles and provide food and habitat to birds and insects. The building service is the primary function of conjoined nature, but the secondary ecological services are equally important because they expand ecological carrying capacity. Natural systems tend to be multivalent in that they provide more than one ecological service (Myers, *Landscape Journal*) and therefore tend to be more resilient than solely engineered systems. Solely engineered systems only perform one way without secondary benefits and perform less efficiently over time.

Conjoined nature has historical roots in vernacular architecture. Green roofs were used to protect shelters from rain more than a thousand years ago (Coffman). Plants have been used for shade and to create a microclimate as well as food and beauty for the building occupants. Deciduous trees have been used to shade south-facing walls in summer while admitting solar warmth in winter. Evergreen trees are used to protect buildings from winter winds, and berms are used to deflect wind. Vernacular methods are now being enlisted to perform ecological building services.

Conjoined nature has significant implications for reduced environmental impact of individual and collective buildings at all scales while simultaneously increasing ecological carrying capacity. Conjoined nature breaks the barrier between strictly technological or biological. It is scalable in the sense that plants provide similar ecological services when used in small areas as in large areas, although they perform better in plant communities. An implicit expectation of "engineered nature" is that it can be made to perform better than the nature that was there in the first place, since the building process generally results in less space for nature. The question is, how much can natural performance be enhanced by engineering? Extensive green roofs can be designed to grow in very light medium to reduce structural loads, but deeper mediums provide better storm water management and opportunity for biodiversity and other secondary ecological services. Significant work on landscape performance is being done by the Landscape Architecture Foundation (Myers et al.). They are developing and evaluating tools and metrics to measure the economic benefit of ecological services.

Examples of conjoined nature include:

USING PRODUCERS FOR BUILDING SERVICES

Green roofs provide storm water management as a building service by keeping rainwater in the hydrologic cycles. Storm water runoff is a serious problem in cities. Engineered solutions have historically treated storm water as *waste* diverted or piped to the nearest river to move the problem downstream. Increased development and impervious surfaces have led to flooding and pollution. Philadelphia and other older cities have combined storm and sewer systems. During rain events, the Philadelphia combined sewer system cannot manage the storm and sewer flow, and the combined effluent is dumped into nearby rivers. This is environmentally unsafe and untenable (www.phila.gov/water).

A green roof can manage rainwater falling on its surface, which is a building service. Rainfall is no longer diverted as storm water, but remains in the hydrologic cycle to be absorbed and transpired by the plant material (producers) on the roof. Beyond the building service, green roof plants contribute additional ecological services to the healthy functioning of the carbon cycle, and may, if well designed, provide habitat, reduce urban heat island effect, and encourage biodiversity. They might also be used for food production. In addition, the growing medium provides a thermal barrier and greater roofing material life to the building (secondary building services). Green roofs provide an "island habitat" if they are not connected to the ground. Green walls can be used to connect the ground level environment to the rooftop (Coffman).

Figure 13.2 Aerial view of the Arcos Building, Fukuoka, Japan, designed by Emilio Ambasz

The ACROS Building in Fukuoka, Japan, designed by Emilio Ambasz, has fourteen terraces that step back like a giant stairway to accommodate a large, intensive green roof that provides storm water management, habitat, biodiversity, energy savings, reduced urban heat island effect, and air pollution reduction (Kyushu University). The building integrates the adjacent park into a significant urban green space and public environment. "Its terraced south façade is utilized by many in the area for exercise and rest, affording views of the city and the harbor beyond" (Wood, Bahrami, & Safarik). See aerial image (EmilioAmbasz. com).

Passive Indoor Air Quality   Building HVACs (Heating, Ventilation, and Air Conditioning) are major consumers of energy. HVAC systems recycle conditioned air *and* add outside air to freshen and remove stale air. Outside air introduced into the system must be conditioned to the same temperature as the interior by heating in winter and cooling in summer. Conditioning outside air represents a building energy load. Plants are being used to reduce the need for outside air and thereby reduce the size and energy usage of HVAC systems. Kamal Meattle has done extensive research on improving indoor air quality with houseplants (producers) in India (TED talk, How to Grow Fresh Air). Meattle uses plants to remove CO_2 and oxygenate air in buildings, thereby improving air quality and reducing the need to bring in "fresh" air from outdoors. This is important because the air in large cities is more polluted than the air one can "grow" in a building. Indoor plants provide better air quality and reduce the HVAC energy load because the internal air recycled by the plants is already conditioned. Green walls may be used on the interior to enhance air quality in a similar way.

Exterior green walls on buildings are being used as rain screens to protect the building envelope from the elements and to provide a cool enclosure. They have been used as auto underpasses in Europe to remove CO_2 from the air. There are now exterior building skin materials designed to support growth of lichens and moss. It is not yet clear whether these wall materials will be merely aesthetic or provide building services because their design and usage is evolving.

Solar Load   Located in Sydney, Australia, One Central Park by Jean Nouvel and Patrick Blanc is a thirty-four-story high-rise building. The project includes green walls, roof gardens, and courtyards, but the distinctive feature is the continuous surrounding planters at each floor level. The planters are like a shawl that has been wrapped around the building to provide solar comfort and beautify the appearance.

> This building reduces its cooling energy load with a five-kilometer-long system of linear slab-edge planters that function like permanent shading shelves and reduce thermal impact in the apartments by 20%. Additional shading from the plant foliage itself can further diminish heat gains by [an] additional 20%. By contrast to the metallic louvers, plants trap carbon dioxide, emit oxygen and reflect less heat back into the city. The choice of the species is critical for the success of the system, because some of the façade's microclimates have extreme levels of sun and wind exposure. Since the plants climb on vertical steel cables from slab to slab, their leaves are ideally positioned for shading even on western exposures, and they can be custom-tailored to the thermal needs of each resident. The plants grow in Polyethylene (a material that can be recycled) planter boxes that are roto-molded into proprietary double-walls containers to assure proper drainage and avoid

bacterial and fungal buildup in the substrate. They are also irrigated with water from the on-site storm water collection tanks and the central recycling plant. The building organically grows its own shading with its own recycled water and saves cooling energy. (CTBUH)

Figure 13.3 One Central Park by Jean Novel and Patrick Blanc located in Sydney, Australia

Secondary ecological services include aesthetic benefit, reduced urban heat island effect, and reduced air pollution.

Outdoor Air Quality   Bosco Verticale (Vertical Forest) was designed by architect Stefano Boeri with an ecological vision to revitalize and "green" Milan, Italy. "This design utilizes metropolitan *reforestation* [to *regenerate*] the environment and urban biodiversity without the implication of expanding the city upon the territory." Vertical Forest consists of two towers hosting 480 large and medium trees, 300 small trees, 11,000 perennial and covering plants, and 5,000 shrubs. The cumulative surface area of all the green space is 1,500 (15 hundred) to 20,000 (20 thousand) square meters, more than the footprint of the site.

The Vertical Forest increases biodiversity. It promotes the formation of an urban ecosystem. Various birds and insects inhabit the space (the initial estimate is 1,600 specimens of birds and butterflies that frequent the vertical environment). The green breathing facade develops the microclimate which produces humidity, absorbs CO_2 and particles, produces oxygen, filters air and protects against radiation and noise pollution. The plants and trees produce 'clean' air for inhabitants to use, increasing comfort. The plants replace standard air handling systems, saving money and energy. Plant irrigation is provided via a water filtration system that utilizes grey-water from sinks, showers, and air conditioning. This diagram shows how water is collected and filtered throughout the building. The first image illustrates the distribution of water (*Dezeen* magazine).

It was also important that the correct trees were selected for this project. Botanical consultant, Laura Gatti, "considered the trees' wood type, size, rooting and form of branching" to make sure they would be durable enough to withstand the limited size of the balconies. "The plants used in the project were grown specifically for the building, pre-cultivated so that they would gradually acclimate to the conditions they would experience once placed on the building" (*Dezeen* magazine).

Figure 13.4 Bosco Verticale designed by architect, Stefano in Milan, Italy

The design has been criticized on two counts. First, the benefits provided by the plants are offset by the negative impact of additional concrete needed to support them. This is a fallacious argument; given a building life expectancy of fifty to one hundred years, the plants will offset the carbon footprint of the concrete many, many times over and provide numerous other benefits. Second, stating the plants are only decorative is another false argument; notwithstanding their beauty, plants continually provide ecological services, which can be measured (Myers).

Bio-Facade Arup and other researchers have recently integrated algae panels as a "bioreactor" on the SolarLeaf facade, which was installed for the first time on the BIQ house for the International Building Exhibition (IBA) 2013 (ARUP.com). Algae is grown between layers of glass in a "bio-skin" that can be "used to produce biomass energy, and control solar load by providing shade." The bio-skin is located outside the weather envelope of the building, and algae is grown with water and CO_2 circulated between the glass panes. The algae is harvested and transformed in a bioreactor to a gas that can be used to provide energy to the building. The process is analogous to making biodiesel on an individual building scale and may lead to designs where buildings actually grow their own energy. In this scenario, the building is actually growing biomass for energy, a provisioning ecological service, and consuming the provisioning it produces, a building service.

Food production is another rapidly emerging area of conjoined nature. Green roofs have been used for food production, and there are many examples of vertical farming, particularly in Japan and Singapore. And it is an obvious next step for the bio-facade to grow algae for human consumption. Agriculture per se does not provide building services, so it will not be discussed further as conjoined nature.

Courtyards and atria, while not part of nature themselves, are important because they are frequently used to provide indoor habitat for nature. Plants that provide building services have historically grown in courtyards. The courtyards were originally open, as in a Roman house, and enclosed as structural technology advanced. The space of a courtyard can be designed as a greenhouse and frequently contains plant and water features. A courtyard admits light needed by the plants, and the light brings heat that cannot escape due to the greenhouse effect. The courtyard becomes part of the HVAC system when heated air may be used to warm the space in winter, or the convective currents of heated air are used to ventilate the space in summer.

DECOMPOSERS FOR BUILDING SERVICES

There is no waste in nature (McDonough & Braungart). Decomposers found in living soil recycle matter to be reused by other living things. Decomposers have been used in numerous conjoined nature systems to provide building services.

Figure 13.5 **BIQ** house for the International Building Exhibition (IBA) 2013 by Arup in Hamburg, Germany

Composting is an engineered version of what happens in nature. Nutrients have value, which is demonstrated by cities that sell composted sewage. Composting toilets, such as those found in the five-story Bullitt Center in Seattle, manage human waste—a building service. The recycled nutrients that result from the ecological service decomposers can be fed to the plants off- or onsite. Bathroom waste becomes food (McDonough & Braungart). Nutrients for onsite plants suggest the possibility of integrated conjoined nature systems in buildings, where a green roof might be fertilized by composted waste from the occupants.

Living Machines were designed by John Todd to clean wastewater, including black water from buildings. A living machine has several stages, including an underground chamber, where anaerobic bacteria decompose solid waste, and a series of oxygenated tanks, where aerobic bacteria and plant material further clean the water until it is suitable for reuse. Todd's concept has been developed further in "tidal" living machines that use gravel-filled basins as a home for bacteria. Black water fills and empties from the basins in a series of cleaning stages. Both systems have been used in buildings and often have a constructed wetland such as that found at the Lewis Environmental Center or the Omega Center as a finishing component. The tidal system may be as effective as Todd's Living Machine with less maintenance and odor and more easily integrated into a building design.

Constructed wetlands, such as those designed by Andropogon landscape architects and KieranTimberlake architects for the Sidwell Friends School, include green roofs, rainwater harvesting, and a constructed wetland. The constructed wetland provides waste management and gray water reuse in landscape irrigation, toilets, and the cooling system as building services. The decomposers that live in the water and roots of the plants in the constructed wetland provide the ecological service of cleaning the water. There are additional ecological services, including biodiversity, habitat, and support of the biogeochemical cycles related to the conjoined nature. The design provides exterior space to the students for science and relaxation. The design integrates engineered natural components outside the building with internal building water and waste systems. There are two separate systems, one for rainwater harvesting and reuse and one for black water recycling and reuse. They occupy a terraced courtyard that slopes toward the L-shaped building. (See diagram 13.6.)'

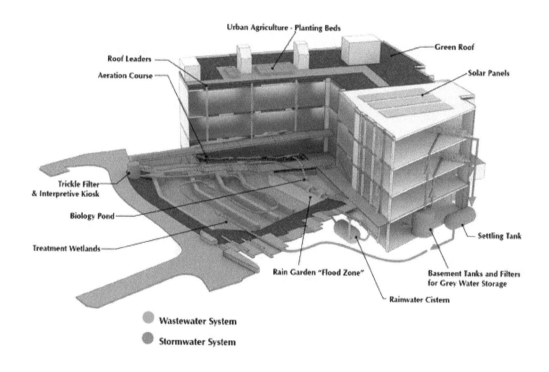

Figure 13.6 Sidwell Friends School diagram

"Proper sizing of the constructed wetlands and cistern

- ensures that the system is capable of treating all wastewater
- minimizing the risk of contaminating the adjacent stormwater system
- Wastewater collected from the building's toilets and faucets is treated on-site
- Settling tanks
- Solids are collected before water is released underground into the constructed wetland
- Tiered wetlands treat roughly 3,000 gallons of wastewater per day using biological processes
- Once water has passed through the wetland, treatment components include a trickling filter, a recirculating sand filter and a UV disinfection unit
- The cleansed wastewater is collected in greywater storage tanks
- Captures 68% of rainfall from a 1-year storm, 9,820 gallons, in the green roof on the middle school addition
- Reduces potable water consumption by an average of 8,500 gallons per month by reusing treated wastewater to flush toilets
- The amount of water that the building recycles is equal to the reduction in the amount of city-supplied water used.
- Reduces heat island effect
- Promotes biodiversity"
(Landscape Performance Series, LAF)

Biowalls are another example of using decomposers to provide building services. A 75-foot-tall biowall is located in the atrium of the Papadakis Integrated Science Building at Drexel University. The biowall is a green wall with specialized epiphytes (air-breathing plants) that are located to filter return air as part of the HVAC system. Plants are arranged in pockets in a porous fabric that is hung on the wall of a space, typically an atrium to daylight the biowall. Water is circulated to the top of the fabric and allowed to drip-irrigate the plants. The water is collected at the bottom of the biowall and recirculated. Water consumption and supplemental lighting are significant due to the size of the wall. The atrium functions as an air-return plenum. The wall behind the biowall has air-return ducts for the HVAC system, which is designed so return air flows through the biowall. Thus, the biowall is part of the HVAC system. Decomposer microbes and bacteria that naturally inhabit the plant roots remove (eat) VOCs and impurities from the HVAC return air as it moves through the biowall. The plants also contribute to oxygenating the air. The resulting return air is better quality and cleaner than outside makeup air brought into the building (Nedlaw). The building services are the energy savings associated with a reduced requirement for outside air that needs to be tempered and the air quality benefit to the occupants. The biowall creates the potential for a closed-loop internal air system to clean and improve the air quality while saving the energy of circulating and conditioning outside air, although this potential is not yet recognized by building codes.

Figure 13.7 Papadakis Integrated Science Building at Drexel University

CONCLUSION

As you read this, the future of conjoined nature is being written around the world in designs of all scales. These and other projects offer a powerful model to reduce the impacts of buildings and cities on the environment and carrying capacity of the planet. The concept of conjoined nature suggests we should no longer think of buildings and nature as separate entities, but seek ways they can work together to provide building services and reduce our ecological footprint and enhance the carrying capacity of the planet. The examples above indicate a wide range of opportunity that is expanding as designers accept the challenge of sustainability. Living organisms are now being incorporated as active components of building systems like HVAC systems and may be combined with passive elements such as solar load control to further enhance building performance and human well-being. Unlike mechanical systems, living systems tend to perform better over time. A green roof will perform better when plants mature than when first planted. Living systems need to be maintained like mechanical systems, but they require less input of matter and energy. The text proposes the IPAT formula can be modified to IPAT − R, where R = ecological restoration, resilience, and/or regenerative design. Conjoined nature embodies R because it contributes to ecological restoration, regeneration, and resilience and uses nature's services to replace mechanical services.

It is time to stop seeing nature in isolation, separate from the built environment. Using ecosystem services to provide building services creates multiple sustainable benefits. More conjoined nature equals less environmental impact and increased carrying capacity. One imagines a future city where green roofs manage the storm water; green facades control solar load and reduce pollution and heat island effect; biowalls clean indoor air; and living machines and constructed wetlands recycle wastewater.

QUESTIONS

1. What can we do to prevent further loss of carrying capacity?
2. Can we have population growth and actually increase carrying capacity?
3. Can buildings and cities provide ecological services?
4. Can you think of examples of and/or opportunities for conjoined nature?
5. Can you implement these ideas at home or work? Vertical farming and aquaculture are related ideas. Can you think of other closely related ideas?

REFERENCES

"Bosco Verticale/Boeri Studio." ArchDaily. N.p., 2015. Web. 21 Mar. 2016.

Braungart, Michael, and William McDonough (2002). Cradle to Cradle: Remaking the Way We Make Things.

Carrington, K. Daryl, and Mary Myers. 2012. "The Fidelity Hypothesis." Abstract. Finding Center: Council of Educators in Landscape Architecture conference. March 28–31, 2012.

Coffman, Reid. January 2009. "Elevating Habitat" in Landscape Architecture Magazine, pp. 72–77.

CTBUH Journal, Case Study: One Central Park, Sydney, 2014. Issue IV.

CTBUH Research Report (2015). Vertical Greenery: Evaluating the High-Rise Vegetation of Bosco Verticale, Milan. Elena Giacomello and Massimo Valagussa.

Darlington, A. "Nedlaw: Living Walls."

Ehrlich, Paul R., and John P. Holdren (1971). "Impact of Population Growth." Science, 171:1212–17.

http://emilioambaszandassociates.com/portfolio/Fukuoka-Prefectural-International-Hall.

http://www.epa.gov/oaintrnt/projects. Green Building Council statistics.

Miller, G.T. (2007). Living in the Environment. Thomson-Cole.

Myers, Mary. "Multivalent Landscape: The Salvation Army Kroc Center Case Study." Landscape Journal, 33:141–17. February 1, 2014.

Odum, E. (1997). Ecology: A Bridge Between Science and Society. Sinauer Associates.

"Sidwell Friends Middle School." Landscape Performance Center. Web. 20 Mar. 2016.

"Sidwell Friends Middle School—Washington, D.C. Methodology for Landscape Performance Benefits." Landscape Performance Series. Web. 20 Mar. 2016.

"Sidwell Friends Middle School Renovation." Sidwell Friends Middle School Renovation. Green Education Foundation, n.d. Web. 17 Mar. 2016.

"Stefano Boeri's 'Vertical Forest' Nears Completion in Milan." Dezeen, Stefano Boeri's Vertical Forest Nears Completion in Milan Comments. N.p., 15 May 2014. Web. 21 Mar. 2016.

Todd, J., E.J.G. Brown, and E. Wells (2002). Ecological Design Applied.

Vakili-Ardebili, A., and Boussabaine, A. "Ecological Building Design Determinants." Architectural Engineering and Design Management, ISSN 1745-2007, 05/2010, Volume 6, Issue 2, pp. 111–31.

Wood, Antony, Payam Bahrami, Daniel Safarik, and Council on Tall Buildings and Urban Habitat. Sustainability Working Group. 2014. Green Walls in High-Rise Buildings. Mulgrave: Images Publishing.

CREDITS

1. Fig. 13.1: Adapted from: E. Tyler Miller, Matter and Energy Flows in Ecosystems from Living in then Environment, "Figure 4-17 Natural Capital, pg 67: *Living in the Environment*, 14th Edition, Annotated Instructor's Edition, Thompson Higher Education.

   Fig. 13.1a: Copyright © Depositphotos/eveleen.

   Fig. 13.1b: Copyright © Depositphotos/logos2012.

   Fig. 13.1c: Copyright © Depositphotos/vectorguy.

   Fig. 13.1d: Copyright © Depositphotos/alegria.

   Fig. 13.1e: Copyright © Depositphotos/insima.

   Fig. 13.1df: Copyright © Depositphotos/insima.

2. Fig. 13.2: Copyright © Kenta Mabuchi (CC BY-SA 2.0) at https://commons.wikimedia.org/wiki/File:ACROS_Fukuoka_2011.jpg.

3. Fig. 13.3: Copyright © Sardaka (CC by 3.0) at https://commons.wikimedia.org/wiki/File:(1)Central_building_Broadway_Sydney-2.jpg.

4. Fig. 13.4: Copyright © Urban Kalbermatter (CC by 2.0) at https://commons.wikimedia.org/wiki/File:Bosco_Verticale_(17830612035).jpg.

5. Fig. 13.5: Gerhard kemme, "BIQ house for the International Building Exhibition (IBA) 2013 by Arup in Hamburg, Germany," https://commons.wikimedia.org/wiki/File:Algae_House.JPG. Copyright in the Public Domain.

6. Fig. 13.6: Copyright © Andropogon Associates, Ltd.

Designing Sustainable Cities and Suburbs

EXTREME SUSTAINABLE CITY MAKEOVER: NEW YORK

BY MICHAEL SORKIN

Imagine New York City being completely sustainable-all food and energy production contained within its borders, with a net zero carbon footprint. Sure, it may be a dream, but the effort is yielding practical, long-term thinking about how we should be planning sustainable cities.

Most of us are familiar with the concept of the "ecological footprint." Originally developed by Canadian academics Matthis Wackernagel and William Rees, the idea embodies a series of algorithms (numerous versions are available on the web) that convert a wide variety of consumption inputs into a single quantity: area. Using this model, one can compare how much of the Earth's surface is required to build a car, heat a house, produce a meal, sink the carbon from a coal-burning power plant, etc.

Figure 14.1 Envisioning a green N.Y. skyline: Artist rendering of a midtown Manhattan skyline dotted with food hubs.

The information yielded by the calculations is revelatory, and sometimes shocking. For example, some simple footprinting produces the scary conclusion that if everyone on Earth were to consume at the rate at which we do in the U.S., the surface area of an additional three or four planets would be required to support us all! This vividly begs the questions both of the equitable distribution of resources globally and throws the matter of self-sufficiency into high relief at the local level.

The real issue, though, is what to do. Too many solutions are caught up in negotiations about how to apportion responsibility and blame. China pollutes massively, but less per capita than the U.S. does. Negotiations also break down in the effort to find suitable economic instruments to address environmental harm, such as the cap-and-trade regime, which monetizes emissions but doesn't actually do anything to lower them.

Part of the problem with taking suitably radical steps is that questions of both politics and efficiency intervene. As the variety of essentially failed environmental summits since 1992 have demonstrated, cooperative global action by nation states is elusive. Even at the individual level, most countries are incapable of mitigating their pollution, generating their energy indigenously and cleanly, or curbing their consumption.

WHAT IS TO BE DONE?

Figure 14.2

All images courtesy of Terreform

There are strong reasons for looking to cities as a primary component of the transition to a sustainable environment and economy. Given the dys- functionality of many national governments and the frequently callous and irresponsible behavior of many transnational corporations, cities are logical spaces for democratic governance, resistance to predatory economic behavior, and environmental organization and action.

Cities, in their physical and social density, are uniquely sustainable environments. They deploy their infrastructures with special efficiency and concentrate activities that are unusually productive—and there are many systems only cities can support. For example, although it seems counterintuitive, New York City is not simply a roaring hive of activity but is also at the top of U.S. cities in energy efficiency. There is a single reason for this: New Yorkers are the greatest mass transit users in the United States. Subways, which only make sense economically when there is a sufficient density of population to support them, also offer other environmental advantages: reducing vehicular pollution,

Figure 14.3 Breathing room: A re-imagined view of Fulton Street in Manhattan (left), and a bird's-eye view of (Steady) State's linear production towers (right).

limiting the extent of other infrastructures, and contributing to the conviviality and convenience of the walking city.

For a number of years, Terreform, our non-profit research organization, has been working on a thought experiment. Given the idea that cities are—from both the political and the technical sides—such excellent elements of both accountability and organization, we set out to imagine a redesign for New York City that would create an ecological footprint precisely coterminus with its political boundaries. Relying on the great urbanist Jane Jacobs, we have drawn heavily on the idea of import substitution for economic logic, a process she held was central to urban development in general and one with profound implications for urban environmental behavior.

With all this in mind, we began the New York City (Steady) State project half a dozen years ago. Our intention was to see if we could effectively redesign and retrofit the City of New York for complete self-sufficiency, to test whether a city as complex as ours could be self-sustaining and to discover the degree to which we could unburden the planet. Our larger purpose was to compile an encyclopedia of the forms and technologies that might be used by other cities around the world that seek to take greater responsibility for their environmental impact.

We focused our work on a series of specific "respiratory" functions of the city: air, temperature and micro-climate, water, energy, movement, manufacturing, waste production, and building. Embedded in each of these categories are profound implications for social and other distributive arrangements in the city. The core of our study is an attempt to assess the implications for urban life of each of these activities, all of which also have deep architectural, planning and technological implications. One of our guiding propositions is the idea that urban autonomy will be best achieved through local organization, which we feel is potentially more resilient, malleable and personal. While cities' functions must necessarily be defined by efficiencies of scale, our endeavor begins with the belief that the sort of transformation we are seeking should be disaggregated and visible, and should offer the possibility of community engagement and control.

Thus, we see the neighborhood as the key component of urban organization. Neighborhoods are political entities that enable meaningful democracy not only by face-to-face contact but also by the shared interest of people working to secure and improve a tangible commons. Our proposal is for neighborhoods that are maximally autonomous, meaning that each would contain not simply housing but would "harmonize" its resident population with numbers of jobs and commercial, recreational and cultural facilities—including schools, parks, sources of energy, and means of waste remediation.

This has many obvious implications. It would mean, for one, that the question of transportation would first be addressed on the demand side (where environmental research must always begin). If everything necessary for daily life were within walking distance from home, the need for extensive transportation infrastructures would be reduced. Likewise, it would end the often destructive class divisions and distinctions among neighborhoods. Establishing a community as the center of economic activity would require providing living space for a mixed group of wage earners, ranging from janitors and teachers to farmers, IT workers and entrepreneurs. The idea of harmonization is crucial and is meant to suggest a balanced idea about design and planning, rather than a coercive insistence on assigning people to specific places within the city.

At the other end of the scale, it's also clear that local autonomy can never be achieved in certain key functions, and these help to establish the place of all cities in a global environment and to set the parameters of urban networks. The planet will always depend on the Amazon Basin to produce a vast portion of its oxygen to sink lots of its carbon. To support another primal need, New York City has made remarkable provision for harvesting drinking water from watersheds and reservoirs it owns upstate, and for transporting it through massive pipes (one of which has recently been completed at the cost of billions—a remarkable project of truly Roman grandeur).

But we handle our water poorly when it arrives. New York, like many other cities, has a combined sewer system. That is, both sewage and storm water are gathered by the same pipes. During intense storms, the system is overwhelmed. Huge quantities of raw waste are dumped directly into the city's rivers, fouling environments far downstream. The sustainable solution doesn't involve simply disentangling the pipes to create two separate systems. It implies rethinking waste as an asset, which in turn underlines the imperative of transforming our culture from a focus on consumption and disposability to a more respectful and canny attitude to global resources.

Indeed, by designing systems that are cyclical rather than linear, the very idea of waste can become an anachronism. In the case of water, rain should be collected and recycled, whether gathered on rooftops and conveyed to cisterns, or percolated through bio-swales (landscape elements that provide drainage) and newly permeable ground to recharge the aquifer. At the same time, human waste need not be carried to the massive treatment installations that characterize the city of today; it can be remediated at more local scales—via "living machines," biological remediation systems that operate at building, block and neighborhood levels, and that can recover waste's potential to transmute into water, fertilizer, fuel, and other raw materials.

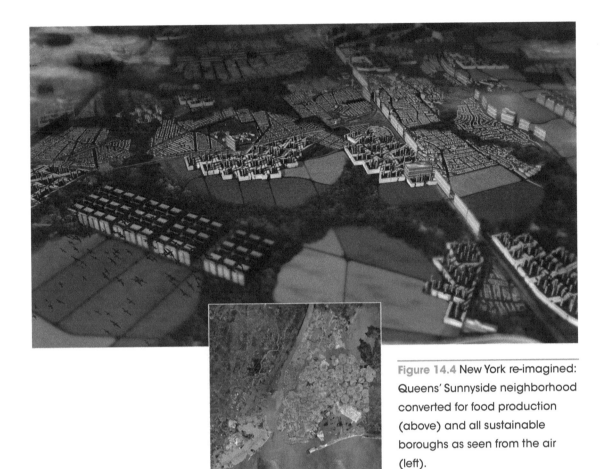

Figure 14.4 New York re-imagined: Queens' Sunnyside neighborhood converted for food production (above) and all sustainable boroughs as seen from the air (left).

As we do not anticipate placing the city under a dome *a la* Bucky Fuller, moving toward self-sufficiency is complicated by the need for mobility and transportation inside and outside municipal boundaries. It is far easier for a city to move to a post-fossil-fuel, post-combustion environment than it is for larger entities of governance and organization, such as the nation state. The city will not have a literal wall, but its edge should be the starting point for a conceptual transformation—an organizational boundary within which people will move differently. One possibility is that New York could be ringed (at various distances)—as Venice is—with intermodal transfer points. Cars would be left outside those boundaries and travel within them would instead be based on more public or shared transportation.

This will have additional knock-on effects. Without cars, there will be no need for wide motorways within the city. The vast spaces they currently occupy can be converted to other uses—agriculture, greenways, housing, etc.—and the vast quantities of steel and concrete used to build them can be recycled for use by the city's future construction and industry.

MORE THAN A THEORY

Although we are doing our project in a literal- minded way, it is informed by the techniques of "patch dynamics," a form of ecological study that is founded in the essential arbitrariness of the boundary of the area being investigated. As with the political boundaries of the city, the patch functions as a kind of controlled experiment that can reveal an order of relationships that might otherwise be obscured by the expansiveness of the systems and their interactions.

Cities are, after all, complex ecosystems, and a large measure of the interest in our project is looking at the way in which a boundary that is the result of a collusion of both physical barriers—two of the city's boroughs, Manhattan and Staten Island, are islands—and political barriers—the other three boroughs, the Bronx (on the U.S. mainland), and Brooklyn and Queens (part of the Long Island land mass) are hemmed by borders without such material justifications. These borders have economic, cultural, morphological, and political implications. The question of the permeability of the urban membrane— which must certainly be transparent to ideas and to people—is at the very center of our investigation.

We have recently completed work on one of the fundamental topics in our project: food, a growing obsession in the United States. Our preoccupation includes consumption—witness the status of chefs and the burgeoning of our locavore culture—as well as production and nutrition. This interest stems, in part, from anxiety about the domination of the food chain by agribusiness, with its energy-intensive, mono-cropping, highly polluting practices and its displacement of family farming. There are also technology-induced fears— the result of the use of pesticides, fertilizers and GMOS. At the same time, trade agreements such as the North American Free Trade Agreement (NAFTA) have depressed local production to the benefit of predatory corporate producers. Finally, obesity rates are now greater than those of malnourishment. Ironically, both heavily correlate with poverty.

Thus, in thinking about how to introduce food production into our model, we knew that our vision had to embrace food justice, localism and the forms of sociability and organization arising from growing, preparing and eating food. With this in mind, we first investigated the possibility of ensuring that every input to the city's consumption came from within its boundaries. We considered that it would be necessary to grow 100 percent of the basic requirement of 2,000 to 2,500 nutritious calories a day for 8.5 million people. We soon discovered that it was possible to achieve this by deploying the full range of growing environments— including rooftops, building facades, repurposed street spaces, vacant lots, over-decked rail yards, basements, rivers, and by the introduction of—everybody's favorite—vertical farms in substantial numbers. But it also proved impractical.

The idea of generating very high rates of food production within a city's fabric is itself not unreasonable, depending on site and circumstances. Havana, taxed by inefficiency, shortages and the U.S. embargo, is nevertheless "blessed" by low wages and a 12-month growing season. As a result, it has been able to introduce a system of very low-tech *"organiponicos"—small* urban farm plots—that now produce nearly 90 percent of the fruit and vegetables for the city. Many Chinese cities—despite their size—have, until recently, produced the majority of their vegetable and livestock supplies in their near hinterlands, as was the pattern in many European cities well through the nineteenth century.

> It is far easier for a city to move to a post-fossil-fuel, post-combustion environment than it is for larger entities of governance, such as the nation state.

From the standpoint of climate and density, New York City is a little more challenging.

Our study looked first at the possibility of 100 percent production. Some of the formal results are illustrated here. This required the extensive deployment of vertical farming which, as a purely spatial matter, was do-able and not out of line with other very large-scale building projects, such as the vast archipelago of housing projects that could be built by the city in a matter of decades. By using vacant lots, abandoned buildings, unused space near infrastructure and industrial buildings, the waterfront, and a variety of other found opportunities, the problem was nominally solved.

But only nominally. The production of grains, for example, (which are grown extremely cheaply in the U.S. Midwest) were not economical as an urban enterprise, nor was it immediately clear how the very large-scale style of growing food—a 30-story tower the size of a Manhattan block using advanced hydroponics could feed around 12,000 people—could be organized as a series of smaller-scale enterprises. And, perhaps most telling, we discovered that the amount of energy required to power these farms (including heating, lighting and the energy embodied in construction) demanded an input equivalent to the output of 25 nuclear plants. This, needless to say, was somewhat contrary to the spirit of the exercise!

SWEET SPOTS

Having proved the marginal possibility of a completely autonomous system, we are now looking at a series of "sweet spots" of greater practicality. We have looked at a scheme for a 100-mile (161-kilometer) hinterland, and at another based on statewide production using a recovered Erie Canal, once the principal water route for goods from the Hudson River to Lake Erie. And we've looked at the way in which agriculture can be more localized in neighborhoods to produce something on the order of 30 percent of demand.

One of our first sketches proposed a "figure-ground" switch—the migration of buildings into street space and the freeing up of block interiors for farming and other public activities. While the image was attractive, the numbers were unimpressive. We estimated that no more than 2 to 3 percent of food requirements could be satisfied in this liberated space. This led us to a serious examination of the underused infrastructure of the city.

We selected several blocks in Queens and, holding the population constant, we calculated solutions that ranged from 100 percent to 30 percent and 10 percent of local food needs. That called our attention to a massive, little-used rail yard nearby that could be used to supplement food production by turning it into an energy farm to harvest solar and wind power. A scheme of growing 30 percent of food demand on the spot yielded both a new, green interior for the blocks and produced a refreshed idea of the urban street, much inspired by Islamic and medieval urbanism, with their tight circulation spaces in which pedestrian and commercial life flourishes.

> **A city conceived with a sense of self-responsibility can play a role in solving economic, political and environmental problems.**

New York City (Steady) State is an ongoing exercise. We look forward to learning a great deal about both the limits and the expansive possibilities for developing urban autonomy. While cities grown too large can be toxic, degrading and ungovernable, a city conceived with a heightened sense of independence and self-responsibility can also play a role in solving the economic, political and environmental problems confronting the planet.

We are now investigating how to mitigate the urban heat island, how to clean the city's air, how to imagine new architectures that will collect sunlight, gather water, generate energy, and remediate their wastes. By looking at these questions in an ecological way, we are able to generate synergistic ideas and a vision about other questions, including neighborhood forms, the possibility of manufacturing the technologies with locally sourced materials, and the kinds of lives we could (and should) lead in a city that truly takes responsibility for itself and all who live in it.

COMMUNITY GARDENS

BY PETER HARNIK

Community gardens are a vastly underappreciated and underprovided resource for cities, both at ground level and on rooftops. As reported by University of Illinois Landscape Architecture Professor Laura Lawson in her excellent book *City Bountiful,* surveys from the 1970s and 1980s revealed that while gardening was Americans' favorite outdoor leisure activity, somewhere between 7 million and 18 million people wanted to garden but weren't able to because they did not have the space. With today's higher population, including millions of immigrants who live in cities but still have deep cultural attachments to agriculture, the situation is now unquestionably more severe. In a nation engulfed by profligate use of land, the irony is hard to miss. Americans traveling in urban areas overseas are often struck by the fact that even small patches alongside railroad tracks and roads, and odd plots between buildings—spaces that are almost invariably wasted in the United States—are intensively cultivated for flowers, vegetables, and spices. In most European countries trains routinely pass hundreds of garden plots in the several miles between city centers and true farm fields on the outskirts.

Community gardens do not have full-fledged pedigrees as parks, but they are certainly members of the extended family, and they are overwhelmingly urban. Coming in a diversity of forms, they can provide beauty, supply food, educate youth, build confidence, reduce pesticide exposure, grow social capital, preserve mental health, instill pride, and raise property values. Although the number of community gardens in the United States is not known, a 1996 survey of thirty-eight major cities by the American Community Gardening Association revealed 6,020 gardens, and the national total may be three times that. In 2008, The Trust for Public Land's survey of the park systems of the seventy-seven largest cities revealed 682 gardens (and 12,988 individual garden plots) specifically owned by park departments and located on urban parkland.

The national movement has a great deal of exuberant vitality, demonstrated even by place names and their fostering organizations: the Garden of Eatin', Queen Pea Garden, Harlem Rose Garden, Jes' Good Rewards Children's Garden, Paradise on Earth, Garden Resources of Washington (GROW), Denver Urban Gardens (DUG), Boston Urban Gardeners (BUG), San Francisco League of Urban Gardeners (SLUG), and Los Angeles' Gardening Angels. But the movement is also severely underfunded, poorly organized, and subject to a bruisingly high level of burnout and turnover. (GROW, SLUG, and BUG have all gone out of business.) Put simply, between the legalities, the neighbors, and the typical challenges of soil and weather, urban agriculture is extraordinarily difficult, even more difficult than running normal public parks.

Vegetables, fruits, and flowers require protection from theft or inadvertent damage, and this entails unsightly fences and unneighborly locks. Because of this, gardens require close control and, in some cities, end up being rationed by way of waiting lists and small fees. Finally, community gardens have a particular look that is very much in the eye of the beholder. For every wannabe farmer who delights in seeing rows of seedlings, pyramids of compost, a shock of vegetable stakes, and dripping irrigation hoses, there is a City Beautiful purist who laments the unkempt prospect and the loss of a potential manicured lawn. On the other hand, the gardeners with their planting, watering, weed-pulling, and harvesting are the everyday users who can help make a park more inviting, busier, and safer. Plus, community gardens make extremely efficient use of space. An area that could barely fit a single tennis court might hold 75 garden plots; a soccer field might be replaced with 300 or more. Moreover, gardens can be placed close to streets and railroads because they have no errant balls bouncing into traffic.

Depending on a host of external factors, the demand for community gardens fluctuates like a pendulum. Every economic downturn sees people trying to save money by growing their own (and then often reverting to supermarket simplicity when good times return). Same with pesticide scares—each frightening headline drives a few more people off "the agro-chemical grid," though it doesn't always last. Most recently, the new interest in saving energy by eating locally has made some easterners and northerners swear off produce from places like California,

Arizona, and Florida. All these factors could spur a renaissance in park gardens, particularly if troublesome ownership and management issues can be solved.

For the purposes of this book, there are two major classes of community gardens: those within existing parks and stand-alone gardens that have sprung up in vacant spaces. The former group does not, of course, represent an increase in the overall park acreage in a city, but it sometimes puts existing parkland to a higher-intensity use or otherwise improves it. The latter effectively increases the size of a city's system of parks and park-like spaces. There are numerous opportunities for an enormous expansion of both kinds of garden lands.

Most cities have plenty of underused or even unused chunks of parks that could be developed into community gardens. Even super crowded places like Jersey City and San Francisco have parkland that is essentially unvisited. That doesn't automatically mean it's perfect for gardening—it may be too shady or too deep within a big park to be reachable by potential gardeners—but those drawbacks might be fixable through tree trimming or park redesign. Chances are that underused "backwater" park areas became that way because they are frightening or have safety issues that need to be dealt with comprehensively, and a garden might be one piece of the larger revival puzzle. Gardens need to be near edges where they can be seen and where people, vehicles, and irrigation water can easily reach them. But putting a garden near an edge helps open up the next internal ring of the park to greater use, thus gradually reclaiming what might be a no-man's land in the interior. There is no guarantee that the dozens of challenging factors that make for a successful community garden—leadership, community involvement, well-enforced rules, adequate funding, stable management, good soil, sufficient sun and water, and much more—can all be provided within a city park by a city park department. But overall, official park department gardens are more stable (if perhaps also a bit more staid) than stand-alone gardens operated on vacant lots by community groups and land trusts.

On the other hand, putting a community garden into an existing park could well mean not putting in a soccer field, dog park, or memorial grove that some other constituency wants. Thus, developing a new, stand-alone community garden leaves existing parkland unmolested and raises the tide for everyone. (It also provides a boost to home values in the surrounding community; a 2007 study by the New York University Furman Center for Real Estate and Urban Policy found that gardens in New York's poorest neighborhoods lifted property values by up to 9.4 percent after five years.) Opportunities abound. Buffalo, St. Louis, Detroit, Cleveland, and Pittsburgh—all of them less than half as populated as they were in 1950—contain thousands of vacant lots, many municipally owned because of nonpayment of taxes. Even in less hard-hit places like Chicago and Kansas City, or resurgent places like Atlanta, New York, Denver, and Seattle, there are still numerous gaps in the urban fabric that are doing little more than collecting cars, weeds, and garbage.

Of the 18,000 or however many community gardens, most of them stand-alone gardens, the great majority operate in humble, contented obscurity, providing their microfarmers with fruits for the eye or the stomach, sociality for the heart, and pleasant breathing spaces for the neighborhood. But every now and then, an issue flares. In both New York in the late 1990s and Los Angeles in the early 2000s community garden battles became front-page showdowns, complete with rallies, arrests, Hollywood celebrities, and multimillion-dollar fundraising campaigns. In Seattle, thanks in part to the P-Patch Trust, a formal land trust that owns land and does organizing, gardeners defeated an effort to convert a longstanding garden into a golf course driving range. But the average urban gardener is a libertarian communalist, happy to share her tiny piece of green earth with compatriots but also happy to not be bothered.

This is actually a problem. Without robust engagement in politics and the public process, gardeners do not bring themselves into the park's mainstream. They regularly become trapped in the romantic but vicious cycle now found in many ramshackle neighborhoods with numerous abandoned properties in legal limbo: stand-alone gardens are created entrepreneurially and extralegally; the gardens receive support from civic-minded nonprofits and begin to generate buzz; artists, gay people, and other urban pioneers discover the area; developers promote the trend; middle-class professionals move in; demand expands; construction swells; gardens are bulldozed.

A community garden program cannot be left to operate reactively. It must be designed to protect gardens at the beginning of the process, not at the end. Gardens must be clearly recognized as an integral part of a city's park system, and they should be included in all redevelopment projects—particularly those that are high-density and that are marketed to former suburbanites who may love all aspects of the city except its lack of gardening space. This is surprisingly rare. Even Arlington, Virginia, poster community of the smart growth movement with scores of new high-rises along its Rosslyn-Ballston subway line, has not created a single new community garden for the 20,000 or so residents who have flocked there in the past thirty years. (The county has responded by dividing many garden plots in half, but the waiting time to get a garden in Arlington is still three to four years.)

As of 2009, the only city that has a truly sophisticated garden structure is Seattle. Chicago, New York, Philadelphia, and several other places have relatively strong private-sector agencies or public-private partnerships that own, hold, and support significant numbers of community gardens, but only Seattle's P-Patch program proactively plans, sites, negotiates, sets rules, and protects gardens throughout the city. P-Patch, which began in 1973 and was named after Rainie Picardo, the farmer who first allowed residents to begin gardening on his land, once even counted as a gardening member Mayor Wes Uhlman. Today P-Patch has sixty-eight gardens, an annual budget of $650,000, and a staff of six, and Seattle has more garden plots per capita than any other major city. Even more impressive, Seattle's City Council passed a formal resolution supporting community gardens and recommending their colocation on other city-owned property. The city's comprehensive plan calls for a standard of one garden for every 2,000 households in high-density neighborhoods (known in Seattle as "urban villages"). Nevertheless, despite this abundance, P-Patch still has a waiting list of 1,900 persons; in crowded neighborhoods that translates to three to four years.

Finding a numerical balance between houses and gardens is tricky. Moribund neighborhoods drowning in vacant lots certainly benefit from greening programs, but it would be shortsighted to lock in every temporary garden in perpetuity. These neighborhoods frankly need economic vitality and the increase in population and buildings that accompanies it. Conversely, economically overheated neighborhoods are tremendous revenue and tax drivers for the city, but politicians need to make sure that these "golden goose" places aren't overbuilt and eventually suffocated by their growth.

Stand-alone gardens need not be slotted only to old home sites. One particularly promising locale is along rail lines, both abandoned and active. Community gardens have already been created alongside the Washington and Old Dominion Railroad Trail in Arlington, Virginia; the Ohlone Trail in Berkeley, California; and the Capital City Trail in Madison, Wisconsin. In Queens, New York, the Long Island City Roots Garden was created directly over the tracks of the unused- but-not-abandoned Degnon Terminal Railroad. (To prevent official abandonment the railroad required that the tracks be retained, so the gardeners bulldozed out 140 cubic yards of garbage and covered the rails with 160 cubic yards of clean dirt; the garden is a train-shaped 26 feet wide and 145 feet long.)

While gardens alongside rail trails are fine, they don't actually increase the amount of parkland in a city. To do that requires moving up to the next level: creating community gardens alongside *nonabandoned* rail lines. This is a tougher challenge but has an added benefit since there are few parts of a city less attractive than the edges of a railroad. From Philadelphia to Los Angeles, as dumping grounds for all manner of modern detritus, the edges of urban rail corridors provide depressing vistas for train riders and local residents alike. Some analysts are convinced that rail ridership would jump up a few notches solely if the view was pleasanter. Back in the 1960s, Lady Bird Johnson spearheaded the remarkably successful highway beautification program, but no subsequent first lady (or anyone else) has taken on what might today be called an extreme track makeover program. Could gardens lead the way?

Because of railroad industry reluctance and disinterest, bolstered by issues of liability and a generally impenetrable bureaucracy, the number of agreements between railroads and gardeners in the United States is very small. For a time there was a market garden alongside tracks in Baltimore, but when the B&O Railroad Museum decided to expand, the garden was removed. For several years in the late 1980s the Pennsylvania Horticultural Society had a "Ribbon of Gold" competition whereby railroads would get a prize for planting fields of yellow flowers alongside active lines, but that ultimately evolved into other programs, and Philadelphia's many tracks reverted to eyesore status.

One notable success is in Madison, Wisconsin, where the St. Paul Avenue Garden operates under a license with the Wisconsin Central Railroad, a subsidiary of Canadian National Railways. The line is lightly used by low-speed freight traffic, so there is not even a fence alongside the tracks. The 72-plot, 25-foot-wide garden runs for about two blocks in an intense utility corridor that includes a buried fiber-optic cable and an overhead high-tension line. "It used to be a dumping ground sort of place," explained Joe Mathers, garden specialist with the Community Action Coalition for South Central Wisconsin. "Then, in the early 1980s Madison got a lot of Hmong refugees from Southeast Asia so we started looking for land for them to farm. We were in a recession so there was land available. When the economy improved development resumed and we lost some spaces. But we should always be able to hang on to this garden—nothing is permitted to be built here."

There are a scattering of community gardens alongside rail lines in Chicago, some consisting of flower gardens to beautify station areas, and there is a garden in the Bronx, New York, alongside a large railroad storage yard. In both those cities, the rail owners are public agencies— Metra and the MTA, respectively. Public rail agencies may be more amenable to leasing or licensing trackside space than private train operators, although no detailed study of opportunities has yet been carried out.

THE HUMAN ADAPTATION TO AND NEED FOR NATURE

Findings from Psychology and Evolutionary Biology

BY MARY MYERS

Humans, like all species, have evolved in nature to absorb and respond to environmental information. The human relationship with the environment is studied by a variety of scientific disciplines. Physicians study the human body, brain, and sensory development. Ecologists and evolutionary biologists research evolutionary aspects. Psychologists, cognitive scientists, and health scientists explore the relationship between emotional and physical health and environment. Research results from all of these domains can inform sustainable design's objectives of working *with* the environment, providing functional purpose and aesthetic satisfaction.

SENSORY DEVELOPMENT—
HOW HUMANS GATHER INFORMATION ABOUT THE WORLD AROUND THEM

We receive information about the world through our senses. Humans have what anthropologist E.T. Hall describes as **immediate** and **distant** sensory receptors. Immediate receptors are touch and taste. The skin is the chief organ of touch and is also sensitive to heat gain and loss. Researchers believe that there is a general relationship between the evolutionary age of the receptor system and the amount

Figure 16.1 How is this little girl learning about the object? Photo by KD Carrington.

Figure 16.2 Crowd at Occupy Wall Street, New York, 2011. If there is tension it will be communicated with the olfactory sense, which detects adrenal changes.

and quality of information it conveys to the central nervous system. (Turner, Hall). The sense of touch is very old in terms of human evolution.

Vision is relatively recent. Likewise, the development of the senses in infants seems to follow the general evolutionary pattern. Human development and perception of the world begins with immediate receptors of touch and taste. Infants learn about the world through handling and tasting objects. They need and respond to the touch of their parents or other adults. Vision became more important in our evolution when human ancestors left the ground due to interspecies competition and changes in the environment, and took to the trees (Hall). Dependence on smell is important to terrestrial animals but stereoscopic vision is essential in arboreal life, because without it, jumping from branch to branch becomes very dangerous (Hall, p. 42).

Vision is the most sophisticated human sense. The eye is about a thousand times as effective as the ear at picking up information. An interesting aspect of eyes is that they also *communicate* information as well as receive information. Feelings, such as love, hate, fear, acceptance, or repugnance are expressed through eyes. Visual information is less ambiguous than auditory information. One reason for this is the rapid speed of light. Light waves travel at 186,282 miles/second, much faster than sound waves, which travel at about 1126 feet/second or one mile in five seconds. Thus, humans have the ability to quickly read a scene or setting, to take in complex data, and to make judgments based upon what we see. We might be less confident of making similar judgments based upon what we hear.

Odor is one of the earliest and most basic methods of sensory communication. It differentiates individuals and makes it possible to identify the emotional states of other people. However, in humans, it is a relatively weak sensory receptor, which in some ways is not a bad thing. "One consequence of weaker olfaction," according to Hall," is that it may have endowed humans with a greater capacity to withstand crowding. If we had noses like rats, we would be forever tied to the full array of emotional shifts occurring in people around us" (Hall, p. 39). Rats with their stronger olfactory sense can detect the anger, frustration, and anxiety communicated in adrenal glands. Humans are less sensitive to smell and thus avoid some of the pleasures but also anxieties associated with smell. In very close crowds, we can sense the emotional state of others through their adrenal glands. If people are tense, this is communicated to others and can increase tension and hostility.

It is possible that the current human population explosion is partly based upon the human capacity to withstand crowding and to live in cities. Currently more than 50% of humans live in city environments. More and more people will live in cities in the future. The link between humans and the outdoor "natural" environment is becoming increasingly affirmed even as we retreat into indoor and human made environments. Physiological and psychological health are linked with elements in the natural environment.

Figure 16.3 Fountain near Philadelphia's Art Museum increases negative ions in the air and the sound drowns out traffic noise. Photo by KD Carrington.

THE EFFECT OF WATER

Being around streams, standing at the edge of the ocean, or near a fountain makes people feel more energetic. This is because the negative ions of moving water suppress serotonin, a chemical associated with drowsiness. Fountains add a dynamic quality to any urban space and are found in cities throughout the world. They were found on many street corners in ancient Rome, and were used as sources of potable water and social gathering places. In the USA, New York, Washington, D.C., Philadelphia, and many other cities, fountains became emblems of civic pride in the nineteenth and early twentieth centuries. Las Vegas, NV, would probably not have flourished as a major tourist destination without the creative and expansive use of fountains. As the world's climate grows warmer, fountains and other water features will be even more important to urban design.

THE NEED FOR SUNLIGHT

Humans need access to sunlight. For millennia we were active outdoor creatures who went to sleep at sunset. Like plants, our physiologies are adapted to and need sunlight. Sunlight boosts vitamin D and triggers

Figure 16.4 Central Park, NYC. Looking northeast from Belvedere. View of pond, open fields, and trees with cityscape beyond. Photo by KD Carrington.

the human endocrine system. "Most cases of Vitamin D deficiency are due to lack of outdoor sun exposure. At least 1,000 different genes governing virtually every tissue in the body are now thought to be regulated by 1,25-dihydroxyvitamin D_3 the active form of the vitamin"(Mead, 2008, p. 160). Vitamin D is important to the production of calcium and is associated with bone development.

Melatonin is a hormone that sets the circadian rhythm (24-hour "clock") of humans, other animals, and plants. Sleep is induced by melatonin whose release is timed through exposure to sunlight (or bright artificial light) in the morning. This exposure is also effective against insomnia, premenstrual syndrome, and seasonal affective disorder (SAD) (Mead, p. 162). While excessive exposure to sunlight is associated with skin cancer, too little sunlight can result in other diseases and problems. It is important to be prudent by using sunscreen and wearing hats and shirts in bright sunlight. Likewise, it appears crucial to human sleep patterns, sense of well-being, and immune systems to be in sunlight. There is debate among researchers and physicians about the amount of solar exposure a person needs. The present consensus calls for at least 15–20 minutes day.

Landscape architect Frederick Law Olmsted designed "pastoral" scenes of large shade trees, gently undulating terrain and turf, and calm lakes to restore calmness to city dwellers. He understood the need for sunshine and fresh air and felt that such scenes provide an antidote to the stressful environment of congested streets and looming buildings. Designing between 1856 and 1872, Olmsted and his partner Calvert Vaux understood the innate need and desire of people for "natural" environments. They designed a park that has been in place nearly150 years, providing active recreation space for millions of New Yorkers. More important is its continued function as a passive open space, containing scenes and elements that humans appear to be hardwired to appreciate. Many places in the 840-acre park also offer prospect and refuge. They are places where people can "look out on the action" (the prospect) from a bench, chair, or blanket near some trees bordering an open space (the refuge).

ENVIRONMENTAL PREFERENCES

Prospect and Refuge

Large cities have existed for only a few thousand years. But people have lived in the natural environment for millennia. We are familiar with and at home in certain types of landscapes. The tree-dotted plains of the African savannah are universally appreciated across all cultures (Kaplan, et al.). The savannah setting provides both *prospect* and *refuge*. Prospect allows us to see the opportunities, such as food and water, and the challenges, such as the presence of human enemies or animal predators, in the distant landscape. Refuge shows places where we can hide from threats or seek shelter from storms.

Figure 16.5 This scene in lower Central Park shows a tree-dotted landscape (similar to the African savannah). The photo appears to have been taken from a position of refuge.

Prospect and refuge theory was developed by Appleton (1996). It has been seminal in defining certain aspects of landscape that appear to be universally appreciated, across time and culture. The biological theories of Lorenz, Morris, and Spenser and on animal behavior in the environment informed the development of the theory. Appleton writes that survival is based upon both the ability to see and the ability to hide in a landscape. Prospect and refuge links us to our early ancestors who had less control over the environment and who might just as easily be prey as predator. Appleton bases his argument on habitat theory, postulating "that aesthetic pleasure in landscape derives from the observer experiencing an environment favorable to the satisfaction of his biological needs" (Appleton, p. 66).

Environmental psychologists Kaplan, Kaplan, and Ryan (1998) followed up on prospect and refuge theory by testing for landscape preferences. They agree with Appleton that exploration and understanding what a landscape holds are basic human needs. The psychologist team researched landscape preference by asking people to rate different scenes (on photographs and slides) using a five-point Likert scale. Thousands of ratings indicated that preferences have "a great deal to do with how the space in a picture is organized" (Kaplan, Kaplan, Ryan, p. 11). Scenes that were rated highly had spaced trees and smooth ground. This is essentially the landscape of the African savannah where humans originated. The open landscape seems to invite exploration because there is prospect. Yet the trees also offer refuge and a focus for the view.

Key Factors That Communicate Landscape Information

Figure 16.6 Ngorongoro Crater, Kenya, exemplifies a prospect and refuge scenery. There is much open space but there are also scattered trees offering refuge.

Four key informational factors were identified by Kaplan, Kaplan, and Ryan: **coherence** and **legibility**, having to do with understanding a setting; and **complexity** and **mystery**, having to do with exploration of a setting. Ideally, landscapes would have all of these factors. Coherence or unity within a design gives a feeling of comfort and predictability. Legibility results in our being able to "read" a setting and immediately understand what it has to offer. Complexity ensures that a scene will not be too boring or overly sterile. Mystery is that which makes us want to move into a landscape, to experience the thrill of discovery.

The Importance of Mystery

Mystery was the most effective factor in making a scene highly favored by respondents. "The desire to explore a place is greatly enhanced if there is some promise that one can find out more as one keeps going. The suggestion that there is more to see is very compelling" (Kaplan, Kaplan, Ryan, p. 16).

Kaplan, Kaplan, and Ryan's findings are important to designers because they provide a basis for including specific elements in a landscape. Mystery can be heightened through use of a curving path or roadway where views around the bend are obscured. Tranquil and serene scenes are particularly favored.

Soft Fascination

Kaplan (1995) uses Henry James' (1892) theory of "voluntary attention," re-terming it "directed attention" in keeping with more recent neurological research. Directed attention requires conscious focus and effort and must be employed when something in itself cannot attract attention. When humans use directed attention, they must control distractions, focusing on "the task at hand," and this takes work. It is fatiguing. Kaplan believes that there may be an evolutionary explanation for this because paying attention to any one thing for a long time would make humans vulnerable to surprises. "Being vigilant, being alert to one's surroundings may have been far more important than the capacity for long and intense concentration" (Kaplan, p. 170). He thinks that directed-attention fatigue may be a relatively recent phenomenon. Others may see it as a particular problem of industrialization, which removed people from rural environments to focus on particular tasks within indoor environments.

Although sleep is recognized as an antidote to fatigue, Kaplan finds restoration of effectiveness to require more than sleep. He believes that effortless or involuntary attention (James 1892) allows directed attention to rest. Kaplan calls this cognitive trait "fascination" (Kaplan, p. 172). Kaplan distinguishes between "hard" and "soft" fascination. "There is the 'hard' fascination of watching auto racing and 'soft' fascination of walking in a natural setting. Soft fascination—characteristic of certain natural settings—has a special advantage in terms of providing an opportunity for reflection, which can further enhance the benefits of recovering from directed attention" (Kaplan, p. 172).

Figure 16.7 A curving road or path adds mystery by suggesting that there is more to see around the bend. Photo by KD Carrington.

These physical and psychological characteristics, along with concern for the biogeochemical cycles and biodiversity, should guide the design of open spaces in cities. Parks can be important antidotes to hectic environments, restorative places encouraging soft fascination. Many areas in Central Park, New York City, were deliberately designed to encourage peacefulness and respite from the hustle/bustle of the city. Olmsted described the stress he felt on the streets of New York in the mid 1800's:

> (I)f we consider that whenever we walk through the denser part of a town, to merely avoid collision with those we meet and pass upon the sidewalks, we have constantly to watch, to foresee and to guard against their movements ... Our minds are thus brought into close dealings with other minds without any friendly flowing toward them, but rather a drawing from them ... It is upon our opportunities of relief from (this effect), therefore, that not only our comfort in townlife, but our ability to maintain a temperate, good natured and healthy state of mind, depends. (Olmsted, pp. 65–66)

He seems to have aimed at countering stress and restoring a sense of peacefulness through design.

Central Park includes the necessary elements for attention restoration with broad lawns dotted with trees (offering prospect and refuge); intimate spaces with diverse plantings; and curving paths (offering mystery). Smaller urban parks, like the vest pocket Paley Park, NYC, are restorative through creative use of natural elements that work directly on human physiology. Paley Park's large water wall blocks the sound of traffic and increases negative ions. It also creates a fascinating visual screen of moving water. Sunlight, water, and vegetation can also be brought into building design, as explained in the chapter on "Conjoined Nature." Perhaps one day, cities will be seamless environments where buildings and nature work together to support positive human and environmental functions.

QUESTIONS

1. What *other* design preferences do you think humans (across all cultures) share?
2. What are optimal urban densities?
3. What do you think is the optimal distance to green space for an urban apartment dweller?
4. What percentage of open space and what sort of open space should cities contain?
5. What is your favorite urban green space? Why?
6. Imagine a small vacant lot, 20' wide by 40' long, in the middle of a city, surrounded by apartments. What elements would you use to design a restorative setting?

REFERENCES

Appleton, Jay. 1996, ed. *The Experience of Landscape* John Wiley & Sons: Chichester, UK.

Jellicoe, Geoffrey and Susan Jellicoe. 1982. *The Landscape of Man: Shaping the Environment from Prehistory to the Present Day.* Van Nostrand Reinhold Company: New York.

Hall, Edward T. 1966. *The Hidden Dimension,* Doubleday & Company, Inc., New York.

Kaplan, R., S. Kaplan, and R. Ryan. 1998. *With People in Mind: Design and Management of Everyday Nature*, Island Press, Washington, D.C.

Kaplan, Stephen. 1995. "The Restorative Benefits of Nature: Toward an Integrative Framework. *Journal of Environmental Psychology* 1995 15, pp. 169–182.

Stamps III, A.E. 2007. "Mystery of Environmental Mystery: Effects of Light, Occlusion and Depth

CREDITS

THE LINK BETWEEN GREEN SPACE AND HEALTH

BY MARY MYERS

Landscape architects, architects, and planners have been concerned about the effects of cities, especially industrial cities, since the 18th century. Industrialization occurred earlier in England and Europe than in the USA. Cities like London and Liverpool were unprepared for the influx of people moving from the countryside to seek work in newly established mills and factories. The basic housing and sanitation infrastructure necessary for the increased population was lacking. This resulted in the spread of disease and low life expectancy. Long working hours inside factories limited contact with sunshine, fresh air, fresh water, and green space, further impairing health. Lack of access to sunshine affected children, too. Children who do not get enough Vitamin D develop rickets, a disease that causes skeletal deformities. "By the late 1800's, approximately 90% of all children living in industrialized Europe and North America had some manifestation of the (rickets)...." (Mead, p. 162).

City officials, planners, and physicians began to recognize that something must be done to effect better public health. A reform movement, originating in England in the 19th century and then spreading to the USA, called for the creation of public parks to facilitate active recreation in the open air and sunshine. Central Park, New York City, (c. 1856–1872) was created for reasons of public health because New York, like London, had seen a rapid increase in population without sufficient green space. One of its designers, landscape architect Frederick Law Olmsted, argued that the park would be an antidote to the mental stress associated with city living.

Empirical evidence is mounting that supports Olmsted's (and others') notion that spending time in, or even just looking at, green space is healthy.

NATURE AND HEALING

Ulrich wrote about the positive effects of hospital views upon length of hospital stay, based upon records of patients recovering from cholecystectomies (surgical removal of the gall bladder) in a suburban Pennsylvania hospital. He hypothesized that "a hospital window view could influence a patient's emotional state and might according affect recovery" (Ulrich, 1985, p. 420). Ulrich accordingly explored the hypothesis by examining the records of patients assigned to rooms on the second and third floors of a three-story wing of the hospital between 1972 and 1981. Windows on one side of the wing looked out on a small stand of deciduous trees. Windows on the other side overlooked a brown brick wall. Rooms were identical in other ways and were served by the same nurses. "Only cholecystectomies performed between 1 May and 20 October were identified because the trees have foliage during those months. Patients with of the same sex, age (within 5 years), being a smoker or nonsmoker, being obese or within normal weight limits, general nature of previous hospitalization and other characteristics were matched" (Ulrich, 1985, p. 420).

Data indicated that "23 surgical patients assigned to rooms with windows looking out on a natural scene had shorter postoperative hospital stays, received fewer negative evaluative comments in nurses notes and took fewer potent analgesics than 23 matched patients in similar rooms with windows facing a brick building wall" (Ulrich, 1985, p. 420).

Hartig and Cooper Marcus (2006) write that justification for including gardens in hospital design might be based upon cost-reduction of health care (in the form of drugs or length of stay in the hospital). However, there is little research that explores a direct link between clinical health benefit and spending time in hospital gardens. Ulrich (1992) points out that hospitals are stressful places where patients, families, and staff all feel an absence of control. He suggests that positive distractions are effective in "reducing patient stress and promoting wellness. A positive distraction is an element that produces positive feelings, effortlessly holds attention and interest and therefore may block or reduce worrisome thoughts.... The most effective positive distractions are mainly elements that have been important to humans through a million years of evolution: (1) nature elements such as trees, plants and water; (2) happy, laughing or caring human faces; and (3) benign animals such as pets" (Ulrich, 1992, p. 24).

Ward Thompson (2011) traces the link between landscape and health through western history, tracing practice and theories from the ancient world, and the urban parks movement of the 19th century to the current research linking health to natural environments. She is interested in the ways that landscape may act as a prophylactic against disease, as well as its potential to mitigate disease (Ward Thompson, p. 188). The ancients described paradise as a garden in which people dwell easily and healthfully. "A recurring characteristic in these descriptions of paradise is the healthful nature of the garden, supporting human beings in every way, providing delight to every sense" (Ward Thompson, p. 188).

Increasingly, research findings support proximity to urban green space's positive effect on mental and physical health. Additionally, neuroscientists have found that beauty triggers activity stimulating a pleasure center of the brain. Thus, if the restorative benefit of being in *any* green space is coupled with the additional benefit of being in a *beautiful* green space, the combined outcome may be that much higher (better).

Landscape aesthetics may be particularly important in urban domains. As human population continues to expand, more people will live in cities. Those cities are likely to be dense. Thus, open space may vary in size, and while large parks may be created, many green spaces may be quite small in size. So what are the limitations of size and scope? How can an overarching ecological plan for restoring the urban forest be carried out at the same time as park design? What elements need to be present for maximization of human health and soft fascination?

It is interesting that the origins of western philosophy emerged from walking, discussing, and reflecting among the sacred groves of Greece. Is it possible that walking in a natural environment allows the mind to dwell on "larger" questions, that deeper cognitive processes are stimulated through perambulation in the natural environment? Researchers have also found that there is additional benefit to mental states (depression) when walking outdoors is done in the company of others (Pretty et al., 2007).

Large-scale studies exploring the relationship of green space to health have been conducted in northern Europe and England.

GENERAL HEALTH AND PROXIMITY TO GREEN SPACE

DeVries et al. (2003) conducted one of the first large-scale inquiries related to the amount of green space in the living environment and public health. They hypothesized that people living in green areas are healthier than people living in less-green areas. Using national data in the Netherlands, they tested the hypothesis by combining data on the self-reported health of over 10,000 people with land-use data on the amount of green space in their living environment. They looked at urbanity, socioeconomics, and demographics as indicators of health and found that living in a green environment was positively related to all three.

The Dutch study included gardens, or small green spaces, as contributors to the environment. The authors considered a garden as primarily a private green space that may compensate for the absence of other, often public, green areas (DeVries et al., p. 1719). It was found that people living in a greener environment, regardless of its size, appear to be significantly healthier than others.

The authors point out the ramifications for planning policy decisions in the Netherlands, a densely populated country. Instead of continuing the trend toward building densely compact urban areas surrounded by green rings of nature, they contend that it might be better to introduce green space within easy access of society. The findings seem to value the greening of vacant lots and creation of neighborhood gardens and pocket parks as a means of providing green space.

Mitchell and Popham (2008) studied the link between disease and access to green space for the population of England under retirement age An important aspect of the study is the large number of data (N=40,813,236) and the clear conclusions that could be drawn from the data. "Health inequalities related to income deprivation in all cause mortality and mortality from circulatory diseases were lower in populations living in the greenest areas" (Mitchell and Popham, p. 1655). The authors estimated that the lower inequality in mortality for the population with the highest exposure to green space saved 1,328 lives per year when compared with the same income group having the lowest exposure to green space. It was concluded that *access to green space positively affects life expectancy in low-income populations in England.*

GREEN EXERCISE AND MENTAL HEALTH

A link has been made between mental health and exercise. Silveira et al. (2013) conducted a meta-analysis of 1292 articles, eventually narrowing the study to 10 articles that investigate the effect of physical exercise in reducing depressive symptoms. They found that aerobic exercise improves response to depression treatment. Elderly patients benefited most from exercise. Blumenthal et al (1999) verified that aerobic training is as effective as antidepressant medication (sertraline) in reducing depressive symptoms.

Pretty et al. (2007) wished to find out the effect of nature and green space on health in the UK. They conducted a survey of 262 participants taking part in a variety of green exercise initiatives in England, Scotland, Wales, and Northern Ireland. The green exercise activities were walking (45%); cycling (32%); conservation (9%); horse riding (3%); boating (4%); woodland activities (4%); and fishing (3%). Respondents were asked about their physical and psychological health, as well as their level of physical fitness and lifestyle. They were also asked to rate their self-esteem and mood pre- and post-exercise activity. It was found that *regardless of type, duration, or intensity of physical activity, psychological well-being improved from doing that activity in nature* (Pretty et al., p. 222).

MIND (originally the National Association for Mental Health) is a large UK non-profit agency dedicated to mental health. The agency is using Pretty et al.s' (and other) research to advocate for green exercise therapy. Green exercise, or "ecotherapy," is viewed as a legitimate treatment for depression and other mental health ills. It can serve as an alternative therapy or complement to standard pharmaceutical treatment. MIND argues that one of the many positive aspects of ecotherapy is that it has few or none of the negative side effects associated with psychiatric drugs, which can include muscle spasms, loss of energy, restlessness, sleeplessness, and Parkinsonism, among others. In fact, ecotherapy has *positive* side effects, because regular exercise offers "protection from type II diabetes, coronary heart disease and lowers blood pressure" (MIND, 2007, p. 5). To this end, MIND recommends that design for mental well-being should be a high priority for planners and designers (MIND, p. 30).

HUMAN PREFERENCE FOR GREEN

Akers et al. (2012) wanted to find out a cognitive mechanism responsible for benefiting from exercise in a green environment. They had fourteen cyclists perform three moderate-intensity five-minute cycling tasks while watching video footage of a rural cycling course that simulated cycling in a real natural environment. One of the videos was unedited (green-color predominant), another was gray, and another red. Lower total mood disturbance and ratings of perceived exertion were found during the green video compared with the gray or red videos. This is one of the first studies to show that the color green has a contributory effect toward positive green exercise outcomes.

PHILADELPHIA:
RELATION BETWEEN GREENING VACANT LOTS AND CRIME REDUCTION

The results of a decade-long study of vacant lots in Philadelphia showed significant social and health benefits associated with landscape. Branas et al. (2011) studied five sections of Philadelphia, using green lots that were cleaned of debris, planted with grass and trees, and surrounded by picket fences. The lots were improved and maintained by Pennsylvania Horticultural Society (PHS) beginning in 1999. Control lots in the same sections received no improvements.

The authors developed a database of 54,132 vacant lots present in the city from 1999 to 2008 (assembled from the Philadelphia Bureau of taxes and other agencies). They used crime data provided by the Philadelphia Police Department that included dates and longitude–latitude coordinates for several types of crimes and arrests during that time period. The Philadelphia Health Management Corporation provided data from the Southeastern Pennsylvania Household Health Survey, which is administered randomly every two years to a new cohort of approximately 5,000 Philadelphians.

In all sections, across the entire city, gun assaults were reduced after the greening treatment.

Interestingly, while gun assaults decreased, disorderly conduct increased after the greening of vacant lots. The authors speculate that this may be due to larger groups of people coming together in lots or that community interest in maintaining a newly greened lot may have increased calls to the police and arrests for disorderly conduct.

North Philadelphia, one of the most impoverished areas of the city, showed reduction in stress associated with presence of green lots (Branas et al., p. 7). This finding may lend impetus for Temple University campus, located in North Philadelphia, to extend its landscape beyond the university borders. Sending green "fingers" of trees and rain gardens out into the streets of the surrounding neighborhoods will complement the urban farms springing up on vacant lots. It will be interesting to study the effects of this greener environment upon health and crime over the coming decades.

Increasingly, these research findings support the positive effect of urban green space upon mental and physical health. Recently, neuroscientists have found that beauty triggers activity stimulating a pleasure center of the brain. If the restorative benefit of being in *any* green space is coupled with the additional benefit of being in a *beautiful* green space, the combined outcome may be much higher (better). Future research should examine the effect of different landscape designs upon mood and pleasure in order to improve sustainable design.

QUESTIONS

1. Do you think humans have innate environmental preferences?
2. Are there universally preferred landscapes and landscape characteristics?
3. What are optimal urban densities?
4. What percentage of open space and what sort of open space should cities contain?
5. How would you improve your local neighborhood to effect better health?
6. What is a good research question to help inform and improve future sustainable design?

REFERENCES

Akers, A., J. Barton, R. Cossey, P. Gainsford, M. Griffin, and D. Micklewright. 2012. "Visual Color Perception in Green Exercise: Positive Effects on Mood and Perceived Exertion." *Environmental Science and Technology* 46: 8661–8666.

Appleton, J. 1996, ed. *The Experience of Landscape* John Wiley & Sons: Chichester, UK.

Barton, J. and J. Pretty. 2010. "What Is the Best Dose of Nature and Green Exercise for Improving Mental Health? A Multi-Study Analysis." *Environmental Science and Technology.* 44: 3947–3955.

Branas, C., R. Cheney, J. MacDonald, V. Tam, T. Jackson, and T. Ten Have. July 18, 2011 "A Difference-in-Differences Analysis of Health, Safety and Greening Vacant Open Space." *American Journal of Epidemiology* 1–11. (http://aje.oxfordjournals.org).

De Vries, S., R. Verheij, P. Gorenewegen, and P. Spreeuwenberg. 2003. "Natural Environments—Healthy Environments? An Exploratory Analysis of the Relationship Between Greenspace and Health." *Environment and Planning* (35)1717–1731.

Jellicoe, G. and S. Jellicoe. 1982. *The Landscape of Man: Shaping the Environment from Prehistory to the Present Day.* Van Nostrand Reinhold Company: New York.

Hall, E.T. (1966) *The Hidden Dimension,* Doubleday & Company, Inc., New York.

Hartig, Terry and Clare Cooper Marcus. December 2006. "Healing Gardens: Places for Nature in Health Care." *Lancet* 368:536–537. (www.thelancet.com).

Kaplan, R., S. Kaplan, and R. Ryan. (1998) *With People in Mind: Design and Management of Everyday Nature.* Island Press: Washington, D.C.

Mead, M.N. 2008. "Benefits of Sunlight: A Bright Spot for Human Health." *Environmental Health Perspectives* 116:4: A160–A167. (www.ncbi.nim.nih.gov/pmc/articles).

MIND. May 2007. "Ecotherapy: the Green Agenda for Mental Health." (http://www.mind.org.uk).

Mitchell R. and F. Popham. 2008. "Effect of Exposure to Natural Environment on Health Inequalities: An Observational Population Study." *Lancet* 372: 1655–60.

Nielsen, T.S. and J.B. Hansen. 2007. "Do Green Areas Affect Health? Results from a Danish Survey on the Use of Green Areas and Health Indicators." *Health and Place* 13, 839–850.

Olmsted, F.L., Jr. and T. Kimball, ed., 1922. *Forty Years of Landscape Architecture: Being the Professional Papers of Frederick Law Olmsted, Seniori.* New York and London: G.P. Putnam's Sons.

Pretty, J., J. Peacock, R. Hine, M. Sellens, N. South, and M. Griffin. 2007. "Green Exercise in the UK Countryside: Effects on Health and Psychological Well-Being, and Implications for Policy and Planning." *Journal of Environmental Planning and Management* 50:2, 211–231.

Stamps III, A.E. 2007. "Mystery of Environmental Mystery: Effects of Light, Occlusion and Depth of View." *Environment and Behavior* 39: 165–199.

Van den Berg, A.E., T. Hartig, and H. Staats. 2007. "Preference for Nature in Urbanized Societies: Stress, Restoration and the Pursuit of Sustainability." *Journal of Social Issues* 63 1:79–96.

Ward Thompson, C. 2011. "Linking Landscape and Health: The Recurring Theme." *Landscape and Urban Planning* 99:187–195.

Ulrich, Roger S, 1985. "View Through a Window May Influence Recovery from Surgery." *Science* 224:4647:420–421.

Ulrich, Roger S. 1992. "How Design Impacts Wellness." *Healthcare Forum Journal* September/October 20–26.

Ward Thompson, C. 2011. "Linking Landscape and Health: The Recurring Theme." *Landscape and Urban Planning* 99:187–195.

ELEVATING HABITAT

A Quasi-traditional Green Roof Design Can Increase Biodiversity in Cities

BY REID COFFMAN

While green roofs have been lauded for their technical advances in stormwater management and mitigation of the urban hear island effect, efforts to create local habitat on green roofs remain modest. The style of green roofs popular today—shallow, engineered soil mixes and a limited palette of plants (typically sedum) considered tough enough for rooftop conditions—generally ignores local ecosystems. It is difficult to see these "technologically advanced" green roofs as any thing but exotic, manufactured islands set atop an urban matrix.

The traditional method of green roof construction is an economical method relying exclusively on local materials. For centuries in some of the Nordic countries, simple roofing systems were made from nearby materials with waterproofing membranes made from a variety of local resources including bark and straw, usually stacked on top of one another and held down with rocks. Occasionally, soil alone was used. The soil's existing seed bank of native plants was the sole source of vegetation, and plants were allowed to self-organize into a unique community. Maintenance consisted of occasionally weeding out saplings.

In contrast, the modern, conventional method developed over the past few decades has been influenced by the imperative to reduce risk of failure and emphasizes imported materials. Measures to protect the building's structural integrity and prevent leaks at all costs predominate. The system typically begins with a petroleum based waterproof membrane, topped with root-barrier fabric and drainage layers. Often a thin water-retention layer is added. Occasionally roof insulation is used. Then comes a lightweight, water-retentive, sterile substrate, manufactured from shale, slate, or clay and blown unto the roof. Nutrients may be added via recycled agricultural products or compost. The plants are usually a monoculture of sedum species or other exotics. Maintenance includes seasonal watering, fertilizing, and weeding all plants not in die original palette.

Although biodiversity studies in the United States and Europe confirm that ail green roofs create habitat, some believe that mimicking the local environmental conditions can create more valuable habitat. With the goal of optimizing local habitat, green roof projects have been created using a "quasi-traditional" method of construction, a method that incorporates local soils and planes to connect to the local ecosystems. Although there has been some interest in North America in the quasi-traditional method, the real innovation has come from Switzerland and the United Kingdom.

THE SWISS EXPERIMENTS

In Switzerland, quasi-traditional green roofs are becoming the preferred method because of their use of local materials and creation of creation of habitat. This was accidentally discovered after several contemporary green roofs failed to keep vegetation alive, and designers and researchers turned toward adding local compost as topdressing. The result was a unique plant community.

One of the most influential precedents has been the green roof on the Moos Lake Water Plant near Zurich, which was constructed in 1914 using the traditional method. At the time Moos Lake was conceived, the soils would keep the water filtration processes inside the building cooler, thus preventing bacteria from developing in the municipal water supply. The ceiling stab is eight centimeters of concrete copped with two centimeters of mastic asphalt, five centimeters of sand, and 15 to 20 centimeters of on-site topsoil. The topsoil is original and was taken from the site where the building was being built, which at the time was a seasonal wet prairie. Over time the surrounding environment developed into the city, and, consequently, the green roof now possesses numerous extirpated and rare plant species including nine species of orchid. It is home to the only population of *Orchis moro* left in the region. The plant biodiversity is so unusual the green roof is being considered as a national wildlife site. It thrives today with minimal maintenance. Replacement of plants and soils has not been necessary. Only small improvements to the waterproofing have been required.

Due to the Moos Lake success, quasi traditional green roofs began appearing that use local soils or a combination of manufactured substrate and local amendments placed on top of contemporary membranes. In 1998 experimental test plots were constructed on the Irchel Tram Depot near Zurich to examine plant survival in these conditions. A variety of substrates varying in consistency and depth was planted with the same conservation seed mix. The findings showed that deeper substrates amended with local topsoil allowed for both greater plant growth and diversity. As a result of this study, this method of seeding native grasses and forbs has become a regular practice. Retrofit experiments began for existing contemporary green roofs, and new projects required innovative design for biodiversity.

One retrofit is the University of Basel Library green roof, which was originally constructed with the contemporary method of uniform substrates and sedums in the mid-1980s. The original design failed to keep plants alive due to low nutrient availability; consequently, in the late 1990s the roof was amended with the dual purpose of improving its visual quality and its plant performance. Several topdressings were applied to the existing substrate, including compost and local clay topsoil. The top topdressing was then seeded with an off-the-shelf local conservation seed mix containing several sixties of concern. The results showed improved plant as well as insect diversity.

During the late 1990s the Swiss began a four-year study observing 24 green roofs in two cities and found higher biodiversity levels (via species richness) in systems that possessed substrate diversify, topographic diversity, and plant diversity.

Engineered substrates "are just too poor in nutrients and too shallow to grow many plants," says Stephan Brenneisen, director of Basel's green roof program. While it is true that adding amendments and increasing soil depth can increase weight loads that are usually antithetical to lightweight green roof design, Brenneisen points out that top-dressing lightweight soils with organic amendment provides necessary habitat for invertebrate life to complete the ecosystem nutrient cycle in these systems.

When it comes to biodiversity, two other elements have been shown to be important: stones and mounds. Stones of various size placed on the substrate surface or worked into the substrate create areas with unique thermal qualities that allow insects to heat or cool themselves as well as hide from predators. "Stones are very important," Brenneisen says. "When stones are used with mounds and local soils, the chances for insect colonization and bird usage will rise."

A green roof on the Rossetti Building (built in 1998) in Basel was one of the first of its kind to employ and test local soils and vegetation to form small mounds, ranging from three to 15 inches in depth. The soils have diverse aggregate component—60 percent stones, gravel, and sand—along with line particles and humus. The system was seeded with a local meadow seed mixture. After three years, coverage was 100 percent on the mounds and 50 percent on the three-inch areas between the mounds. This patchy vegetation coverage was considered acceptable for the mission of biodiversity, because it provides variety in plant habitat. It is hoped that the three-inch areas will achieve no more than 70 percent coverage, allowing continual patchiness that will attract a variety of insects and birds.

Efforts to protect native fauna have spurred recent innovative projects. The Sihlpost Platform in the Zurich main railway station was designed to provide a "desertlike" habitat for lizards and birds that live in the rock-covered river basins next to the tracks. Topographic diversity and plant diversity were created by constructing hummocks over support columns that provide habitat patches for insects, lizards, and birds. Terrestrial linkage for the lizards was maintained by creating gabion baskets tilled with local stone. This linkage has so far been successful—I observed several lizards using this system.

In a mixture of art and ecology, the root of Nordtangente, an elevated expressway in downtown Basel, was designed as habitat mitigation for a nearby dry meadows that was being developed. Dry meadows are species-rich environments of national significance in Switzerland. This green roof began with an artist's interpretation of the Swiss-inspired Helvetica font, constructed on raised shelves of aggregate so as to be visible from nearby residential flats. Local meadow topsoil (half-inch to one-and-a-half-inch depth) was added to random shelves to provide habitat. The random display makes the alphabet appear through a quilted patchwork.

The seeds in the soils of the dry meadows established on the roof.

Today, all new green roof projects in Basel go through design review for quasi-traditional techniques that improve habitat, which is overseen by Brenneisen. "We are trying to find homes for rare species on these roofs," Brenneisen says "After all, the tops of the buildings don't matter to most architects. But they can matter to the local plants and animals if they are designed correctly."

ENGLISH AND CANADIAN INTERPRETATIONS

Using the quasi-traditional method in London would meet two objectives: The urban suits are habitat to numerous species of concern, and using on-site materials furthers the project's sustainability goals.

The soils in London are urban soils; therefore, green roof projects are being built with die "rubble" from local sites. On the new Laban Center, home of a famous dance school, a quasi-traditional green roof was built with contemporary membranes, and on-site materials were used for the substrate to provide habitat mitigation, but very little organic material was added to determine its potential as a unique bird habitat.

The "rubble roof," which includes crushed brick, concrete chunks, various aggregates, and stones, provides a patchy vegetated habitat for the black redstart, an endangered bird that has adapted to living in the city's vacant lots. (As it happens, this same bird was also the most abundant species found on Swiss ecoroofs.)

This does not surprise Dusty Gedge, green roof designer and director of LivingRoofs.com, an independent research and advocacy organization in the United Kingdom. "Black redstarts are endangered in London and in conflict with redevelopment efforts," he says. "Why build a roof with aggregate and plants from out of town, when the birds like the local rubble better? Plus, it's more sustainable." On new projects he is overseeing in London's Canary Wharf, the green roofs include local "rubble" but also more organic material and a wider variety of aggregate sizes to achieve the desired patchy vegetation mosaic.

In North America, at least one project has been recognized for using quasi-traditional ecoroofing methods and applying landscape restoration practices. Oak Hammock Marsh Interpretive Center near Winnipeg received a 2003 international Award of Excellence from Green Roofs for Healthy Cities, a North American nonprofit whose mission is research and advocacy of green roofs. The design team, including Ten Architectural Group and local naturalists, used an ecological restoration approach in creating this roof. A local prairie soil was preconditioned to eliminate weed seeds, installed on the roof, and then seeded and plugged with a combination of native grasses and forbs to from a short-grass prairie community. Located within a wetlands complex, the roof attracts such bird species as mallards, pinmils, gadwalls, and killdeer, which seasonally build nests and hatch their young in the short-grass prairie environment of the roof. Maintenance is seasonal hand weeding, spot spraying when necessary, and periodically burning the green roof to maintain the nutrient recycling of a short-grass prairie system.

DESIGN CONSIDERATIONS

Some fear that specifying on-site or local material will cause some green roofs to fail. Inventorying and assessing on-site materials can reduce this risk. Designs for all green roofs should meet the international standards known as the FLL Standards, which specify the physical properties of drainage and support courses. On-site materials can be used in each of the courses if they meet the specifications in provide essential functions, such as drainage allowance or plant rooting area.

As more communities place green roofs into stormwater regulations as best management practices, the quasi-traditional roof may encounter resistance, as local materials are unproven. One advantage to most contemporary substrates is that they clean the water through the use of expanded clays and shale, which act as filters. Unknown entities such as untested local topsoil could become pollutant sources that could leach nutrients, including nitrates, into the storm sewers from the building downspouts. If this is shown to be the case, quasi-traditional green roofs could become anathema to water quality goals. It is important to lab test soil and substrate for retention and chemical properties.

Very little is known about how elevated habitats will function for wildlife. Size, location, and elevation are all variables that could affect wildlife usage. Some migratory birds are using the roofs as stopover habitat where they rest and forage for food, while a few bird species are successfully nesting on the roofs. At this time most researchers believe green roof habitat is advantageous for all species of wildlife. One way of preventing species decline is by providing adequate resources for targeted at-risk species.

Also, retaining waterproofing membrane warranties may be difficult with local materials. Many distributors will warrant their waterproofing membrane only if their green roof system is specified, though some don't have that requirement. Early communication with suppliers and contractors will alleviate problems in this area.

In the end, the quasi-traditional method may contribute to urban biodiversity and wildlife habitat, which may come with its own challenges. Because much innovation hits been created around storm water issues, it is reasonable to assume similar innovation can occur with habitat in mind. Quasi-traditional practices can be effective for habitat creation and may possibly be useful for the future of green roof design.

RESOURCES

- Conference proceedings from Greening Rooftops for Sustainable Communities 2003–2008 available at Greening Rooftops for Healthy Cities, www.greenroofs.org
- FLL Guidelines for the Planning, Execution, and Upkeep of Green Roof Sites, *www.f-l-l.delenglish.html*
- *Green Roofs: Ecological Design and Construction,* edited by Seina Chrisman with Earth Pledge; Altglen, Pennsylvania: Schiffer Publishing, 2005.

- *Green Roofs in Sustainable Landscape Design* by Steven Cantor, New York: W. W. Norton & Company, 2005.
- *Win-Win Ecology: How the Earth's Species Can Survive in the Midst of Human Enterprise,* by M. L. Rosenzweig; New York: Oxford University Press, 2003.

RETROFITTING A SUBURBAN GARDEN:

Biodiversity Starts at Home

BY MARY MYERS

The American suburban dream centers on living in a "green" environment with all of the advantages (and none of the disadvantages) of an urban environment. However, suburbia is unsustainable due to the amount of matter, land and energy required to build and maintain buildings, roads and landscapes.

Additionally, wooded or agricultural sites ("green fields") are converted to "grey fields" (pavement and structures) with decreased capability to provide ecological services. Suburban landscapes are frequently comprised of exotic plant spaces and do not support native biodiversity. How can suburbia be modified or retrofit to promote greater biodiversity and increased ecosystem services? The author examined this question and decided to put some of this book's ideas into effect in her own suburban yard.

BACKGROUND

The American suburban lifestyle is one that was once only available to the highest levels of society. Suburbanites live in large homes (castles) with labor saving devices to facilitate cooking and cleaning (mechanical servants). Residents frequently do not use all of the rooms in their houses on a daily basis but heat and cool them nonetheless. A car is necessary to navigate the vast transportation network of roads because houses, shops, schools and work are far apart. Walking between destinations is time consuming and frequently unsafe. Bicycles would be useful to cover 5 – 10 mile distances but cyclists frequently must ride alongside, and at the mercy of cars and trucks.

Designers and planners are now examining the unsustainable aspects of suburbia and proposing ideas to improve the environment. Greenways are being built to provide safe travel routes for bicyclists and pedestrians. Energy saving appliances and heating and cooling modes are being integrated into houses. Some suburbanites opt to draw their energy from renewable sources. The renovation of older houses is reducing sprawl and conserving virgin resources used for new houses.

SUBURBAN LANDSCAPES

What about the suburban yard? Suburban land holdings typically range from ¼ acre to 10 acres or more. The "estate" is often comprised of lawn and ornamental trees and flowers. The trees and shrubs are frequently exotic aliens—meaning they are non-native species. This landscape has quite low diversity and ecosystem service potential. The lawn requires lots of mowing to keep it in a consistently juvenile state (3" height). Any fallen leaves are quickly removed with leaf blowers or rakes to ensure that the grass is not smothered with leaf litter. Chemicals that can seep into groundwater, are applied to the lawn, flower beds and shrubs to kill unwanted "weeds" and to promote vigor. Considerable matter and energy inputs are needed to keep this garden looking the same year in and year out.

The economic and environmental costs associated with American lawns are significant. Haydu, et.al (2006) state that the turfgrass industry, including sod farms, lawn care services, lawncare retail stores, lawn equipment manufacturing and golf courses generated $62.2 billion collectively. This figure today would likely be about $100 billion. Banks and McConnell (2015) studied the contribution of gasoline-powered lawn and garden equipment (GLGE) to air pollution in the USA. They found that "In 2011, approximately 26.7 million tons of pollutants were emitted by GLGE (VOC=461,800; CO=5,793,200; NOx=68,500, PM10=20,700; CO_2=20,382,400), accounting for 24%–45% of all non-road gasoline emissions (Banks and McConnell, p. 1). If lawns can be reduced or eliminated at the national level, Carbon dioxide, volatile organic compounds and other pollutants will be reduced.

Suburbanites are rarely seen using their yards and the overall societal trend seems to be toward spending more time indoors. (Driessnack, Tremblay, et.al) However, the suburban landscape has the potential to improve ecosystem health and/or provide food. Inhabitants can benefit physically and emotionally from actively managing the ecosystem and/or food production.

BIODIVERSITY AND ECOSYSTEM SERVICES

Miller (2005) views biological diversity, or biodiversity as "one of the earth's most important renewable resources....providing the biological wealth or capital that helps keep us alive and supports our economies (Miller 2005, 67)." This idea is extended in the concept of ecosystem services. "Ecosystem services are the benefits that people gain from ecosystems (Millennium Ecosystem Report, 2005, "Ecosystems and Their

Services", p. 57)." These services can be immediately linked to survival, such as the provisioning of food and water; or they may be related to regulating services, such as climate and flood regulation, or the maintenance of water quality; or they may be related to cultural services, such as the beauty and wonder of the natural world. Sustainable design should seek to incorporate and overlap as many services and benefits as possible.

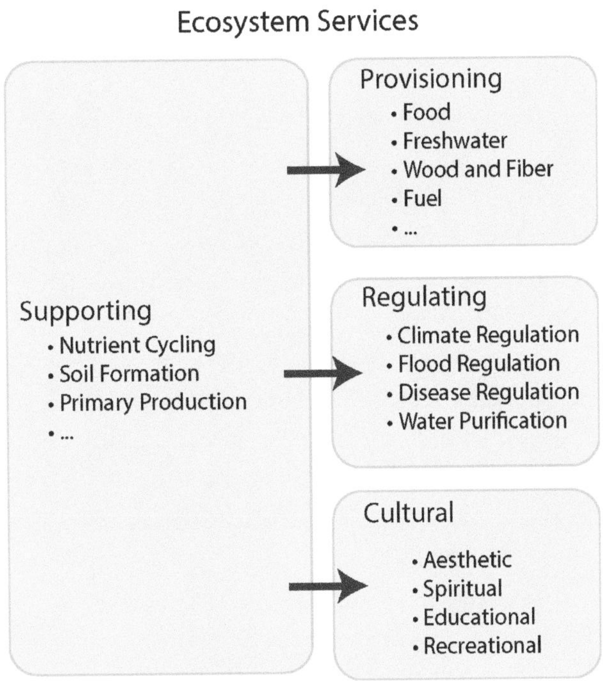

Ecosystem Services

Supporting
- Nutrient Cycling
- Soil Formation
- Primary Production
- ...

Provisioning
- Food
- Freshwater
- Wood and Fiber
- Fuel
- ...

Regulating
- Climate Regulation
- Flood Regulation
- Disease Regulation
- Water Purification

Cultural
- Aesthetic
- Spiritual
- Educational
- Recreational

Figure 19.1 Diagram from Millenium Ecosystem Report 2005.

Tallemy (2007) writes about the loss of biodiversity in the USA:

> "(W)ell over 70 percent of the forests along our eastern seaboard are gone. We have reduced the enormous land mass that, over millions of years, created the rich biodiversity we can still see today in this country to tiny habitat islands (with) high rates of species extinction and emigration and low rates of speciation and immigration (Tallamy, 29)."

We have transformed native forests to highly simplified systems for industrial scale agriculture, or paved them over with roads and parking lots and buildings, or through our approach to suburban gardens, which replace native with non native plants. Tallamy links loss of biodiversity to exotic (or alien) plant species introduced from other parts of the world. As an entomologist, he observed that there was very little insect damage to the exotic plants (Norway maple, Bradford pear, autumn olive, etc.) in his own back yard in Southeastern Pennsylvania. Hypothesizing that this was due to native insects' preference for native plants, he began to investigate the question. He studied the insect herbivore biomass produced by native versus non-native plants. He found that native plants produced nearly *four* times more insect biomass than alien plants produced. "This difference resulted entirely from the inability of insects with chewing mouthparts to eat alien plants (Tallamy, p.328)." There is a co-evolutionary relationship between the native insects and plants, just as there is between many birds and insects (and on up the food chain). Tallamy's findings propelled him to think about the potential for suburbia to increase, rather than decrease, biodiversity.

ASPIRATION

As I looked around my neighborhood, like Tallamy, I noticed the prevalence of non-native species, particularly the exotic shrubs, lawn grasses and herbaceous plants in the understory of the large native Beech, Tulip Trees, Oak and Hickory. Few of my neighbors had native shrubs, groundcovers or vines. While there were birds in the leafy canopies above and mosquitoes, fireflies and gnats during the summer months, was it possible that more birds, butterflies and other insects ought to be flourishing? An idea took shape—to create an aesthetically pleasing, ecologically based landscape design with multiple plant species. It would be an opportunity to see native plants in the suburban setting, plants that ought to be present in the local landscape. It could also serve as a model to educate to neighbors and passersby about locally native plants and habitats. I reasoned that the impetus to grow local food and buy local products might logically extend to local flora. Growing locally native plant species, especially those local to the county, seemed both the right thing to do and a well-timed effort. I worked with landscape contractor and Temple University alum, Brad Scherff to design the rain gardens. Brad's company installed the landscape and cleaned out the invasive plants. Diane Ehrich, TU alum in horticulture, assisted with new plants.

EXISTING CONDITIONS

When we moved into our house in the Philadelphia suburbs in the mid 2000's, my family liked the diversity of architectural types, dating from the 1930's, and walkable neighborhood. Tall native American Beech trees (*Fagus grandifolia*) grew in our yard and were part of a shared neighborhood grove. I have always called the Beech, "Queen of the Forest" for its quality of stately grace. Below the beech grew native Rhododendron (*Rhododentron maximum*), Blue Phlox (*Phlox divaricata*) and a native Mountain Laurel (*Kalmia latifolia*) that bloomed in late spring. A Flowering Dogwood (*Cornus florida*) grew near the street. Aside from these five species, the plants were exotic. They included numerous Japanese azaleas, (*Rhododendron japonica*), Chinese Forsythia, (*Forsythia sinensis*), False Cypress (*Chamecyperus sp*) from Japan, European Privet (*Ligustrum vulgare*), Japanese Kwanzan Cherry (*Prunus serrulata "Kwanzan"*), Bugle weed (*Ajuga reptans*) from Europe, Japanese Azalea (*Rhododendron japonicum*), English Yew (*Taxus baccata*) and Spreading Yew (*Taxus x media "Densiformis"*).

Two extremely aggressive ground covers Wintercreeper (*Euonymous fortunii*) from Asia and English Ivy (*Hedera helix*) had taken over large areas of the side yard and infiltrated (along with those planted by our neighbors) the shared woodland. A less aggressive ground cover, Japanese Pachesandra (*Pachesandra procumbins*) was springing up here and there. European Lesser Celandine (*Ranunculus ficaria*) was marching up the hill from the nearby Tookany Creek, appropriating lawns and any open patch of land under the canopy of tall trees. These exotics, along with invasive Japanese Stiltgrass, Crabgrass and Garlic Mustard were forming dense mats and suppressing the diversity of the woodland floor—once strewn with spring ephemerals, ferns and other shade tolerant native plants.

Figure 19.2 The original landscape was characterized by lots of lawn and exotic shrubs packed tightly against the building. Behind is a Beech, Tuliptree, Oak, Hickory woodland shared with the neighbors.

The lawn species included Zoysia, a creeping grass from Asia and other non-native species. Despite its name, Kentucky Blue Grass, (*Poa pratensis*) is of European origin. Fescue *(Festuca rubra)* and Canada Rye *(Elymus Canadensis)* are from N. America.

Table 19.1

NATIVE TO N. AMERICA (N = 7) NATIVE TO MONTGOMERY COUNTY, PA (N = 5)	NON-NATIVE (ASIA OR EUROPE) (N = 16)
American Beech	Bugle weed
Blue Phlox	Chinese Forsythia
	Crabrass
Flowering Dogwood	English Ivy
Mountain Laurel	English Yew
Rosebay Rhododendron	European Privet
	Garlic Mustard
Canada Rye	False Cypress
Red Fescue	Japanese Azalea
	Japanese Kwanzan Cherry
	Japanese Pachysandra
	Japanese Stiltgrass
	Kentucky Blue Grass
	Spreading Yew
	Wintercreeper
	Zoysia

Table 20.1 Plant species on site when the house was purchased. The non-native species, or exotics, were probably purchased by the former owner(s) at local plant nurseries. Many or most plant nurseries do not carry native species but sell exotic, non-natives. 23 total species; 16 (70%) are exotic aliens from other continents); 5 are native to PA; 2 are native to N. America but not to PA.

DESIGN GOALS

The overarching design goal was to increase ecosystems services over the existing conditions. The new garden would exemplify the revised I=PAT – R formula (Environmental Impact = Population x Affluence x Technology – Restoration) by restoring plants native to the southeastern Pennsylvania Piedmont setting. The resulting increase in biodiversity ought to enhance ecological service delivery at the local scale. Although the site is not large, the change was hypothesized to result in measurable improvement over the original lot (over time).

The specific design goals for this suburban landscape were:
1. Increase biodiversity in order to support a stable, resilient ecosystem capable of providing a variety of services (at the local scale).
2. Infiltrate stormwater on site in order to reduce runoff entering nearby Tookany Creek. This action would contribute to the flood regulation ecosystem service.
3. Improve carbon dioxide sequestration contributing to climate regulation ecosystem services.
4. Educate the public about the beauty and function of native plants, contributing to the educational ecosystem service.
5. Create functional and beautiful outdoor spaces using diverse native plants, contributing to the aesthetic ecosystem service

Methods of measuring the degree to which the goals have been met:

1. Biodiversity can be measured with the Plant Stewardship Index.
2. Stormwater infiltration can be measured with observations over time.
3. Carbon dioxide sequestration can be measured with an online calculator developed by the National Forest Service and Casey Trees.
4. Public education can be measured through numbers of tours/presentations and articles about the project
5. Function and beauty of the spaces could be measured through use and survey of residents and visitors using the space.

Due to the recent installation of the landscape (2012-13), it was difficult to measure items 2,4 and 5. Stormwater should be monitored with instruments over a period of years. We have observed the function of the rain gardens during large storms to see if stormwater is spilling over into the street. But we may need to employ other methods. The cultural benefits related to education and beauty require time to develop and administer: i.e. offer and teach classes; write articles; survey users and visitors. One measure of the public education is that the garden was featured in an article for the New York Times, October, 9 2014 titled "One Woman's Pipedream: A Rain Garden Even the Neighbors seem to Like". Author Anne Raver wrote compellingly of both the function and aesthetics associated with the new garden. Her article reached many readers.

DESIGN APPROACH

Increasing Biodiversity

A design premise was that the landscape would not be static, or held in check. Often, a designer desires to control the composition s/he has created but this has never been completely possible. Even Versailles, the estate of French King Louis XIV, could not be frozen in time. Plants grow: some faster than others. The ground layer, or herbaceous layer frequently expresses the greatest change with certain species dominating one year, and others the next. Cultural expectations must adjust to accept and appreciate change and evolution within the garden. An ecologically based landscape will look more complex, perhaps messier, than the standard "mow and blow" setting suburbanites are accustomed to.

Redundancy

Our redesigned garden would be diverse, containing many different plant species. A diverse ecosystem has redundancy with several plant species serving the same function and having the same niche. Redundancy ensures that the system won't collapse if one species is lost. It is also interesting from an aesthetic point of view because it results in visual interest for there is always something in bloom or fruit during the growing season.

The design is based upon a plant community approach. "A plant community is defined as an assemblage of plant populations sharing a common environment and interacting with each other, with animal populations and with the physical environment (Fike, 1)." The majority of plants would be native to Montgomery County, Pennsylvania. If any "escaped" into the wild, there would be no lasting devastation as has occurred with the escape of ornamental exotics. "To date, over 5,000 species of alien plants have invaded the natural areas of North America (Tallamy, 82)." Aliens greatly reduce native biodiversity by outcompeting natives. If a plant escaped from my residential landscape, it would in effect be returning "home" to its native woodland habitat.

PLANT SELECTION

Several sources were used to develop the plant list: *Terrestrial & Palustrine Plant Communities of Pennsylvania* by Jean Fike (1999), *Montgomery Count, Pennsylvania Natural Areas Inventory Update 2008* by Ann Rhoads and Timothy Block and *Vascular Flora of Pennsylvania* by Ann Rhoads and William Klein (1993). Observations and plots from field trips to reference sites with ecologist colleague John Munro and graduate students of landscape architecture, also provided information about the plant communities associated with our sloping woodland habitat and wetland habitats suited to the rain garden concept. It must be stressed that the new landscape is not a pure restoration but a design that uses native species. It establishes a trajectory of growth but that growth will be managed for multifunctional purposes—ecosystem services, aesthetics, and family recreation. The result is still a suburban landscape.

Terrestrial plant community

The terrestrial plant community model that best fit the site is the tuliptree-beech-maple forest which occurs on "Fairly deep, not strongly acidic soils, at a mid-to-lower slope position...The most consistent tree species for this often very mixed type are red maple (*Acer rubrum),* tuliptree (*Liriodendron tulipefera*) and American beech *(Fagus grandifolia)* (Fike, 12)." These species were present on the site or in the immediate vicinity.

Palustrine plant community (wetland)

The red maple, mixed shrub palustrine plant community was used as a model for the rain garden because it occurs in more southern parts of the state (such as the site's location in Montgomery County). Trees include: red maple (*Acer rubrum*); black-gum (*Nyssa sylvatica*); eastern hemlock, (*Tsuga canadensis*). Shrubs include: spice bush (*Lindera benzoin*); and winter berry (*Ilex verticillata*) silky willow (*Salix sericea*); swamp rose (*rosa palustris*) and buttonbush (*Cephalanthus occidentalis*). According to Fike, ferns usually dominate the ground layer. Species include: marsh fern (*thelypteris palustris*); sensitive fern (*Onoclea sensibilis*); royal fern (*Onoclea regalis*); crested shield fern (*Dryopteris cristata*). Other herbs include marsh marigold (*Caltha palustris*), beggar ticks (*Bidens species*); skunk cabbage (*Symplocarpus foetidus).*

The landscape plan defines native, as plants native to Pennsylvania. Since Pennsylvania is large and includes diverse regions, natives of Montgomery County, PA are preferred. The new landscape has a total of 153 plant species. 123 (80.4%) species are native to Montgomery County, PA; 9 (5.9%) species are native to Pennsylvania but not to Montgomery County; 13 (8.5%) are native to the USA but not Pennsylvania. Eight species (or about 5.2% of the total) are preexisting plants from Eurasia. These eight will be phased out over time and replaced with native species. None of the retained non-native species is considered invasive at the present time.

DESIGN CONCEPT AND IMPLEMENTATION

The house is located on the corner of two streets. The 0.30 acre property is unusual in that it lacks a traditional back yard. Instead, it has a very large front yard with smaller side yards. The different areas accommodate different design treatments.

Patio and east side garden

The site has about a 12' change in elevation. The building makes use of the elevation change by placing the garage below grade at basement level, with a patio terrace above it. The patio is shaded by large beech trees and has a view into the shared neighborhood beech woodland. Rosebay Rhododendron (*Rh. Maximum)* line the driveway, extending under the Beech trees on the south and east side of the lot.

A red maple seedling had rooted near the north side of the patio where it was left to grow. Red maples are adaptable and this tree provides a buffer between the street and patio. Tuliptree saplings and hickory saplings had taken hold in the east side garden. These too, were left alone to add diversity to the woodland setting. It is important to have a diversity of age and size among plants, just as it is important to have diversity of species. As the mature trees, like the beech, decline, the younger shade trees will replace them.

Moss garden. An upper side garden facing west/southwest is damp and mossy, shaded by oak, hickory and beech trees. That garden has been planted with ferns and spring ephemerals, such as Bloodroot, Bluebells and Jack in the Pulpit. Perennials such as Native Columbine, Wood Geranium bloom later in spring. The summer emphasis is on texture and shades of green with Wild Ginger, Maidenhair Fern and Lady Fern.

Figure 19.3 Cardinal flower brings brilliant color to the shady moss garden in summertime. This moisture loving plant is also found in the rain gardens. Photo by Mary Myers.

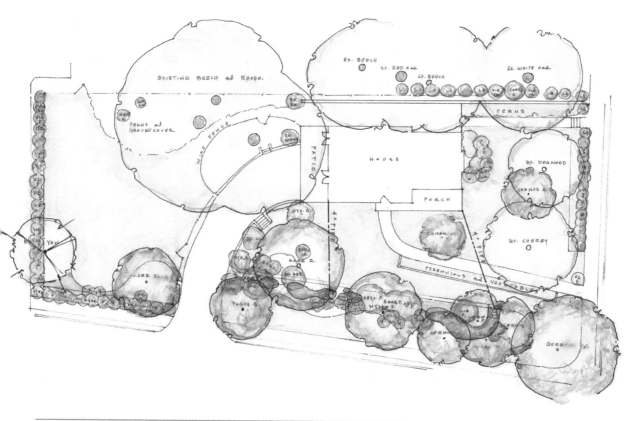

Figure 19.4 The site plan shows the rain gardens in blue, with two - 4" pipes leading to them. The pipes drain the entire roof surface into the rain gardens. Large beech and oak occurred on the south side of the property located on the upper edge of the plan. These trees provide a lot of summer shade which keeps the interior temperatures low. Plan by Mary Myers.

Lower garden/dog run

The lower garden serves as a dog play or dog run area. It could also be a playground for little children as it is visible from the patio and kitchen. The lower garden is bounded by a 3' high wire mesh fence with a ¾" thick fence of dried heather twigs overlaid on top. The heather fence faces the street and serves as a backdrop to native shrubs bordering the sidewalk and neighbor's drive.

Perennial Border

A narrow 3' wide border runs alongside the stone walk to the front door. The border contains perennials, such as Coneflower and Blazing Star which can be observed close up. Some perennials, such as Goldenrod and Blackeyed Susan are also found in the rain garden. The repetition is meant to create a harmonious effect between the perennial border which is more obviously cultivated and formal, and the "wilder" rain garden.

Rain gardens and front garden

The front garden is most extensive in terms of area and elevation change. It includes a long stone retaining wall. The four rain gardens are located at the base of the wall. Pipes draining into the rain gardens outlet in the lower part of the wall. The pipes were left white and visible, to enhance public understanding of the stormwater function. The rain gardens are planted for showy summer bloom to attract and educate the public about designing with native plants. Plants include Goldenrod, Blue Vervain, Milkweed, Cardinal Flower, Mistflower and Hibiscus.

Between 25% and 33% of the original lawn area was removed, replaced with shrub beds topped with leaf compost. Leaf compost breaks down more rapidly than bark compost and has a more refined texture than bark. Compost adds beneficial nutrients to the soil obviating the need for fertilizer.

INFILTRATING STORMWATER

Four small rain gardens were created to store and infiltrate stormwater coming from the roof of the house. Like many suburban houses, the roof's stormwater was collected in gutters and leaders then piped underground to the street. The stormwater on the street was directed into storm drains piping the water to the Tookany Creek. This creek has seen enormous rates of

Figure 19.5 Fluted Swallowtail Butterfly on Coneflower. Photo by Mary Myers

Figure 19.6 Milkweed blossom with bee. This plant is also the sole food source for the Monarch butterfly. The Monarch lays its eggs on milkweed sprouts. The emergent caterpillars eat the plant's milky sap which is acidic. The sap is stored for life and protects the butterflies from being eaten. (http://ed.fnal.gov/) Photo by Mary Myers

erosion and pollution due to the high volumes and velocities of water during peak storms. If more suburban houses hold and infiltrate their stormwater onsite, stream conditions will improve.

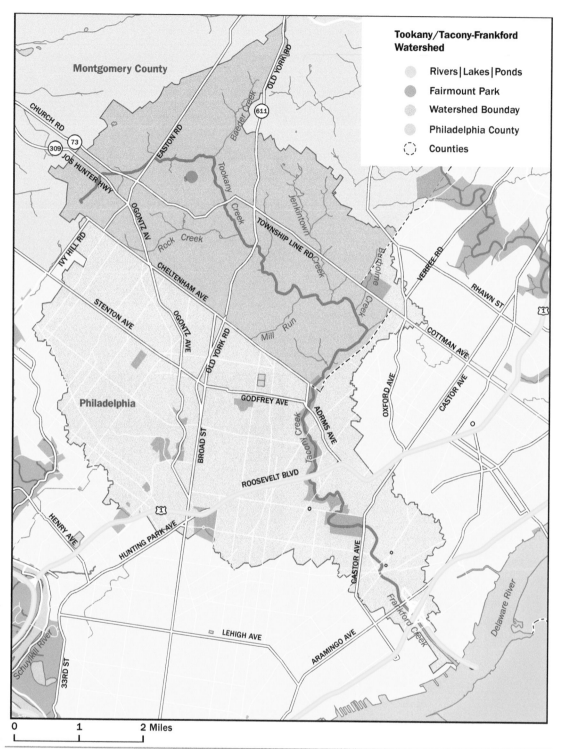

Figure 19.7 The site (shown as a red dot) lies in the Tookany-Frankford watershed. The stormwater was piped to the Tookany where it accumulated with the flood waters from other sites to speed its way to the Delaware River, blowing out storm drains, trees and eroding the creek banks.)ttfwatershed.org/)

Adapted from: Tookany-Frankford watershed," http://www.phillywatersheds.org/maps/Tookany_Tacony_Frankford_Watershed.pdf.

The roof leaders were attached to new 4" diameter flexible plastic pipes, that outlet into rain gardens, instead of the street. Based upon standard formulae, about 200 square feet of rain garden, at 12" average depth, was necessary to absorb a 1.15" storm. About 90% of the storms in our area are in this category.[1]

ECOLOGICAL QUALITY

Ecological quality was measured using the Plant Stewardship Index, a free calculator provided by Bowman's Hill Wildflower Preserve, New Hope, PA. www.bhwp.org/psi. Total PSI for the site was 41.82. Prior to planting the PSI was 5.23. The new approach increased ecological quality 8 times over the pre 2012 condition.

CARBON SEQUESTRATION

The carbon sequestered by the trees on the site totals 8,029 pounds/year. This is due to the presence of existing large beech and oak trees. The trees that we planted were fairly small in size (between 1 – 2" diameter) resulting in less carbon sequestration benefit than if larger trees were planted. However, my experience in practice indicated that small trees get established and adjusted to their new situations more easily than older trees. Also, planting smaller trees is less expensive and easier. I used an online free calculator, the National Tree Benefit Calculator ,to determine the amount of carbon sequestered.

The calculator puts carbon sequestration into perspective stating:

> "Most car owners of an "average" car (mid-sized sedan) drive 12,000 miles generating about 11,000 pounds of CO2 every year. A flight from New York to Los Angeles adds 1,400 pounds of CO2 per passenger. "http://www.treebenefits.com/calculator/ Accessed June 12, 2013).

My family uses only one car, (a hybrid Toyota Prius), and averages about 14,000 miles per year. We use regional rail for commuting. However, we fly for business and also for vacations. This would indicate that our carbon footprints from travel alone are in the 30,000 lb/yr range, more than triple the carbon sequestered by our trees. This finding indicates that we should be doing more to curb our transportation use and fuel used to heat our house. On the positive side, the small plants that were installed in 2012-13 are growing rapidly. Some –in the rain garden—have doubled or tripled their size. With additional planting, growth and care; and energy conservation strategies within the house, our carbon footprint can be significantly reduced—perhaps as much as 75-90% in the years ahead.

---

1   Our region receives about 40" of precipitation annually according to the National Climatic Data Center http://www.ncdc.noaa.gov/cag/time-series/us

CONCLUSION

Tallamy writes about balanced ecosystems which accommodate some defoliation but whose overall effect is healthy and beautiful.

"In a balanced community, with rare exceptions, no one member of the food chain dominates another, and if one species in an essentially sound system does start to run rampant, it is soon brought back into equilibrium by the other members of the community. That is why all of the leaves in native forests aren't eaten by insects, why we usually don't see huge defoliation events that rage unchecked through the woods (except when an alien species like the gypsy moth is on the loose), and why a forest in balance brings us a sense of aesthetic pleasure. If you carefully inspect individual leaves in a forest, you will find that a small portion of most of them have in fact, been eaten by insects; but the overall effect is still one of beauty, not destruction (Tallamy, 95)."[2]

The important thing to remember when designing with a native plant community approach is that change is inevitable. Natural landscapes display "almost infinitely complicated patterns of variation, occurring at many scales, and changing constantly over time (Fike, 1)." This complexity and variation occurs with a defined spectrum of plants that thrive within the climatic and geologic (soil) conditions of a place.

Our landscape includes diversity of plants and also wet areas (rain gardens). During its first spring 2013, we observed a few species we had

Figure 19.8 Curving beds display the variety of flowers, shrubs and small trees associated with the rain gardens. These plants offer much more seasonal interest to the garden than the previous lawn and forsythia plantings. Photo by Mary Myers

2   Tallamy provides an idea of plant species that sustain wildlife, beginning at the base of the food chain—examining which plants support insects. The more insects that are supported, the more birds and mammals will be supported. Tallamy shows the numbers of *Lepidotora* species (moths and butterflies) supported by native plants. Lepidoterans are a large taxon (11,500, or 50% of all insect species in North America). It was thought that understanding the host plants of this taxon would provide a good estimate of host use by all herbivores. (Tallamy, p. 146). A sampling of the findings showed that: native oak trees support 534 lepidotera species; blueberry/cranberry support 288; maple support 285; hickory support 159; and beech support 125. (Tallamy, p. 147)."

not seen previously: Red and Grey backed Salamanders and a Garden Snake. We take great delight in the variety of plants—composed within a natural plant community construct---and are finding that diversity has brought stability to the system with fewer weeds to pull. Many suburban communities in the eastern USA have Whitetail Deer populations. Ours is no exception. Deer browse in the garden, along with insects, birds and squirrels. However, because of the numerous plant species, the browse does not affect the overall aesthetic or function of the garden.

IMPLICATIONS

This new, diverse landscape has measureable benefits in increased ecological quality (biodiversity); stormwater mitigation; and carbon sequestration. Many of the plants provide food for insects, birds, small and large mammals (including humans). Useful and aesthetic space has been added to the site through the creation of a flower/vegetable border; rain garden; shade garden and dog run area.

This approach based upon establishing and meeting sustainable design goals, can be applied at different scales. It is as useful for a college or corporate campus as for a residential lot. Smaller sites, such as streetside rain gardens or green roofs can also be designed to maximize ecological and stormwater benefits. Their aggregate value may add up to considerable benefit in a city or suburban locale. For example, trees and plants on multiple small sites can contribute to the larger urban or regional forest. Stormwater that is managed through rain gardens helps regulate flooding and but also serves as a plant resource---nourishing the growth and life of trees and plants. Human well being also benefits from proximity to green space so adding biodiversity to the suburban and urban realm is desirable for its potential preventative or ameliorative health benefit. Finally, it is clear that design approaches that benefit other forms of life (plants and animals) benefit humans, too. Leopold (1949) describes land as a "fountain of energy flowing through a circuit of soils, plants and animals...native plants and animals keep the energy circuit open (Leopold, p. 254-255)." The ecological approach to designing sites is supportive of keeping the energy circuit open and in so doing enhances ecological services, including enjoyment in watching a fuller orchestration of nature's bloom and fruit cycles than in observed in a standard suburban garden.

QUESTIONS

1. What additional items might be added to the list of goals?
2. Can you think of other ways of measuring whether the goals have been met?
3. Are there ecosystem services that the garden is not currently addressing?
4. What percentage, or acreage of American suburban gardens should be retrofit to impact markedly improved biodiversity?
5. What methods could be used to encourage the transition to native biodiversity?

REFERENCES

Banks, Jamie and Robert McConnell. 2015. "National Emissions from Lawn and Garden Equipment". https://www.epa.gov/sites/production/files/2015-09/.../banks.pdf

Driessnack, Martha. 2009. "Children and Nature Deficit Disorder". Journal for Specialists in Pediatric Nursing. January 1, 2009, pp73-74.

Fike, Jean. 1999. Terrestrial and Palustrine Plant Communities of Pennsylvania, Pennsylvania Natural Diversity Inventory. http://www.naturalheritage.state.pa.us

Haydu, John, Hodges, Alan and Charles Hall. March 2006. "Economic Impacts of the Turfgrass and Lawncare Industry in the United States." University of Florida Extension Services, Institute of Food and Agricultural Sciences. http://edis.ifas.ufl.edu/

Leopold, Aldo. 1949. A Sand County Almanac. Oxford University Press, Inc.

Lundgren, J. 1995. A Natural Areas Inventory of Montgomery County, PA
http://www.naturalheritage.state.pa.us/cnai_pdfs/montgomery%20county%20nai%202008%20update%20web.pdf

Millennium Ecosystem Assessment. Millennium Ecosystem Assessment Synthesis Reports. 2005. http://www.unep.org/maweb

Miller, G. Tyler, Jr. 2005. Living in the Environment. Fourteenth Edition. Brooks Cole/Thomson Learning: Pacific Grove, California

National Climatic Data Center. http://www.ncdc.noaa.gov/cag/time-series/us. Accessed January 2014.

Raver, Anne. October 8, 2014. "One Woman's Pipe Dream: A Rain Garden Even the Neighbors Seem to Like" in The New York Times. http://www.nytimes.com/2014/10/09/garden/a-rain-garden-that-even-the-neighbors-seem-to-like.

Rhoads, Ann and Block, Timothy. 2008. Montgomery County, Pennsylvania Natural Areas Inventory Update 2008. Montgomery County Planning Commission, Norristown, PA.

Tallamy, Doug. 2007. Bringing Nature Home: How you can sustain wildlife with native plants. Timber Press: Portland, Oregon.

Tremblay Mark Stephen, Rachel Christine Colley, Travis John Saunders, Genevieve Nissa Healy, and Neville Owen. 2010. "Physiological and health implications of a sedentary lifestyle". Appl. Physiol. Nutr. Metab. 35: 725–740 (2010)

APPENDIX ONE - LIST OF PLANTS

NATIVE TO MONTGOMERY COUNTY, PA TREES (N = 13)	NOT NATIVE PRE-EXISTING EURASIAN TREES (N = 2)
Red Maple (Acer rubrum) Came in as seedling (Native to Montgomery County)	English Yew (retained to screen view of street/neighbor) not identified as invasive (UK)
Hornbeam (Carpinus caroliniana) (Native to Montgomery County)	Japanese Kwanzan Cherry (retained but new native Pagoda Dogwood planted as replacement) (Asia)

Hickory, mockernut (Carya tomentosa) Sapling in beech woodland (Native to Montgomery County)	
Eastern redbud (Cercis canadensis) (Native to Montgomery County)	
Fringe tree (Chioanthus virginicus) (Native to Montgomery County)	PA threatened
Pagoda dogwood (Cornus alternifolia) (Native to Montgomery County)	
Flowering dogwood (Cornus florida) (Native to Montgomery County)	
American beech (Fagus grandifolia) (Native to Montgomery County)	
Tulip tree (Lireodendron tulipifera) Sapling in beech woodland (Native to Montgomery County)	
Black gum (Nyssa sylvatica) (Native to Montgomery County)	
Black oak (Quercus nigra) (Native to Montgomery County)	
Red oak (Quercus rubrum) Sapling in beech woodland and mature tree near lot line (Native to Montgomery County)	
White oak (Quercus alba) (Native to Montgomery County)	
SHRUBS NATIVE TO MONTGOMERY COUNTY, PA (N = 19) **SHRUBS NATIVE TO PA (N =3)**	**NON NATIVE SHRUBS (N = 7)** **2 PRE-EXISTING EURASIAN, 5 FROM SOUTHERN PIEDMONT USA)**
Shadblow (Amelanchior canadensis) (Native to Montgomery County)	Bottlebrush buckeye (Aesculus parviflora) Native to southeastern piedmont (Georgia, Alabama)
Pepperbush (Clethra alnifolia) (Native to Montgomery County)	Oakleaf Hydrangea (Hydrangea quercifolia). Native to southeastern piedmont.
Red willow or Silky Dogwood (Cornus amomum) Native to central and western PA	
Hazelnut (Corylus Americana) (Native to Montgomery County)	
Native bush honeysuckle (Diervilla lonicera) (Native to Montgomery County)	
Witch hazel (Hammamelis virginiana) (Native to Montgomery County)	
Native hydrangea (Hydrangea arborescens) (Native to Montgomery County)	
Virginia sweetspire (Itea virginica) (thought to be native to Montgomery County but believed to be extirpated)	
Spicebush (Lindera benzoin) (Native to Montgomery County)	

Smooth Azalea (Rhododendron arborescens) (Native to western PA)	Pinkshell Azalea (Rhododendron vaseyii), native to Blue Ridge Mountains, NC and TN
Rosebay (Rhododendron maximum) (Native to Montgomery County)	Rhododentron catawbiense "alba" Hybrid, original stock native to southeastern piedmont
Fragrant sumac (Rhus aromatica) (Native to western PA)	Japanese Azalea (reduced by 50%) (Asia)
American elder (Sambucus canadensis) (Native to Montgomery County)	
Red berried elder (Sambucus racemosa var Pubens) (Native to Montgomery County)	
Meadow sweet (Spiraea alba var. latifolia) (Native to Montgomery County)	Spreading Yew (retained for evergreen interest) not identified as invasive (UK)
Lowbush blueberry (Vaccinium angustifolium) (Native to Montgomery County)	
Highbush blueberry (Vaccinium corymbosum) (Native to Montgomery County)	
Mapleleaf Viburnum (Viburnum acerifolium) (Native to Montgomery County)	
Arrowwood IViburnum dentatum) (Native to Montgomery County)	Arrowood "Chicago Lustre" (Viburnum dentatum 'Chicago Lustre' hybrid) original stock native to PA.
Viburnum nudum, Swamp Haw Native to Montgomery County)	PA endangered
Blackhaw (Viburnum prunifolium) (Native to Montgomery County)	
Highbush Cranberry (Viburnum trilobum) (Native to Montgomery County)	PA rare
FERNS NATIVE TO MONTGOMERY COUNTY, PA (N = 8)	**NON NATIVE FERNS**
Maidenhair fern (Adiantum pedatum) (Native to Montgomery County)	
Ebony spleenwort (Asplenium platyneuron) (Native to Montgomery County)	
Northern Lady fern (Athyrium filix-femina) (Native to Montgomery County)	
Wood fern (Dryopteris burgessi) (Native to Montgomery County)	
Sensitive fern (Onoclea sesibilis) (Native to Montgomery County)	
Cinnamon fern (Osmunda cinnamomea) (Native to Montgomery County)	
Christmas fern (Polystichum acrostichoides) (Native to Montgomery County)	
New York Fern (Thelypteris noveboracensis (Native to Montgomery County)	
VINES NATIVE TO MONTGOMERY, COUNTY, PA(N = 4)	**NON NATIVE VINES**

American bittersweet (Celustrus scandens) (Native to Montgomery County)	
Virgin's bower (Clematis virginiana) (Native to Montgomery County)	
Native honeysuckle (Lonicera sempervirens) (Native to Montgomery County)	
Virginia creeper (Parthenocissus quinquefolia) (Native to Montgomery County)	
SPRING EPHEMERALS NATIVE TO MONTGOMERY COUNTY, PA (N = 13), NATIVE TO PA (N = 1)	**SPRING EPHEMERALS NOT NATIVE TO PA (N = 1 FROM EURASIA)**
Putty Root (Aplectrum Hyemale) (Native to Montgomery County)	PA rare species
Jack in the Pulpit (Arisaema triphyllum) (Native to Montgomery County)	Celandine Poppy (Styloporum diphyllum) Introduced -apparently naturalized from cultivated sources.
Shooting star (Dodecatheon meadia) (Native to Montgomery County)	PA endangered species
Dwarf crested iris (Iris crestata) (Native to Montgomery County)	PA endangered species
Twinleaf (Jeffersonia diphylla) (Native to Montgomery County)	
Canada mayflower (Maeanthemum canadense) (Native to Montgomery County)	
Virginia bluebells (Mertensia virginica) (Native to Montgomery County)	
Mayapple (Podophyllum peltatum) (Native to Montgomery County)	
Jacob's ladder (Polemonium reptans) (Native to Montgomery County)	
Bloodroot (Sanguinaria canadensis) (Native to Montgomery County)	
Allegheny foam flower (Tiarella cordifolia) (Native to Montgomery County)	
Trillium (Trillium grandiflorum) (Native to Montgomery County)	
Merrybells (Uvularia grandiflora) Native to western PA.	
Common violet (Viola sororia var.) (Native to Montgomery County)	
HERBACEOUS PERENNIALS/BIENNIALS NATIVE TO MONTGOMERY COUNTY, PA (N = 63), NATIVE TO PA (N = 5)	**HERBACEOUS PERENNIALS/BIENNIALS NATIVE TO N. AMERICA (N = 4 EASTERN PIEDMONT USA; N = 2 CENTRAL USA), (N = 1 FROM EURASIA)**
Purple Giant Hyssop (Agastache scrophularifolia) (Native to Montgomery County)	Pink Turtlehead, (Chelone lyonni), native to southeastern USA
Canada anemone (Anemone Canadensis) Native to central and western PA	Longstalk tickseed (Coreopsis verticillata "Moonbeam") Sp. native to eastern USA
Native columbine (Aquiligea Canadensis) (Native to Montgomery County)	Purple coneflower (Echinacea purpurea) Native to central USA

Wild ginger (Asarum canadense) (Native to Montgomery County)	
Swamp mallow (Asclepias incarnata) (Native to Montgomery County)	Rattlesnake master (Eryngium yuccifolum) (Native to Midwest and east USA but not PA)
Butterfly Weed (Asclepias tuberosa) (Native to Montgomery County)	Slender Cranesbill Geranium (Geranium Pusillum) (Introduced to North America)
Blue Wood Aster (Aster cordifolius) (Native to Montgomery County)	
White wood aster (Aster divericata) (Native to Montgomery County)	Prairie Coneflower Ratibida pinnata (native to Midwestern USA)
New England Aster (Aster novae-angliae) (Native to Montgomery County)	Carolina lupine (Thermopsis caroliniana) Native to southeastern USA
New York Aster (Aster novaebelgii) (Native to Montgomery County)	
Aromatic Aster (Aster oblongifolius) (Native to Montgomery County)	
Blue False Indigo (Baptisia australis) (Native to western PA)	
Wild Indigo (Baptisia tinctoria) (Native to Montgomery County)	
Showy bur weed (Bidens laevis) (Native to Montgomery County)	
Tall Bellflower (Campanula Americana) (Native to Montgomery County)	
Blue cohosh (Caulophyllum thalictroides) (Native to Montgomery County)	
Fairy Wand (Chamelelinum luteum) (Native to Montgomery County)	
White Turtlehead (Chelone glabra), (Native to Montgomery County)	
Green and gold (Chrysogamum virginianum) Native to south central PA.	
Golden corydalis (Corydalis flavula) (Native to Montgomery County) - biennial	
Wild bleeding heart (Dicentra eximea) Native to central and western PA.	
Elephant's foot (Elephantopus carolinianus) (Native to Montgomery/Phila. County)	PA endangered species
Firewort, (Erchtites hieracifolia), (Native to Montgomery County)	
Mistflower (Eupatorium coelestinum) (Native to Montgomery County)	
Little Joe Pyeweed, (Eupatorium dubium "Little Joe", (Sp native to Montgomery County)	
Boneset (Eupatorium fistulosum) (Native to Montgomery County)	

Grass leafed goldenrod (Euthamia graminifolia (Native to Montgomery County)	
Queen of the Prairie (Filipendula rubra) "Venusta") (Sp. native to PA, Bucks County)	
Bedstraw (Galium aprine) (Native to Montgomery County)	
Wood Geranium (Geranium maculatum) (Native to Montgomery County)	
Sneezeweed (Helenium autumnale) (Native to Montgomery County)	
Alum root (Heuchera Americana "Dale's Strain") (Sp.native to Montgomery County)	
Rose mallow (Hibiscus moscheutos) (Native to Montgomery County)	
Great St. John's Wort (Hypericum pyramidatum) Native to central, eastern and southern PA	
Jewelweed (Impatiens capensis) (Native to Montgomery County)	
Dwarf Crested Iris (Iris crestata) (Native to Montgomery County)	PA endangered
Blue flag (Iris versicolor) (Native to Montgomery County)	
Blazing star (Liatris spicata) (Native to Montgomery County)	
Cardinal flower (Lobelia cardinalis) (Native to Montgomery County)	
Great blue lobelia (Lobelia siphilitica) (Native to Montgomery County)	
Monkey flower (Mimulus ringens) (Native to Montgomery County)	
Partridgeberry (Mitchella repans), (native to Montgomery County	
Oswego Tea (Monarda didyma) (Native to Montgomery County)	
Bergamot Monarda fistulosa) Native to Montgomery County	
Wood sorrel (Oxalis stricta) (Native to Montgomery County)	
Parthenium integrifolium, Wild Quinine (Native to Montgomery County)	PA Extirpated
Wood Phlox (Phlox divaricata "Blue Moon" (Sp native to Montgomery County)	
Meadow Phlox (Phlox maculata) (Native to Montgomery County)	
Phlox "David" and Phlox("Jeana", (Phlox paniculata "David" and "Jeana") (Sp native to Montgomery County)	

Downy Phlox (Phlox pilosa) (Native to Montgomery County)	PA Endangered
Moss pink (Phlox subulosa cultivar) (Sp native to Montgomery County)	
Obedient Plant (Physostegia virginiana "Pink Manners") (sp native to Montgomery County)	
Pokeweed (Phytolacca Americana) (Native to Montgomery County)	
Clearweed (Piilea pumila) (Native to Montgomery County)	
Solomon's seal (Polygonatum biflorum) (Native to Mont- gomery County).	
Mountain mint (Pyncathemum muticum) (Native to Montgomery County)	
Cone flower (Rudbeckia fulgida) (Native to Montgomery County)	
Wild Senna (Senna hebecarpus) (Native to Montgomery County)	
Blue stemmed Goldenrod (Solidago caesia)(Native to Montgomery County)	
Canada Goldenrod (Solidago canadensis) (Native to Montgomery County)	
Gray goldenrod (Solidago nemoralis) (Native to Mont- gomery County)	
Wrinkle leaf goldenrod (Solidago rugosa "Fireworks" and Solidago rugosa "Little Lemon") (Sp. Native to Montgomery County)	
Tall Meadowrue (Thalictrum pubescens) Native to Montgomery County	
Spiderwort (Tradescantia ohioensis 'Concord Grape'). (Sp.native to Montgomery County	
Blue vervain (Verbena hastata) (Native to Montgomery County)	
Culver's root (Veronicastrum virginicum) (Native to Mont- gomery County)	
New York Ironweed (Vernonia noveboracensis) (Native to Montg. Co.)	
Barren Strawberry, (Waldsteinia fragaroides or Geum fragaroides) (Native to Montgomery County)	
SEDGES NATIVE TO MONTGOMERY COUNTY, PA (N = 1)	**NON NATIVE SEDGES**
Pennsylvania sedge (Carex pennsylvanica) (Native to Montgomery County)	
Grasses native to Montgomery County, PA (n = 1)	Grasses not native to PA (n = 4) (pre existing Eurasian, n = 2 and pre existing N. American n = 2)
Prairie Dropseed (Sporobolus heterolepsis) (Native to serpentine barrens, lower Montgomery County, PA)	PA endandgered

	Red fescue (*Festuca rubra*) from N. America (retained in reduced lawn area)
	Kentucky Blue Grass (*Poa pratensis*) is from Europe (retained in reduced lawn area)
	Zoysia sp. from Asia (retained in reduced lawn area)
	Canada Rye (*Elmis canadensis*) from N. America (retained in reduced lawn area)

APPENDIX TWO CARBON SEQUESTRATION USING NATIONAL TREE BENEFIT CALCULATOR

TREES (N = 16)	POUNDS OF CARBON SEQUESTERED PER YEAR
Red Maple (Acer rubrum) 3" diameter	51 lbs.
Hornbeam (Carpinus caroliniana) 1" dia.	6 lbs.
Hickory, mockernut (Carya tomentosa) 3"	52 lbs.
American Chestnut, (Castena dentata) 1" dia.	6 lbs.
Eastern redbud (Cercis canadensis) 1 @ 3" dia., 1 @1" dia.	52 lbs + 6 lbs. = 58 lbs.
Fringe tree (Chioanthus virginicus 4" dia. multistem	56 lbs.
Pagoda dogwood (Cornus alternifolia) 1@ 2.5" dia., 1@ 1" dia.	29 lbs + 6 lbs = 35 lbs.
Flowering dogwood (Cornus florida) 1 @ 9" diam. 1 @ 1.5" dia.	170 lbs + 12 lbs = 182 lbs.
American beech (Fagus grandifolia) 1 @ 36" dia, 1 @ 30" dia. 3 @ 24" dia.	926 lbs. + 839 lbs. + 2,169 = 4,931 lbs.
Tulip tree (Lireodendron tulipifera) 2 @ 3" dia.	104 lbs.
Black gum (Nyssa sylvatica) 1@ 2" dia.	23 lbs.
Black oak (Quercus nigra) 1 @ 1" dia.	6 lbs.
Red oak (Quercus rubrum) 1 @ 2" dia., 1 @ 30" dia.	31 lbs. + 1,137 lbs. = 1,168 lbs.
White oak (Quercus alba) 1@ 30" dia.	1,264 lbs.
English Yew (Taxus) 6" dia.	49 lbs.
Japanese Kwanzan Cherry (Prunus sp.) 10" dia	119 lbs.
TOTAL	lbs.

Ethics

THE LAND ETHIC

BY ALDO LEOPOLD

When god-like Odysseus returned from the wars in Troy, he hanged all on one rope a dozen slave-girls of his household whom he suspected of misbehavior during his absence.

This hanging involved no question of propriety. The girls were property. The disposal of property was then, as now, a matter of expediency, not of right and wrong.

Concepts of right and wrong were not lacking from Odysseus' Greece: witness the fidelity of his wife through the long years before at last his black-prowed galleys clove the wine-dark seas for home. The ethical structure of that day covered wives, but had not yet been extended to human chattels. During the three thousand years which have since elapsed, ethical criteria have been extended to many fields of conduct, with corresponding shrinkages in those judged by expediency only.

THE ETHICAL SEQUENCE

This extension of ethics, so far studied only by philosophers, is actually a process in ecological evolution. Its sequences may be described in ecological as well as in philosophical terms. An ethic, ecologically, is a limitation on freedom of action in the struggle for existence. An ethic, philosophically, is a differentiation of social from anti-social conduct. These are two definitions of one thing. The thing has its origin in the tendency of interdependent individuals or groups to evolve modes of co-operation. The ecologist calls these symbioses. Politics and economics are advanced symbioses in which the original free-for-all competition has been replaced, in part, by co-operative mechanisms with an ethical content.

The complexity of co-operative mechanisms has increased with population density, and with the efficiency of tools. It was simpler, for example, to define the anti-social uses of sticks and stones in the days of the mastodons than of bullets and billboards in the age of motors.

The first ethics dealt with the relation between individuals; the Mosaic Decalogue is an example. Later accretions dealt with the relation between the individual and society. The Golden Rule tries to integrate the individual to society; democracy to integrate social organization to the individual.

There is as yet no ethic dealing with man's relation to land and to the animals and plants which grow upon it. Land, like Odysseus' slave-girls, is still property. The land-relation is still strictly economic, entailing privileges but not obligations.

The extension of ethics to this third element in human environment is, if I read the evidence correctly, an evolutionary possibility and an ecological necessity. It is the third step in a sequence. The first two have already been taken. Individual thinkers since the days of Ezekiel and Isaiah have asserted that the despoliation of land is not only inexpedient but wrong. Society, however, has not yet affirmed their belief. I regard the present conservation movement as the embryo of such an affirmation.

An ethic may be regarded as a mode of guidance for meeting ecological situations so new or intricate, or involving such deferred reactions, that the path of social expediency is not discernible to the average individual. Animal instincts are modes of guidance for the individual in meeting such situations. Ethics are possibly a land of community instinct in-the-making.

THE COMMUNITY CONCEPT

All ethics so far evolved rest upon a single premise: that the individual is a member of a community of interdependent parts. His instincts prompt him to compete for his place in that community, but his ethics prompt him also to co-operate (perhaps in order that there may be a place to compete for).

The land ethic simply enlarges the boundaries of the community to include soils, waters, plants, and animals, or collectively: the land.

This sounds simple: do we not already sing our love for and obligation to the land of the free and the home of the brave? Yes, but just what and whom do we love? Certainly not the soil, which we are sending helter-skelter downriver. Certainly not the waters, which we assume have no function except to turn turbines, float barges, and carry off sewage. Certainly not the plants, of which we exterminate whole communities without batting an eye. Certainly not the animals, of which we have already extirpated many of the largest and most beautiful species. A land ethic of course cannot prevent the alteration, management, and use of these 'resources,' but it does affirm their right to continued existence, and, at least in spots, their continued existence in a natural state.

In short, a land ethic changes the role of *Homo sapiens* from conqueror of the land-community to plain member and citizen of it. It implies respect for his fellow-members, and also respect for the community as such.

In human history, we have learned (I hope) that the conqueror role is eventually self-defeating. Why? Because it is implicit in such a role that the conqueror knows, *ex cathedra*, just what makes the community clock tick, and just what and who is valuable, and what and who is worthless, in community life. It always turns out that he knows neither, and this is why his conquests eventually defeat themselves.

In the biotic community, a parallel situation exists. Abraham knew exactly what the land was for: it was to drip milk and honey into Abraham's mouth. At the present moment, the assurance with which we regard this assumption is inverse to the degree of our education.

The ordinary citizen today assumes that science knows what makes the community clock tick; the scientist is equally sure that he does not. He knows that the biotic mechanism is so complex that its workings may never be fully understood.

That man is, in fact, only a member of a biotic team, is shown by an ecological interpretation of history. Many historical events, hitherto explained solely in terms of human enterprise, were actually biotic interactions between people and land. The characteristics of the land determined the facts quite as potently as the characteristics of the men who lived on it.

Consider, for example, the settlement of the Mississippi valley. In the years following the Revolution, three groups were contending for its control: the native Indian, the French and English traders, and the American settlers. Historians wonder what would have happened if the English at Detroit had thrown a little more weight into the Indian side of those tipsy scales which decided the outcome of the colonial migration into the cane-lands of Kentucky. It is time now to ponder the fact that the cane-lands, when subjected to the particular mixture of forces represented by the cow, plow, fire, and axe of the pioneer, became bluegrass. What if the plant succession inherent in this dark and bloody ground had, under the impact of these forces, given us some worthless sedge, shrub, or weed? Would Boone and Kenton have held out? Would there have been any overflow into Ohio, Indiana, Illinois, and Missouri? Any Louisiana Purchase? Any transcontinental union of new states? Any Civil War?

Kentucky was one sentence in the drama of history. We are commonly told what the human actors in this drama tried to do, but we are seldom told that their success, or the lack of it, hung in large degree on the reaction of particular soils to the impact of the particular forces exerted by their occupancy. In the case of Kentucky, we do not even know where the bluegrass came from—whether it is a native species, or a stowaway from Europe.

Contrast the cane-lands with what hindsight tells us about the Southwest, where the pioneers were equally brave, resourceful, and persevering. The impact of occupancy here brought no bluegrass, or other plant fitted to withstand the bumps and buffetings of hard use. This region, when grazed by livestock, reverted through a series of more and more worthless grasses, shrubs, and weeds to a condition of unstable equilibrium. Each recession of plant types bred erosion; each increment to erosion bred a further recession of plants. The result today is a progressive and mutual deterioration, not only of plants and soils, but of the animal community subsisting thereon. The early settlers did not expect this: on the ciénegas of New Mexico some even cut ditches to hasten it. So subtle has been its progress that few residents of the region are aware of it. It is quite invisible to the tourist who finds this wrecked landscape colorful and charming (as indeed it is, but it bears scant resemblance to what it was in 1848).

This same landscape was 'developed' once before, but with quite different results. The Pueblo Indians settled the Southwest in pre-Columbian times, but they happened *not* to be equipped with range livestock. Their civilization expired, but not because their land expired.

In India, regions devoid of any sod-forming grass have been settled, apparently without wrecking the land, by the simple expedient of carrying the grass to the cow, rather than vice versa. (Was this the result of some deep wisdom, or was it just good luck? I do not know.)

In short, the plant succession steered the course of history; the pioneer simply demonstrated, for good or ill, what successions inhered in the land. Is history taught in this spirit? It will be, once the concept of land as a community really penetrates our intellectual life.

THE ECOLOGICAL CONSCIENCE

Conservation is a state of harmony between men and land. Despite nearly a century of propaganda, conservation still proceeds at a snail's pace; progress still consists largely of letterhead pieties and convention oratory. On the back forty we still slip two steps backward for each forward stride.

The usual answer to this dilemma is 'more conservation education.' No one will debate this, but is it certain that only the *volume* of education needs stepping up? Is something lacking in the *content* as well?

It is difficult to give a fair summary of its content in brief form, but, as I understand it, the content is substantially this: obey the law, vote right, join some organizations, and practice what conservation is profitable on your own land; the government will do the rest.

Is not this formula too easy to accomplish anything worth-while? It defines no right or wrong, assigns no obligation, calls for no sacrifice, implies no change in the current philosophy of values. In respect of land-use, it urges only enlightened self-interest. Just how far will such education take us? An example will perhaps yield a partial answer.

By 1930 it had become clear to all except the ecologically blind that southwestern Wisconsin's topsoil was slipping seaward. In 1933 the farmers were told that if they would adopt certain remedial practices for five years, the public would donate CCC labor to install them, plus the necessary machinery and materials. The offer was widely accepted, but the practices were widely forgotten when the five-year contract period was up. The farmers continued only those practices that yielded an immediate and visible economic gain for themselves.

This led to the idea that maybe farmers would learn more quickly if they themselves wrote the rules. Accordingly the Wisconsin Legislature in 1937 passed the Soil Conservation District Law. This said to farmers, in effect: *We, the public, will furnish you free technical service and loan you specialized machinery, if you will write your own rules for land-use. Each county may write its own rules, and these will have the force of law.* Nearly all the counties promptly organized to accept the proffered help, but after a decade of operation, *no county has yet written a single rule.* There has been visible progress in such practices as strip-cropping, pasture renovation, and soil liming, but none in fencing woodlots against grazing, and none in excluding plow and cow from steep slopes. The farmers, in short, have selected those remedial practices which were profitable anyhow, and ignored those which were profitable to the community, but not clearly profitable to themselves.

When one asks why no rules have been written, one is told that the community is not yet ready to support them; education must precede rules. But the education actually in progress makes no mention of obligations to land over and above those dictated by self-interest. The net result is that we have more education but less soil, fewer healthy woods, and as many floods as in 1937.

The puzzling aspect of such situations is that the existence of obligations over and above self-interest is taken for granted in such rural community enterprises as the betterment of roads, schools, churches, and baseball teams. Their existence is not taken for granted, nor as yet seriously discussed, in bettering the behavior of the water that falls on the land, or in the preserving of the beauty or diversity of the farm landscape. Land-use ethics are still governed wholly by economic self-interest, just as social ethics were a century ago.

To sum up: we asked the farmer to do what he conveniently could to save his soil, and he has done just that, and only that. The farmer who clears the woods off a 75 per cent slope, turns his cows into the clearing, and dumps its rainfall, rocks, and soil into the community creek, is still (if otherwise decent) a respected member of society. If he puts lime on his fields and plants his crops on contour, he is still entitled to all the privileges and emoluments of his Soil Conservation District. The District is a beautiful piece of social machinery, but it is coughing along on two cylinders because we have been too timid, and too anxious for quick success, to tell the farmer the true magnitude of his obligations. Obligations have no meaning without conscience, and the problem we face is the extension of the social conscience from people to land.

No important change in ethics was ever accomplished without an internal change in our intellectual emphasis, loyalties, affections, and convictions. The proof that conservation has not yet touched these foundations of conduct lies in the fact that philosophy and religion have not yet heard of it. In our attempt to make conservation easy, we have made it trivial.

SUBSTITUTES FOR A LAND ETHIC

When the logic of history hungers for bread and we hand out a stone, we are at pains to explain how much the stone resembles bread. I now describe some of the stones which serve in lieu of a land ethic.

One basic weakness in a conservation system based wholly on economic motives is that most members of the land community have no economic value. Wildflowers and songbirds are examples. Of the 22,000 higher plants and animals native to Wisconsin, it is doubtful whether more than 5 per cent can be sold, fed, eaten, or otherwise put to economic use. Yet these creatures are members of the biotic community, and if (as I believe) its stability depends on its integrity, they are entitled to continuance.

When one of these non-economic categories is threatened, and if we happen to love it, we invent subterfuges to give it economic importance. At the beginning of the century song birds were supposed to be disappearing. Ornithologists jumped to the rescue with some distinctly shaky evidence to the effect that insects would eat us up if birds failed to control them. The evidence had to be economic in order to be valid.

It is painful to read these circumlocutions today. We have no land ethic yet, but we have at least drawn nearer the point of admitting that birds should continue as a matter of biotic right, regardless of the presence or absence of economic advantage to us.

A parallel situation exists in respect of predatory mammals, raptorial birds, and fish-eating birds. Time was when biologists somewhat overworked the evidence that these creatures preserve the health of game by killing weaklings, or that they control rodents for the farmer, or that they prey only on 'worthless' species. Here again, the evidence had to be economic in order to be valid. It is only in recent years that we hear the more honest argument that predators are members of the community, and that no special interest has the right to exterminate them for the sake of a benefit, real or fancied, to itself. Unfortunately this enlightened view is still in the talk stage. In the field the extermination of predators goes merrily on: witness the impending erasure of the timber wolf by fiat of Congress, the Conservation Bureaus, and many state legislatures.

Some species of trees have been 'read out of the party' by economics-minded foresters because they grow too slowly, or have too low a sale value to pay as timber crops: white cedar, tamarack, cypress, beech, and hemlock are examples. In Europe, where forestry is ecologically more advanced, the non-commercial tree species are recognized as members of the native forest community, to be preserved as such, within reason. Moreover some (like beech) have been found to have a valuable function in building up soil fertility. The interdependence of the forest and its constituent tree species, ground flora, and fauna is taken for granted.

Lack of economic value is sometimes a character not only of species or groups, but of entire biotic communities: marshes, bogs, dunes, and 'deserts' are examples. Our formula in such cases is to relegate their conservation to government as refuges, monuments, or parks. The difficulty is that these communities are usually interspersed with more valuable private lands; the government cannot possibly own or control such scattered parcels. The net effect is that we have relegated some of them to ultimate extinction over large areas. If the private owner were ecologically minded, he would be proud to be the custodian of a reasonable proportion of such areas, which add diversity and beauty to his farm and to his community.

In some instances, the assumed lack of profit in these 'waste' areas has proved to be wrong, but only after most of them had been done away with. The present scramble to reflood muskrat marshes is a case in point.

There is a clear tendency in American, conservation to relegate to government all necessary jobs that private landowners fail to perform. Government owner ship, operation, subsidy, or regulation is now widely prevalent in forestry, range management, soil and watershed management, park and wilderness conservation, fisheries management, and migratory bird management, with more to come. Most of this growth in governmental conservation is proper and logical, some of it is inevitable. That I imply no disapproval of it is implicit in the fact that I have spent most of my life working for it. Nevertheless the question arises: What is the ultimate magnitude of the enterprise? Will the tax base carry its eventual ramifications? At what point will governmental conservation, like the mastodon, become handicapped by its own dimensions? The answer, if there is any, seems to be in a land ethic, or some other force which assigns more obligation to the private landowner.

Industrial landowners and users, especially lumbermen, and stockmen, are inclined to wall long and loudly about the extension of government ownership and regulation to land, but (with notable exceptions) they show little disposition to develop the only visible alternative: the voluntary practice of conservation, on their own lands.

When the private landowner is asked to perform some unprofitable act for the good of the community, he today assents only with outstretched palm. If the act costs him cash this is fair and proper, but when it costs only forethought, open-mindedness, or time, the issue is at least debatable. The overwhelming growth of land-use subsidies in recent years must be ascribed, in large part, to the government's own agencies for conservation education: the land bureaus, the agricultural colleges, and the extension services. As far as I can detect, no ethical obligation toward land is taught in these Institutions.

To sum up: a system of conservation based solely on economic self-interest is hopelessly lopsided. It tends to Ignore, and thus eventually to eliminate, many elements in the land community that lack commercial value, but that are (as far as we know) essential to its healthy functioning. It assumes, falsely, I think, that the economic parts of the biotic clock will function without the uneconomic parts. It tends to relegate to government many functions eventually too large, too complex, or too widely dispersed to be performed by government.

An ethical obligation on the part of the private owner is the only visible remedy for these situations.

THE LAND PYRAMID

An ethic to supplement and guide the economic relation to land presupposes the existence of some mental image of land as a biotic mechanism. We can be ethical only in relation to something we can see, feel, understand, love, or otherwise have faith in.

The image commonly employed in conservation education is 'the balance of nature.' For reasons too lengthy to detail here, this figure of speech falls to describe accurately what little we know about the land mechanism. A much truer image is the one employed in ecology: the biotic pyramid. I shall first sketch the pyramid as a symbol of land, and later develop some of its implications in terms of land-use.

Plants absorb energy from the sun. This energy lows through, a circuit called the biota, which may be represented by a pyramid consisting of layers. The bottom layer is the soil. A plant layer rests on the soil, an insect layer on the plants, a bird and rodent layer on the insects, and so on up through various animal groups to the apex layer, which consists of the larger carnivores.

The species of a layer are alike not in where they came from, or in what they look like, but rather in what they eat. Each successive layer depends on those below it for food and often for other services, and each in turn furnishes food and services to those above. Proceeding upward, each successive layer decreases in numerical abundance. Thus, for every carnivore there are hundreds of his prey, thousands of their prey, millions of insects, uncountable plants. The pyramidal form of the system reflects this numerical progression from apex to base. Man shares an intermediate layer with the bears, raccoons, and squirrels which eat both meat and vegetables.

The lines of dependency for food and other services are called food chains. Thus soil-oak-deer-Indian is a chain that has now been largely converted to soil-corn-cow-farmer. Each species, including ourselves, is a link in many chains. The deer eats a hundred plants other than oak, and the cow a hundred plants other than corn. Both, then, are links in a hundred chains. The pyramid is a tangle of chains so complex as to seem disorderly, yet the stability of the system proves it to be a highly organized structure. Its functioning; depends on the co-operation and competition of its diverse parts.

In the beginning, the pyramid of life was low and squat; the food chains short and simple. Evolution has added layer after layer, link after link. Man is one of thousands of accretions to the height and complexity of the pyramid. Science has given us many doubts, but it has given us at least one certainty: the trend of evolution is to elaborate and diversify the biota.

Land, then, is not merely soil; it is a fountain of energy flowing through a circuit of soils, plants, and animals. Food chains are the living channels which conduct energy upward; death and decay return it to the soil. The circuit is not closed; some energy is dissipated in decay, some is added by absorption from the air, some is stored in soils, peats, and long-lived forests; but it is a sustained circuit, like a slowly augmented revolving fund of life. There is always a net loss by downhill wash, but this is normally small and offset by the decay of rocks. It is deposited in the ocean and, in the course of geological time, raised to form new lands and new pyramids.

The velocity and character of the upward flow of energy depend on the complex structure of the plant and animal community, much as the upward flow of sap in a tree depends on its complex cellular organization. Without this complexity, normal circulation would presumably not occur. Structure means the characteristic numbers, as well as the characteristic kinds and functions, of the component species. This interdependence between, the complex structure of the land and its smooth functioning as an energy unit is one of its basic attributes.

When a change occurs in one part of the circuit, many other parts must adjust themselves to it. Change does not necessarily obstruct or divert the flow of energy; evolution is a long series of self-induced changes, the net result of which has been to elaborate the flow mechanism and to lengthen the circuit. Evolutionary changes, however, are usually slow and local. Man's invention of tools has enabled him to make changes of unprecedented violence, rapidity, and scope.

One change is in the composition of floras and faunas. The larger predators are lopped off the apex of the pyramid; food chains, for the first time in history, become shorter rather than longer. Domesticated species from other lands are substituted for wild ones, and wild ones are moved to new habitats. In this world-wide, pooling of faunas and floras, some species get out of bounds as pests and diseases, others are extinguished. Such effects are seldom intended or foreseen; they represent unpredicted and often untraceable readjustments in the structure. Agricultural science is largely a race between the emergence of new pests and the emergence of new techniques for their control.

Another change touches the flow of energy through plants and animals and its return to the soil. Fertility is the ability of soil to receive, store, and release energy. Agriculture, by overdrafts on the soil, or by too radical a substitution of domestic for native species in the superstructure, may derange the channels of flow or deplete storage. Soils depleted of their storage, or of the organic matter which anchors it, wash away faster than they form. This is erosion.

Waters, like soil, are part of the energy circuit. Industry, by polluting waters or obstructing them with dams, may exclude the plants and animals necessary to keep energy in circulation.

Transportation brings about another basic change: the plants or animals grown in one region are now consumed and returned to the soil in another. Transportation taps the energy stored in rocks, and in the air, and uses it elsewhere; thus we fertilize the garden with nitrogen gleaned by the guano birds from the fishes of seas on the other side of the Equator. Thus the formerly localized and self-contained circuits are pooled on a world-wide scale.

The process of altering the pyramid for human occupation releases stored energy, and this often gives rise, during the pioneering period, to a deceptive exuberance of plant and animal life, both wild and tame. These releases of biotic capital tend to becloud or postpone the penalties of violence.

This thumbnail sketch of land as an energy circuit conveys three basic ideas:

1. That land is not merely soil.
2. That the native plants and animals kept the energy circuit open; others may or may not.
3. That man-made changes are of a different order than evolutionary changes, and have effects more comprehensive than is intended or foreseen.

These ideas, collectively, raise two basic issues: Can the land adjust itself to the new order? Can the desired alterations be accomplished with less violence?

Biotas seem to differ in their capacity to sustain violent conversion. Western Europe, for example, carries a far different pyramid than Caesar found there. Some large animals are lost; swampy forests have become meadows or plow-land; many new plants and animals are introduced, some of which escape as pests; the remaining natives are greatly changed in distribution and abundance. Yet the soil is still there and, with the help of imported nutrients, still fertile; the waters flow normally; the new structure seems to function and to persist. There is no visible stoppage or derangement of the circuit.

Western Europe, then, has a resistant biota. Its inner processes are tough, elastic, resistant to strain. No matter how violent the alterations, the pyramid, so far, has developed some new *modus vivendi* which preserves its habitability for man, and for most of the other natives.

Japan seems to present another instance of radical conversion without disorganization.

Most other civilized regions, and some as yet barely touched by civilization, display various stages of disorganization, varying from initial symptoms to advanced wastage. In Asia Minor and North Africa diagnosis is confused by climatic changes, which may have been either the cause or the effect of advanced wastage. In the United States the degree of disorganization varies locally; it is worst in the Southwest, the Ozarks, and parts of the South, and least in New England and the Northwest. Better land-uses may still arrest it in the less advanced regions. In parts of Mexico, South America, South Africa, and Australia a violent and accelerating wastage is in progress, but I cannot assess the prospects.

This almost world-wide display of disorganization in the land seems to be similar to disease in an animal, except that it never culminates in complete disorganization or death. The land recovers, but at some reduced level of complexity, and with a reduced carrying capacity for people, plants, and animals. Many biotas currently regarded as lands of opportunity" are in fact already subsisting on exploitative agriculture, i.e. they have already exceeded their sustained carrying capacity. Most of South America is overpopulated in this sense.

In arid regions we attempt to offset the process of wastage by reclamation, but it is only too evident that the prospective longevity of reclamation projects is often short. In our own West, the best of them may not last a century.

The combined evidence of history and ecology seems to support one general deduction: the less violent the man-made changes, the greater the probability of successful readjustment in the pyramid. Violence, in turn, varies with human population density; a dense population requires a more violent conversion. In this respect, North America has a better chance for permanence than Europe, if she can contrive to limit her density.

This deduction runs counter to our current philosophy, which assumes that because a small increase in density enriched human life, that an indefinite increase will enrich it indefinitely. Ecology knows of no density relationship that holds for indefinitely wide limits. All gains from density are subject to a law of diminishing returns.

Whatever may be the equation for men and land, it is improbable that we as yet know all its terms. Recent discoveries in mineral and vitamin nutrition reveal unsuspected dependencies in the up-circuit: incredibly minute quantities of certain substances determine the value of soils to plants, of plants to animals. What of the down-circuit? What of the vanishing species, the preservation of which we now regard as an esthetic luxury? They helped build the soil; in what unsuspected ways may they be essential to its maintenance? Professor Weaver proposes that we use prairie flowers to re-flocculate the wasting soils of the dust bowl; who knows for what purpose cranes and condors, otters and grizzlies may some day be used?

LAND HEALTH AND THE A-B CLEAVAGE

A land ethic, then, reflects the existence of an ecological conscience and this in turn reflects a conviction of individual responsibility for the health of the land. Health is the capacity of the land for self-renewal. Conservation is our effort to understand and preserve this capacity.

Conservationists are notorious for their dissensions. Superficially these seem to add up to mere confusion, but a more careful scrutiny reveals a single plane of cleavage common to many specialized fields. In each field one group (A) regards the land as soil, and its function as commodity-production; another group (B) regards the land as a biota, and its function as something broader. How much broader is admittedly in a state of doubt and confusion.

In my own field, forestry, group A is quite content to grow frees like cabbages, with, cellulose as the basic forest commodity. It feels no inhibition against violence; its ideology is agronomic. Group B, on the other hand, sees forestry as fundamentally different from agronomy because it employs natural species, and manages a natural environment rather than creating an artificial one. Group B prefers natural re-production on principle. It worries on biotic as well as economic grounds about the loss of species like chestnut, and the threatened loss of the white pines. It worries about a whole series of secondary forest functions: wildlife, recreation, watersheds, wilderness areas. To my mind, Group B feels the stirrings of an ecological conscience.

In the wildlife field, a parallel cleavage exists. For Group A the basic commodities are sport and meat; the yardsticks of production are ciphers of take in pheasants and trout.

Artificial propagation is acceptable as a permanent as well as a temporary recourse—if its unit costs permit. Group B, on the other hand, worries about a whole series of biotic side-issues. What is the cost in predators of producing a game crop? Should we have further recourse to exotics? How can management restore the shrinking species, like prairie grouse, already hopeless as shootable game? How can management restore the threatened rarities, like trumpeter swan and whooping crane? Can management principles be extended to wildflowers? Here again it is clear to me that we have the same A-B cleavage as in forestry.

In the larger field of agriculture I am less competent to speak, but there seem to be somewhat parallel cleavages. Scientific agriculture was actively developing before ecology was born, hence a slower penetration of ecological concepts might be expected. Moreover the farmer, by the very nature of his techniques, must modify the biota more radically than the forester or the wildlife manager. Nevertheless, there are many discontents in agriculture which seem to- add up to a new vision of 'biotic farming.'

Perhaps the most important of these is the new evidence that poundage or tonnage is no measure of the food-value of farm crops; the products of fertile soil may be qualitatively as well as quantitatively superior. We can bolster poundage from depleted soils by pouring on imported fertility, but we are not necessarily bolstering food-value. The possible ultimate ramifications of this idea are so immense that I must leave their exposition to abler pens.

The discontent that labels itself 'organic farming,' while bearing some of the earmarks of a cult, is nevertheless biotic in its direction, particularly in its Insistence on the importance of soil flora and fauna.

The ecological fundamentals of agriculture are just as poorly known to the public as in other fields of land-use. For example, few educated people realize that the marvelous advances in technique made during recent decades are improvements in the pump, rather than the well. Acre for acre, they have barely sufficed to offset the sinking level of fertility.

In all of these cleavages, we see repeated the same basic paradoxes; man the conqueror *versus* man the biotic citizen; science the sharpener of his sword *versus* science the searchlight on his universe; land the slave and servant *versus* land the collective organism. Robinson's injunction to Tristram may well be applied, at this juncture, to *Homo sapiens* as a species in geological time:

Whether you will or not

You are a King, Tristram, for you are one

Of the time-tested few that leave the world,

When they are gone, not the same place it was.

Mark what you leave.

THE OUTLOOK

It is inconceivable to me that an ethical relation to land can exist without love, respect, and admiration for land, and a high regard for its value. By value, I of course mean something far broader than mere economic value; I mean value in the philosophical sense.

Perhaps the most serious obstacle impeding the evolution of a land ethic is the fact that our educational and economic system is headed away from, rather than toward, an intense consciousness of land. Your true modern is separated from the land by many middlemen, and by innumerable physical gadgets. He has no vital relation to it; to him it is the space between cities on which crops grow. Turn him loose for a day on the land, and if the spot does not happen, to be a golf links or a 'scenic' area, he is bored stiff. If crops could be raised by hydroponics instead of farming, it would suit him very well. Synthetic substitutes for wood, leather wool, and other natural land products suit him better than the originals. In short, land is something he has 'outgrown.'

Almost equally serious as an obstacle to a land ethic is the attitude of the fanner for whom the land is still an adversary, or a taskmaster that keeps him in slavery. Theoretically, the mechanization of farming ought to cut the farmer's chains, but whether it really does is debatable.

One of the requisites for an ecological comprehension of land is an understanding of ecology, and this is by no means co-extensive with 'education'; in fact, much higher education seems deliberately to avoid ecological concepts. An understanding of ecology does not necessarily originate in courses bearing ecological labels; it is quite as likely to be labeled geography, botany, agronomy, history, or economics. This is as it should be, but whatever the label, ecological training is scarce.

The case for a land ethic would appear hopeless but for the minority which is in obvious revolt against these 'modern' trends.

The 'key-log' which must be moved to release the evolutionary process for an ethic is simply this: quit thinking about decent land-use as solely an economic problem. Examine each question in terms of what is ethically and esthetically right, as well as what is economically expedient. A thing is right when it tends to preserve the integrity, stability, and beauty of the biotic community. It is wrong when it tends otherwise.

It of course goes without saying that economic feasibility limits the tether of what can or cannot be done for land. It always has and it always will. The fallacy the economic determinists have tied around our collective neck, and which we now need to cast off, is the belief that economics determines *all* land-use. This is simply not true. An innumerable host of actions arid attitudes, comprising perhaps the bulk of all land relations, is determined by the land-users' tastes and predilections, rather than by his purse. The bulk of all land relations hinges on investments of time, forethought, skill, and faith rather than on investments of cash. As a land-user thinketh, so is he.

I have purposely presented the land, ethic as a product of social evolution because nothing so important as an ethic is ever 'written.' Only the most superficial student of history supposes that Moses 'wrote' the Decalogue; it evolved in the minds of a thinking community, and Moses wrote a tentative summary of it for a 'seminar.' I say tentative because evolution never stops.

The evolution of a land ethic is an intellectual as well as emotional process. Conservation is paved with good intentions which prove to be futile, or even dangerous, because they are devoid of critical understanding either of the land, or of economic land-use. I think it is a truism that as the ethical frontier advances from the individual to the community, its intellectual content increases.

The mechanism of operation is the same for any ethic: social approbation for right actions: social disapproval for wrong actions.

By and large, our present problem is one of attitudes and implements. We are-remodeling the Alhambra with a steam-shovel, and we are proud of our yardage. We shall hardly relinquish the shovel, which after all has many good points, but we are in need of gentler and more objective criteria for its successful use.